'Other' Austrians

Mackinlay, E. 2004. "Without a song you are nothing". Lecture presented at Queensland University of Technology, 9 August, Brisbane, Queensland, Australia.

—. 2005. Moving and dancing towards decolonisation in education: An example from an Indigenous Australian performance classroom. *Australian Journal of Indigenous Education* 34: 113-122.

Marett, A. 2005. *Songs, Dreamings and ghosts: The wangga of North Australia.* Lebanon, NH: Wesleyan University Press.

McLuhan, M. 1967. *The medium is the massage.* London: Routledge and Kegan Paul.

Ministry of Education (Schools Division). 1988a. *The arts framework: P-10.* Carlton, VIC: Curriculum Corporation of Victoria.

Ministry of Education (Schools Division). 1988b. *The school curriculum and organisation framework: P-12.* Carlton, VIC: Curriculum Corporation of Victoria.

Mussen, P. H., Conger, J. J., and J. Kagan. 1974. *Child development and personality*, 4th ed. New York, NY: Harper and Rowe.

Nakata, M. 2002. Indigenous knowledge and the cultural interface: Underlying issues at the intersection of knowledge and information systems. Paper presented at the 68th International Federation of Library Association Council and General Conference, 8-24 August, Glasgow, Scotland.

Papert, S. 1980. *Mindstorms, children, computers and powerful ideas.* New York, NY: Basic Books Inc.

—. 1994. *The children's machine: Rethinking school in the age of the computer.* New York, NY: Harvester Wheatsheaf.

—. 1996. *Constructionism.* Mahwah, NJ: Lawrence Erlbaum and Associates.

Paynter, J., and P. Aston. 1970. *Sounds and silence: Classroom projects in creative music.* Cambridge, MA: Cambridge University Press.

Perkins, D. N. 1986. *Knowledge as design.* Hillsdale, NJ: Lawrence Earlbaum Associates.

Perkins, D. N. 1988. Teaching for transfer. *Educational Leadership* 46(1): 22-32.

Pratt, G. 1990. *Aural awareness: Principles and practice.* London: Open University Press.

Reimer, B. 1989. *A philosophy of music education*, 2nd ed. Englewood Cliffs, NJ: Simon and Schuster.

Reimer, B., and R. A. Smith. 1992. *The arts, education and aesthetic knowing.* Chicago, IL: National Society for the Study of Education, distributed by the University of Chicago Press.

Reimer, B., and J. E. Wright. Eds. 1992. *On the nature of musical experience.* Niwot, CO: University Press of Colarado.

Robinson, K. 2001. *Out of our minds*. New York, NY: John Wiley.

Rusinek, G., P. Burnard, F. Evelein, N. Economidou-Stavrou, and E. Sæther. 2005. *PROSIME: Promoting social inclusion through good practice in music education*. Madrid: Universidad Compluense de Madrid.

Saatchi and Saatchi. 2000. *Australians and the arts*. Sydney, NSW: Australia Council.

Schon, D. 1984. *The reflective practitioner*. New York, NY: Basic Books, Harper Colophon.

—. 1987. *Educating the reflective practitioner*. San Francisco, CA: Jossey Bass Publishers.

Schusterman, R. 1992. *Pragmatist aesthetics: Living beauty, rethinking art*. New York, NY: Blackwell Publishers.

Simpson, A., P. Bodlovich, I. Harvey, and J. Owens. 2003. *The power and the passion (or It's a long way to the top if you want to rock n roll)*. Melbourne, VIC: The Australian Contemporary Music Working Group.

Sloboda, J., and J. A. Howe. 1992. Transition in the early musical careers of able young musicians: Choosing instruments and teachers. *Journal of Research in Music Education* 40(4): 283-294.

Spirovski, D. 2004. Stories of transformation through meaningful music making. *Queensland Journal of Music Education* 11(1): 68-93.

Swanwick, K. 1981. *A basis for music education*. London: NFER-Nelson Publishing Co. Ltd.

—. 1984a. Further notes on sociology of music dducation. *British Journal of Sociology of Education* 5(3): 303-307.

—. 1984b. Problems of a sociological approach to pop music in schools. *British Journal of Sociology of Education* 5(1): 49-56.

—. 1988. *Music, mind and education*. London: Routledge.

—. 1994. *Musical knowledge: Intuition, analysis and music education*. London: Routledge.

—. 1999. *Teaching music musically*. London: Routledge.

Swanwick, K., and Franca, C. C. 1999. Composing, Performing and Audience-listening as indicators of musical understanding. *British Journal of Music Education* 16(1): 5-19.

Swanwick, K., and J. Tillman. 1986. The sequence of musical development: A study of children's composition. *British Journal of Music Education* 3(3): 305-339.

Vella, R. 2000. *Musical environments: A manual for listening, improvising and composing*. Sydney, NSW: Currency Press.

Victorian Certificate of Education. 1991. *Music craft study design*. Melbourne, VIC: Victorian Curriculum Assessment Board.

Vulliamy, G. 1981. Music education and Music language. *Australian Journal of Music Education* 26: 25-28.

Vulliamy, G., and E. Lee. 1976. *Pop music in schools*. 1st ed. London: Cambridge University Press.

—. 1982. *Pop, rock and ethnic music in schools*. Cambridge: Cambridge University Press.

—. 1982. *Popular music: A teachers guide*. Cambridge: Routledge and Kegan Paul.

Vulliamy, G., and T. Shepherd .1984. A response to Swanwick. *British Journal of Sociology of Education* 5(1): 57-76.

—. 1985. A further response to Swanwick. *British Journal of Sociology in Education* 6(2): 225-229.

Walker, C. 2000. *Buried country: The story of Aboriginal country music*. Sydney, NSW: Pluto Press.

Walker, R. 1990. *Musical beliefs: Psychoacoustic, mythical and educational perspectives*. New York, NY: Teachers College Press.

—. 1996. Music education freed from colonialism a new praxis. *International Journal of Music Education* 27: 2-15.

Will, U. 2000. Oral memory in Australian Aboriginal song performance and the Parry-Kirk debate: A cognitive ethnomusicological perspective. In *Proceedings of the International Study Group on Music Archaeology* (Vol. X), ed. E. and R. Hickmann, 1-29. Columbus, OH: Ohio State University, Columbus.

Zillmere State School. 2002. *Aim high: From little things big things grow...* [Unpublished video recording]. Brisbane, QLD: Zillmere State School with Lifeline Brisbane City Council and Education Queensland.

Allyson Fiddler (ed.)

'Other' Austrians
Post-1945 Austrian Women's Writing

*Proceedings of the conference
held at the University of Nottingham
from 18–20 April 1996*

Peter Lang · Berne

Die Deutsche Bibliothek – CIP-Einheitsaufnahme

'Other' Austrians: post–1945 Austrian women's writing :
proceedings of the conference held at Nottingham from 18–20 April 1996 /
Allyson Fiddler (ed.). – Bern : Lang, 1998
ISBN 3-906756-40-8

ISBN 3-906756-40-8
US-ISBN 0-8204-3446-9

© Peter Lang AG, European Academic Publishers, Berne 1998

All rights reserved.
All parts of this publication are protected by copyright.
Any utilisation outside the strict limits of the copyright law, without
the permission of the publisher, is forbidden and liable to prosecution.
This applies in particular to reproductions, translations, microfilming,
and storage and processing in electronic retrieval systems.

Printed in Germany

Acknowledgements

I would like to record my heartfelt thanks to Emil Brix and Ulla Krauss-Nussbaumer of the Austrian Institute in London. I am grateful to the Austrian Institute and to the University of Nottingham for their generous support, both of the conference itself and of this publication. The European Social fund also supported the conference – in this context, I wish to express my warmest thanks to Joan Bradshaw and Dianne Rooksby at the Centre for Continuing Professional Development for their tremendous organizational expertise. Thanks, too, are owed to Hinrich Siefken and colleagues in the Department of German at Nottingham and to my colleagues here at the University of Lancaster. Christine Compton provided much needed assistance with some of the more fiendishly difficult aspects of word-processing. The friendship and advice of friends and colleagues in Women in German Studies (WIGS) was also warmly appreciated. Finally, I should like to thank Anna Mitgutsch and Elisabeth Reichart for their inspiring contributions to the conference.

Table of Contents

Introduction: the 'Other' Austrians   9
Allyson Fiddler

Representing Abuse: Elisabeth Reichart's 'La Valse' and   15
Marlen Haushofer's 'Wir töten Stella'
Juliet Wigmore

Insanity, Inspiration and Insight: Considering 'weibliche Denkweisen' in
Elisabeth Reichart's *Sakkorausch*   25
Laura Ovenden

Utopia, Dystopia, and Realism in Christine Nöstlinger's Children's Books   35
Gabriela Steinke

Christine Nöstlinger and the Force of Tradition   47
Mike Rogers

Prelude(s) oder Portrait of the Authoress as a Little Girl: Kindheit in Margit
Schreiners Geschichten. Mit Ausblicken auf other Austrians.   57
Hubert Lengauer

Klösterreich – Memories of a Catholic Girlhood   71
Petra M. Bagley

Erika Mitterer as a Christian Writer: A Study of the Novel   83
Der Fürst der Welt as a Precursor of the Later Poetry
Margaret Ives

'Die Liebe zu den Modellen': Barbara Frischmuth's Myths   91
Mererid Puw Davies

The Sounds of Silence: Ilse Aichinger's *Die größere Hoffnung*,   105
Der Gefesselte, and *Kleist, Moos, Fasane*
Brigid Haines

Inszenierungen des unendlichen Gesprächs: Zu Friederike Mayröckers
langer Prosa   115
Andreas Kramer

Hilde Spiel and the Possibility of a Multicultural Society: 129
Die Früchte des Wohlstands and *Mirko und Franca*
Andrea Hammel

Marginalization and Memories: Ceija Stojka's Autobiographical Writing 141
Susan Tebbutt

Ruth Beckermann und die jüdische Nachkriegsgeneration in Österreich 153
Andrea Reiter

Anna Mitgutsch's *Abschied von Jerusalem*: An Austrian Writer's
Presentation of a Divided City 167
Margaret Stone

Der unbewohnbarste Ort: Über den Begriff der Grenze bei Anna Mitgutsch 179
Petra Günther

Offene, utopische Stadt: Zur Darstellung Roms in Ingeborg Bachmanns
Kurzprosa 189
Christina Ujma

The Question of Subjectivity in Bachmann's *Frankfurter Vorlesungen* and
Das Dreißigste Jahr 201
Ingrid Stipa

The Cost of Loving: Love, Desire, and Subjectivity in the Work of
Marlen Haushofer 211
Margaret Littler

Die Klavierspielerin: on Mutilation and Somatophobia 225
Tobe Levin

Wasser, hinunter, wohin? Elfriede Jelineks *Kinder der Toten* 235
– ein Flüssigtext
Juliane Vogel

Index 243

Notes on Contributors 245

Introduction: the 'Other' Austrians

Allyson Fiddler

The decision to hold a conference on Post-1945 Austrian Women's Writing was informed by several considerations. To my knowledge there had not been such a conference in the United Kingdom,[1] and, given the number of Austrian women writers and the diversity of their writing, it seemed highly likely that a conference with this focus would attract a great deal of interest. Happily, this intuition was correct and delegates from Austria, Belgium, Germany, Great Britain, Ireland, and the United States signed up to attend. The conference, held at the University of Nottingham in April 1996, was made possible by the generous assistance of the Austrian Institute in London and by a grant from the European Social Fund.

Thankfully, books on twentieth-century Austrian literature now strike the reader as odd if they do not include articles on some of the many important Austrian *women* writers, but until recently it was unusual to find the post-1945 period being represented by anyone other than Peter Handke or Thomas Bernhard. The title of the present volume, *'Other' Austrians*, is in part an ironic reminder of this male monopoly. It borrows from feminist and from psychoanalytic theory the concept of the Other. As Toril Moi explains, 'woman is not only the Other, as Simone de Beauvoir discovered, but is quite specifically *man*'s Other: his negative or mirror-image. This is why Irigaray claims that patriarchal discourse situates woman *outside* representation: she is absence, negativity, the dark continent, or at best a lesser man' (Moi 1985: 133-4). The title should be seen as a celebration of women's contribution to Austrian literature. Whatever qualms some readers and critics may have about the selective focus of the present volume – the *female* monopoly – the sub-title should serve to indicate that this is not intended to be a universal study of post-war Austrian literature *per se*, but a timely attempt to redress the balance. In any case, many of the contributors took up the invitation issued in the call for papers to explore parallels and comparisons with male Austrian writers or indeed with German women writers.

Two of the high points of the conference were the literary readings by Anna Mitgutsch and Elisabeth Reichart which took place on both evenings of the conference. After reading extracts from their recent works, the writers responded to the interested questions and comments from the other participants, and, in their turn, contributed throughout the event to discussions on others' papers. Elisabeth Reichart read from her two most recent publications, *Nachtmär* (1995) and *Sakkorausch* (1994). In her paper in the present volume, Juliet Wigmore looks at the earlier *Erzählung* 'La Valse' (1992), exploring the strategies for representing incest in this work and in the much earlier short story by Marlen Haushofer, 'Wir töten Stella' (1958). Wigmore explores some of the intertextual components of the stories and suggests that the pre-texts to which the narrators of both stories have recourse, all 'classic indices of the patriarchal order: the Bible, Greek legends and mythology, and *Märchen*', underpin and legitimize women's victimization. However, the friction between these pre-texts and their new setting in these short stories, is one which is mobilized to good effect by Reichart and Haushofer to help produce a better understanding of sexual abuse and, indeed, of women's and society's collusion in it. *Sakkorausch* (1994) is another highly intertextual work, a text, as Laura Ovenden underlines, with *two* authors. Ovenden revisits Romantic conceptions of 'genius' and the psychological discourse of madness and shows how the future knowledge brought to the text by the narrator's voice makes of Druskowitz's supposed insanity in fact a more incisive and subversive kind of perceptiveness.

Both Mike Rogers and Gaby Steinke concern themselves with the children's literature of Christine Nöstlinger. Rogers considers Nöstlinger to have written subversions, and in certain cases, inversions of traditional adult-child behavioural patterns. He argues that Nöstlinger negotiates the fine line of attacking certain traditional values and promoting others: 'Sharing a tradition does not have to be simply indoctrination; it can be a step towards communication between the generations'. Gaby Steinke explores the hybrid texture of realism and fantasy in Nöstlinger's children's books. Where Nöstlinger's earlier children's books had offered their readers models of a 'freundliche Utopie', the later works show an increasingly dystopian tendency, Steinke argues.

Hubert Lengauer looks not at children's literature but at the theme of childhood in three collections of short stories by Margit Schreiner and asks, with Jean-François Lyotard, whether the stories are appealing precisely because they are feminine, regression fantasies. The appeal, then, is borne of envy: 'eine Schöpfung der Eifersucht, die der Mann gegenüber dem empfindet, was er nicht sein darf' (Lyotard). In his discussion of the elongation of time in the perspective of the child, Lengauer casts a sensitive eye over works by Schreiner and a range of other contemporary Austrian writers and considers the different ways in which they deal with the subject of childhood. Schreiner's stories are revealed to be often charmingly banal, sometimes infused with the melancholy of adult retrospection. But, Lengauer feels, Schreiner's predominant theme of the development of childhood has been exhausted; he looks forward to the unfolding of new themes in Schreiner's writing.

The novels by Austrian and German women writers considered by Petra Bagley also deal with childhood and, in particular, with the education and gender drilling of the convent school. Bagley demonstrates the effects of stifling moral and religious strictures on the sense of identity and guilt expressed by the narrators in these autobiographically-inspired texts. Barbara Frischmuth, Brigitte Schwaiger, and Jutta Richter all present voices which challenge the dogmatic approaches of their Catholic upbringing and demonstrate the ultimate irony of how patriarchal values are inculcated in the all-female environment of the convent. Margaret Ives looks at a novel by Erika Mitterer which was originally published in 1940 but was republished in 1988 and is illuminating in the way it points forward to some of the themes of Mitterer's later poetry. Rereading *Der Fürst der Welt* with hindsight and with the messages of Mitterer's poetry in mind, Ives argues that the novel's conclusion can be read as a positive message of hope and redemption.

Mererid Puw Davies reads three novels by Barbara Frischmuth with a view to providing a differentiated critique of the author's use of myth. Drawing on and augmenting Barthes's theories of myth and the discourse or language of myth, 'mythology', Davies refutes Frischmuth's supposedly representative status within Austrian women's writing. In considering the political dimension in Frischmuth's use of myth, Davies argues that the author's work reveals a progression away from the ironizing of myth and towards the adoption of 'a mode of narration which, in assigning great prestige to myth, effectively becomes "mythological" itself'.

Ilse Aichinger and Friederike Mayröcker are two Austrian writers whose work is extremely difficult to pin down. Brigid Haines tackles Aichinger's impenetrability by drawing attention to some of the creative paradoxes of her writing. The aim of Haines's essay is to try to unpick Aichinger's dichotomous conception of 'Schweigen'. On the one hand, there is the negative dimension of silence which is to be overcome, demonstrating Aichinger's oppositional, one might say political stance. On the other hand, 'Schweigen' is to be seen as a positive goal – 'because, despite writing against the grain of history, she does not wish to install new narratives in place of old ones'. Andreas Kramer brings to bear the concept of 'Textur' on Mayröcker's writing. Underlining the difficulty of categorising Mayröcker, Kramer argues that she does not fit into either of the opposing, theoretical models of deconstruction and radical constructivism. Rather, the concept of 'Textur' is a better way of positioning Mayröcker's aesthetics and Kramer outlines a revised understanding of Baßler's term.

The volume continues with a sequence of essays dealing with the issue of racial and religious minorities. Andrea Hammel addresses Hilde Spiel's project of multiculturalism in the novels *Die Früchte des Wohlstands* (1981) and *Mirko und Franca* (1980) which, although set a hundred years apart, throw up important parallels and demonstrate the author's conviction that European society must come to terms with its past. This message is brought home most emphatically in Susan Tebbutt's essay on the autobiographical writings of Ceija Stojka. The persecution and marginalization of the Roma both in the past – Stojka's writings present traumatic memories of the Nazi holocaust – and in post-war society, too, are important but neglected themes in discussions of Austrian literature. Stojka's work reminds us that Austrian women's writing is far from homogeneous, and Tebbutt explores the various facets of Stojka's identity as woman, as Roma, and as Austrian. Andrea Reiter looks at the essayist and filmmaker Ruth Beckermann, whose personal biography and attitude to her own Jewishness, Reiter argues, is representative for the post-war generation of Jews in Austria. Gender is not the determining factor in Beckermann's exploration of her own identity. Instead, the avenues which she explores in her films and in her essays are the Austrian and Jewish axes of her present and of her past. Reiter compares Beckermann's work with writings by Lea Fleischmann and Chaim Noll, exploring the central role of the essay in the work of Jewish writers and noting in contrast with these others who chose to leave Austria, the positive side to Beckermann's relationship with Austria. A further dimension which Reiter explores here is the therapeutic function of Beckermann's explorations of the holocaust and the function of the video camera as 'weapon' against her own initial speechlessness.

Anna Mitgutsch is a writer who has also recently started to explore her Jewish identity. Dvorah, her central character in *Abschied von Jerusalem* (1995) is on a journey of self-discovery, ostensibly holidaying in Jerusalem as part of her quest to find out what happened to her aunt who disappeared from Austria during the war. It is from *Abschied von Jerusalem* that Anna Mitgutsch read on the first evening of our conference. Margaret Stone looks at this most engaging novel, seeing in it both an accomplished description of Israeli landscapes and moods as captured through its protagonist and a thought-provoking treatment of Jerusalem's complex political landscape. Petra Günther traces the development of the image of the border/threshold/boundary in Mitgutsch's *oeuvre*. She considers its use as physical space, its significance for women (Mitgutsch's protagonists are all women), and its flexibile valency. 'Die Grenze' is sometimes positively and sometimes negatively connoted in Mitgutsch's writing.

Christina Ujma charts Ingeborg Bachmann's relationship to her *Wahlheimat* Rome. Ujma discusses Bachmann's writings on Rome and on Italian culture and politics both against the backdrop of the 'German' tradition of the Italian experience and with reference to the main locus of Bachmann's creativity, Vienna. In a second paper on Bachmann, Ingrid Stipa considers conceptions of subjectivity in Bachmann's theoretical writings and how the author translates these into her stories in the collection *Das dreißigste Jahr*. Stipa traces the steps toward a more positive – or should one say less negative? – structuring of gender relationships in Bachmann's stories, concluding with a look at the story 'Alles'. With Kristeva, Bachmann is pointing towards the possibility of communication between the sexes via alternative, non-verbal means, not governed by the patriarchal order. Marlen Haushofer was also exercised by the impasse of heterosexual relationships and her protagonists became less, not more autonomous subjects. Margaret Littler addresses the complex ways in which female desire is presented in Haushofer's work and posits Haushofer's subject

– as evinced in her later works – as a model of ethical existence based on responsibility and love. Littler draws on the theories of Luce Irigaray to underpin this argument.

In her campaigning piece against female mutilation, Tobe Levin suggests potential parallels between the genital mutilation practised on more than 80 million women throughout the world and the self-inflicted genital mutilation carried out by Erika Kohut in Elfriede Jelinek's *Die Klavierspielerin* (1983). Levin controversially posits the 'shared oppression' that is female genital mutilation and argues that Erika's acts, like those of mothers who inflict clitoridectomies and the like on their own daughters, amount, not to an emphasis of sexual difference but to its erasure. Once again, women's complicity is a theme here as it has been in other papers in this volume. The final paper in this volume looks at Jelinek's most recent novel, *Die Kinder der Toten* (1995). Juliane Vogel reveals the true subject or agent of Jelinek's novel to be water. In fact, *Die Kinder der Toten* is a fluid text, Vogel argues. Underneath the surface playing with biblical, literary, mythical models, water, in its multifarious manifestations – the flood, mudflows and landslides – is both a metaphorical vehicle to transport the sins of the past into the present but also a mode of writing. Jelinek liberates the hidden fluid content of words, 'um die Festkörpergrenzen von Personen und Dingen aufzuweichen'.

The papers in this collection do not set out to establish parameters for Austrian women's writing or to characterize its defining features. They do, however, demonstrate the heterogeneous nature of women's writing and the methodological pluralism which is the hallmark of contemporary women's studies. It is hoped that the new approaches taken here and the breadth of authors considered will stimulate interest in the rich and diverse contribution of women writers to the literary landscape of Austria in the second half of the twentieth century.

Notes

[1] Kleiber and Tunner 1986 is based on a conference held in Mulhouse in 1985. There are other useful volumes on the subject, notably Vansant 1988 and Walter-Buchebner-Gesellschaft 1991. The results of two other conferences on contemporary Austrian literature held in the U.K. in the 1990s can be consulted in Schmidt and McGowan 1993 and Finlay and Jeutter forthcoming. Naturally, women writers feature in both.

Bibliography

Finlay, Frank and Ralf Jeutter. Forthcoming 1998. *Contemporary Austrian Drama*, Amsterdam, Rodopi

Kleiber, Carine and Erika Tunner (eds). 1986. *Frauenliteratur in Österreich von 1945 bis heute*, Berne, Peter Lang

Moi, Toril. 1985. *Sexual/Textual Politics: Feminist Literary Theory*, London, Methuen

Schmidt, Ricarda and Moray McGowan (eds). 1993. *From High Priests to Desecrators: Contemporary Austrian Writers*, Sheffield, Sheffield Academic Press

Vansant, Jacqueline. 1988. *Against the Horizon: Feminism and Postwar Austrian Women Writers*, Connecticut, Greenwood

Walter-Buchebner-Gesellschaft (ed.). 1991. *Das Schreiben der Frauen in Österreich seit 1950*, Vienna, Böhlau

Representing Abuse: Elisabeth Reichart's 'La Valse' and Marlen Haushofer's 'Wir töten Stella'

Juliet Wigmore

The two stories 'La Valse' and 'Wir töten Stella' were published at a space of 34 years, in 1992 and 1958 respectively (Reichart 1992 and Haushofer 1990). Both are *Erzählungen* of some length and each tells a story of what we would now call 'sexual abuse'. In 'La Valse' the story takes the form of father-daughter rape, in earlier parlance 'incest' (Driver and Droisen 1989: 17-18); in the other story, a foster child is abused by her substitute father in a family setting which itself appears incestuous. This similarity of subject matter is the basis on which I shall compare the way in which abuse is represented in the two stories. First, I shall briefly mention the external context against which we read these narratives. I shall then consider questions of responsibility, the outcomes of the two stories, and particularly the role of the narrator in each case. I shall seek to show that the narrators make use of various intertextual relationships in particular, which contextualize the events and relate them in varying degrees to patriarchal social norms.

The way in which abuse is represented in these narratives, as well as the way in which we read the stories, is conditioned by perceptions of child abuse in society. In the course of this century, the topic has been subject to a variety of approaches, both by professionals and by society at large: from having been 'discovered' to be widely prevalent and subsequently being dismissed as fantasy by Freud, to being treated as a symptom of the dysfunctional family, to being interpreted as an expression of patriarchal oppression, followed by the inevitable backlash, including, for instance 'False Memory Syndrome' (Armstrong 1996). A notable development has been that, since around the mid-1970s, women who suffered abuse in childhood have been more willing to state their case publicly, while some feminist theorists have treated physical and sexual violation of women as being central to the maintainence of male power (Waldby et al. 1989 and Rich 1981). In both the stories to be discussed, the patriarchal structures are called to account: however, scarcely surprisingly in view of the dates of publication, the confrontational aspect figures more explicitly in 'La Valse', as one would expect from a story of the 1990s, than it does in 'Wir töten Stella' (1958). The difference of emphasis is apparent not least in the position of each narrator. I shall first consider 'La Valse' and then bring hindsight to bear upon relevant aspects of 'Wir töten Stella'.

'La Valse'

In 'La Valse' the story is narrated by the abused woman herself, who exposes the abuse she suffered as a child. As she narrates, she develops from seeing herself as a victim to representing herself as a survivor,[1] in the end achieving a sense of release and an optimistic view of the future. The story spans a period of seven days, during which the narrator, Briscilla, nurses her dying father through the last week of his life. She tells how she and her sister Hanna were sexually abused by their father, leading eventually to Hanna's suicide as a young adult. As narrator, Briscilla tackles the tradition of abuse both in her own family and as a well-established pattern in patriarchal society, through various types of dialogic structure: these consist, on the one hand, of imaginary personal diatribes against her father, who is now silent, and debates with her sister, who answers her back. Hanna, the dead sister, can be interpreted as one part of Briscilla's fragmented personality. She both represents the part of Briscilla which succumbed, while Briscilla herself survived, and acts as an alter ego, who calls for revenge. The imaginary dialogues with Hanna and with other people from Briscilla's life are complemented by passages in which Briscilla engages with extraneous textual material, which is incorporated into the text of 'La Valse' and results in confrontational dialogue with the pervasive ideologies represented by the pre-texts. In this way, the battle between Briscilla and the force of patriarchal oppression, represented in her family by her father, are played out.

Textual material from three different sources is incorporated into the narrative, and is linked by Briscilla's developing thoughts on her situation. First, she recalls Hanna's suicide note; of all the texts, this one emanates from the position closest to Briscilla, while the others come from sources at an increasing remove, demonstrating her progression from the particular problem in her family to the general issue of patriarchal power, manifested as abuse. The development of Briscilla's ideas is triggered by Hanna's farewell message, in which she called for revenge. The idea of vengeance brings to Briscilla's mind a second text, which she now sees as a potential tool of revenge against her parents. This book, lent to her by a man named Paul, with whom she had a brief relationship, is a text of alternative medicine. Paul, with missionary zeal, had hoped that with its challenge to traditional medicine, it would help to cure someone of serious illness. What Briscilla gains from it is not a new cure for her father's cancer, however: instead, its questioning of established medical authority prompts in her a sceptical attitude towards Paul's book itself. Above all it seems to be the authoritative tone of this book which puts her on her guard, because it reminds her of the reverence she was supposed to show towards Biblical scripture, and to her parents, who used the Bible as a means of underlining their own authority. Addressing Hanna, Briscilla first quotes Paul's book and then indicates, through her sarcastic tone, that she herself has made a connection between these two authorities: 'Hanna hast du das gehört! Das gefällt dir, stimmt's. Noch immer keine Antwort. Es muß dir einfach gefallen, denk doch an unser Gebet, das wir zu spät beten lernten: – Du sollst Vater und Mutter ehren – und ihre Geschäfte lieben, wie sie dich lieben' (17-18). Briscilla's scepticism about anything that demands unqualified belief is based in the actual betrayal of trust by her parents in the form of sexual abuse. This topic itself is then introduced by an interpolated text. This script, the one most central to the story, is a passage from Genesis which tells the story of Lot and his daughters, an ancient model of an incestuous family.

Two lengthy passages from this story are incorporated into the text of 'La Valse', on day 2 (18) and day 5 (34). On the first occasion, the verses cited out of context point to the gender bias of the story, first shown by Lot's own words to the men of Sodom (Genesis 19.7-8), in which, from Briscilla's point of view, he condemns himself: 'Ach, liebe Brüder, tut nicht so übel! Siehe, ich habe zwei Töchter, die wissen noch von keinem Mann; die will ich herausgeben unter euch, und tut mit ihnen, was euch gefällt' (18). The Biblical Lot offered up his daughters to the men of Sodom in order to prevent them from raping two male visitors, who, according to the omniscient narrator of Genesis, were actually angels. (His action has usually been interpreted as being the lesser of two evils![2]) Taking this passage out of its original context has the effect of highlighting its anti-woman bias: the critique is emphasized by the fact that it is immediately followed by a verse from much later in the Lot story, which concerns the fate of Lot's unnamed wife: 'Und sein Weib sah hinter sich und ward zur Salzsäule' (18). The juxtaposing of these two, originally separate, sections of the story shows Briscilla reshaping the received text, and so revealing the patriarchal values which inform this perspective on incest, which, as a Biblical text, also formed part of the system of belief in Briscilla's family.

Later in the story, a longer quotation from the story of Lot is incorporated, including verses describing how Lot's daughters seduced their father with the deliberate aim of becoming pregnant and so continuing his line. In the Genesis account there is no indication of any abuse of the daughters by their father; in fact it is they who practise deceit upon him, although the attitude of the narrator is usually seen as being ambivalent in this respect. Lot himself is clearly exonerated first by the fact that he was made drunk and secondly, because his daughters were deliberately seductive. (The cultural impact of this story is clear from the fact that there are many paintings of this subject, in which the daughters are always presented as seductive, suggesting a pervasive male fantasy.[3]) By recontextualising the story of Lot within events in her own family, Briscilla suggests that the Bible story seems to justify the unjustifiable, and thus reveals the model authoritative situation to be flawed.

These textual interpolations are further supported by a range of quotations and less direct allusions to other texts which had a formative influence in Briscilla's childhood, including *Märchen* and classical motifs.[4] These, too, it is implied, were tools which helped to inculcate a patriarchal view of women and so, indirectly, they bear some of the blame for the abuse which has occurred. By challenging their authority, Briscilla is eventually able to see the tyranny represented by her father in a wider historical context. It is also stated at the outset that Briscilla's father belongs to the generation which colluded with fascism, and thus, it may be suggested, the abuse of women is also to be seen within the wider context of the political abuse of power. Further support for this interpretation is found if one takes into account other stories of the collection entitled *La Valse*, some of which deal directly with the legacy of the fascist period.

'Wir töten Stella'
Marlen Haushofer's story 'Wir töten Stella' is narrated from a markedly different angle. Once again, a female narrator is the central protagonist, but instead of having been a victim/survivor, she presents herself as having colluded with abuse which was perpetrated upon the young woman, Stella. Anna, the narrator, attempts to set down Stella's story retrospectively, out of a sense of duty to her, shortly after her death. Although Stella's death was accidental – she died in a road accident – it is presented as tantamount to suicide, as it was consistent with her state of mind at the time. Unlike Hanna, or Briscilla, in 'La Valse', Stella does not testify in her own words to her maltreatment. We know little of her true feelings; she remains exclusively a victim, and there is no sign of regeneration.

Unlike Briscilla, Stella was not a young child at the time in question: at nineteen years old, she was apparently closer to Briscilla's age at the time of telling her story, although she is depicted as childlike and vulnerable. In contrast to 'La Valse' too, Stella, who is a guest in Anna's house, is not the biological daughter of the abuser, Richard, husband of the narrator and an inveterate pursuer of young women. Yet the incest motif, apparently excluded by the lack of genetic relationship between Richard and Stella, is represented metaphorically in the configurations which pertain within this dysfunctional family, particularly in Anna's obsessive love for her son Wolfgang and the parallel closeness between Richard and their daughter Annette (Venske 1987: 103). However, it is Stella, the outsider in this paradigm, who becomes the main victim of it. That the blame is shared by the family as a whole is one implication of the plural subject 'wir' in the title of the story, which also draws attention to the inward-looking aspect of the family. Anna has reservations about taking Stella into the family, because of what she calls 'die unzähligen Tabus, die wir im Umgang miteinander beachten müssen' (63). Despite her misgivings, she agrees to have Stella to stay when her mother goes away with a new man. Here too, there is a parallel with 'La Valse', where the mother figure also fails to protect, having left the family, like Lot's wife before her, and whose absence meant that the daughters were exposed to abuse.

Anna's role in Stella's destruction can be seen as falling into three phases: having first accepted Stella as a guest, against her better judgement, Anna secondly creates the conditions for Stella to become a victim of abuse by her husband, Richard. Taking pity on Stella's neglected state – or perhaps merely trying to make her conform to prevailing feminine norms – she encourages Stella to make more of her appearance, apparently in an attempt to prepare her for the adult world. At this point, Anna has little awareness of what exactly she is preparing Stella for, still less that it will turn into a threat to her. As a result of Anna's endeavours, Stella becomes preoccupied with her quest for attractiveness and is flattered by Richard's attentions. Like any needy child, she welcomes the offer of what passes for love. The reader is given to understand that Stella is raped or at least seduced by Richard, and then cast off, as part of a recurrent pattern on his part. Anna, who finds Stella awkward and evasive, makes little attempt to intervene to protect her. The third aspect of Anna's contribution to Stella's demise, therefore, consists in her collusion in what occurs. It is her sense of guilt which prompts her to write the story and suggest to the reader that she has been aware of her own part in Stella's destruction to a greater extent than she at first admits.

By contrast with 'La Valse', 'Wir töten Stella' makes no extensive use of extraneous material. Nevertheless, this story also comprises explicit allusions to an ancient, authoritative text, the *Iliad*, which Anna's fifteen-year-old son, Wolfgang, is studying in his schoolwork. Anna, desperately trying to ignore what is going on under her own roof, takes refuge with him. Having always kept a wary eye on his reading, she is at first surprised to find that the figure who attracts him most in this story is not Achilles, the hero, but Cassandra, but then she concedes: 'warum soll er nicht geahnt haben, daß sie die wahre Heldin ist?' (73). Anna's reaction that Cassandra is 'die wahre Heldin' suggests that she admires Cassandra's courage, presumably for the fact that she spoke out about what she knew, despite knowing that her words would go unheeded. It is not entirely clear to what extent Anna actually identifies Cassandra's dilemma with her own and her attitude towards the Greek heroine is certainly ambivalent. She is mentioned again when, one night, Anna dreams that she meets Cassandra, but instead of heeding her prophetic warning, throws stones at her. Thus Cassandra seems to represent the site of Anna's own conflict. Yet even her admiration of Cassandra's apparent heroism is problematic: much as Anna, in her waking hours, admires Cassandra, she also knows that she achieved nothing by speaking out, just as she herself believes – as she did even at the time of these events –

that it was pointless to try to prevent what was happening between Richard and Stella. However, she does not consider the fact that, in the ancient story, Cassandra's hopeless position is fate, dictated by the gods, whereas Anna's own is one that she herself has chosen. Her desire to identify with Cassandra can therefore be regarded as part of her attempt to justify her own actions, but it reveals her guilt all the more clearly.

Anna's tendency to escapism is reflected in her wistful attitude towards reading the *Iliad*: it takes her back to her own childhood, when the future looked more positive, before she became disillusioned. This idyllic quality is also reflected in her final mention of the *Iliad*, when Anna thinks back nostalgically to the time before Stella's death (or before her arrival?) when she was able to read the *Iliad* in peace with Wolfgang. Using the present tense, she muses, 'wir sprechen von Achill und Kassandra, und ich bin glücklich' (101). Yet here again it is clear that her quest for an idyllic past is pure escapism, since her family life showed signs of disturbance, even before it was actually disrupted. Thus, the classical text is the means used by Anna both to avoid confrontation with reality and to delude herself about the actual circumstances.

Between the war hero Achilles (not yet 'Achill das Vieh'[5]), and Richard, there is also a parallel which implies a mismatch: for Achilles was betrayed by a woman, whereas it is Richard, as substitute father, who betrays Stella's trust. This disparity helps to reveal the author's criticism of the authoritative text itself. Like the negative influence of the Bible in 'La Valse', the *Iliad*, as part of institutionalized education, has a formative influence on the young, such as Wolfgang. It perpetuates a traditional myth (starting, in Judaeo-Christian history, with Eve), according to which men, the heroes, are betrayed by women, while women who know the truth, like Cassandra, are disregarded. The behaviour of the narrator, Anna, in relation to this text suggests, however, that she is less critical of the text than is the author herself.

It is not made entirely clear what is the main reason for Anna's failure to warn or to protect Stella. At various points Anna gives different indications: her need to preserve the integrity of the family, and to protect Wolfgang especially, is one underlying motive. Others mentioned or implied include inertia, resignation, fear and perhaps even satisfaction at being left alone by Richard. Although she knew that Stella would suffer, she could not have known that the outcome would be Stella's death. As Anna says, death is for her the only moral boundary (71), and thus, one may infer, it is the overstepping of this moral limit which has prompted her to reflect on her own motives. Her sense of vision as narrator is partially conditioned by hindsight and the realization that she colluded, a moral failing which emerges all the more clearly by contrast with her model heroine, Cassandra.

However, the story also hints at a secret in Anna's own past, which is never fully explained. She at first states, and then reformulates more speculatively, that something unknown or unmentionable 'muß mir vor Jahren geschehen sein' (67). This event – vague as it is – caused her to fear for her person. On the one hand, this horror seems to be rooted in fear of destruction instilled during the war, which resulted in her establishing clearer boundaries between good and evil. One entirely plausible interpretation of the story explains it as a metaphor for the morality of fleeing from political responsibility in the time following the Anschluß (Roebling 1991). Seen in the context of recent discussions of sexual abuse, however, we may also speculate that Anna herself was possibly the victim of abuse, 'vor Jahren', in her own childhood. If so, this may explain why she is so unwilling or unable to take control of the situation in her own household: she appears to have successfully repressed her own trauma, and at the time of writing is already in constant danger of forgetting Stella and her suffering. Thus, despite the evident difference in narrative position from that of 'La Valse', it seems plausible to regard this narrator too as a possible victim of abuse. Whatever it was that afflicted her in the past, we must conclude that, unlike the narrator in 'La Valse', Anna remains trapped in the role of victim. The parallel between the personal experience of abuse and the devastation practised in the wider political context represents a further point of comparison between this story and 'La Valse'.

Apart from the classical motif from the *Iliad*, the main intertextual relationship, there are also allusions to a range of extraneous sources similar to those mentioned in connection with 'La Valse': for example, an evocation of the Garden of Eden after the Fall. As Anna writes, she says that her garden has lost its attraction for her. She now feels like a lodger in her own home, an outsider, as Stella was previously. She can, therefore, be interpreted as having taken on Stella's role as victim.

Both 'Wir töten Stella' and 'La Valse' also allude to *Märchen* motifs: in 'La Valse' some well-known *Märchen* are mentioned by name and are championed by Briscilla and Hanna respectively: the Frog King is played off against Sleeping Beauty, for instance (39). In 'Wir töten Stella', no specific *Märchen* are mentioned by title, but typical motifs are invoked, such as Anna's formulation for Richard and Stella as 'der gute Onkel und das törichte Mädchen' (75), while Stella, dressed in her new outfits, is said by Anna to look 'wie eine Prinzessin' (75). These motifs again suggest that Anna is aware, if only dimly, that the make-believe situation, in which they are all living, cannot last and that disillusionment is inevitable.

The various texts which express the narrator's consciousness in these two accounts of abuse can all be regarded as classic indices of the patriarchal order: the Bible, Greek legends and mythology, and *Märchen*; and this list is not exhaustive. In both stories it becomes clear that the relevant pre-texts have a formative effect in moulding attitudes within a gender-biased society, in which the sexual abuse of women has long been condoned. Subverting the patriarchal texts is therefore a step towards breaking out of this pattern.

The endings of the two stories strike quite different notes. In 'La Valse', the seven days of Briscilla's father's dying are paralleled by the narrator's own regeneration, and the story ends optimistically. In 'Wir töten Stella', by contrast, the new generation of womanhood is prematurely interrupted by the death of Stella and the resignation of Anna, who has not succeeded in effecting any change and is in danger of even forgetting what has occurred.

Notes

[1] Elisabeth Reichart herself uses similar terminology in her novel about women of the Resistance, *Komm über den See*: 'Nennt uns nicht Opfer! Ich kann dieses Wort nicht hören, es gehört mit zu den Vereinbarungen, die über uns getroffen wurden... Wir waren es doch, die versuchten zu überleben, als Menschen zu überleben' (Reichart 1988: 153). The term 'survivor' has for some time been used by women who suffered sexual abuse, in preference to 'victim', although this usage is not unproblematic. See also Armstrong 1996: 30.

[2] The approval of Lot's anti-woman behaviour is reflected in John Milton's lines:
Witness the streets of Sodom, and that night
In Gibeah, when the hospitable door
Exposed a matron to avoid *worse rape*.
(Milton 1966 [1667]: 224; my emphasis.)

[3] Josephine Rijnaarts mentions a depiction by Alessandro Turchi in the Dresdner Gemäldegalerie (Rijnaarts 1988: 25).

[4] For further details, see Wigmore 1996.

[5] The epithet attached to Achilles in Christa Wolf, *Kassandra* (Wolf 1983: 87).

Bibliography

Armstrong, Louise. 1996. *What Happened when Women said Incest*, London, The Women's Press

Driver, Emily and Audrey Droisen (eds). 1989. *Child Sexual Abuse*, Basingstoke, Macmillan

Haushofer, Marlen. 1990. 'Wir töten Stella' (1958), repr. in *Wir töten Stella und andere Erzählungen*, Munich, dtv

Milton, John. 1966. *Paradise Lost*, Book I (1667), in *Milton Poetical Works*, ed. Douglas Bush, London, OUP

Reichart, Elisabeth. 1988. *Komm über den See*, Frankfurt am Main, Fischer

—. 1992. 'La Valse', in *La Valse*, Salzburg, Otto Müller

Rich, Adrienne. 1981. *Compulsory Heterosexuality and Lesbian Existence* (1980), repr. London, Onlywomen Press

Rijnaarts, Josephine. 1988. *Lots Töchter*, Munich, dtv

Roebling, Irmgard. 1991. '"Wir töten Stella". Eine Österreicherin schreibt gegen das Vergessen', in Christine Schmidtjell (ed.), *Marlen Haushofer, Die Überlebenden. Unveröffentlichte Texte aus dem Nachlaß. Aufsätze zum Werk*, Linz, Landesverlag: 173-88

Venske, Regula. 1987. '"das Alte verloren und das Neue nicht gewonnen...": Marlen Haushofer', in Regula Venske and Sigrid Weigel (eds) *Frauenliteratur ohne Tradition*, Frankfurt am Main, Fischer: 99-130

Waldby, Cathy et al. 1989. 'Theoretical perspectives on Father-Daughter Incest', in Driver and Droisen 1989: 88-106

Wigmore, Juliet. 1996. 'Elisabeth Reichart's "La Valse" and the Text of Abuse', *German Life and Letters*, 49, 4, 1996

Wolf, Christa. 1983. *Kassandra*, Darmstadt and Neuwied, repr. Sammlung Luchterhand

Insanity, Inspiration and Insight: Considering 'weibliche Denkweisen' in Elisabeth Reichart's *Sakkorausch*

Laura Ovenden

Immediately after the television broadcast of the Panorama interview with the Princess of Wales, Nicholas Soames described the Princess as a woman in the advanced stages of paranoia.[1] Whatever one may think of the state of the British monarchy, Nicholas Soames's comment was the perfect example of a man's attempt to disempower a powerful woman by arming himself with the discourse of psychiatry. Whether accused of paranoia or associated with other manifestations of mental illness, the Princess of Wales has something in common with the nineteenth-century Austrian philosopher, Helene von Druskowitz, who was initially diagnosed as suffering from 'Verfolgungswahn', then 'alle paar Jahre wechseln sie [the doctors] wieder zu halluzinatorischem Wahnsinn' (*Sakkorausch*: 20). As a result of her hallucinations, Helene von Druskowitz was incarcerated in an asylum in Austria for the remaining twenty-seven years of her life.

In her study *Women's Madness: Misogyny or Mental Illness?* Jane Ussher writes, 'the Victorian era marked an important change in the discursive regimes which confined and controlled women, because it was in this period that the close association between femininity and pathology became firmly established within the scientific, literary and popular discourse: madness became synonymous with womanhood' (Ussher 1991: 64). Also central to the nineteenth-century discourse on female insanity was the construction of female sexuality and deviancy as madness. Following Foucault, Ussher notes that 'if these sexually nonconformist women could be treated as madwomen their threat to the discourse of femininity was neutralized' (Ussher 1991: 73). A medical textbook of 1848 argued, for example, that the Victorian woman had 'a head almost too small for intellect but just big enough for love' (cited in Ussher 1991: 68). The popularity in Germany at the turn of the century of Dr P J Möbius's book *Über den physiologischen Schwachsinn des Weibes* is well-documented and it also reflects dominant thinking of the time. Dr Möbius writes:

> Nach alledem ist der weibliche Schwachsinn nicht nur vorhanden, sondern auch notwendig, er ist nicht nur ein physiologisches Faktum, sondern auch ein physiologisches Postulat. Wollen wir ein Weib, das ganz seinen Mutterberuf erfüllt, so kann es nicht ein männliches Gehirn haben. Ließe es sich machen, daß die weiblichen Fähigkeiten den männlichen gleich entwickelt würden, so würden die Mutterorgane

> verkümmern, und wir würden einen häßlichen und nutzlosen Zwitter vor uns haben. Jemand hat gesagt, man solle vom Weibe nichts verlangen, als daß es 'gesund und dumm' sei. Das ist grob ausgedrückt, aber es liegt in dem Paradoxon eine Wahrheit. Übermäßige Gehirntätigkeit macht das Weib nicht nur verkehrt, sondern auch krank. Wir sehen das leider tagtäglich vor Augen. Soll das Weib das sein, wozu die Natur es bestimmt hat, so darf es nicht mit dem Manne wetteifern. (Möbius [1905] 1990: 41)

Perhaps it is not, therefore, surprising that a woman, whose behaviour deviated from the prescribed norms of womanly conduct, should fall foul of the discourses represented by Möbius, be diagnosed as insane and incarcerated. Druskowitz displayed her intellect publicly, she refused to wear the corset, part of the strict dress code for women at that time, and she did not want to marry and have children. In the medical notes on Druskowitz from the asylum at Mauer-Oehling, we find the same language and perspective used in Nicholas Soames's comment in the description of Helene von Druskowitz:

> 1.09.05 Unverändert. Patientin ... braucht regelmäßig Hypnotica, von denen sie Paraldehyd als 'schnapsartig' bevorzugt. In ihrem Benehmen vollkommen unverändert, raucht Tabak aus Stummelpfeifen, findet sich fleißig, siedet sich Tee, verfaßt Gedichte zum Lobe des Alkohols, schreibt unleserlich philosophisch konfuse Abhandlungen und Dramen, schickt androphobe Satyren an die Frauenzeitungen, fühlt sich auf der Höhe ihres literarischen Schaffens, leidet sehr unter dem Mangel an Anerkennung von Seiten ihrer Mitwelt, dabei harmlos, gutmütig, dankbar für jedes freundliche Wort – erklärt dann den Betreffenden sofort als Ausnahme seines 'bocksbeuteltragenden' Geschlechts. Halluziniert lebhaft, beschreibt ihre Sinnestäuschungen als tranzendentale Gebilde, führt nachts oft laute Selbstgespräche. (Druskowitz 1988: 90-1)

Helene von Druskowitz was born in Vienna in 1856. She and her mother moved to Zürich so that she could attend the university. At twenty-two, she was the first Austrian woman to be awarded a doctorate for her dissertation on Byron's *Don Juan*. In 1882 she returned to Vienna and, under numerous pseudonyms including 'Sakkorausch', published literary criticism, plays and philosophical tracts.[2] Especially important for Elisabeth Reichart's text *Sakkorausch* is *Drei englische Dichterinnen*, a literary study of Elizabeth Barrett Browning, George Eliot and the Scottish dramatist Joanne Baille, published in 1885. The previous year Helene von Druskowitz had met Friedrich Nietzsche, who was immediately impressed with her. Nietzsche wrote to his sister of Druskowitz, 'Ich meine, es ist ein edles und rechtschaffenes Geschöpf, welches meiner "Philosophie" keinen Schaden thut' (Druskowitz 1988: 82). However, when Druskowitz criticized Nietzsche's philosophical ideas both privately in letters and by returning him the manuscript of the secret 'Zarathustra', then publicly in her treatise *Moderne Versuche eines Religionsersatzes* in 1886, she soon found that she could not rely on the support of her patrons. In 1891 when she was incarcerated in Mauer-Oehling asylum in Niederösterreich, although she proudly did not ask for help, her acquaintances also did not attempt to have her released.

Druskowitz continued to write and have her work published despite these setbacks and in 1905, after fourteen years' incarceration, her philosophical manifesto *Der Mann als logische und sittliche Unmöglichkeit und als Fluch der Welt: Pessimistische Kardinalsätze* appeared in print and she continued to write until her death in the asylum in 1918. The lack of recognition of Helene von Druskowitz by her contemporaries has started to be redressed since the republication of the *Pessimistische Kardinalsätze* by a small feminist publishing house in 1988 and more recently by Elisabeth Reichart's fifth publication *Sakkorausch*. Reichart's text was commissioned for the Wiener Festwochen and an abridged version was performed in May 1994. On the first page of the slim volume Reichart describes Helene von Druskowitz as her 'Mitautorin' and much of the text is based on or directly quoted from the *Pessimistische Kardinalsätze* The second fictional figure in *Sakkorausch* is Elizabeth Barrett Browning, who is portrayed as a silent fellow inmate at Mauer-Oehling, and her poem, 'My Doves', is quoted in part.

Elisabeth Reichart's choice of the title *Sakkorausch* out of the list of possible pseudonyms Helene von Druskowitz adopted during her career, highlights in 'Sakko' the attempt to hide one's sex with a shapeless garment, the equivalent, perhaps, of the male pseudonym many women writers adopted when writing within the male tradition, as well as the suggestion of bisexuality and in 'Rausch' the concept of ecstasy/enthusiasm; that is, prophetic inspiration and its Nietzschean connotations are called to mind. The pseudonym also underlines the playful and humorous element in both Drukowitz's writing and Reichart's text. Both writers seem to be defining themselves in terms of contemporary literary and cultural models of male individuality and female Otherness, while simultaneously resisting those paradigms as they examine what is involved in writing as a woman.

With relation to the form of *Sakkorausch*, if we accept Peter Brooks's thesis in 'The Idea of a Psychoanalytic Literary Criticism' (Brooks 1987: 2) that the text rather than the author ought to be the object of analysis in psychoanalytic criticism, it follows that we should pose the question whether *Sakkorausch* is an insane text? The monologue certainly has no beginning, middle, and end. It is as if the listener is overhearing part of a 'Selbstgespräch' which consists of a varied assortment of texts, including fragments of poems, nursery rhymes, philosophical writings and foreign languages. These fragments are juxtaposed within the text, which thereby resists the illusion of a coherent discourse. The text is visually represented as individual sentences and on the first page the narrator of the monologue seems to confirm the insanity of the text. 'Meine Sätze beweisen meinen Irrsinn' (*Sakkorausch*: 9). Although this can be understood as the ironic standpoint of the narrator, such sentences place the reader in the position of the analyst. Like the analyst, the reader must attempt, in the act of reading, to form a coherent linear discourse. Peter Brooks writes that 'we "intervene" in a text as much by our very act of reading, in our (counter-)transferential desire to master the text, as also in the desire to be mastered by it' (Brooks 1987: 11-12).

Traditionally closely associated with madness is the concept of inspiration. In *Phaedras* Plato describes the poet in terms reminiscent of a shaman. 'If any man comes to the gates of poetry without the madness of the Muses, persuaded that skill alone will make him a good poet, then shall he and his works of sanity with him be brought to naught by the poetry of madness' (quoted in Battersby 1989: 43). In *The Mirror and the Lamp*, an important study on Romantic aesthetics, M. H. Abrams writes in connection with the ancient question of whether a poet is born or made, 'and very early, inspiration – whether regarded as a celestial or mundane form of madness – was said to be either the constant accompaniment or the actual equivalent of the *ingenium* with which a poet is endowed by nature' (Abrams 1953: 188).

It appears, however, that this creative combination of madness and genius was only to be found in male writers. In *Gender and Genius* Christine Battersby carries out a comprehensive study of the historical development of the concept of genius and the extent to which it has been gendered throughout the history of ideas. She illustrates how the two distinct terms 'genius' and 'ingenium' converged during the seventeenth century and it was only in the following century that the term 'genius' began to be used in its modern sense. Battersby concludes that 'by the end of the eighteenth century, "genius" had acquired Romantic grandeur: it had been transformed from a kind of talent into a superior type of BEING who walked a "sublime" path between "sanity" and "madness", between the "monstrous" and the "superhuman"' (Battersby 1994: 148). As Battersby suggests, although Romantic aesthetics exalted the feminine it did not encourage the female, and the effect of this exclusion of women from the aesthetic debate is described by Gilbert and Gubar in *The Madwoman in the Attic*, a study of nineteenth-century women writers. 'If contemporary women do now attempt the pen with energy and authority, they are able to do so only because their eighteenth and nineteenth-century foremothers struggled in isolation that felt like illness, alienation that felt like madness, obscurity that felt like paralysis, to overcome the anxiety of authorship that was endemic to their literary subculture' (Gilbert and Gubar 1979: 51). And if they did not limit themselves to the private sphere, but publicly displayed their intellect, as Druskowitz did, they were certainly not considered geniuses but a threat to society and abnormal.

Both Helene von Druskowitz and Elizabeth Barrett Browning were incarcerated as a direct result of patriarchy. Elizabeth Barrett Browning's father insisted that she be treated as an invalid from the age of fifteen, as a result of her tuberculosis. He was the epitome of Victorian patriarchal tyranny and even forbade his children to marry, although Elizabeth, his favourite, rebelled against this, gaining her freedom only through marriage to Robert Browning and her elopememt to Italy. Helene von Druskowitz could have regained her physical freedom if she had taken the advice of Marie von Ebner-Eschenbach and married, but instead she chose to exercise her intellectual freedom through her radical writings within the confines of an asylum. For both the narrator of *Sakkorausch* and the historical figure Helene von Druskowitz being unmarried is 'das vornehmste Zeichen für die geniale weibliche Verfassung, sie bedeutet das Genie der Frau selbst' (Druskowitz 1988: 74; *Sakkorausch*: 34). Helene von Druskowitz was publishing her opinions on the subject of women writers and genius in 1885. Commenting on Elizabeth Barrett Browning's poems she writes:

> Ihre Neigungen aber haben einen unverkennbar weiblichen Charakter, und dasselbe spezifische Gepräge offenbart ja ihre gesamte Dichtung. Und wir wünschen nicht, daß dies anders wäre. Wir suchen bei einer Frau nicht männliches Fühlen und Schaffen, aus der Tiefe des weiblichen Wesens soll sie schöpfen, um eine Poesie hervorzubringen, welche die natürliche Ergänzung zu den Offenbarungen des männlichen Genies bildet. Denn falsch ist der Ausspruch, daß das Genie kein Geschlecht habe. Dem unerschöplichen Mitgefühl und der gerechtesten Entrüstung eines Frauenherzens nur konnte der Schmerzensgesang 'The Cry of the Children' entquellen. (Druskowitz 1885: 114)

In both *The Madwoman in the Attic* and *Drei englische Dichterinnen* the emphasis is on reclaiming women writers of the past, on finding a voice in the male tradition and perhaps most importantly on seeing literary foremothers as a source of inspiration. In *Sakkorausch* Helene von Druskowitz is both the source of inspiration as well as the 'Mitautorin' of the text. Elisabeth Reichart combines the metaphor of the madwoman as muse with writing as insight. The monologue becomes the vehicle for Druskowitz's 'Selbstgespräche' and the author intervenes in the text by ascribing the narrator with powers of clairvoyance and moments of insight, which draw on the classical tradition of assigning women the sibylline roles of priestess and oracle.

When considering the reader's role, it is clear that his/her historical knowledge also contributes to transforming the narrator's supposed madness into insight and to making the text meaningful. The monologue is located at the beginning of the First World War and one of the textual strategies used to question the construct of madness involves temporality. The narrator of the monologue is beyond the consciousness of the narrated time, which thereby implies authorial intervention. The double voice of a narrator with future knowledge and Helene von Druskowitz means that it is possible to read this text as both the monologue of a woman in the nineteenth century, who makes references to other writers and has moments of insight, and as the representation of the mental landscape of a woman, which is fragmentary and constructed by the author through the montage of texts. As a result of this authorial intervention, an internal dialogue evolves between the fictional Druskowitz of the monologue and the authorial voice, which has a consciousness beyond the narrated time, and consequently the text is shot through with future knowledge and allusion. The following examples of games with time hint playfully at the presence of this consciousness.

The text constantly plays word games which appear associative and on one occasion even breaks down into seemingly nonsensical babble: 'Sag danke. Sag bitte. Danke, bitte, bitte, danke, dankdank, bittbitt, bibi, debil, bite, nana, dada, eda, ade, scheiden tut weh ...' (*Sakkorausch*: 56). Yet, in this example the author has actually opened up the cultural field of possibilities of meaning. Through the use of anachronism as a technical device, the contemporary reader sees the word 'dada' and all the cultural information which comes with the recognition of that term is brought into the present reading of the text. For although the language is breaking down, the modern reader has come to recognize word association as a form of poetry. On another occasion after some reflections the narrator announces 'Den letzten Gedanken hat mir Sigmund Freud gestohlen. Er wird berühmt werden für die Entdeckung des Todestriebes, zurückgenommenes Diebesgut, der Kleinmut ist der Vater der reinen Lehre' (*Sakkorausch*: 48). On these occasions the reader's present-day perspective renders seemingly insane sentences sane. Credibility is given to the outpourings of Reichart's figure, because we can verify her comments from our present historical position, or alternatively the reader recognizes the author's intervention in ascribing to the narrator powers of clairvoyance. In these and other examples the reader may ask, if the author is playing temporal tricks from her postmodern perspective or creating posthumous time in the text we are reading?

Reflecting on the future return of the soldiers, who willingly went to fight in the First World War with the supporting cheers of their women, Reichart's narrator says:

> Die zurückkommen, werden sich dieser Jauchzer erinnern, dieser Ekstase. Sie werden wieder einmal ihre Affenstärke unter Beweis stellen müssen, und ihre Rache wird fürchterlicher sein, als es sich Frauen jemals ausdenken könnten. Mit ihren Stummeln werden sie die Frauen zu Krüppeln schlagen. Mit dem Eiter ihrer nicht verheilenden Wunden werden sie ihre Kinder und Kindeskinder füttern und so für den nächsten Krieg sorgen, mit aller Sorge, der sie fähig sind. (*Sakkorausch:* 42-3)

The sobering effect this graphic, almost fantastic description has on the reader, results from our awareness of the effects of war on women and children. Our historical knowledge of the Weimar and Nazi periods and the more recent conflict in the former Yugoslavia gives credibility to this vision. Depictions of this form of fascism in the family can be found in other Reichart texts and in *Sakkorausch* they suggest insight on the part of the narrator and confirm the insanity of war.[3]

During the narrator's reflections on the events and future of the First World War, she also experiences moments of insight:

> Ich sehe sie Steine aufstellen.
> Grabsteine.
> Doch nur die Namen werden eingemeißelt.
> Die Erde bleibt knochenleer.
> Sie erfinden sogar einen Namen dafür:
> Kriegerdenkmal. (*Sakkorausch*: 43)

Reminiscent of Christa Wolf's *Kassandra*, who has ominous premonitions about the Trojan war and is locked away for being a political liability, the narrator can be regarded as a 'Seherin'. The wider debate concerning insight centres on the question of whether madness offers one insight into a higher world or 'Übersphäre' as Druskowitz describes it. Related to the question of inspiration or enthusiasm – when one is taken from the normal sphere through divine possession – 'Rausch' or ecstasy often describes this state, but the narrator of *Sakkorausch* dispels the theological explanations, complaining that the doctors at the asylum deny her the alcohol she needs to transport her to this creative state. 'Das Trinken beflügelt meinen Geist, erleichtert das Denken. Der Alkohol löst die Verbindung zur Materie'(*Sakkorausch*: 25).

Helene von Druskowitz is first and foremost a philosopher and *Sakkorausch* dramatizes a feminist mode of thinking. It is, therefore, perhaps not surprising that Reichart chose the monologue as the appropriate form of expression. From a feminist perspective, it gives voice to a historical figure, whom others tried to silence and forget, and it does so with a form which avoids objectification. In terms of literary history, the interior monologue can be seen as the form commensurate to the loss of community. Until the First World War, the purpose of language was to communicate and the logical consistency of the world and God was still not questioned by the majority. In the wake of the writings of Darwin, Nietzsche and Freud and the events of the war, that sense of wholeness was lost forever. The interior monologue reflects the metaphysical loneliness of this historical period and the literary form can also be seen to represent another form of incarceration; that is, of being locked inside one's consciousness. The form of the monologue also provides an effective form for the frequent word games which are central to Reichart's text and which emphasize the humour and articulacy of the narrator. The tension in the relationship between the narrator and the figure of Elizabeth in the text expresses the fundamental issue of choosing to articulate one's thoughts. Elizabeth, the articulate poet, chooses to be silent in *Sakkorausch*, while the narrator criticizes her 'Gemurmel' with the birds which fly into the grounds of the asylum. In *Sakkorausch* the power implications of the articulate woman are made clear and consequently rather than embracing a view of female Otherness which suggests a break with consciousness and language due to its patriarchal history, 'Reichart's character is certainly not afraid to say "I"' (Fiddler 1997: 265).

Sakkorausch is a text with two authors. As Bakhtin suggests in his paper 'Discourse in the Novel', often one text takes precedence over another in the process of grafting together different texts; thus literary language, for example, may be used to illuminate another discourse, as is often the case with irony (Bakhtin 1981: 301-31). In *Sakkorausch*, however, the various texts are not placed within a hierarchical order. It is impossible to find a position from which one discourse is set above another. For example, when the figure of 'Elizabeth' dies, suddenly the narrator is able to remember the first three stanzas of the poem 'My Doves'. The poem appears autonomous within the text, rather than subordinate to the will of others. A further technique which works against any concept of hierarchy within the text results in it being practically impossible to work out where Druskowitz ends and Reichart begins. *Sakkorausch* is truly a double-authored text. Benefiting from the literary advances of modernism and developments in feminist theory and psychological debate, Reichart uses a hybrid texture to show Helene von Druskowitz's nonconformity and creativity to be anything but mad, and as a result *Sakkorausch* acts as a historical corrective. In *Sakkorausch* Elisabeth Reichart plays with the discourse of genius and insight. While on the one hand undermining the reader's understanding of the concepts of femininity and madness, the author does not dismiss these concepts but reappropriates and revalues genius and insight within a feminist context. As a result of these various textual strategies, during the act of reading the reader is made aware of the subversive and ultimately empowering quality of the text.

Notes

[1] The Princess of Wales interviewed by Martin Bashir *Panorama* (BBC1, 20 November 1995). Nicholas Soames on *Newsnight* (BBC2, 20 November 1995).

[2] For a detailed biographical essay on Helene von Druskowitz see Gronewald 1992.

Notes continued

[3] Further depictions include the destructive relationship between the returning soldier and his wife in 'Wie nah ist Mauthausen?' and the description of family life in 'Der Sonntagsbraten' both in the collection of stories *La valse* (Reichart 1992) and the story *Fotze* (Reichart 1993).

Bibliography

Abrams, M.H. 1953. *The Mirror and the Lamp: Romantic Theory and the Critical Tradition*, London, OUP

Bakhtin, M. M. 1981. *The Dialogic Imagination: Four Essays*, tr. Caryl Emerson and Michael Holoquist, Texas, University of Texas Press

Battersby, Christine. 1989. *Gender and Genius: Towards a Feminist Aesthetics*, London, The Women's Press

Brooks, Peter. 1987. 'The Idea of a Psychoanalytic Literary Criticism', in Shlomith Rimmon-Kenan (ed.), *Discourse in Psychoanalysis and Literature*, London, Methuen: 1-18

Druskowitz, Helene von. 1885. *Drei englische Dichterinnen*, Berlin

—. 1988. *Der Mann als logische und sittliche Unmöglichkeit und als Fluch der Welt: Pessimistische Kardinalsätze* (1905), originally *Pessimistische Kardinalsätze: Ein Vademekum für die freiesten Geister*, von Erna (Helene von Druskowitz), Wittenberg, Kore

Fiddler, Allyson. 1997. 'Post-war Austrian Women Writers', in Chris Weedon (ed.) *Postwar Women's Writing in German*, Oxford, Berghahn: 243-68

Gilbert, Sandra M. and Susan Gubar. 1979. *The Madwoman in the Attic*, New Haven, Yale University Press

Gronewold, Hinrike. 1992. 'Die geistige Amazone', in Sibylle Duda and Luise Pusch (eds), *WahnsinnsFrauen*, Frankfurt am Main, Suhrkamp: 96-122

Möbius, P. J. 1990. *Über den physiologischen Schwachsinn des Weibes* (1905), Munich, Matthes and Seitz

Reichart, Elisabeth. 1992. *La Valse*, Salzburg, Otto Müller

—. 1993. *Fotze*, Salzburg, Otto Müller

—. 1994. *Sakkorausch*, Salzburg, Otto Müller

Ussher, Jane. 1991. *Women's Madness: Misogyny or Mental Illness?*, London, Harvester Wheatsheaf

Utopia, Dystopia, and Realism in Christine Nöstlinger's Children's Books

Gabriela Steinke

Christine Nöstlinger, born in 1936 into a working-class Viennese family, is one of Austria's best known and most successful contemporary writers. She has published some ninety-odd books to date; the vast majority are books for children and adolescents.[1] Most of these have enjoyed phenomenal success, both commercially and in terms of critical acclaim. Several of her books have been adopted for the school syllabus, not only in German-speaking countries, but also, for instance, in the United States. Her 'realistic' books are usually set in the milieu she knows best, in working-class or petit-bourgeois Vienna, and deal with the everyday concerns of children – family, school, friends, first love. Nöstlinger advocates human rights for children in her books: children must be acknowledged as autonomous human beings and not treated as objects of pedagogical endeavours. Whatever her protagonists' misdemeanours, Nöstlinger never raises a moralizing finger. Her writing style is rooted in the Viennese vernacular and is often extremely funny, but also bitingly ironic, although her linguistic sharpness and immediacy have shown signs of abating in recent years.

Nöstlinger understands most of her books as literature proper. In a blistering attack on mainstream Germanists, who insist on categorising children's books as 'zielgruppenorientierte Trivialliteratur', Nöstlinger argues not only for differentiation in the area of children's books (there are trivial ones but there is also 'literature'), she demands an end to the different criteria used for adult's and for children's books: 'Aber wo es um Bücher für Erwachsene geht, werden ja auch Kritiken geschrieben und keine Gutachten' (1985b: 383). Nöstlinger complains that critics of children's literature have ignored the remarkable changes the genre has undergone since the late sixties and that they still judge a children's book in terms of 'pädagogisch wertvoll' rather than considering it as literature. She has no illusions about her readership, maintaining: 'Auch die Kinder sind ja schon korrumpiert von klein auf. In dem Alter, wo sie lesen können, ham's schon ka Vorstellung mehr von einer freundlichen Utopie'. But this is partly why she writes: 'Ich möcht die Kinder auf die Widersprüche aufmerksam machen. Die Kinder müssen erst einmal erkennen, was an den Zuständen schlecht ist – die meisten nehmen ja die herrschenden Zustände als die einzig möglichen ziemlich kritiklos hin ... Die erste Stufe wäre, den Kindern ihr eigenes dumpfes Unbehagen, das sie net artikulieren können, vorzuformulieren'. The second stage would be to awaken in children the longing for a different order and kindle their imagination as to 'wie es freundlicher und humaner zugehen könnt' auf der Welt' (quoted in Löffler 1983: 61).

In this paper I will concentrate on four of her books with fantastic elements, to which a number of the characteristics relevant to her realistic fiction also apply. Nöstlinger's starting point is, with one exception, always the 'real world', into which fantastic elements intrude. These four books are her first published children's book *Die feuerrote Friederike* (1970), *Konrad oder Das Kind aus der Konservenbüchse* (1975), *Hugo, das Kind in den besten Jahren* (1983) and *Der TV-Karl* (1995). I will argue that Nöstlinger starts with a 'Vorformulierung' of a 'freundliche Utopie', but comes to depicting dystopia as a mirror of 'real life'.

The publication of *Die feuerrote Friederike* was commented on by Klaus Doderer, doyen of critics in this field, as follows: 'Mein Gott, ein neuer Ton in der Jugendliteratur, ein brisantes Thema im Bereich der Kinderwelt – eine keineswegs süßlich geratene Paradies-Utopie im Kinderbuch!' (quoted in Dilewsky 1993: 20). The book tells the story of Friederike, aged about six, who lives with her old aunt and her cat in very modest circumstances, who has exceptionally bright red hair and is rather fat, and who is victimized by the other children because of these physical attributes. The little girl's misery, as well as the surrounding adults' blindness or helplessness, is captured in simple but convincing language and is nowhere belittled. So far, so realistic. The fantastic element appears when the cat begins to talk to reveal that Friederike's red hair, a feature shared by both the aunt and the cat, is magical and can not only be made to glow and burn but also enables the wearer to fly. Friederike finds a letter left by her father in which he invites her to join him in a wonderful country to which he has emigrated. He decribes it as a socialist paradise:

> Es gibt ein Land, dort sind alle Menschen glücklich.... Kein Kind wird ausgelacht. Alle helfen einander. Die Väter und Mütter müssen dort nicht sehr viel arbeiten. Keiner will reicher werden als die anderen. Der Schuster macht Schuhe, weil er das gerne tut. Wer Schuhe haben will, holt sich welche von ihm.... Wenn dort jemand gar nichts arbeiten will, geben ihm die Leute auch alles umsonst. Sie sind nicht geizig. Die meisten Menschen arbeiten aber trotzdem. Es macht ihnen Spaß. Für Arbeiten, die keiner machen will, haben sie Maschinen erfunden. Leider ist der Weg in dieses Land sehr schwierig. Man müßte mit dem Zug, dann mit dem Schiff und dann wieder mit dem Zug fahren.... Aber selbst wenn man das alles tun wollte, gelänge es noch längst nicht, denn man bekommt keine Auskunft, wo der richtige Weg ist. (*Die feuerrote Friederike*: 52)

This is, albeit in very simple terms, the description of a classic literary utopia, an ideal society geographically removed from the writer's own, but reachable under certain circumstances. At the end of the book, Friederike and her aunt and cat escape to this ideal country, taking along the postman and his wife who have helped them throughout. They are able to reach the promised land with relative ease because they can fly; people not endowed with red magic hair would find it almost impossible. Not only is the way long and arduous, the few road signs which exist have been turned by 'böse Menschen': 'Denn die Menschen können nicht glauben, daß es dieses Land gibt. Oder sie glauben, es sei woanders. Sehr wenige wissen davon, sagen aber aus Bosheit nichts' (*Die feuerrote Friederike*: 53).

Nöstlinger is said to have later denounced her book as 'ideologisch überfrachtet' and 'die kindliche Klientel überfordernd' (Dilewsky 1993: 42), a criticism that I regard as only partly justified as the book can certainly be read on several levels. What is of most interest in the present context is firstly that she gives a fairly detailed description of a utopian state and secondly that the solution to the protagonist's problems can only be found there, not in her own reality. We therefore see both hope (escape to utopia) and hopelessness (there is no prospect of a solution to Friederike's dilemma in her reality). Before providing her escapist ending, however, Nöstlinger has managed not only to raise questions about the treatment of outsiders and the complacency and conformism which allow this (mis-)treatment to proceed unchecked; her mentioning of people's general inability and unwillingness to believe in the possibility of such an ideal society challenges readers to examine their own belief in, and resolve to strive for, a better world. Nöstlinger implies that anybody working towards utopia would be swimming against the stream, so Friederike's story and Nöstlinger's description of the ideal society clearly serve to underline the desirability, even necessity of making the attempt to reach utopia. However, an even darker side of human nature than complacency and lack of imagination is hinted at with those individuals who accept the existence of the utopian society, even know its location, but keep it secret out of malice. In this early and hopeful book, they still number very few.

Konrad, in my opinion one of her best books, manages a solution in reality. Frau Bartolotti, a somewhat anarchic single woman who earns her living as a weaver, takes delivery of a parcel which contains, literally, a tin can with a seven-year-old boy in it. A nourishing solution has to be poured over him, and then he is to all intents and purposes a normal human boy. He has, however, in the factory where he was produced, been programmed as an 'ideal' child according to conservative adult standards. He is extremely well behaved, gets physically ill when he hears 'bad' language or sees 'bad' behaviour, in short, he has internalized the rules set by adults to the highest degree possible. Frau Bartolotti, with her own unconventional lifestyle and opinions finds this hard to come to terms with, but she begins to love the boy and tries to do her best by him. Her twice-a-week friend Egon, a dry stick of an apothecary (one of

Nöstlinger's more malicious caricatures), on the other hand is absolutely delighted with Konrad. When the factory notices that Konrad has been delivered to the wrong address, they try to re-appropriate him, and the only way to prevent this is to change the well-behaved Konrad into a normal naughty child.

This book, despite its entertaining storyline and very funny narrative style, presents a disturbing dystopian vision which in these days of gene manipulation and cloning takes on a new relevance. Clearly Nöstlinger's underlying idea was to show how questionable adult ideals of children's behaviour can be and how the kind of socialization which emphasizes conforming to the existing order can restrict and ultimately violate what she considers to be the defining characteristics of a human being: creativity, individuality, playfulness, imagination. If we then look further at the central conceit of a human being manufactured to specification (and one cannot help but wonder who would write the specification), a homunculus who would, if his life had developed as his creators planned, never have had a chance to become a truly autonomous, fully human person, then the full horror of the situation becomes apparent. Konrad does have emotions, he can love, he can be happy or unhappy, but to begin with, these are all conditioned reactions so that he wants what he has been programmed to want. Any truly childlike traits have been ironed out. The factory's employees, when they try to retrieve Konrad, are presented as what can almost be described as fascist henchmen. They all wear the same pale blue uniform, seem to have unlimited reservoirs of information, and at the climax they appear everywhere so that escape appears to be impossible; they seem untouched by any ordinary rules or laws and are genuinely frightening. They are outwitted, of course. Konrad has painfully learned to be a naughty child and is thus rejected by them and the original buyers, but we have been told that Konrad is one of many, and an uneasy feeling remains as to the fate of these others. We need not credit Nöstlinger with any prophetic gift, but in view of the contemporary preoccupation, not only with the above mentioned gene manipulation but also the ramifications in connection with fertility treatment, the increasing possibilities for technical intervention in (for the moment) animal breeding programmes alongside an increasing demand for perfection in human offspring, Konrad poses a number of moral questions about societal ideals which need to be urgently addressed by humanity as a whole. Children are not always a joy and delight to be with, they are not particularly 'user-friendly'. How much intervention is possible, how much, if any, is desirable? How long before we eradicate, along with any perceived imperfections, the human side of human beings?

Hugo, das Kind in den besten Jahren is based on a series of fantastic drawings by Jörg Wollmann. The pictures provided Nöstlinger with inspiration but the story is entirely her own product. Hugo is, according to one leading critic, 'ein nicht leicht verstehbarer und nicht auf den ersten Blick ins Gesamtwerk der

Autorin einzuordnender phantastischer Roman, um den die Kritik bisher einen weiten Bogen gemacht hat' (Dahrendorf 1992: 21).

It is certainly no ordinary children's book. Ordinary children play no part in the action; they clearly exist, but the narrative revolves around adults on the one hand and 'alte Kinder' who cannot grow up on the other. Hugo, 'das Kind in den besten Jahren', is past fifty, and some truly 'alte Kinder' he encounters are even older. These characters live in a society which is near enough our own to be recognisable (Mike Rogers feels reminded of Switzerland [1993: 207], whereas Eva-Maria Metcalf has no doubt that Austria is the model [1989: 174]) but which includes many fantastic elements: animals are sentient members of society, Hugo goes on his illicit journeys in a paper airship, Hugo's parents, Miesmeier 1 and Miesmeier 2, are both male, the 'Zeitdehner' can slow the passing of time, and so forth. The fantastic elements are introduced without comment and thus taken for granted, whereas Nöstlinger exaggerates and caricatures many of the traits which are familiar from 'real life'. This technique results in the portrait of a society which is both realistic and dystopian. Reality is mirrored with the help of a magnifying glass, as it were, the veneer of normality and decency is exposed as just a veneer underneath which we see narrow-minded pettiness, authoritarian structures and multiple, sometimes lethal, discrimination of minorities.

> Hunde standen damals im Ansehen der Bevölkerung nicht gerade sehr hoch. Hunde hatten zwar die gleichen Rechte wie alle anderen auch: aktives und passives Wahlrecht und Recht auf Einleitung von Bürgerinitiativen und Recht auf Bildung und was es sonst noch für Rechte gibt. Sogar ein Extra-Gesetz zum Schutze der Hunds-Minderheit gab es. Aber Gesetze allein bringen noch kein Ansehen! Gesetze schützen nicht davor, daß Nasen gerümpft werden und Abstand gehalten wird ... Daß man auf Hunde hochmütig herabschaute, war ja auch schon daran zu erkennen, daß weder im Parlament noch in irgendeinem Gemeinderat oder Stadtrat ein Hund saß. Wo doch die Hundsminderheit immerhin 10% des Gesamtbestandes an Bevölkerung ausmachte ... Doch außer den Hunden selbst störte niemanden in Ammersbrunn, daß dem nicht so war. Die Ammersbrunner fanden, in ihrer Stadt sei alles in schönster Ordnung. Es störte sie nicht nur die Hundsungerechtigkeit nicht, es störte sie überhaupt nichts. (*Hugo*: 9)

This passage, which comes at the very beginning of the book, introduces a society which is tolerant and liberal on paper but which in practice turns a blind eye to exclusion and discrimination. Although the oppressed minorities are mostly the animal members of society, Nöstlinger is not concerned with a 'be-kind-to-animals' campaign. One could easily substitute 'Jews' or any other oppressed group of people for the animals as becomes obvious in the absurd criteria for discrimination in the case of pigs: 'Haarige Wildschweine bekamen weder Führerschein noch Pilotenschein. Auch vom Hochschulstudium waren sie ausgeschlossen, und in bessere Lokale als Bahnhofswirtschaften ließ man sie überhaupt nicht hinein.... Unbehaarte rosa Hausschweine dagegen waren sehr angesehen! Sie saßen in Direktionsetagen und Anwaltskanzleien und Ordinationen, und niemand verwehrte ihnen den Zutritt in allerhöchste Kreise' (*Hugo*: 129). Nöstlinger does not fall into the trap of depicting the oppressed minority groups as saintly martyrs; there are just as many mean, apathetic, narrow-minded and downright nasty specimens here as in mainstream society. The point is that their individual shortcomings do not justify their collective oppression.

The most significant minority in terms of the book are the 'alte Kinder', children who do not grow up even if they have lived for seventy years and longer. These children are subject to the authority and dependent on the charity of their parents and other adults all their lives, they are therefore regarded as a burden; they have no 'rights', their lives are eternally regimented and restricted, they may be put 'in [ein Kinderheim] für vermischte, unbrauchbare Kinder' (*Hugo*: 22); and even if, in some cases, their physical size allows them to pass as adults and they try this as an attempt at autonomy, they remain unhappy because life as an adult runs counter to their childish nature. And on top of everything, they have to worry about their future because 'Nicht einmal eine Rente gab es für alte Kinder. Alte Kinder waren komplett auf die Freundlichkeit und Güte netter Menschen angewiesen' (*Hugo*: 12). The eradication of this last problem is the eponymous Hugo's main purpose in life. 'Hugo wollte alle alten Kinder, und die in den besten Jahren auch, zu einer Interessengemeinschaft, einer Art Gewerkschaft, zusammenschliessen ... Und die "Alte-Kinder-Rente" war sein Anliegen' (12-13). So he tries to contact as many 'alte Kinder' as possible on his secret nightly flights in a paper airship, a task not made any easier by the fact that, as in classic case studies of many an oppressed minority, some of the old children try to deny their nature, not only to society but also to themselves. Assimilation as a survival strategy, however, is discredited by Nöstlinger and shown to bring misery more often than success.

Hugo is the one who insists on the right even of old children to be children and to be accepted on their own terms without the repression of a straitjacket concept of educating children into 'good' adults. He formulates his creed as follows:' Ich bin ein Kind und habe ein Recht auf alles Kindliche. Ich weigere mich, Ordnung als den höchsten Wert im Leben anzuerkennen! Ich habe ein Recht darauf, glücklich zu sein! Ich muß nicht dauernd Sachen machen, die mir sinnlos vorkommen! Ich muß mich nicht dauernd danach richten, was die Erwachsenen wollen! Ich bin ein freies Kind und weiß selbst am besten, was für mich gut ist!' (*Hugo*: 205-6). It goes without saying that in his society, and by implication in the 'real world' of the reader, the exact opposite is normal practice.

In an interesting article about 'ewige Kinder', Hans-Heino Ewers argues that Hugo and his ilk stand at the end of a long line of eternal children in art and literature. In older works, most notably during the romantic period, childhood was interpreted as embodying a particular state of purity and perfection within the human condition, and the eternal child often appeared as a genius or even as a guardian angel who could re-connect both adults and children to the true nature and original creativity which they had lost in the process of growing up. This idealized concept of childhood has not entirely vanished even now, although it was already subverted by J.M. Barrie and Lewis Carrol.[2] In Nöstlinger's old children 'hat sich der Fall der literarischen Figur vollendet: Aus einem engelhaften Wesen von strahlender ewiger Kindheit ist der pathologische Fall eines anormalen, wachstumsgestörten Kindes geworden ... [Sein] Kindbleiben erscheint als krankhafte Abweichung, als Verkrüppelung, die von Internisten, Orthopäden und Pädagogen mit Attesten bescheinigt werden' (Ewers 1985: 63). And yet there is some potential at least for what a child might see as, in Nöstlinger's words, a 'freundliche Utopie': a society in which animals are integrated members and can easily be communicated with, same-sex as well as mixed-sex marriages, a truly biblical life span for the humans, if not the animals, and, somewhat further along the road to wishful thinking, the ability to fly and to have access to certain kinds of 'magic'. Hugo's reality, of course, has more nightmarish than positive traits.

The dystopian elements are epitomized in the 'Hasenflüchtlingslager' which was originally built as a refuge for hares during a pogrom and is still billed as the ideal sanctuary for misfits and persecuted individuals. It turns out to be a totally regimented society which ironically negates everything its original inmates used to fight for. Ruhe und Ordnung is the motto, and anybody who does not conform is either forcefully evicted or, like a group of 'alte Kinder' who naturally disturbed the peace, sedated and hypnotized into submission. The 'HAFLA' is controlled in a chillingly efficient bureaucratic manner, and the inhabitants are so subdued that they look the other way when Hugo and his friends are marched away for deportation with the comment: 'Wir sind fix, wenn es darum geht, Störenfriede abzubeuteln! Keiner kann uns unsere Ordnung stören!' (*Hugo*: 210). Similarities to certain real-life societies need hardly be spelled out.

A contrasting idea of an alternative society is offered by the 'Wohn-Wahl-Waldschule', clearly modelled on A. S. Neill's Summerhill but without the school fees, where children are not forced to learn, or indeed do, anything and as a consequence want to know so much that demand outstrips supply and instruction will soon have to be rationed. This school represents a vision of utopia, and by its very existence highlights the dystopian elements prevailing elsewhere.

Hugo is a complex book which not only echoes familiar Nöstlinger concerns but also makes reference to many other works (there is more than a hint of Oskar Matzerath in Hugo, for instance); it would merit a detailed analysis.³ In the present context it is obvious that Nöstlinger has gone further towards a dystopian vision of society. Where *Konrad* still provided a happy ending, *Hugo* is open-ended, and there are no solutions to the problems in sight. Hugo might be able to collect enough old children to form his union, but even securing a pension would only alleviate one aspect of their suffering while the fundamental dilemma remains. This society is unlikely to change in such a way as would enable any of its members who do not conform to its standards to live self-determined lives. Hugo's subversive activities are too limited to become the spark for a revolution which could bring about change.

With *Der TV-Karl*, Nöstlinger seems to have finally descended into despair. This slim volume purports to be the diary of 12-year-old Anton who, we learn by-the-by, is a loner without the ability to make friends who lives in truly depressing, though not unrealistic circumstances. His parents are in the last throes of fighting before the inevitable divorce and almost completely ignore the boy, even forgetting his birthday. The only consolation comes from his grandmother who is, however, powerless to change the situation in any significant way. So far we are on familiar Nöstlinger territory, but where in other books she provides her child protagonists with a fighting spirit and a chance to improve their lives to some extent, Anton meets the TV-Karl.

This character is an elderly man who lives in Anton's television set and seems to spend some of his time as an extra in serials. He is able to communicate with anybody in front of the television set when a special blue button on the remote control is pressed. Karl offers Anton solace, advice and help with his homework, and Anton soon becomes completely dependent on his company, thus isolating himself even more from his real-life surroundings. Very quickly he reaches a state where he admits to himself: 'Ohne ihn, habe ich gemerkt, könnte ich gar nicht mehr sein' (*Der TV-Karl*: 21). Karl lets Anton benefit from his knowledge and experience, although he entertains some rather antiquated notions of childhood and family life which Anton refutes from bitter experience.

Anton's only hope is that he may go to live with his grandmother after his parents' divorce; meanwhile it is Karl who provides him with interest in life. Karl is able to leave the television set for short periods although the outside air causes him to shrink gradually; this has near fatal consequences on one occasion when Karl agrees to impersonate Anton's father in order to sort out a problem. Anton's television set is thrown out and while Karl keeps shrinking, Anton and his grandmother desperately try to find another remote control with the crucial blue button. They succeed in the nick of time, but at a price: the grandmother is in imminent danger of being arrested and put in a mental institution because she has been stealing remote controls all over the neighbourhood. Karl offers her asylum in the television ('Dazu braucht man zwar ein TV-Asylrecht, aber das, hat er gesagt, bekommt die Oma sicher' [*Der TV-Karl*: 72]). Anton decides to follow his grandmother into the television, and the book ends with a newspaper entry about their disappearance: 'Die Polizei tappt völlig im Dunkeln, eine Familientragödie wird vermutet' (74).

A tragedy indeed! There are hints of the usual Nöstlinger humour in the narrative, and Anton is potentially a typical Nöstlinger hero. But what of the 'solution'? Is there no alternative to an escape into a world of illusion, a world of manufactured entertainment which does not even represent a potentially viable utopia like the one Friederike escaped to? Karl and his grandmother give up on the real world without being able to imagine any alternative but the pre-fabricated world of television, of make-believe. It seems that Nöstlinger has finally run out of hope. Dahrendorf detects earlier signs of desperation in Nöstlinger's writing which, he claims, she tones down in her children's books but which she articulates in her novel for adults, *Die unteren sieben Achtel des Eisbergs* (Dahrendorf 1985: 37 and 39). Desperation maybe, rage and frustration certainly, are detectable in many of Nöstlinger's books, notably in the four discussed here. Nor does Nöstlinger commit the sin of writing 'in Kniebeuge' which Erich Kästner so deplored in many books for children.[4] She always takes her child protagonists and their problems entirely seriously and reflects dilemmas which are anything but 'childish'. However, for an author who intended to write 'freundliche Utopien' (Löffler 1983: 61), Nöstlinger has come to show a remarkable concentration of pessimistic outlooks, especially in her later 'fantastic' books. She herself admitted in 1985 that her hope and courage were waning, and although this has not restricted her output, her expectations of what she can achieve with children's books have become more modest. In her own words: 'Ich gab den Versuch, an einem Heilungsprozess teilzunehmen, auf und legte mir einen Handel mit Heftpflastern zu' (Nöstlinger 1985a: 12). It can of course be argued that she has thus become more of a realist. Nöstlinger never portrayed a 'heile Welt' in her children's books, but she intended to communicate hope for a better future and the possibility of change through individual initiative. Utopias are meant to give an example of what we should strive to attain. Dystopias can serve as a warning of what might be if we do not resist restrictive tendencies in society, if we conform, no matter what the cost in self-fulfilment and self-determination might be for ourselves and others. Given the present state of the world, Nöstlinger's warnings, whether written on the basis of hope or of hopelessness, are uncomfortably close to the bone.

Notes

[1] The reasons why children's literature is a legitimate field for 'serious' academic analysis have been expounded at great length by such authorities as Malte Dahrendorf (1986), Dagmar Grenz (1990), Maria Lypp (1977) Zohar Shavit (1986) and others; Alison Lurie (1990) has shown the possibilities of subverting societal values in children's books; specifically on Nöstlinger see Mike Rogers (1993).

[2] There are, however, many adaptations of both *Peter Pan* and *Alice in Wonderland* which severely sabotage the originals and offer yet another sanitized view of idealized childhood.

[3] Eva-Maria Metcalf (1989) devotes a considerable portion of her thesis to *Hugo* but only skims several important aspects such as intertextuality and narrative style. Otherwise, as Dahrendorf suggested, critics have given the book a wide berth.

[4] On the occasion of a 'Kundgebung für das Jugendbuch' in Zurich (1950); an often quoted criticism here taken from a quotation in Luiselotte Enderle (1993: 90).

Bibliography

Dahrendorf, Malte. 1985. 'Verschiedene Wahrheiten für Kinder und Erwachsene?', in Freundeskreis des Instituts für Jugendbuchforschung Frankfurt (ed.), *Kinderwelten. Kinder und Kindheit in der neueren Literatur.* Festschrift für Klaus Doderer, Weinheim, Beltz: 21-41
—. 1986. *Jugendliteratur und Politik*, Frankfurt am Main, dipa
—. 1992. 'Geschichten über Kinder in den besten Jahren', *Informationen Jugendliteratur und Medien 1992*, 44, 1: 20-5
Dilewski, Klaus Jürgen. 1993. *Christine Nöstlinger als Kinder- und Jugendbuchautorin. Genres, Stoffe, Sozialcharaktere, Intentionen.* Frankfurt am Main, Haag und Herchen
Enderle, Luiselotte. 1993. *Erich Kästner*. Reinbek, rororo
Ewers, Hans-Heino. 1985. 'Kinder, die nicht erwachsen werden. Die Geniusgestalt des ewigen Kindes bei Goethe, Tieck, E.T.A. Hoffmann, J.M. Barrie, Ende und Nöstlinger', in Freundeskreis des Instituts für Jugendbuchforschung Frankfurt (ed.), *Kinderwelten. Kinder und Kindheit in der neueren Literatur.* Festschrift für Klaus Doderer, Weinheim, Beltz: 42-70
Grenz, Dagmar (ed.). 1990. *Kinderliteratur – Literatur für Erwachsene?* Munich, Wilhelm Fink Verlag
Löffler, Sigrid. 1983. 'Fast wie ein Markenartikel. Die Wiener Kinderbuch-Autorin hat Erfolg mit Anti-Helden', *Die Zeit*, 16 December: 61
Lurie, Alison. 1990. *Not in Front of the Grown-Ups*, London, Sphere Books

Lypp, Maria (ed.). 1977. *Literatur für Kinder. Studien über ihr Verhältnis zur Gesamtliteratur*, Göttingen, Vandenhoek und Ruprecht

Metcalf, Eva-Maria. 1989. 'Children in the Prime of their Lives: Children and Childhood in the Books of Christine Nöstlinger', Ph. D. dissertation, University of Minnesota

Nöstlinger, Christine. 1970. *Die feuerrote Friederike*, Vienna, Jugend und Volk

—. 1975. *Konrad oder Das Kind aus der Konservenbüchse*, Hamburg, Verlag Friedrich Oetinger

—. 1983. *Hugo, das Kind in den besten Jahren*. Roman nach phantastischen Bildern von Jörg Wollmann, Weinheim, Beltz und Gelberg

—. 1985a. 'Die Richtung der Hoffnung', *Fundevogel*, 1: 12-13

—. 1985b. 'Ist Kinderliteratur Literatur?' Festvortrag zur Eröffnung der österreichischen Buchwoche '85 in der Wiener Hofburg, *Anzeiger des österreichischen Buchhandels*, 23, December: 383-5

—. 1995. *Der TV-Karl*, Weinheim, Beltz und Gelberg

Rogers, Mike. 1993. 'Christine Nöstlinger: Kids' Stuff?' in Schmidt, Ricarda and Moray McGowan (eds), *From High Priests to Desecrators: Contemporary Austrian Writers*, Sheffield, Sheffield Academic Press: 201-211

Shavit, Zohar. 1986. *Poetics of Children's Literature*, Athens, University of Georgia Press

Christine Nöstlinger and the Force of Tradition

Mike Rogers

It is a tradition (whether right or wrong) to regard the fairy-tale as the primal form of children's literature. Without discussing the historical, psychological and sociological reasons behind this, I nevertheless find it useful to begin the present paper by mentioning two of the main approaches to the fairy-tale itself, which, I believe, can act as pointers to two major issues involved in considering children's literature. These are Bruno Bettelheim's psycho-analytical view and Jack Zipes's corrective reminder that, before they entered the nursery, fairy-tales originally emerged as folk-tales from a specific historical, social and political context (Bettelheim 1976, Zipes 1979).[1] Thus, the wicked step-mother may indeed reflect the child's unwillingness to attribute negative qualities to the real mother (even though the child perceives her as having them), but the figure's presence in so many stories may equally result from high mortality rates in child-birth. While Bettelheim suggests that the fairy-tale (and, by extension, children's literature) has its major purpose in assisting the child's psychological development, Zipes's attitude would attribute at least equal importance to the socio-political message. In the long run, however, a strict separation of the two is perhaps neither practicable nor desirable, since the socialization of the individual necessarily depends on both internal and external factors.

I should like to parallel Bettelheim and Zipes with another contrasting pair of critical approaches to children's literature itself: those of Alison Lurie and John Stephens. Before applying a predominantly linguistic approach to children's literature, with a comprehensive discourse analysis that concentrates to a fair degree on implied subject positions, Stephens offers us in *Language and Ideology in Children's Fiction* (1992) some general comments on children's literature – a hazardous undertaking, given the vast range of books marketed under that heading. However, he draws attention to one of the basic premises: 'what this otherwise rather amorphous body of texts has in common is an impulse to intervene in the lives of children' (8). Like castor oil, tofu, or Lord Reith's BBC, they will be good for one. Alison Lurie, on the other hand, stresses in her collection of essays, *Not in front of the Grown-Ups* (1990), the subversive element of children's literature, which, in the English tradition of Carroll and Lear, can scarcely be denied.

And here I have arrived at one of the senses of tradition which will be important in the present discussion: tradition as what we expect from a given genre, the models to which we anticipate the books we read will conform. This notion of conforming to models also gives us another relevant sense of tradition, which relates very clearly to the pedagogic function of children's literature: tradition as that which parents hand on to children, with the expectation that they will respect and even venerate it in the same way. After all, they, the parents, received it from their own parents, and they assume their children will behave as they did. However, healthy psychological development demands that children become independent, while healthy social development requires that they learn how to relate to others and others' demands. These two necessities must be balanced against one another, so the wholesale rejection of tradition (which cannot help being 'the parents' tradition') is not a realistic option except for the total solipsist.

To meet these demands, children's literature not only hands on tradition but also mediates between its sense as a set of demands and its sense as a shared body of knowledge and assumptions, inasmuch as a story provides an area within which tradition's claims can be safely investigated and challenged, a space for negotiation where there are no permanent consequences. This becomes clear when we consider the bedtime story, which gives the child a sense of security in the unvarying repetition the child demands, and also a sense of adventure without danger, because everything is 'only a dream' – the story closes the events of the day and opens up the space for dream-work to deal, one hopes, with particular conflicts.

This is, perhaps, the moment to mention the role of the imagination, not least since 'the stimulation of the imagination' is one of the openly acknowledged purposes of children's literature. In some respects, Zipes and Bettelheim agree here that the development of the capacity to fantasize is an extremely important step for the child in grappling with the problems of life, whether this means facing up to spiritual conflicts and working them through, or envisaging the possibility that the socially powerless might one day take power. Maybe one could combine the two in a Goethean vision of Fantasie as the goddess who frees one from all kinds of bonds and boundaries. On the other hand, a fantasy-world can offer an all-too convenient refuge from 'reality' for those who find themselves persecuted or unable to cope with the demands of existence. Indeed, one of the criticisms levelled at Nöstlinger's first book for children was that its heroine took permanent refuge in an idealized fantasy-world, rather than taking up arms against a sea of troubles.

Die feuerrote Friederike (1970) dramatizes the predicament of the 'outsider' child, red-haired Friederike, whose red hair provides both the reason for her exclusion and, inasmuch as it can burn the children who tease her, a means of revenge for that exclusion. Friederike does not live with her parents, but with an aunt and her cat. This arrangement (as in other children's books) avoids the need to portray conflicts between the parent as the authority figure and the child as the subordinate. An adult is present, and is part of the child's world, but as a companion, as a co-conspirator.

On the other hand, the whole of normal society is comprehensively rejected by Friederike, Aunt and Cat, together with a friendly postman and wife, who all fly off together to a Happy Land. The element of social cooperation is only present inasmuch as the hereditarily gifted Aunt, Friederike and Cat put their aeronautical abilities at the service of their non-magical friends. Indeed, Friederike's rejection of human society upset the pedagogically-minded critics of children's literature so much that one of them wrote an article whose title asked whether she really had to fly away (Müller 1973).

Although her later books are by no means exclusively devoted to outsider children, this first book of hers makes it clear that she does not follow the tradition of reconciling the individual and society when such reconciliation would demand too great a surrender on the part of the individual. As I have indicated elsewhere (Rogers 1994), Nöstlinger uses the idea of the child in many positive, not to say subversive, ways, even to the degree of constructing the 'child who never grows up' – or, as one might also suspect, who is never allowed to grow up. The parent figures in *Hugo, oder das Kind in den besten Jahren* (1983) are apparently both male, but their over-protective nature is best defined by their names: Miesmeier 1 and Miesmeier 2. Indeed, positively presented parent-figures are rare in Nöstlinger's works. Ilse Janda, who runs off to Italy for what we all assume is sexual experience, is as much running away from her parents as running to the man in the red sports-car (*Ilse Janda, 14*, Nöstlinger 1974a). The father in *Wir pfeifen auf den Gurkenkönig* (1972b) reveals the Fascist and authoritarian elements inherent in the father's role in the German-speaking world by his unquestioning obedience to the dubious figure of the Gherkin King, who has rightly been ousted by his subjects. In *Konrad oder das Kind aus der Konservendose* (1975) there are pseudo-parental figures who inflict the educational process on the child in their charge. But it is a grotesque inversion of the normal conditioning, inasmuch as the Kid from a Kan has come off the production-line as a 'perfect child' and has to be trained to be 'normal' – and even 'more than normal', since the only chance for the parent-figures to retain him (since it turns out that he has been delivered to them by mistake) is to persuade the men from the factory who come to reclaim him that the factory conditioning has failed completely. The strait-laced male pharmacist is thus obliged to devote his pedagogic zeal to teaching Konrad bad words and worse actions, a process of which he could truthfully have said, 'This is going to hurt me more than it hurts you'.

In these examples, then, Nöstlinger questions tradition, predominantly through the use of fantasy to deform or transcend the expectations of reality. However, choosing to make the 'contact-adult' of the grandparents' and not the parents' generation, as she does in several instances, both in contexts of realism and fantasy, is not enough to constitute an attack on traditional values, inasmuch as it maintains the power-structures between the adult and the child, underlines the value of age and experience, and is more than a little reminiscent of older social models, in which grandparents, as part of the *Großfamilie*, naturally lived with their children and grandchildren and functioned as child-minders while the more physically able parents were engaged in the labour of getting a living – Stifter's *Granit* offers a ready example. On the other hand, the processes and the realities of 'education' are ironized directly and indirectly in several books and the notion that authority automatically deserves respect is comprehensively undermined in the service of the individual's right to form independent judgements.

Nöstlinger is openly conscious of the expressly political implications and origins of this attitude, and draws attention to them in the afterword to the first edition of the autobiographical *Maikäfer, flieg!* (1973), in which she speaks of her preference as a child for the Russian troops of occupation over the Americans, and relates this to her preference at the time of writing for the Vietcong over the Green Berets, making clear that these preferences go against the 'tradition' of conservatism and the preservation of the status quo. However, it is equally clear that these preferences fit with the Viennese left-wing 'tradition' of her own family – or at least the male members of it. Nöstlinger's account in *Zwei Wochen im Mai* (1981), the equally autobiographical companion volume to *Maikäfer, flieg!*, of her preference for her father (and the problematic relationship with her mother) suggests deeply personal origins for her own political attitudes.

Rosa Riedl, Schutzgespenst, in the book of the same title (1979), is the only working-class ghost in Europe, and was run over by a tram as she rushed across the road to help a Jewish friend who was being forced to scrub the pavement with a toothbrush immediately after the Anschluß. In creating this character, Nöstlinger is clearly following the pedagogic tradition of children's literature, trying to hand on to the children of the present-day a sense of the past – the past that she regards as *hers*, the tradition of Austro-Marxism which is also kept alive by the grandfather in *Andreas* (1978), who argues with other old party-members about exactly when everything went wrong, and who disapproves deeply of his daughter's bourgeois behaviour.

Nöstlinger is concerned to convey the feel of the everyday past, not just a particular political message – she reprints some ephemera at the end of *Zwei Wochen im Mai* with an express statement to that effect. Sharing a tradition does not have to be simply indoctrination; it can be a step towards communication between the generations, by sharing a sense of what is valued, familiar, and, in that respect, taken for granted. Her depiction of her own life in the immediate post-war period must be understood in that sense, as an attempt to link the past to the present, stressing both their similarities and their differences. Inasmuch as the child Nöstlinger was a child, modern children can relate to her perceptions; but the world she inhabited was a different one, with different problems that need to be explained. The explanation is not intended to serve the abstract pedagogical purpose of increasing the readers' knowledge of the past. It is designed to show how the youthful experiences of the present older generation have made them what they are, in the hope that the present younger generation will understand them better, and see them not as absolute and unchanging authorities but as part of a process. Adults may attempt to influence the young, who may well resist, but the adults may well have fought – and lost – the same battles in their own formative years.

It is in the same sense that we must consider Nöstlinger's involvement with the fabric of Viennese buildings, and their social implications. This is a tradition which has assumed physical form, as anyone can testify who has ever lived in what is nowadays known as a 'Substandardwohnung'. Previous inhabitants have left tangible signs of their physical presence which affect the people living there now: a nameplate might be easy to remove, but a name inscribed on the flap of the letter box is a lot more permanent, as are the vast number of long-since keyless locks that make the front door of the average flat look like a monument to paranoia.

The opening of *Andreas* describes the house in which the action takes place. The house[2] embodies its own history, its own tradition. An isolated bomber from a bombing raid late in the war was responsible for the destruction of its decorative stucco and for deep cracks in the walls, which repeated applications of plain grey rendering (post-war austerity rejecting any attempt at the previous decoration) can neither heal nor disguise, though the housing inspection team deny that they have any significance in terms of the safety of the structure. Instead of exploiting this description as heavy symbolism, Nöstlinger goes on to provide us with isolated scraps from the childhood memories of Andreas's mother who grew up in the house, and then gives us a brief chronicle of events up to the present, including the determination of Andreas's mother, now married and still living there, to take over the other apartments:

> 1966 starb die Alte, die neben Susanna wohnte. Susanna mietete die Wohnung. Zu ihrem Vater sagte sie: 'Wirst sehen, Papa, ich krieg noch den ersten Stock! Wie ein Wurm werd ich mich durchbohren.' Wozu das gut sein sollte, fragte der Vater. Daß irgend jemand, daß vor allem seine Tochter sechs Zimmer als Ziel anstrebte, war ihm verdächtig. Alle, die zuviel wollten, waren verdächtig. (*Andreas*: 30)

In *Andreas* as a whole, and to a lesser extent in other books as well, Nöstlinger stresses, as she does here, the sources of parental behaviour, and the fact that unsatisfactory child-parent relationships have existed before the one that her target-audience is experiencing. Clearly, she is stacking the cards against Susanna, the would-be bourgeoise who is betraying her father's socialist principles, but at least his disappointment in her gives a timely reminder to any reader of any age that parents do not actually control children, and are not able to make them the mere vessels of tradition. On the other hand, there is a sense in which tradition nevertheless asserts itself precisely in a sequence of unsatisfactory parent-child relationships.

What makes such sequences hard to identify (except for outsiders) and thus hard to break, is that the individuals trapped within them tend to see themselves predominantly in the role which they currently inhabit. Tradition, like time, only flows in one direction in this universe of ours, though Nöstlinger does her best, on occasions, to disrupt the inevitable progression, as in *Mister Bats Meisterstück oder die total verjüngte Oma* (1971) or in *Olfi Obermeyer und der Ödipus* (1984), where a teenage son is surprised that his mother should feel compelled to look away when his biological father is getting dressed.

And yet, such devices are not really subversions of tradition; they are inversions. The child and the parent change roles temporarily, but the relationships persist. If they did not, then (as, for example in F. Anstey's *Vice Versa*) there would be no humorous structure to please the audience. Olfi's reaction to what he sees as his mother's prudery – which is intended to show up her behaviour as 'hypocritical' in some sense – never encompasses the possibility that there might be a very good reason why one would wish to avoid even the appearance of physical (let alone sexual) intimacy with a man one had last slept with some sixteen years previously. His reaction is as superficial and patronising in its inverted way, as is his mother's implied prudery about the facts of sex – which is hardly surprising, given their relationship.

In some senses, then, I am here criticising Nöstlinger's ability as a writer, inasmuch as she only gives us a rather cheap and superficial joke. At the same time, though, I am also praising it (in this instance) for establishing (subconsciously) a truth about the way in which families pass on their attitudes. It may be a matter of style (here a certain superficiality in the interpretation of behaviour) as much as the actual principles concerned.

Of course, the word *family* is very important here. Nöstlinger, herself divorced and remarried, (and I make no apology for bringing her life into relation to her work to the same degree that she does herself – peripherally, and exemplarily, rather than causally) has several works that deal with divorce and its consequences, with varying degrees of tact and realism. It is clear that while *Ein Mann für Mama* (1972a) exploits the sentimentality of the situation, others, such as *Sowieso und überhaupt* (1991) are relatively dispassionate, and even in *Ein Mann für Mama* the subsidiary family members and family relationships are presented in such an acerbic way as to undermine any notion that life in an extended family can be idyllic. While the fact that Nöstlinger acknowledges the existence of divorce removes her from the 'heile Welt' tradition of children's fiction, she is certainly no feminist agitator for free love. Indeed, *Olfi Obermeyer und der Ödipus* (1984) plays ironically with the notion of the only boy in a family that consists entirely of women, and the psychoanalytically-based gender theory which unsettles Olfi comes with its vulgar Freudianism straight from a women's magazine.

Nöstlinger's 'realism' is a realism of small details, not a representative realism of large issues and *Zeitgeist*. In that sense, precise observation can undermine the traditional assumption, and the precise observation can be equally present in her fantasies – indeed, it is what makes them interesting and convincing, the small truths within what may be a greater untruth. The odd couple who become 'parents' of Konrad, the Kid from a Kan, are not a plea for new forms of relationship – they are an embodiment of two forms of existence, the ordered and the disordered, and an acknowledgement that they can actually be brought together by a child's need for love and an adult's need to provide that love. This tradition of mutual dependence, which is often modified and distorted by mutual resentment, is at the core of Nöstlinger's world, even – and perhaps most strongly – when it is made manifest by its absence. One could perhaps discuss it best in terms of the sense of 'home'.

The Frozen Prince, in the novel of that name (1990), attempts to solve the problem of his incompatible parents by placing his bed across the river – into which he falls and is swept away, to disturbing adventures. His home is a broken one. Andreas, as we have seen, comes from a 'home' that is broken because of its expansion through his mother's ambition. His home has no homeliness; the furniture is no longer part of it. The father describes the all-white bedroom suite his wife has selected with the phrase that is the novel's subtitle: 'die unteren sieben Achtel des Eisbergs', while the vast couches on which Andreas has his sexually exploitative way with the fat girl from upstairs are 'eine Wohnlandschaft'.

Clearly, Nöstlinger is mocking shallow modernity, because, I think, it is not *her* home. It does not have the emotional depth and significance that real furniture has, furniture with which people have been associated. Tradition, then, is security – but it is also constriction. This is the emotional conflict and emotional paradox which cannot be resolved by intellectual methods, and from which fantasy gives only temporary respite. However dreadful home may be, it is still home, and everywhere else is alien. For true freedom, one must free oneself from it, yet it alone can give one the strength to do so.

Nöstlinger presents this impasse most powerfully in *Der Spatz in der Hand* (1974b), set in precisely the same kind of apartment house in which she grew up (though on this occasion there are no overt autobiographical allusions). The eleven- or twelve-year-old heroine has achieved her independence to some degree by acquiring a room of her own – in this case, a redundant Klo am Gang, that symbol of the *Bassenahaus* (see note 2), an unlit, unheated water-closet, to which a large iron key gives her unrestricted access. It is, indeed, a world of her own, yet hardly an outward-looking one, even though it clearly represents, in an extreme form, the only place where one can be alone and truly oneself in defiance of those maxims about the importance of social interaction for the development of the individual. The heroine dreams, at the beginning, of furnishing it, and having her own nameplate on the door.

By the end, however, she has effectively renounced it. The boy that she became fascinated with, who was only staying temporarily with his aunt in the house, has left, with his mother, without giving her his address. And he lives in one of those strange streets, enormously long (unlike her own) with huge council-built blocks of flats, where she has no chance of finding him again (see note 2 above). The games she played in her private loo, fantasies (significantly enough) of flying, fantasies over the pictures she could see in the floor-tiles, have no relevance any more: 'Die roten Ecken der gelben Fliesen konnte man durch die Luft fliegen lassen, zum Fenster hinausfliegen lassen. Aber selber blieb man sitzen, selber schwebte man nicht, selber flog man nicht zum Fenster hinaus' (*Der Spatz in der Hand*: 94). She offers the key to the local boy who always trails after, and whom she exploits shamelessly and mercilessly. But he won't accept it. He wants to share the loo with her. She is determined that she will make him pay for it – but she is not sure what for.

In the end, in this novel at least, the imagination that enabled Friederike to fly away does not help and does not liberate. Understanding how the situation has come about only makes the impossibility of escape for this person at this time all the clearer (though it may alert readers to their own situations, both social and psychological, so that the views of Zipes and Bettelheim on the purpose of fairy-tales are both endorsed). In the end there is only reality, the bird in the hand. Nöstlinger's fantasy works definitely subvert the repressive and authoritarian aspects of tradition, but the more realistic ones show and analyse the irresistible power of the personal tradition which one embodies oneself, which is, for good or ill, the source of one's identity, and that one can therefore only play at rejecting. Perhaps by re-living one's childhood as the author of books for children.

Notes

[1] This exclusive opposition gives way to pluralistic complementarity in Zipes 1988.

[2] *Wohnkultur in Wien* needs a little explanation. *Haus* means to any Viennese a building that occupies a particular space on a street. Thus, the *Haashaus* is a large modern building owned by the firm of Philipp Haas, housing a restaurant, shops and prestigious offices. The *Freihaus auf der Wieden* encompassed an entire block and included Schikaneder's theatre where *Die Zauberflöte* was premiered. Smaller 'houses', containing several 'Wohnungen' (which might be no more than single rooms) were built and traded as one of the best possible forms of investment from the early eighteenth century onwards, since the walled nature of Vienna encouraged maximum use of surface area. In the early nineteenth century, as shown in Nestroy's *Zu ebener Erde und erster Stock* (1835), a single 'house' contained clear social divisions, with the poorest on the ground floor, the richest on the first floor, and then increasing impoverishment up to the attic. The development of the suburbs in the late nineteenth century led to more socially unified housing, with piped water (a communal tap and a *Bassena*) available on each floor instead of a well in the courtyard. The next great step forward in Viennese housing were the enormous 'Gemeindebauten' of the late nineteen-twenties and early nineteen-thirties, specifically built to house workers and provide them with all necessary amenities (shops, restaurants, hairdressers) in the one vast block, whose modern style led them to be dubbed 'working-class fortresses' which some of them proved to be when shelled by Dollfuß's troops in the course of the Februaraufstand in 1934. Such blocks might have as many as twenty-four separate staircases; the *Karl-Marx-Hof* in Heiligenstadt, for example, is nearly a mile long and is served by four tram-stops. Small wonder that the heroine of *Der Spatz in der Hand* despairs of finding the young boy again in such a place.

Bibliography

Bettelheim, Bruno. 1976. *The Uses of Enchantment*, London, Thames and Hudson

Lurie, Alison. 1990. *Not in Front of the Grown-Ups*, London, Bloomsbury Publishing

Müller, D. 1973. 'Muß die feuerrote Friederike wirklich fliehen?' *Buch und Spiel in der Praxis*, 1: 4

Nöstlinger, Christine. 1970. *Die feuerrote Friederike*, Vienna, Jugend und Volk

—. 1971. *Mr Bats Meisterstück*, Hamburg, Oetinger

—. 1972a. *Ein Mann für Mama*, Hamburg, Oetinger

—. 1972b. *Wir pfeifen auf den Gurkenkönig*, Weinheim, Beltz und Gelberg

—. 1973. *Maikäfer, flieg!*, Weinheim, Beltz und Gelberg

—. 1974a. *Ilse Janda, 14*, Hamburg, Oetinger

—. 1974b. *Der Spatz in der Hand...ist besser als die Taube auf dem Dach*, Weinheim, Beltz und Gelberg

—. 1975. *Konrad oder das Kind aus der Konservenbüchse*, Hamburg, Oetinger

—. 1978. *Andreas oder Die unteren sieben Achtel des Eisbergs*, Weinheim, Beltz und Gelberg
—. 1979. *Rosa Riedl, Schutzgespenst*, Vienna, Jugend und Volk
—. 1981. *Zwei Wochen im Mai*, Weinheim, Beltz und Gelberg
—. 1983 *Hugo, das Kind in besten Jahren*, Weinheim, Beltz und Gelberg
—. 1984. *Olfi Obermeier und der Ödipus*, Hamburg, Oetinger
—. 1990. *Der gefrorene Prinz*, Weinheim, Beltz und Gelberg
—. 1991. *Sowieso und überhaupt*, Vienna, Dachs-Verlag
Rogers, Mike. 1994. 'Christine Nöstlinger and the Notion of Childhood', in Williams, Arthur and Stuart Parkes (eds), *The Individual, Identity and Innovation*, Berne, Peter Lang: 89-98
Stephens, John. 1992. *Language and Ideology in Children's Fiction*, London, Longman
Zipes, Jack. 1979. *Breaking the Magic Spell*, London, Hutchinson
—. 1988. *The Brothers Grimm: From Enchanted Forests to the Modern World*, London, Routledge

Prelude(s) oder Portrait of the Authoress as a Little Girl: Kindheit in Margit Schreiners Geschichten. Mit Ausblicken auf other Austrians.

Hubert Lengauer

1) Hermeneutische Ausgangslage

Der eingeborenen Oberösterreicherin der Nachkriegsgeneration sind Margit Schreiners Kindheitsorte vertraut, Denkweisen und Atmosphäre geläufig. Spontaner, vielleicht zu schneller Zustimmung folgt freilich die Einsicht in eine gewisse Begrenztheit des thematischen Repertoires und der literarisch-technischen Möglichkeiten. Nach dem knappen Urteil einer britischen Kritikerin sind ihre Geschichten 'quite interesting not to say a touch bizarre in places (and in other places not bizarre enough)' (Fiddler 1996), und man kann dem Urteil, das sich auf den mittleren und bisher erfolgreichsten Erzählband der Autorin, *Mein erster Neger* (1990), bezieht, beipflichten und es auf die andern beiden, *Die Rosen des Heiligen Benedikt* (1989) und *Die Unterdrückung der Frau, die Virilität der Männer, der Katholizismus und der Dreck* (1995) ausdehnen. Der erste Band enthält die frechsten, groteskesten Geschichten, die sehr direkt auf ihre Gegenstände losgehen, z.B. 'Über das Geschlecht' (es geht um das männliche, den – grob zusammengefaßt – faszinierend-ekelerregenden 'Teil' desselben) oder die sodomitische Beziehung des Sennen Jörg zu seinem Schaf Mizzi ('Der Senner von der Kargeralm'), die sich der besonderen Zuwendung des Kritikers Ludwig Harig erfreut (Harig 1990), – nebenbei auch ein Fall literarischer Blasphemie, von der Germanistin Schreiner an Paul Celan verübt: das Schaf, so heißt es im Bericht des Senns Jörg, habe einen 'Fadensonnenlaut' ausgestoßen, 'ein unglaublich herrlicher, reiner Laut, den kein Instrument der Welt hervorbringen könne ... ein jenseits der Musik liegender Ton ... ein Wunder' (*Die Rosen des Heiligen Benedikt*: 28-9). Die Sado-Maso-Geschichte 'Bergheimerstraße 3' führt zu einem gewaltsamen, grotesk-ratlosen Ende, sie 'rinnt' gewissermaßen 'aus' und wird in einer letzten Geste – trotz der Ungeheuerlichkeit der dargestellten Vorfälle – abgetan, fertig gemacht: ein beinahe kafkaeskes 'Gib's auf!' angesichts der zunehmenden, zunehmend evidenten Sinnlosigkeit des Vorgangs. Weit in die Groteske hinaus mäandernde Geschichten werden, und das ist geradezu das Markenzeichen der Erzählerin, oft in einer Weise verlassen, daß man zunächst an erzählerische Unfähigkeit glaubt; es ist aber, bei genauerem Hinsehen, die dargestellte Unfähigkeit der Welt, sinnvolle, sinnvoll endende Geschichten hervorzubringen, jedenfalls auf dem Gebiet der Liebe, der sexuellen Beziehungen oder wie man jenes weite, unscharf begrenzte Feld bezeichnen will, das die Geschichten der Margit Schreiner durchstreifen.

Das Bizarre ist aber sichtlich im Abnehmen begriffen, das Freche ist im jüngsten Band aus den Geschichten, so scheint es, auf das Cover (Mel Ramos' *Banana Split*) gerückt, während die Geschichten nicht selten etwas schmalere Problemfelder wie Kauf und Anwendung eines Schwangerschaftstests ('1990', 'Der Apotheker', *Die Unterdrückung der Frau*: 142-54 und 154-62) beackern; aber diese Einschätzung mag auch eine Frage der geschlechtsspezifischen hermeneutischen Voraussetzungen sein. Auch der Versuch einer Etüde in einer Männerperspektive, worüber vielleicht kompetenter geredet werden kann, mißglückt: 'Der alte Mann' (*Die Unterdrückung der Frau*: 163-74) ist die Frauenphantasie einer Männerphantasie, die Erzählerin versucht, mit den Augen eines Mannes zu sehen, dem die Beinverschlingung eines Liebespaars (der jüngere Bruder ist involviert) nicht aus dem Kopf geht und der schließlich der Liebhaber seiner Schwägerin wird. Motivation und Rechtfertigung driften ins Naturmythische, die Geliebte wird schließlich schwanger und desparat, der Bauer hingegen, es liest sich fast wie eine Kontrafaktur zu einer Johann Peter Hebel-Kalendergeschichte – 'bearbeitete weiter das Land, ackerte und pflügte und grub die Erde um, säte, band auf, was wuchs, und pflückte und erntete, begoß die Pflanzen, deren unstillbaren Durst nie jemand löschen kann, und trug abends Obst und Gemüse in der Tragtasche, die er um die linke Schulter trug, hinunter ins Dorf zu seiner Frau, damit sie es verarbeite und die ihren ernähre' (*Die Unterdrückung der Frau*: 173). Das Natur-Pathos beherrscht die Erzählung bis zum bitteren, triefenden Ende.

Das erzählerische Werk der Margit Schreiner ist, das sollte mit der kurzen Revue angedeutet werden, inhomogen in der Qualität, um das mindeste zu sagen. Ihre Geschichten sind kaum formale oder inhaltliche Innovationen. Es sind, um einen Untertitel von Harold Brodkey zu strapazieren (allerdings auch ohne damit die Qualität anzugeben) 'stories in an almost classical mode', meist in konventioneller Erzählstrategie, aber in manchen unerwarteten Wendungen sie auch überschreitend. Dennoch ist die Autorin in der literarischen Kritik überwiegend positiv aufgenommen worden. Nach dem Erzählband *Mein erster Neger* wurde sie von manchen Zeitungen zur 'literarischen Neuentdeckung der Saison' (Herbst 1990) erklärt, die 'alle deutschen Feuilletonfürsten und Könige der Kritik' begeistert habe (Zimmermann 1991: 40-1). Die Startauflage des Buches war bereits kurz nach ihrem Erscheinen ausverkauft. Diesem Erfolg war ein Eklat beim Ingeborg Bachmann-Preis im Sommer 1990 vorausgegangen, bei dem die preisverdächtige Autorin disqualifiziert wurde. 'Die Schreiner mußte nach Hause fahren. Das Publikum aber war neugierig geworden und die Jurymitglieder zeigten sich sichtlich bemüht, ihre umstrittene Entscheidung wiedergutzumachen. Der neue Erzählband *Mein erster Neger* kam liebevoll gestreichelt durch die sonst gefährlich angespitzten Fingernägel des Feuilletons.' (Zimmermann 1991: 41). Die hier maliziös apostrophierten 'angespitzten Fingernägel' mögen sich auf die Bachmannpreisjurorin Verena Auffermann beziehen, die das Buch sehr positiv in der *Süddeutschen Zeitung* besprochen hatte (Auffermann 1991); wohl weniger auf Volker Hage in der *Zeit* (Hage 1990) oder andere der zahlreichen positiven Besprechungen.

Neben diesem Faktum öffentlicher Anerkennung warnt auch Margit Schreiners theoretische Kompetenz vor zu schnellem Urteil. Im Essay zu Meta Merz, der sensibel und auch bewundernd die Kompromißlosigkeit in Gedichten und Prosa der jüngeren, früh verstorbenen Dichterin bespricht, finden sich Hinweise auf Schreiners eigene Präferenzen: daß eine Geschichte, klar und einfach erzählt, geheimnisvoll bleiben kann, 'ein moralischer Appell, niemand weiß, von wem, gegen wen oder für wen ... Produkt einer ganzen Reihe von Zweifeln' (Schreiner 1993: 151); Margit Schreiners eigene Geschichten streben diesem Modell des Erzählens nach, und auch thematische Sympathien lassen sich erkennen: 'Verfolgt man die Fährte des Unglücks des Kindes,' so heißt es zu einer Geschichte von Meta Merz, 'stößt man auf die Nacktheit (du sollst nicht), den kalten Steinfußboden (du sollst nicht), auch Tiere sind Lebewesen wie Pflanzen, Menschen und Kinder auch, du sollst nicht vergnügt sein, die Herbstgrenze ist längst überschritten, am Anfang ist alles schon zu Ende' (1993: 153). Margit Schreiners Kindergeschichten stellen sich sehr deutlich in die Tradition des Schreibens über den kindlichen Zustand als Ursprung und Voraussetzung der produktiven Phantasie. In diesem allgemeineren Sinn ist dieses Schreiben 'autobiographisch', nicht im Sinn der 'autobiographischen Fallen', jener Köder, die die Erzählerin auslegt, um zu Vermutungen über ihren Lebenslauf oder Lebenswandel zu verleiten. So ist das Paradox zu begreifen, das Margit Schreiner an der Literatur von Meta Merz kennzeichnet: 'alle Literatur ist schmerzlichste Autobiographie und hat nichts zu tun mit Autobiographie. Es geht um den wahren Satz – oder?'(1993: 164).

2) Das Reich der Kindheit.

Was ist an diesen Kindergeschichten, mit ihrer Mischung des Läppischen mit dem Raffinierten, die Margit Schreiner beherrscht, nun der 'Einsatz in den Kämpfen der Frauen' (Lyotard 1990)? Ist es die Versuchung des Philosophen, angesichts der Aporien im Denken des Geschlechtergegensatzes

> die Feder dem zu reichen, was einem fragenden erwachsenen Mann am weitesten entgegengesetzt ist – *einem kleinen Mädchen*. Aber man wendet ein, daß kleine Mädchen nicht schreiben, daß sie wie die Wilden seien. Und dann sind sie, wie die Wilden auch, zweifellos nur eine Schöpfung ihres vermeintlichen Gegenteils, der ernsten Männlichkeit, die im Grunde auch ihr Richter ist: eine Schöpfung der

Eifersucht, die der Mann gegenüber dem empfindet, was er nicht sein darf. (Lyotard 1990: 142-3)

Liegt der Reiz von Margit Schreiners Geschichten darin, daß sie diese Regreßphantasie anbietet und variiert? Die Erzählerstimme in einer der Geschichten (bezeichnenderweise heißt sie 'Ankunft in Afrika' und eröffnet den Band *Mein erster Neger*) ruft erwachsen-melancholisch diesen ursprünglichen Zustand hervor, in der Anrede an den verschollenen, unwiederbringlichen Gefährten der frühen Spiele:

> Auf dem harten Lehmboden haben wir uns also gewälzt. Das Hemd habe ich ausgezogen, um meinen Rücken an den kühlen Wänden zu reiben, und die Hose habe ich ausgezogen und mich auf die kleine Erhöhung am Boden gesetzt. Zwischen meinen Schamlippen war die glatte Erde. Du hast eine Grube in den Boden gegraben; dazu hast du die Schaufel also mitgenommen. Über die Grube habe ich mich gehockt und reingepinkelt. Die Flüssigkeit ist wie ein goldener See stehengeblieben und nicht versickert. Du hast zornig an die Wände geschifft. (*Mein erster Neger*: 11)

'Der männliche Imperialismus ist kriegerisch und pädagogisch', würde der Philosoph wohl dieser Szene interpretatorisch abgewinnen (Lyotard 1990: 147); und: 'Die Männer – zumindest im Abendland – lieben nicht die Liebe, sondern den Sieg. Unter ihnen herrscht eine ironische Verachtung des Körpers und der Sinne, der Gerüche, der Berührungen, der Ausscheidungen, des Geschehen-Lassens, der Klänge; diejenigen unter ihnen, die sich dem überlassen, nennen sie 'Künstler'. Aber die Künstler sind weiblich' (Lyotard 1990: 146). Näher als hier, in der kleinen Figur des Franzi Brandlmüller in Schreiners Erzählung, der vielleicht das Zeug zum Künstler hatte, bei all den evidenten Unterschieden der Geschlechtsrollen und dem hier in der Tat klein gehaltenen Unterschied der physischen Voraussetzungen, – näher werden Männer und Frauen bei Schreiner einander nie mehr kommen, nicht in der dazu kalt kontrastierten Deflorationsszene in der selben Geschichte und nicht in all den anderen Geschichten, die notwendig als defizient gegenüber diesem atavistischen Szenario erscheinen müssen. 'Kennzeichen der Männlichkeit ist der Anspruch, die Ordnung herrschen zu lassen; Kennzeichen der Weiblichkeit der Zwang, darüber zu lachen', mahnt Lyotard (143). In Margit Schreiners Geschichten Ordnung stiften zu wollen, birgt das Risiko, mit einem Gelächter übrig zu bleiben, jenem Lachen, dem manche ihrer männlichen Figuren ausgesetzt werden, wenn sie trivial scheitern, nachdem sie einen halben Tag lang die Welt erklärt haben (*Die Unterdrückung der Frau*: 102-18), aber auch Frauen, die über die vier Hauptübel Italiens, wenn nicht gar der Menschheit, Bescheid wissen, als da sind: die Unterdrückung der Frau, die Virilität der Männer, der Katholizismus und der Dreck, aber nicht, wie diese Übel zu unterlaufen und – etwa unter Zuhilfenahme eines einschlägig motivierten Mönchs – zum eigenen Nutzen zu verwenden seien. Lachen würde Margit Schreiner vermutlich auch über Lyotards Ordnungsversuch oder seine Anwendung auf ihre kindlichen (und erwachsen werdenden) Mädchenfiguren; keineswegs sind sie aus 'sugar and spice and all things nice' (wenn wir Lyotard polemischerweise einmal so übersetzen), sondern meist geradezu pueril in ihrem Zugriff auf 'slugs and snails and puppy dogs' tails', in ihrem insistierenden Interesse an Onkeln, Vätern oder kumpelhaften Altersgenossen. Die Dinge liegen also, selbst in so vergleichsweise simplen Erzählungen, komplizierter als die philosophische und politische *correctness* es will. Ich vermute das Schreinersche Gelächter auch in der Unbekümmertheit, mit der sie Geschichten oder Themen wiederverwendet und so, mit einem vielleicht nicht sehr großen literarischen Pfunde, ziemlich erfolgreich auf dem Markte gewuchert hat.

Der romantische Ursprung der Poesie im Wilden, Animalischen, im *prelude* des Vorzivilisatorisch-Kindlichen als einem paradiesisch frühen 'Ganzen' der Erfahrung, ist als Topos altehrwürdig. Und auch was generell die Thematisierung von Kindheit in der österreichischen Literatur nach 1945 angeht, befindet sich Margit Schreiner in guter Gesellschaft. Christine Lavants Erzählung *Das Kind* (1948) müßte zuallererst genannt werden. Frauen haben allerdings keineswegs das Monopol. Peter Turrini hat in einem Gedichtband das schreckliche Reich der Kindheit beschworen und die erlittenen Demütigungen zum Ursprung seiner Literatur erklärt. Für Peter Handke hat Gerhard Melzer die Kindheit als poetische Daseinsform im Werk erforscht und mit guten Gründen und Beispielen die fundierende Bedeutung des 'erschriebenen Paradieses' erwiesen (Melzer 1993); Franz Innerhofer (*Schöne Tage*, 1974), Josef Winkler (*Menschenkind*, 1979 u.ö.) und Werner Kofler (*Guggile. Vom Bravsein und vom Schweinigeln*, 1975), Waltraud Anna Mitgutsch (*Die Züchtigung*, 1985) haben Kindheitsmuster bearbeitet. Das Thema ist also generell kein spezifisch weibliches, auch und gerade nicht in der Betonung der Sexualität als jener Grunderfahrung, die Literatur (als ihre nötige Bearbeitung) produziert.

Mit großer Raffinesse entfaltet Marlen Haushofer in der Kindheitsgeschichte des Mädchens Meta das ödipale Dreieck, auf das sich Erziehungsarbeit und Sublimation gründet.

> Diese Käfer sind nicht ganz bei Trost; immer setzt sich einer auf den andern und versucht, in sein Hinterteil hineinzukriechen. Seit Tagen bemüht sich Meta, dieses Bürgerkriegs Herr zu werden und die unterdrückten Briefträger [i.e. Käfer, H.L.] von den angriffslustigen zu befreien.... Wenigstens ein paar Käfer werden ihr dankbar sein für die Befreiung. Im Küchenkalender steht: "Man muß das Unrecht bekämpfen, wo

man es antrifft." ... Während Vater im Lusthaus schläft, hat Meta mindestens hundert Käfer gerettet. (Haushofer 1986 a: 80)

Als Repräsentantin der Mutter (Küche), hinter der ein gewalttätiger Großvater als unausrottbares Über-Ich steht, tut das Kind das vermeintlich Gute in der Natur, während der Vater, der auch sonst Milde, Großzügigkeit und pädagogische Inkonsequenz walten läßt und das Kind vor dem strengen Zugriff der Mutter schützt, im Lusthaus schläft. Seine Abwesenheit läßt die moralischen Prinzipien dominieren, in seiner Präsenz ist er von wohltuender körperlicher Kompaktheit, wie manche der Onkel, die das Haus bevölkern und zu Entdeckungen Anlaß geben:

> Und dann entdeckt Meta noch etwas, die beiden Onkel haben sehr viel Fleisch an sich. Nicht daß sie fett wären, sie haben nur eine besondere Art von Fleisch, das zugleich fest und blühend ist. Meta stellt fest, daß sie diese Art von Fleisch mag. Sie möchte die beiden tätscheln wie die Kühe oder Stasis kleine Kälbchen. Die Onkel merken nichts von ihren Gedanken, und darüber ist sie froh, wer weiß, ob es ihnen angenehm wäre, mit Kühen verglichen zu werden. Es ist überhaupt ein Glück, daß die Großen nicht Gedanken lesen können. Meta säße dann in einem schönen Schlamassel. (1986 a: 146)

Was 'die Großen' aus Haushofers frühen Kindheitsgeschichten herausgelesen haben: daß das 'kleine Glück' der Kindheit 'im Zeichen von Asexualität' stehe und daß diese Kindheit als 'Flucht- und Regressionsraum' antiautoritär und 'ungeschlechtlich (wenn man vom Naturgesetz der Fortpflanzung absieht)' verfaßt sei (Frei 1991: 143), ist für die Erzählung *Himmel, der nirgendwo endet* (1969) angesichts der zitierten Stelle zu bezweifeln.

Das Erzählen in den Kindergeschichten Margit Schreiners ist dem bei Marlen Haushofer strukturell am nächsten, vielleicht sogar inhaltlich, wenn man die erweiterte Öffentlichkeit des Sexuellen von den Sechzigerjahren bis jetzt rechnet. Anders als bei Schreiner ist bei Marlen Haushofer der Bereich der Kindheit zugleich als ein Ort gefaßt; Konstanze Fliedl spricht daher vom 'regressive[n] Zug zum verlorenen Kindheitsort, wo die Ambivalenz von paradiesischer und unheimlicher Erinnerung durchaus gewahrt bleibt' (Fliedl 1994: 625). Die 'melancholische Insel', als die Konstanze Fliedl (1986) Kindheit bei Marlen Haushofer sieht, hat sich bei Schreiner zum melancholischen Kontinent 'Afrika' (*Afrikanische Erinnerungen* heißt der Untertitel zu *Mein erster Neger*) gedehnt, einer Kindheits- Phantasiewelt, die von der erwachsenen Ich-Erzählerin variiert wird, mit anderen Ängsten, Lüsten und Alpträumen ausgestattet wird, aber mit der kindlichen durch erzählerische Konstanten verbunden bleibt. Erzählerische Konstante ist eine Art 'simplizianisches' Erzählen, wie es auch die zitierte Haushofer-Stelle kennzeichnet. Die Differenz zwischen kindlicher Perspektive und Benennung und gleichzeitig induziertem (nicht formuliertem) erwachsenen Wissen (des Lesers) macht den ästhetischen Reiz aus. Die Grenzen des Verfahrens liegen dort, wo 'die Diskontinuität von Kindheit und Erwachsensein nicht reflektiert' wird und die Rückkehrwünsche eine Jugend, der man entkommen ist, zu einer trivialisierten, verklärten 'Kindheitsheimat' zurechtschreiben. Karl Wagner (den ich zitiert habe), hat diese Beschränkungen an Peter Rosegger beschrieben und seiner lebenslangen Beschwörung der ländlichen Kindheit George Eliots kritische Erinnerung an 'the strangely perspectiveless conception of life' in der Kindheit entgegengesetzt, 'that gave bitterness its intensity' (Eliot 1979: 122f.; Wagner 1991: 226). Die soziale Distanz des urbanen Lesers zur ländlichen Simplizität verdoppelt das Vergügen, und Rosegger hat es am besten verstanden, die Effekte von Kindheit und Ländlichkeit literarisch zu summieren. In seinem Verriß der *Unterdrückung der Frau* Margit Schreiners zielt Wendelin Schmidt-Dengler auf genau dieses Verfahren der Schreiner und kennzeichnet es (an manchen Beispielen nicht ganz zu Unrecht) als verschleppte, anachronistische Roseggertechnik (Schmidt-Dengler 1996: 101).

Das urbane Gegenstück dazu hat Walter Benjamin entwickelt. Im Exil werden jene Bilder wie eine Impfung appliziert, 'in denen die Erfahrung der Großstadt in einem Kinde der Bürgerklasse sich niederschlägt', ohne daß dabei 'das Gefühl der Sehnsucht ... über den Geist ... Herr' wird. Auf Kontinuität biographischer Erfahrung wird zugunsten der Tiefe der Erfahrung in der Diskontinuität der Bilder verzichtet. Ergebnis ist geradezu die Umkehrung des simplizianischen Verfahrens und 'der geprägten Formen, wie sie im Naturgefühl seit Jahrhunderten den Erinnerungen an eine auf dem Lande verbrachte Kindheit zu Gebote stehen' (Benjamin 1987: 9). Die Erinnerung, vom Wissen um den Nationalsozialismus überschattet, der zwischen Kindheit und exiliertem Erwachsenen liegt, kann oder will nicht leisten, was häufig (und so auch bei Haushofer) Ziel der Kindheitserinnerungen vom Lande ist: Neubegründung vom Ursprung Kind-Natur her.

Die 'melancholische Insel' Kindheit ist aber nicht nur ein anderer Raum, wie das die Metapher nahelegt, sondern auch und vor allem die Enklave einer anderen Zeiterfahrung. 'Es schien dem Kind, als habe es nie etwas anderes gegeben als Schnee und Winter. Oder war es auszudenken, daß das Schneegebirge im Hof jemals schmelzen sollte', heißt es in einer früheren Kindheits-Erzählung der Marlen Haushofer, die das 'fünfte Jahr' im Leben eines Kindes im Wechsel der Jahreszeiten beschreibt (1986 b: 5). Marlen Haushofer hat damit ein Merkmal von Kindheit erfaßt, das die Erzählung davon kategorial poetisch macht. Am genauesten hat dies John Berger als 'elongation of time' bestimmt, welche zusammen mit der Erfahrung des Verlusts und der Irreversibilität jene 'terrible beauty' herstellt, in die Erwachsene nur in der Krise zurückkehren:

> When we suffer anguish we return to early childhood because that is the period in which we first learnt to suffer the experience of total loss.... It was the period in which we suffered more total losses than in all the rest of our life put together.... the man or woman in anguish is trapped in the time-scale of childhood without a child's protection, suffering a uniquely adult agony. (Berger 1967: 122-4)

In der Erzählung Marlen Haushofers beherrscht diese intensivierende Elongation die Zeit vor dem Sündenfall, der dennoch – als pädagogische Drohung – die kindlichen Nächte bestimmt und ausdehnt.

> Sie konnte nicht begreifen, wozu der große, nackte Sohn Gottes gut sein sollte... Irgendwo in der Schwärze der Nacht hing er und füllte den Raum; groß, schweigend und bedrohlich.... Man konnte nur flüstern: 'Sei nicht böse, weil ich dir den Rücken gezeigt hab, bis ich groß bin und viele Sünden habe, dann werde ich dich anschauen beim Abendgebet. Nur jetzt laß mich wieder einschlafen, ich bin ja noch klein.' (1986b: 6-7)

Wenn je eine Autorin Elongation der Zeit und kindliche Verlusterfahrung radikal inszeniert hat, dann ist es Marie Thérèse Kerschbaumers Roman *Die Fremde*. Die sprachlich weit ausschwingende Detaillierung der Erinnerung kompensiert jetzt die zugefügte, erlittene Sprachlosigkeit des Kindes. Es ist eine Passionsgeschichte in einem rücksichtslos vorwärtsdrängenden, herrisch die größte Aufmerksamkeit erzwingenden Text. Eine iterative Dynamik, ein Kreisen und Wiederholen, eine Massierung der Bildlichkeit, bestimmen ihn und lassen die Zeitdeiktika fast verschwinden, die sonst einen Erzähltext segmentieren und in seiner Logik, die jene der Chronologie ist, durchsichtig und lesbar machen. Kein märchenhaft tröstliches 'Es war einmal ... und dann' leitet die Lektüre und knüpft die Episoden aneinander. Es ist vielmehr eine bestürzend *simultane* Kindlichkeit, die hier exponiert wird, so wie (nach J. Berger) die eingekrümmte Körpersprache der Erwachsenen, die unkontrollierte Mimik, den kindlichen Zustand unmittelbar herstellen. Kerschbaumers Schreiben erlöst nicht aus der Beschränktheit und Perspektivelosigkeit dieses Zustands, die Sprachbewegung erfaßt als Form die quälende Elongation der Zeit, kein augenzwinkernder Erzähler kostet die Differenz zwischen kindlicher Erfahrung und erwachsenem Wissen (auch des Lesers) aus. Die Beschämung *ist* die Beschämung, der Schmerz *ist* der Schmerz, das Leiden *ist* das Leiden, und nicht etwas anderes, was das Kind nur nicht versteht, wir aber schon. Das Kind ist nicht 'dieses kleine, alberne, ichige Scheusal' Musils (Musil 1962: 129; Šlibar 1995: 92); nicht 'Mir wie ein Hund, unheimlich stumm und fremd' (Hofmannsthal 1963: 17), sondern unmittelbare Präsenz, obwohl Kerschbaumer nicht 'ich' zu diesem Kind sagt, sondern es als 'Barbarina' hinausstellt, um es in einer doppelten Weise (grammatikalisch und durch den Namen) fremd zu machen. Das Ende der

Kränkung wäre das Ende des Erzählens, Spaltsinnigkeit läßt überleben und begründet das Schreiben:

> Barbarina, die kein Opfer sein wollte, entkam, oder entkam bedingt und nur zeitweilig, weil sie sich zum Schein opferte und sich dabei sagte, das bin nicht ich, das ist nur ein Traum. Und sie sagte sich weiter, was wißt ihr von mir, die ich von weit zu euch gekommen bin, von fremden Gewalten unter euch geworfen, eine Fremde. (Kerschbaumer 1992: 23-4)

Die künstlerische Berufung ist die säkulare Version des Messianischen; in der Erinnerung der Kindheit ordnet sich dazu ein 'Knabenspiel mit unsichtbarer Monstranz, Barbarina in untergeordneter Stellung, kniend und eine Glocke läutend, während sie selbst die Monstranz zu halten aufs heftigste begehrte, was ihr verwehrt war, worauf sie sich in einem dunklen Wald ausgesetzt fand' (24). Opferrolle und Widerstand machen die Pubertierende zur 'blasphemische[n] Ausnahme inmitten selbstgefälliger Übereinkunft' (25), die in Träumen, Erinnerung, Phantasie (als Autorin also gewissermaßen) kompensiert, was ihrer Paria-Existenz angetan wurde und noch jetzt angetan wird: Literatur ist die Bühne für die säkularisierte Form dieser Leidensrolle. Dies gilt ähnlich für einen Text wie Christine Lavants Erzählung *Das Kind*, auch wenn seine umgekehrte Bewegungsrichtung als 'Heimweh im geistigen und religiös-existenziellen Sinne nach dem Zuhause in der Selbstverständlichkeit eines begnadeten Daseins, in der Ungebrochenheit einer Existenz als "Kind Jesu"' gedeutet wird, wie dies in Neva Šlibars Interpretation dieser Erzählung überzeugend geschieht (Šlibar 1995: 122).

Geht man an die Anfänge des Werks von Marlen Haushofer, so stößt man auf eine Erzählung, die im Jahr 1945 ganz gründlich und mit überladener Landschafts- und Natursymbolik den Anfang inszeniert: 'Das Morgenrot', die Geschichte einer Geburt. Die Gebärende ist von Flüchtlingen zurückgelassen worden, bringt im Wald bei brennendem Morgenrot ein Kind zur Welt, hüllt es in ihre Kleider, setzt es am Paßübergang aus und kehrt selbst nackt in die Natur zurück. Das Kind kann – schon hört man ein Pferdegespann – gewissermaßen voraussetzungslos neu beginnen. Der physische Übergang (Geburt, Paß) weist auf den historischen, der Tod der Kindeseltern ist das Ende eines geschichtlichen Abschnitts, des Kriegs, der mit mystifizierender Einfalt erklärt wird:

> Alle Menschen waren ja gut, nur zeitweise ein wenig verwirrt, daß sie sich gegenseitig totschlugen.... Weshalb hätten sie sonst ihren Mann totgeschossen? An seinem dreiundzwanzigsten Geburtstag, in einem fremden Land, genau acht Monate vor der Geburt ihres Kindes. Es hatte keinen Sinn, darüber nachzudenken, sie würde doch nie hinter das Geheimnis kommen, und heute erübrigte es sich und wurde unwichtig wie alles andere. (Haushofer 1990: 9-10)

Alle andern Fragen (Wie kam der Soldat ins fremde Land? Was wollte er dort, wer hat es ihm befohlen, wen hat *er* erschossen?) werden nicht gestellt, tragen nichts zur Neubegründung bei; der kräftige Sohn aber wird blaugraue Augen haben wie der Vater und blondes Haar wie die Mutter.

Es kann nun nicht darum gehen, eine verdienstvolle Autorin durch Entblößung bedenklicher Elemente in ihrer Erstlingserzählung zu denunzieren. Mit der Symbolik ihrer Geschichte war sie vermutlich im *mainstream* bildlicher und literarischer Darstellungen der Wiederaufbauzeit nach dem 2. Weltkrieg (Kos 1994: 87, 123 et passim). Es sollte vielmehr nur angedeutet werden, daß Begründungsregresse dieser Art geschichtlich sehr unterschiedliche Motivationen und Ausprägungen haben.

Eine Erzählung von Margit Schreiner befaßt sich ebenfalls mit der Geburt als begründendem Anfang; sie bildet den schärfsten denkbaren Kontrast zu Marlen Haushofers Geschichte.

> Ich bin durch einen Kaiserschnitt zur Welt gekommen. Das Kind vor mir hat meine Mutter verloren, weil es eine Steißlage war und die Ärzte nicht operieren wollten. Aus irgendeinem Grund, wahrscheinlich aus Neugier oder aus Sportgeist, wollten sie das Kind unbedingt während der Geburt drehen. Was nicht gelang. Das Kind, das Marlies heißen sollte, blieb stecken. Nicht nur, daß es im Bauch meiner Mutter erstickte, es saß auch fest. Die Ärzte überlegten, es zu zerstückeln. Aber dann schafften sie es doch irgendwie, das tote Kind aus meiner Mutter zu ziehen. Sie wurde dabei so verletzt, daß sie nicht mehr auf natürliche Weise gebären konnte. (*Die Unterdrückung der Frau*: 9)

Die Geburt erfolgt zu Weihnachten, der Krankenhauschor singt Stille Nacht, heilige Nacht, sodaß die Mutter, 'vom Morphium noch ganz benommen, alles durcheinanderbrachte und gar nicht mehr richtig unterscheiden konnte zwischen dem holden Knaben im lockigen Haar und mir. So etwas kann zur Belastung werden. Am Tag meiner Geburt erhielt Neruda den Stalinpreis, und am Dachstein ging eine Lawine nieder, die drei Menschen unter sich begrub' (*Die Unterdrückung der Frau*: 9).

Weder Natur noch Zivilisation sind milde zum Zeitpunkt dieser Geburt, die Koinzidenz der natürlichen, historischen und heilsgeschichtlichen Ereignisse ist absurd und allenfalls blasphemisch auf den Gebieten der Poesie (Neruda), Politik (Stalin) und Religion (Jesus). Die diesem 'Anfang' folgenden Geschichten könnten pathetisch als das Abarbeiten der Belastung gelesen werden, die durch die Konjunktion der Leit-Sterne (Stalin, Neruda) zum Zeitpunkt der Geburt und durch den Mangel, kein 'Knabe im lockigen Haar' zu sein, erwachsen. Das Abarbeiten selbst geschieht aber unpathetisch, ja mit den pathosbrechenden Mitteln von Groteske, von Ironie und Zynismus gegenüber ideologischen Vorgaben (dem üblichen Katholizismus einer durchschnittlichen österreichischen

Jugend, später dem Marxismus der Studentengruppen, dem Feminismus der Frauengruppen) und, damit verbunden, der Ausbildung einer reservatio mentalis gegenüber der Wirklichkeit, soweit sie sich von diesen Konstrukten bestimmen läßt. Die vorformulierten Lebens- und Politikkonzepte laufen ins Leere, bleiben in ihrer absurden Widersprüchlichkeit stehen oder werden von den unkommentierten Wahrnehmungen und Aktionen der Ich-Figur widerlegt. An dem stummen Kind fliegen die widersprüchlichen Beurteilungen der Vergangenheit seiner diversen Onkel vorbei, ob der eine Lagerarzt war, wie der Vater meint, oder Tierarzt, wie die Mutter sagt (*Die Unterdrückung der Frau*: 22); ob der andere seine Kristallschale 1944 zur Geburt seines Sohnes von der Partei geschenkt bekommen hat oder von der Landesregierung wegen seinem Buckel und seinem Klumpfuß (28), bleibt unentschieden, das Ungelöste ist aber gerade so aufschlußreich als 'Vergangenheitsbewältigung' im *understatement*. Unter den Onkel-Geschichten gibt es eine, die das Auslaufen in die Stille und Leere besonders eindrucksvoll inszeniert. Es ist die Geschichte von Hugo ('Bescherung', *Die Unterdrückung der Frau*: 74-6), der nur mehr als Stimme gegenwärtig ist, auf einer Schallplatte, mit der der Soldat Weihnachtswünsche übermittelt, welche die Familie nun hört, bis die Ente durchgebraten ist. Die Ich-Erzählerin (das erzählte Ich) spielt diese Platte aus weichem Material zu Ende, bis die Stimme gelöscht ist, in dieser 'Stillen Nacht'. Mit dieser Tilgung der Vergangenheit bringt die jugendliche Akteurin auf den Punkt, was ohnehin passiert, aber unmerklich, aus Trägheit, Vergeßlichkeit oder sonst lebenspraktischen Gründen, und sie negiert es zugleich.

Die Struktur der Darstellung solcher Widersprüchlichkeiten bleibt ähnlich, auch wenn, mit dem Fortschreiten im biographischen Modell, die Themen wechseln. Später wird es um Sexualität und Politik gehen (z.B. 'Mitgliederversammlung', *Die Unterdrückung der Frau*: 83-6; 'Der Club der politisch interessierten Frau': 91-102). Das bevorzugte Ausdrucksmittel der Mentalreservation ist negativ: Reduktion, Verweigerung von Kommentar, Auslassung. Positiv bestimmt sie sich allenfalls durch Phantasiegebilde wie den unsichtbaren Elefanten Hendrich, der die Ich-Figur in *Mein erster Neger* begleitet, das vielgestaltige, mitwachsende Konstrukt 'Afrika' als Kontinent der Phantasie, der Lust, der Alpträume, oder auch durch das Hindeuten auf Poesie (etwa einen Pasolini-Text in 'Die Eskimorolle', *Die Unterdrückung der Frau*: 102-18), mit dem die ideologische Debatte unwiderleglich beendet wird: die Poesie spricht letzte Worte.

Oder die Banalität spricht sie. Das ist ein Zug in den Schreinerschen Erzählungen, der zu Mißverständnissen führt, indem die dargestellte Banalität der Autorin unmittelbar angelastet wird. Daran ist ihre Darstellungstechnik nicht ganz unbeteiligt: ungeschickt und gewollt naiv daherkommende Geschichten mit autobiographischem Duktus laden dazu ein. In vielen Fällen erscheint die erzählte

(Ich-) Figur als *odd girl out* in einer Wolke banaler Gefühle, und der erzählenden Ich-Figur bleibt nichts als das Eingeständnis solcher Banalität. Eine Halbwüchsige fährt zu einer Tante, die Anhängerin der Zeugen Jehovas ist und Kitschmalerin; auf der Fahrt durch eine Vorstadtgegend, die einer großen Müllkippe gleicht, wird der Einmarsch der Warschau-Pakt-Truppen in die Tschechoslowakei im Radio durchgesagt; der Vater, der den Tschechen immer ein ähnliches Schicksal gewünscht hatte wie den Deutschen nach '45, fährt auf einen Supermarktparkplatz und weint; nach der Ankunft verwickelt er die Tante in einen Disput über das ewige Leben. 'Ich lehnte mich auf das Polster im Fenster und sah zum Eingang der Flughafenkaserne hinüber. Dort stand ein großer blonder Junge mit geschultertem Gewehr und lächelte mir zu. Er war sehr hübsch, und während mein Vater auf seine Schwester einredete, zum katholischen Glauben ihrer Väter zurückzukehren, wäre ich am liebsten hinuntergelaufen und hätte mich an den Schlagbaum gelehnt' (*Die Unterdrückung der Frau*: 73-4). Solche Geschichten sind nicht dumm, jedenfalls nicht so dumm wie die in ihr erzählten Personen. Sie erzählen einen konfusen Zustand, an dem Dummheit und Banalität ihren Anteil haben und meiden gerade so jeden Betroffenheitskitsch. So wie sie auf das autobiographische Erzählmuster einlädt, so lädt die Autorin auch auf Erwartungen und Deutungsmuster anderer Art ein, um diese dann ebenso erbarmungslos wie unpathetisch abzumurksen. Dieses Reich der Kindheit ist nicht pathetisch furchtbar, und die Erzählung davon kann also nicht so furchtbar pathetisch sein. Es ist oft langweilig, banal, enttäuschend und gerade deshalb verletzend und beschämend. Der Vergleich mit den Kindheitswelten der Aichinger, Kerschbaumer, Mitgutsch ist erhellend und potentiell ungerecht zugleich, indem die Schwere und Ernsthaftigkeit des Dargestellten grundsätzlich kein Maß für das literarische Gelingen darstellt. Margit Schreiners Geschichten sind (bis auf ganz wenige Ausnahmen) keine Tragödien, höchstens Tragikomödien. Sie sind auch keine Erziehung des Herzens und jedenfalls kein Erziehungsroman, auch wenn die Autorin, etwa durch die Gattungsangabe 'Roman in Geschichten' dies für die *Unterdrückung der Frau* so haben möchte. Sie sind ein in Episoden gegliederter 'simplizianischer', pikaresker Bericht von den mäandernden Entwicklungswegen einer Kindheit und Jugend in den Fünfziger- und Sechzigerjahren, durch die Niederungen Oberösterreichs in die Untiefen Salzburgs. Von den mäßigen Höhen Latiums aus, auf denen der bisher letzte Erzählband ankommt, ist allerdings die Grenze von Margit Schreiners Themen und Darstellungsmöglichkeiten sichtbar geworden: Zeit, daß etwas anderes kommt.

Bibliographie

Auffermann, Verena. 1991. 'Menschen und liebe Elefanten. Neue Erzählungen von Margit Schreiner', *Süddeutsche Zeitung*, 46, 23.-24. Februar: 188
Benjamin, Walter. 1987. *Berliner Kindheit um 1900*, mit einem Nachwort von Theodor W. Adorno, Frankfurt am Main, Suhrkamp
Berger, John. 1967. *A Fortunate Man*, London, Allan Lane, Penguin
Eliot, George. 1979. *The Mill on the Floss*, hrsg. A. S. Byatt, Harmondsworth, Penguin
Fiddler, Allyson. 1996. e-mail, (unveröffentlicht), 15. Januar
Fliedl, Konstanze. 1986. 'Die melancholische Insel. Zum Werk Marlen Haushofers', *Vierteljahresschrift des Adalbert Stifter-Instituts*, 35, 1/2: 35-51
—. 1994. 'Marlen Haushofer', in Hartmut Steinecke (Hrsg.), *Deutsche Dichter des 20. Jahrhunderts*, Berlin, Erich Schmidt: 624-34
Frei, Norbert. 1991. 'Marlen Haushofer. Die frühen Erzählungen', in Christine Schmidjell (Hrsg.) *Marlen Haushofer. Die Überlebenden. Unveröffentlichte Texte aus dem Nachlaß. Aufsätze zum Werk*, Linz, Landesverlag: 139-58
Hage, Volker. 9.11.1990. 'Alle Wege führen nach Afrika. Eine eigenwillige Erzählerin: Margit Schreiner und ihr "Erster Neger"', *Die Zeit*: 2
Harig, Ludwig. 1990. 'Ein langes Zucken, ein langes Verbluten. Liebes- und Haßgeschichten von Margit Schreiner', *Süddeutsche Zeitung*, 17.-18. Februar: xvi
Haushofer, Marlen. 1986a. *Himmel, der nirgendwo endet*, Frankfurt, dtv
—. 1986b. 'Das fünfte Jahr', in Marlen Haushofer 1986. *Schreckliche Treue*, Düsseldorf, Claassen: 5-54
—. 1990. 'Das Morgenrot', in Marlen Haushofer, *Die Frau mit den interessanten Träumen*, München, dtv
Hofmannsthal, Hugo von. 1963. *Gedichte und lyrische Dramen*, Hrsg. Herbert Steiner, Frankfurt am Main, S. Fischer
Innerhofer, Franz. 1974. *Schöne Tage*, Salzburg, Residenz
Kerschbaumer, Marie Thérèse. 1992. *Die Fremde*, Klagenfurt, Wieser
Kofler, Werner. 1975. *Guggile. Vom Bravsein und vom Schweinigeln. Eine Materialsammlung aus der Provinz*, Berlin, Wagenbach
Kos, Wolfgang. 1994. *Eigenheim Österreich. Zu Politik, Kultur und Alltag nach 1945*, Wien, Sonderzahl
Lavant, Christine. 1948. *Das Kind*, Stuttgart, Brentano-Verlag
Lyotard, Jean-François. 1990. 'Ein Einsatz in den Kämpfen der Frauen', in *Aisthesis. Wahrnehmung heute oder Perspektiven einer anderen Ästhetik*. Leipzig, Reclam: 142-56

Melzer, Gerhard. 1993. 'Das erschriebene Paradies. Kindheit als poetische Daseinsform im Werk Handkes', in Gerhard Fuchs und Gerhard Melzer (Hrsg.), *Peter Handke. Die Langsamkeit der Welt*, Graz, Droschl: 47-62

Mitgutsch, Waltraud Anna. 1985. *Die Züchtigung*, München, dtv

Musil, Robert. 1962. 'Die Amsel', in Robert Musil, *Nachlaß zu Lebzeiten*. Reinbek, Rowohlt

Schmidt-Dengler, Wendelin. 1996. 'Schweres Banana Split', *Literatur und Kritik*, 305/306, Juli: 100-1

Schreiner, Margit. 1989. *Die Rosen des Heiligen Benedikt. Liebes- und Haßgeschichten*, Zürich, Haffmanns

—. 1990. *Mein erster Neger. Afrikanische Erinnerungen*, Zürich, Haffmanns

—. 1993. 'Meta Merz', in Elisabeth Reichart (Hrsg.), *Österreichische Dichterinnen*, Salzburg, Otto Müller: 145-66

—. 1995. *Die Unterdrückung der Frau, die Virilität der Männer, der Katholizismus und der Dreck. Roman in Geschichten*, Zürich, Haffmanns

Šlibar, Neva. 1995. 'Ein Kind Jesu: Jesuskind und Krüppelchen. Die Kinderperspektive in Christine Lavants Erzählungen', in Arno Rußegger und Johann Strutz (Hrsg.), *Die Bilderschrift Christine Lavants*, Salzburg, Otto Müller: 87-123

Wagner, Karl. 1991. *Die literarische Öffentlichkeit der Provinzliteratur. Der Volksschriftsteller Peter Rosegger*, Tübingen, Niemeyer

Winkler, Josef. 1979. *Menschenkind*, Frankfurt am Main, Suhrkamp

Zimmermann, Peter. 1991. '"Geschmacklos? Dann bin ich nicht weit genug gegangen!"', *Wienerin*, Februar: 40-1

Klösterreich[1] – Memories of a Catholic Girlhood[2]

Petra M. Bagley

The I-narrator of Jutta Richter's *Himmel, Hölle, Fegefeuer* (1982), an 18-year-old student of theology, makes what for her has been an anxiety-ridden, difficult decision, namely to leave the Catholic church of her own free will. She does so to attain:

> Die Freiheit, mit gutem Gewissen und Stolz ich sagen zu können. Ohne belauert zu werden von einem Gott, der alles sieht. Ohne aus dem Hinterhalt bestraft zu werden. Ohne zu denken: an letzter Stelle. Ohne zu denken: Schuld. Ich und Schuld, ich und nicht würdig, ich und Staub, ich und Reue, und ganz klein (so klein mit Hut), und ganz zuletzt, und Abschaum und Schmutz, und triebhaft, und niedrig, und gering, und böse, und verdorben. Wie dieser faule Apfel, der die anderen Äpfel ansteckt. Ohne all das zu denken oder auch nur ahnen ich sagen können. (*Himmel, Hölle, Fegefeuer*: 17)

It is the intention of this paper to consider, with reference to a number of Austrian and German contemporary women writers who have experienced a convent school education, to what extent the notion of God and guilt being inseparable prevents female freedom and individuality. In order to do this we shall consider the interplay between religious, in our case, Catholic education, and women's social and sexual role by focusing on the relationship that the female protagonists, the I-narrators, have with God as portrayed by Austrian writers, such as Barbara Frischmuth (*Die Klosterschule*, 1968), Brigitte Schwaiger (*Der Himmel ist süß*, 1986) and Andrea Wolfmayr (*Pechmarie*, 1989), as well as German writers, such as Jutta Richter (*Himmel, Hölle, Fegefeuer*, 1992) and Christel Keiderling (*Eine Rose für eine Nonne*, 1993).

On 10 July 1995 Pope John Paul II made an unprecedented apology for the Roman Catholic Church's marginalization of women and discrimination against them. In this apostolic letter to all the world's women the Pope declared the liberation of women as 'positive' and went on to say: 'Women's dignity has often been unacknowledged and their prerogatives misrepresented; they have often been relegated to the margins of society and even reduced to servitude' (Bunting 1995: 6). Whilst the Pope also thanked working women and urged the need for equal pay for equal work, protection for working mothers, fairness in career advancements and equality of spouses with regard to family rights, he continued to place emphasis on women's roles as mothers and wives. This is no less true of convent education, where so much of the teaching was and is bound up with dogmas. Indeed, for this very reason, it can be accused of failing to keep pace with the times.

In Frischmuth's *Die Klosterschule* (1968) young girls are educated to become either the 'possession' of a man, namely by being his wife, or enter the service of the Church as a nun, with the possibility of undertaking missionary work. The role of the woman as being subordinate to that of men is constantly alluded to, be it in the form of the nuns' teaching – the girls are told to serve their husbands and be subservient to them (*Klosterschule*: 40), or in the author's intentional use of predominantly masculine pronouns and possessive adjectives. Frischmuth points to a human order in which thought and behaviour are male-oriented: 'Wir sollen, ob wir wollen oder nicht, unseren Willen einem höheren unterordnen, da dieser uns gewollt und wir ihn mit dem unseren stets wollen sollen' (*Klosterschule*: 15). Ambivalence exists regarding to whom 'einem höheren', 'dieser' and 'ihn' refer, whether it is to God or to man in his role as husband. The narrator's scepticism illustrates the author's ability to undermine masculine (by association God's) authority via the language used. It does seem somewhat ironic that women, here the nuns, are applying and reinforcing old-fashioned conceptions about women's subordinate role in life by dint of outdated, disciplinarian methods of upbringing, all under the guise of serving a 'higher power'. The nuns appear to have become functionaries of a moribund, patriarchal system, espousing an authoritarian, orthodox Catholic philosophy of life, which is resrictive, in almost a military manner, both on a psychological and physical level. As Marina Warner points out: 'For Catholicism, what is vitally important, is the idea that authority does not lie within, it is not the inner voice but the outer voice, the voice of the Pope, the bishop, the priest and to some extent the nun' (Warner 1976: 181). At the earliest opportunity this hierarchy is impressed upon the impressionable, young girls' minds. The following example from *Himmel, Hölle, Fegefeuer* illustrates the antiquatedness of this male-dominated structure: 'Der liebe Gott, sagte Schwester Lioba im Kindergarten, kommt zuerst, dann kommt der Papst, dann der Kardinal, dann der Bischof, der Herr Pfarrer als nächster, dann die Schwester Oberin, dann Vater und Mutter, dann kommt ganz lange nichts. Und ganz zum Schluß kommst du, sagte Schwester Lioba im Kindergarten' (*Himmel, Hölle, Fegefeuer*: 8).

In *Die Klosterschule* Frischmuth also evokes the atmosphere of an authoritarian regime, that is, a way of life where discipline, self-control and rigid conformity hold sway. This is evident at the very start of the book with a quotation from the Augustinian monk, Abraham a Santa Clara, whose words are disparaging of women, yet characterize the education the convent girls receive: 'Eine rechte Jungfrau soll sein und muß sein wie eine Spitalsuppe, die hat nicht viele Augen, also soll sie auch wenig umgaffen' (*Klosterschule*: 5).[3] Virginity is considered to have the greatest value according to the sexual morals expounded in this convent education, so that the best path to God is to remain a virgin and become a nun. As mentioned above, the other option open to the girls in *Die Klosterschule* is marriage, where they will become not a servant of God but of their husband. Moreover, their sexuality will exist only for the purpose of procreation and they will be completely at the beck and call of their husband, since in this contract of marriage the woman becomes his property. Even in the games the girls play they show their acceptance of this stereotypical state of affairs, where the man has the power and strength which he may abuse, and the woman is meek and supplicating. The I-narrator and her friend, Milla, pretend to be Anthony and Cleopatra: 'Wir rücken ganz eng zusammen, legen je eine Hand auf den Stamm der Buche, wobei die von Milla auf der meinen zu liegen kommt, was ich in der Ordnung finde, schließlich ist sie der Mann' (*Klosterschule*: 59-60).

It is not just some quirk of Catholic dogmatism, promoting these gender roles which are demeaning and detrimental to women. The basis is, of course, the Bible in which women are consistently portrayed in a negative light 'as appendages of men; as possessions of men; as goods which may be sold, disposed of, given away, traded, or just ordered about by men; as things which might better be seen but not heard; and even as things which, in particular situations, are better not even seen' (Harris 1984: 30). The apostle Paul, for example, justifies his opinion of the proper role of women in the depiction of creation:

> Now I want you to realise that the head of every man is Christ, and the head of the woman is man, and the head of Christ is God. (1 Corinthians 11. 3)

> A man ought not to cover his head, since he is the image and glory of God; but the woman is the glory of man. For man did not come from the woman, but woman from man; neither was man created for woman, but woman for man. (1 Corinthians 11. 7-9)

His words are reflected in what the nuns teach their pupils in *Die Klosterschule*, namely that women are inferior to men; that they must live in a submissive relationship to men; that through humility and subservience they can earn respect and that ultimately their salvation is to be found in childbearing (1 Timothy 2, 11-15).

According to the Bible, then, the characteristics of a good woman as measured in relation to how well she serves her husband, are loyalty, piety, fidelity and the ability to keep house and rear children. In the convent teachings these qualities are further enhanced by passivity and obedience, as Frischmuth's I-narrator notes, whilst thinking about the day when she will leave the convent:

> Bis dahin aber ist noch eine lange Zeit, in der sie uns zurechtbiegenwerden – wer sein Kind liebt, der züchtigt es ... Jedermann sei der Obrigkeit untertan! Denn es gibt keine Gewalt, die nicht von Gott stammt. Wo immer eine besteht, ist sie von Gott angeordnet. Wer sich also gegen die Obrigkeit auflehnt, lehnt sich gegen die Anordnung Gottes auf! (*Klosterschule*: 88)[4]

With the Bible as a foundation stone, it could, therefore, be claimed that sexism permeates almost every facet of the major traditional Christian religions. Religious institutions are for the most part dominated by men. Such ideological reinforcement has clearly contributed to a large extent to the tragedy that has often been women's history. In *Die Klosterschule* Frischmuth illustrates the dangers behind such teachings by highlighting the hiatus between such a traditional, religious education and modern-day attitudes towards the role of women in society.

The indoctrination of young minds is particularly evident in these overtly religious-oriented works by Frischmuth, Richter and Schwaiger. Through their female I-narrators and the power of language each author makes explicit the persuasive hold, primarily in a negative sense, the Catholic church has over these young girls courtesy of its pedagogical system. In Richter's *Himmel, Hölle, Fegefeuer* it is the fact that the convent education, supported by the Catholic church, stifles the girls' freedom of thought and behaviour in such a hypocritical manner which infuriates the I-narrator. She describes her anger as:

> Die Wut darüber, daß ich es nie gewagt hatte, den Nonnen zu widersprechen, daß ich nie gesagt hatte, was ich unter Christentum verstand. Ich hätte sagen müssen, ... daß es nicht christliche Erziehung sein könne, die Heucheln lehre. Nein, christliche Erziehung müßte die Erziehung zur Wahrhaftigkeit sein, nicht zum lächelnden Grüß Gott, Schwester. (*Himmel, Hölle, Fegefeuer*: 98-9)

For many convent girls a common experience has been the problem of deciphering religious facts from the religious fervour. In Frischmuth's book prayers shape the daily routine. In the very first chapter entitled 'Ora et labora' (prayers and work) over forty prayers are named in just one sentence covering nearly one and a half pages. The listing of prayers invokes endless chanting, the repetition and the rhythm of monotony. The purpose of prayer has evidently lost all meaning: 'Wir beten, wie man uns zu beten gelehrt hat' (*Klosterschule*: 8). Without reflection the girls reproduce the drummed-in phrases and prejudices, as Richter's I-narrator says of the Catholic church: 'Sie lehrt das Nachbeten, nicht aber das Selbstdenken' (*Himmel, Hölle, Fegefeuer*: 34). When doubts begin to emerge in the mind of Frischmuth's I-narrator, she comments: 'Und zum erstenmal habe ich auch eine Art Widerwillen gegen die zahllosen Gebete' (*Klosterschule*: 86). The fact that praying is such an intrinsic and time-consuming part of this convent education does mean that the girls are encouraged to focus their thoughts solely on God and discouraged from letting their minds wander and having private, by association 'sinful' thoughts, particularly if these thoughts were to result in questioning their training for life.

Even the I-narrator in Schwaiger's *Der Himmel ist süß* whose naivety and the fact that she is an exemplary pupil allow for the most positive attitude towards a Catholic upbringing, in comparison to the other I-narrators examined here, makes the comment: 'Ich glaubte nicht mehr, daß meine Gebete galten' (*Der Himmel ist süß*: 167). In an interview in 1990 Schwaiger described her own childhood experience of the Catholic church as 'terrible'. She had, in fact, intended initially to entitle the book 'Die verzauberten Kinder' because in her words: 'Ich denke, daß Religion Magie ist, ein dunkler Zauber, der die menschliche Substanz angreifen kann wie ein Virus' (Kuschel 1990: 21). With reference to her time spent at the convent school she, too, makes the point: 'Da war kein Denken und kein Fragen mehr, sondern nur Glauben und Fürwahrhalten. Auch absolutes Vertrauen' (Kuschel 1990: 21). For the novice nun the validity of this life is ultimately a matter of absolute faith: 'You have to believe that prayer has an effect. It might seem desperately introspective, but we all need to turn away at some points in order to turn back with something to pour into the world' (Bunting 1996: 7).

For the I-narrators in the works considered here there is no intention of entering a strict contemplative order of nuns. For them prayer is one aspect of the rigid, inflexible routine of their Catholic schools. Rules and regulations are plentiful and illustrate every area of existence: be it at mealtime, during daily walks, during class, at bedtime. The rules are all for the good of the girls in that they are intended to prepare them for life. In *Der Himmel ist süß*, for instance, serious training begins in class in the 'Kindergarten', where the girls are told to sit up straight, keep their clean hands on the table and write with their good hand, that is, their right hand (*Der Himmel ist süß*: 37). Good girls also eat up all their food, do not get themselves dirty and do not tell tales (*Himmel, Hölle, Fegefeuer*: 9). In *Die Klosterschule* one-hour daily walks on weekdays take on a military feel: 'Hand in Hand, zwei und zwei, Schritt für Schritt... Die Richtung wird ausgegeben ...Wir sollen Disziplin halten', the narrator comments, 'die Gebote des Anstands nicht außer Acht lassen' (*Klosterschule*: 15). The reasoning behind and the consequence of such regimented discipline appear to be to surpress any individuality. This is because it is in the interest of the nuns, in their role as teachers and moral guardians to create uniformity, a collective consciousness, and at the same time keep their charges under control. Both at school and in the home, in accordance with what has been termed 'Schwarze Pädagogik', those in authority are determined to break the will of the child.[5] For example, in Andrea

Wolfmayr's *Pechmarie* (1989) the discipline of Catholic education is reflected in the home:

> Zuerst einmal gehört der Wille des Kindes gebrochen, sagt der Großvater. Und dann gehört das Gute, Wahre und Schöne in die Kinderseele gepflanzt. Das sei Erziehung. Das mache den Menschen zu einem Charakter. Und das sei wahre Liebe, seine Kinder zu Charakteren zu machen ... Kinder gehören in erster Linie zur Ordnung erzogen, und zur Folgsamkeit, zum Gehorsam. (*Pechmarie*: 74-5)

The overwhelming suggestion being made by all the writers in this study is that unconditional obedience is a necessary feature of the tightknit community of the convent school as well as beyond the walls. It is achieved through humiliation, fear and threats: 'Wer sich absondert, stellt sich den Einflüsterungen des Bösen' (*Klosterschule*: 71).

In Keiderling's *Eine Rose für eine Nonne*, the I-narrator is banned from visiting for a fifth time the deathbed of Sister Germana, with whom she had formed a close friendship over 33 years. The reason given by the nuns is that this special attention upsets the other elderly women, who had befriended this nun. The I-narrator refers to these nuns as 'die Wölfinnen', who at this late stage of the friendship of what was once a teacher/pupil relationship, are attempting to keep the two apart: 'Man ist gegen uns, Sr. Germana, man belauert, bespitzelt uns wie Feinde' (*Eine Rose für eine Nonne*: 67). Suffering from pneumonia at the age of 88, this now dying nun is weak and without power, after having run the convent for fifty years. The nuns clearly show that they are jealous, not only because this nun had had such an influential position, but also on account of the loving relationship between one of their sisters and her former pupil.

The situation portrayed by Keiderling is not uncommon. In every religious community of women there have always been written and enforced prohibitions against particular friendships. Firstly, preferential love has been viewed as tending towards exclusive love which could lead to the demise of religious life. Secondly, it violates the vow of chastity, whereby nuns promise to 'avoid undue familiarities, to guard modesty in all their actions, to mortify the senses'. From the nuns' point of view, order maintains a certain balance between the individual and the group. The danger, however, is that 'the zeal for order is often achieved at the expense of female freedom and friendship' (Raymond 1986: 93 and 109). What complicates the issue in Keiderling's work is that the intimate friendship is not between two nuns but between the former Mother Superior and a former pupil, who is not a member of the sisterhood. The sense of being an outsider and certainly not being made welcome by the nuns is evident at the end of the book when the I-narrator stands at the grave of Sister Germana for the first time since the funeral. She imagines that she is not alone but in the presence of numerous nuns, all singing the night prayer 'Hail, Holy Queen, Mother of Mercy': 'In geschlossenen Reihen standen sie um das Grab. Geballt wie eine Mauer- schwarz – bedrohlich – undurchdringlich' (*Eine Rose für eine Nonne*: 108). From the perspective of the nuns the pupil had overstepped the mark and could be conveniently blamed for breaking the rules and ignoring the legislated well-being of this social organism: 'Wir sollen uns nicht absondern, nicht einzeln und schon gar nicht zu zweit. Wer sich absondert, entbehrt des Schutzes der Gemeinschaft' (*Die Klosterschule*: 71). For Keiderling's I-narrator there is a sense of being castigated and paying the price for love. Behind all this is, of course, the fear of lesbianism and that the intense passion of friendship and love could surpass the boundaries of moderation within the convent.[6]

It is not just the freedom to express love for another female which is condemned by the nuns. Love of oneself is also taboo in the sense that recognition and acknowledgement of one's own identity is actively surpressed. In *Die Klosterschule* this manifests itself in the lack of mirrors in the school on the grounds that vanity would become rife. More significantly, looking in the mirror would mean projecting one's self and attaining self-identification which could be considered a rebellious act against the order. The ego is not permitted to exist; the collective is paramount. Frischmuth emphasizes this in her predominant use of the pronoun 'wir' (the very first word of the book). In Schwaiger's work, too, the girls are taught by the catechist to speak as one voice in order to show their dismissal of the devil and their belief in God.[7]

According to all the texts considered here, the convent girls are discouraged from asking any questions which might suggest that they are querying what is the accepted truth. Any dissenting voice is reprimanded: 'Im Religionsunterricht lasen wir die Apostelgeschichte. Rektor Koop redete ohne Unterbrechung, er stellte keine Fragen, er rief niemanden auf, zwischen ihm und uns bestand ein schweigendes Abkommen: Wer Zweifel an der Lehre der Kirche äußerte, würde keine gute Note bekommen. Wir lernten das Schweigen' (*Himmel, Hölle, Fegefeuer*: 37). This instilling of non-questioning is already encouraged in the 'Kindergarten': 'Und wir wollen nicht fragen ...sondern wir wollen gut zuhören!' (*Der Himmel ist süß*: 38).[8] To compensate in some way for the lack of freedom of expression and freedom of movement the girls in *Die Klosterschule* invent stories. Opportunity for this occurs during their daily walks, when instead of practising their English, they tell each other stories, communicating on their terms about fairy tales and legends. On Sundays, however, when they are not being so carefully watched over, they become more daring and adventurous in their stories, telling of real people and their cultures in far-flung corners of the world, such as Alaska, Mauritius, Tibet. By letting their imaginations run free, the world beyond the walls of the convent is experienced as being one of freedom, fascinating and exotic, since it is unknown to them.

For Frischmuth's I-narrator imagining what it is like to be free becomes more than just a fun thing to do at the weekend. Returning to school after the summer vacation she feels uncomfortable about the prefect wanting to know every detail about her friendships at home. As mentioned earlier, she begins to have doubts about the purpose of the endless prayers. Her uncertainty suggests that she no longer feels that she is part of the community: 'Es ist ein seltsames Gefühl, hier zu sein und doch nicht hier wie früher' (*Klosterschule*: 87). In a letter to a friend, a former pupil, to whom she is not supposed to write, she poses numerous questions about what life is like outside the convent. Her final comment accentuates the imprisonment she is experiencing:'Und vor allem mußt du mir schreiben, ob du tust, was dir Spaß macht, und wenn du es nicht tust, warum du es nicht tust. Ich würde es ganz bestimmt tun, wenn ich frei wäre, so wie du' (*Klosterschule*: 89). The motto to Wolfmayr's *Pechmarie* likewise addresses this issue of freedom: 'Lange vor unserer Geburt haben die Eltern beschlossen, wer wir sein sollen ... Auch die Gedanken sind nicht frei. Manchmal ist ICH sehr schwer'.

This brings us full circle to the very first quote in this paper by Richter's I-narrator, namely: 'Die Freiheit, mit gutem Gewissen und Stolz ich sagen zu können' (*Himmel, Hölle, Fegefeuer*: 17). The Catholic education of all the protagonists in the works quoted here, be it in the confines of the convent school and/or at home, focuses on the fact that guilt constantly pervades their thoughts. Each I-narrator struggles with her conscience to come to terms with feelings of inadequacy and failure. In *Himmel, Hölle, Fegefeuer* the I-narrator had wanted to bring about changes in the church, even if it was only on the superficial level of introducing different music or a different service into the church, but nothing could change as long as the minds of those in authority resisted change. In *Eine Rose für eine Nonne* the I-narrator had, similarly, come up against a wall of intolerance and had failed to keep her promise to Sister Germana, namely to be at her bedside when she died. In *Der Himmel ist süß* with its subtitle 'Eine Beichte', Gitti lies during her first confession to the priest, saying that she stole buttons and not money from her mother: the recognition of her sin weighs heavy on her mind. In *Die Klosterschule* the I-narrator associates freedom with the relinquishing of religious principles, and therefore cannot imagine what kind of morals will apply to her future life. Whilst she is unable to distinguish between the dogmatic teachings of the Catholic convent school and Catholicism as a faith, she does recognize that as a person she will have to change. Yet she is afraid of the repercussions, if she turns her back on all she has been taught and trained to do. This fear is also linked to her understanding of God. An integral aspect of the girls' education is the ultimate authority of an all-powerful, omniscient God: 'Ob in Schule, Haus oder Garten, Gott sieht und hört alles, seinem Wissen bleibt nichts verborgen, seine Allmacht ist zu allem imstande' (*Klosterschule*: 77).

Again in the 'Kindergarten', this time in *Pechmarie*: 'Der Liebe Gott hockt als oberste Kontrollinstanz in meinem Kopf, und man hat keine Ruhe vor ihm, niemals, immer ist da dieser Liebe Gott und verfolgt argwöhnisch, was man tut, schüttelt den Kopf und droht mit dem Finger' (*Pechmarie*: 33-4). Thus, in the mind of Wolfmayr's I-narrator, punishment results from God and a sense of threat prevails throughout her early years of schooling.

The questions that these I-narrators begin to ask about the nature of God and the ideology with which they are being indoctrinated do indicate that these convent girls are making an attempt to achieve personal freedom and independence. The subtitle of *Himmel, Hölle, Fegefeuer* reads 'Versuch einer Befreiung' and is attributable to the author's own conviction, namely: 'Man kann aus einer Institution oder einer Partei austreten; ob man aber aus einer christlich geprägten Erziehung austreten kann, bezweifle ich' (Richter quoted in Bernhard 1993).[9] Her I-narrator signs the official forms for leaving the Catholic church and thereupon automatically goes to a Catholic church for peace and quiet in order to reflect on what she has done – such is the twist in the tale.

In each book convent schooling is shown to be inflexible in the face of any real changes in society due to the fact that its philosophy has its roots in dogmas. Whilst this is a small, closed-off world, it is training adults of the future for a larger world. These literary works based on their writers' own experiences of Austrian/German convent education do challenge the content and methods of these pedagogical institutions by highlighting the needs of individual girls against a background of a Christian religion. Sometimes the challenge is a loud and forceful protest as in Richter's *Himmel, Hölle, Fegefeuer*; sometimes it is a quiet, yet persistent confrontation, as in Frischmuth's *Die Klosterschule*. In spite of this being an all-female community, the girls are educated according to how men define women. The education portrayed should, therefore, be seen from the perspective of exploring another dimension of women's emancipation, one which has its roots in the spiritual but is not divorced from women's social quest. By focusing on the fact that Catholicism can be a source of oppression, these women writers do draw attention to the sexual politics of theology. Twenty-five years lie between Frischmuth's *Die Klosterschule* and Keiderling's *Eine Rose für eine Nonne*, yet the freedom to be true to one's female self remains a contentious issue in the contemporary literature of women from German-speaking countries.

Notes

[1] The term 'Klösterreich' was coined by Klaus Zeyringer in his study of Austrian literature of the 1980s. See Zeyringer 1992: 212.

Notes continued

[2] My title recalls Mary McCarthy's autobiographical work *Memories of a Catholic Girlhood* (1957).

[3] One of the things that the German writer, Karin Struck, originally found attractive about Catholicism was the fact that Catholics address the Virgin Mary in their prayers: 'Was ich damals so verführerisch fand, war eben die Tatsache daß dort auch noch eine Frau im Spiel war'. Interestingly, the Virgin Mary is not mentioned in a work such as *Die Klosterschule*, possible because her presence would have undermined the male-oriented teachings. Struck was also fascinated by the smell of incense and the sensuous side of religion in general. See Kuschel 1985: 53. Mary McCarthy makes the point of how Catholicism provided her with an aesthetic outlet in the words of the Mass, the litanies, Easter lilies around the altar, the rosaries and votive lamps (McCarthy 1957: xxv).

[4] The reference is to 'He who spares the rod, hates his son, but he who loves him is careful to discipline him' (Proverbs 13:24). Such an upbringing prevails in Waltraud Anna Mitgutsch's *Die Züchtigung* (1985). For further discussion see Bagley 1996: 57-87.

[5] For a historical depiction of 'Schwarze Pädagogik', see Rutschky 1977, and for a psychoanalytical discussion of the principles of this method of upbringing see Miller 1990.

[6] It is interesting to note that recent writing on the subject of friendships in convent communities by authors such as Curb and Manahan (1985), advocates that nuns should not fear intimacy and even intensity of feeling with other women; that particular friendships should 'come out of the closet'.

[7] A group mentality can also have its advantages because when one of the group misbehaves she does have the support of the others and no individual takes the blame on her own. From the nuns' point of view this would be seen as an additional form of punishment and should prevent individuals from misbehaving.

[8] A point worth noting here is that in the past Catholicism dispensed with people with different visions by labelling them heretics. There was no room for disobedient souls who needed to live their own myths and whose imagination could not fit into standardized categories.

[9] Recent studies show that in the past thirty years approximately half a per cent of Catholics have been leaving the church in Germany, one per cent the Protestant church. In today's Germany 24 per cent of Catholics have considered at least once seriously leaving the church, 23 per cent of Protestants. A quarter of these intend to put this into practice. Faith without a church is a growing trend because the church is viewed as nothing more than a powerful institution. See Kistenfeger and Robers 1996: 52-60.

Bibliography

Bagley, Petra M. 1996. *Somebody's Daughter: The Portrayal of Daughter-Parent Relationships by Contemporary Women Writers from German-speaking Countries*, Stuttgart, Akademischer Verlag Hans-Dieter Heinz
Bernhard, Renate. 1993. 'Versuchter Abschied von gestern. Autorin Jutta Richter las aus *Himmel, Hölle, Fegefeuer*', *Rheinische Post*, 23 March
Bunting, Madeleine. 1995. 'Pope says sorry to all women', *Guardian*, 11 July: 6
—. 1996. 'Within these walls', *Guardian*, 1 February: 7
Curb, Rosemary and Nancy Manahan (eds) 1985. *Lesbian Nuns: Breaking Silence*, Tallahassee, Naiad
Frischmuth, Barbara. 1986. *Die Klosterschule*, Reinbek bei Hamburg, rororo
Harris, Kevin. 1984. *Sex, Ideology and Religion: The Representation of Women in the Bible*, New Jersey, Barnes and Noble Books
Keiderling, Christel. 1993. *Eine Rose für eine Nonne. Abschied von einer Freundin*, Frankfurt am Main, Ulrike Helmer
Kistenfeger, Hartmut and Norbert Robers. 6 April 1996. 'Glaube ohne Kirche', *Focus*, 15: 52-60
Kuschel, Karl-Josef. 1985. *Weil wir uns auf dieser Erde nicht ganz zu Hause fühlen: 12 Schriftsteller über Religion und Literatur*, München, Piper
—. 1990. '"Auf diesem Gott bin ich nicht neugierig": Interview mit Brigitte Schwaiger', *Publik-Forum*, 24 August: 21
McCarthy, Mary. 1957. *Memories of a Catholic Girlhood*, London, Heinemann
Miller, Alice. 1990. *Am Anfang war Erziehung*, Frankfurt am Main, Suhrkamp
Mitgutsch, Waltraud Anna. 1988. *Die Züchtigung*, Munich, dtv
Raymond, Janice. 1986. *A Passion for Friends: Toward a Philosophy of Female Affection*, London, The Women's Press
Richter, Jutta. 1992. *Himmel, Hölle, Fegefeuer: Versuch einer Befreiung*, Munich, Goldmann
Rutschky, Katharina. 1977. *Schwarze Paedagogik: Quellen zur Naturgeschichte der bürgerlichen Erziehung*, Frankfurt am Main, Ullstein
Schwaiger, Brigitte. 1986. *Der Himmel ist süß. Eine Beichte*, Reinbek, rororo
Warner, Marina. 1976. *Alone of all her Sex: The Myth of the Virgin Mary*, London, Picador
Wolfmayr, Andrea. 1989. *Pechmarie*, Graz, Verlag Styria
Zeyringer, Klaus. 1992. *Innerlichkeit und Öffentlichkeit: österreichische Literatur der achtziger Jahre*, Tübingen, Francke

Erika Mitterer as a Christian Writer: A Study of the Novel *Der Fürst der Welt* as a Precursor of the Later Poetry

Margaret Ives

Erika Mitterer is perhaps best known outside Austria for her contribution to the *Briefwechsel in Gedichten mit R. M. Rilke* (Rilke 1957) which, although dating from the early 1920s, did not appear in print until 1950 (see Mason 1953 and Brown 1990). Born in 1906, and thus just eighteen years old when she began to send poems to Rilke in May 1924, she had been writing poetry since the age of twelve, and in 1930 was awarded the Julius Reich prize for her first published collection *Dank des Lebens*. A second collection *Gesang der Wandernden* followed a few years later (1935). By this time she was already working on a major novel, *Der Fürst der Welt* (Mitterer 1980), which sold 49,300 copies within four years of its publication in 1940. Other works include the novels *Wir sind allein*, begun in the pre-war period but not published until 1945, *Die nackte Wahrheit* (1951) and *Alle unsere Spiele* (1977), an English translation of which appeared in 1988, shortly after the commemoration in Austria of her 80th birthday, under the title *All Our Games*. While these latter novels probe the extent of Austrian collaboration within the Third Reich and can be viewed as 'Vergangenheitsbewältigung' (Wigmore 1991), *Der Fürst der Welt* is primarily concerned with the insidious nature of evil and our human failure to recognize its various manifestations. It is also a powerful plea for a renewed spirituality and Christian commitment, and as such foreshadows several themes of Mitterer's later poetry, particularly those expressed in the two collections *Entsühnung des Kain* (1974) and *Das verhüllte Kreuz* (1985).

Der Fürst der Welt is set in Germany in the late Middle Ages at the time of the Inquisition. Following an outbreak of smallpox, several unfortunate women are denounced as witches, and after a long period of interrogation and torture are finally burnt at the stake. The style and narrative techniques could strike us today as curiously old-fashioned. This is not the experimental prose of a Jelinek; the all-seeing narrator and some rather strained interior monologues remind us more of Marie von Ebner-Eschenbach and the late nineteenth-century realist tradition. Yet the narrative technique is more subtle than it appears. Mitterer clearly indicates her allegorical intentions when she writes: 'Durch die Darstellung der Zeitenwende des ausgehenden Mittelalters wollte ich meine Zeit besser begreifen, wie, in einem scheinbar intakten Gemeinwesen und in den Herzen der Menschen, die Machtergreifung des Bösen möglich wird.'[1]

Satan, the Prince of the title, is, according to Mitterer, ever-present among us. The forms of his appearance may differ, but the ways in which he corrupts us are inextricably rooted in our fallen human condition. In this context, therefore, the novel can be read as a veiled commentary on the evils of the Third Reich, also a time of denunciations and witch-hunts, and this helps to explain the relatively slow unfolding of the plot and the all-seeing overview provided by the narration. In order to see how innocent actions can be mis-interpreted and contorted into something sinister, in order to understand how ordinary, decent people can be persuaded to betray each other, the same events must be illuminated from a number of different angles. The reader, for instance, is aware of the true parentage of a baby boy discovered on the threshold of the local convent and is thus all the more appalled as chance remarks overheard by one of the nuns are twisted and then repeated so as to condemn a totally innocent person. The account of a friendly gesture towards a child in a queue at the butcher's shop may seem too long-winded and out of proportion, yet when this same gesture is later cited as an example of sorcery, the extent of the suspicion and mistrust that has engulfed the townsfolk is forcefully revealed. In this way 'die *Machtergreifung* des Bösen' (my italics) is shown to be not some instantly recognizable cataclysmic catastrophe, but a gradual process of innuendo and attrition that creeps up on us unawares and is therefore all the more difficult to resist.

Within this framework it is possible to discover many other coded messages. Perhaps the boldest of these is the mention, in the latter half of the novel, of the prison known as the 'Judenkeller', where the unfortunate women accused of witchcraft are being held and questioned. Everyone knows that this dungeon exists; everyone knows what happens to people who are detained there; but no one is prepared to make any kind of protest, and the whole subject is taboo. At another point an appeal is made to a foreign lawyer to come and save the town from the consequences of its folly. 'Und jetzt schrieb er mit schmerzenden Augen, daß nur die Gegenwart des großen Gelehrten die Stadt vom Wahne befreien, Unschuldige vom Tode erretten, die Geschichte vor einem Schandmal bewahren könne, das sonst über Jahrhunderte hinaus alle großen Taten, alle glorreichen Erfindungen, alle herrlichen Kunstwerke dieser Zeit entstellen würde' (*Der Fürst der Welt*: 506). At a time when many thousands of innocent people were disappearing daily from the streets of Vienna these words must indeed have signalled a grim prophecy. In post-war Austria they again raise the theme of collective guilt and responsibility, a topic which is further explored in Mitterer's portrayal of Bishop Ulrich who, although deeply troubled by the arrests and imprisonments, does not denounce them publicly and thus appears to condone them. The final picture is truly sombre: there is no happy end and only the merest hint of a possible Christian redemption.

Nevertheless, the different perspectives of today's generations reveal much more than a confrontation with the recent past. From a feminist viewpoint the novel clearly shows women as the victims of men's arrogance, selfishness, thoughtlessness and malice. The two central female characters are both betrayed by the machinations of the male hierarchy and condemned out-of-hand on trumped-up charges. The younger one, Theres, herself without guile, is compromised against her will when she is followed by a young man who insists on accompanying her, and she is from that moment onwards regarded as a *femme fatale* who, on account of her flaming red hair, is 'die rote Hexe' who steals other women's sweethearts. Accused of sorcery and thrown into prison, she believes to the end that the one man she has come to trust, the kind and humane Dr. Fabri, will intervene on her behalf and convince the courts of her innocence. He makes only a very feeble attempt to do so, and she goes to her death totally disillusioned 'daß er ihren Blick nicht erwidern kann. Daß er machtlos ist und sie längst preisgegeben hat' (*Fürst der Welt*: 607). Her sister, who has entered a religious order and is later elected Prioress, is persuaded by her own father-confessor, with whom she has fallen in love, to feign the stigmata in order to bring fame to the convent and money to the town. When the duplicity is discovered, this hypocritical priest takes the lead in humiliating and exposing her, demanding that she be mercilessly punished, cast out of her order, and sent into exile. She, for her part, makes no counter-denunciation, coming at the very end of the novel to see her former desire for sexual fulfilment and male human companionship as a purely selfish kind of love which has led her away from her true vocation. She is therefore willing to accept her penance and emerges in the last chapter as a guilt-ridden and tragic figure, but still morally superior to Pater Alexander who is finally depicted as 'ein müder und unzufriedener Priester, der nicht Abt werden konnte, weil die Brüder ihn haßten' (*Der Fürst der Welt*: 551). If Dr. Fabri depicts the failure, in Mitterer's view, of the values of liberal humanism and the subsequent Enlightenment in face of unmitigated evil, the portrayal of Pater Alexander contains some equally strong criticism of the medieval Church hierarchy, particularly as regards its attitudes towards women.

There is also a sense in which *Der Fürst der Welt* can further be interpreted as part of Erika Mitterer's ongoing debate with institutionalized Christianity in general. It is not merely that the Church is here shown as riddled with corruption and guilty of sharp practice: it is also suggested that it, too, is under the sway of Satan in that the most terrible atrocities are carried out by the Inquisition ostensibly in the service of Christ. There is, in addition, a strong theological undertow throughout the novel. Maria Michaela, as Prioress, continually looks back to her childhood when, as Hiltrud von der Ried, she had listened to the well-known folk-tale of the orphan child adopted by the Virgin Mary, a story which she is now convinced holds the secret of the Godhead. (*Die dreizehnte Kammer*, which refers to this story, was in fact the working title of the novel in its early stages.) Several other scenes are set in the Bishop's Palace where the Bishop himself poses the question 'Wessen Macht ist größer – die Macht Gottes, oder die des Satans?' *(Der Fürst der Welt*: 399) and if the answer favours Satan, then – according to Mitterer – it is because human beings have as yet still not grasped the true meaning of Christian love. 'Wir alle lieben nicht genug' (*Der Fürst der Welt*: 599), words spoken by one of the more saintly priests as Maria Michaela seeks absolution, seem at first puzzling, challenging the reader to go back over the events of the narrative to discover their meaning. Matthias Nothaft, the wealthy merchant who adopts Theres, is then seen to have had no real understanding of her, regarding her more as an unpaid servant than as a kinswoman. Dr. Fabri, although brave and compassionate enough to treat the sick during the smallpox epidemic, conspicuously lacks 'Zivilcourage' and is afraid of entering into any kind of committed relationship. His flight to Nuremberg at a crucial turning-point must be re-assessed not as a voyage of self-discovery, but as self-centred escapism. Maria Michaela's refusal to admit Theres into the convent, thereby abandoning her to the malice of the townsfolk, is now shown as a decision taken out of a desire to conceal her own illicit passion rather than out of any true concern for her sister's welfare. The townspeople themselves are portrayed throughout as riddled with envy and jealousy, only too eager to witness the downfall of their fellows and denounce them to the Inquisition. On the fringes of society outside the city walls the poor and outcast in their hovels are easy victims of superstition and ignorance and, denied any kind of help by the prosperous, are the source of the disease that wreaks so much havoc. Had they too been treated with reverence and respect, had there been a more equitable distribution of wealth, there would perhaps have been no smallpox epidemic, no search for scapegoats, no Inquisition, and no persecution of the innocent.

'Wir alle lieben nicht genug' thus becomes an expression of Erika Mitterer's burning social conscience and is indeed the main theme of her later poetry. Particularly in the collection *Entsühnung des Kain* there are meditations on the belief that evil arises because we do not love each other as we ought and because we fail to have adequate trust in the generosity and grace of God. The poems depict a bleak world, a world grown sceptical and shallow, superficial, frivolous and irreverent. Consequently we no longer experience any real joy in life and, as Rilke put it in the *Duineser Elegien*:

> ... die findigen Tiere merken es schon, daß wir nicht sehr verläßlich zuhaus sind in der gedeuteten Welt. (*Erste Elegie*, ll. 11-13)

However, whereas Rilke saw the great medieval cathedrals as genuine expressions of human striving and searching for God, Erika Mitterer feels alienated by them. In the poem 'Spät' she tells us that she has admired the basilicas and columns and frescos, but there seems to be no meaning behind them, for the faith that once inspired them has been lost. Only very late in life has she herself come to learn true reverence, that overwhelming sense of awe that forces us to our knees in total submission. Everywhere else the evils of modernity seem to have corrupted religious practice. The bitterly sarcastic 'Mission heute' chastises western Christians for daring to export the so-called benefits of civilization to so-called undeveloped parts of the world:

> Wir teilen mit ihnen:
> unsere Zeit und all unsere
> Errungenschaften.
> Einst war es der Schnaps,
> jetzt sind es die Zigaretten,
> der Kunstdünger,
> die Motorfahrzeuge
> und die Aufklärungsfilme.
>
> Ein Schelm gibt mehr, als er hat ...
>
> Wir haben
> Impstoff und Vitamintabletten,
> Sozialfürsorge, Geburtenkontrolle.
> (Von allem zu wenig). Wir haben
> die Menschenrechte deklariert,
> die Chancengleichheit,
> die Frauenbefreiung als Zielvorstellung;
> Meinungsumfragen,
> Wahlarithmetik und Schlankschlemmersuppen
> als Mittel zum Zweck.
> Wahrlich, Mut haben wir nötig,
> um zu fernen Völkern zu gehen!
> (*Entsühnung des Kain*: 11-12)

Mitterer is prepared to admit that there are perhaps still one or two very sincere missionaries who will go to live and work alongside needy people and who will totally commit their lives in this way. Nevertheless, even such totally committed people lack, in Mitterer's opinion, the courage to preach Christianity where it is today most needed. In the latter part of 'Mission heute' she asks a pertinent question: how dare we preach the love of God to primitive peoples when all around us, in our own society, there is cruelty and violence, neglect and sheer despair? Who indeed could be presumptuous enough to speak of a loving father-figure God to the victims of child abuse?

> Wer aber hat den Mut und geht
> hinüber ins Nebenhaus, wo der Vater
> die Mutter erschlug und dem Knaben
> Schweigen befahl, und ihn nachher
> ständig allein ließ?
> Bis ihn die 'Fürsorge' aufgriff und er
> immer wieder davonlief–?
> Wer hat den Mut, *den* beten zu lehren:
> 'Vater unser!' Wer
> verhüllt nicht sein Antlitz?
> (*Entsühnung des Kain*: 12-13)

In the final poem 'Entsühnung des Kain', from which the collection takes its name, it is Eve who speaks. She acknowledges her guilt in favouring the younger son Abel over the first-born Cain and in fostering that jealousy in Cain that drives him ultimately to murder his sibling:

> Wir haben ihn alle
> immer zu wenig geliebt.
> Mußte er nicht seinen Bruder
> hassen- den Fröhlichen, Neidlosen,
> Furchtlosen, Arglosen?
> (*Entsühnung des Kain*: 67)

The adjectives are significant, for we find them again and again in Mitterer's work. These are the affluent, the well-to-do, the respectable citizens who do not realize that material well-being and prosperity can be seedbeds of evil in that they encourage selfishness and judgmental attitudes towards others who may one day seek a terrible revenge. While this is not entirely adequate as an explanation of fascism or Right-wing extremism, it does point to Mitterer's belief in an insidious canker at work within society, a self-seeking individualism which, by gaining access to traditional values and institutional religion, can destroy all our defences against the Evil One and lead us all into forms of collective madness and depravity. It is a dark picture, the picture of a world sorely in need of redemption, otherwise the Prince of this world will surely triumph and destroy us. Are there, therefore, any grounds for hope? In the poem 'Hoffnung', taken from the collection *Das verhüllte Kreuz*, we find Mitterer moving towards her own feminist theology, one which many feminists and theologians will find uncomfortable. For her the hope of the world is that the unconditional, truly Christian love which alone can bring salvation will be kept alive, nurtured and lived out by women, for it is women who supremely experience such self-sacrificial giving in their biological life-cycles as mothers:

> Frauen erkennen das Heil
> anders als Männer: sie spüren's!
> Und sie wissen und danken,
> brauchen nicht zu verstehn
> (*Das verhüllte Kreuz*: 51)

At the end of *Der Fürst der Welt* Maria Michaela, reduced to the status of a beggar-woman, sets out on a lone pilgrimage to Jerusalem as an act of penance. As she passes through the city gates a young man, Beatus, who is about to enter the monastery as a novice, is so struck by her resolute appearance that he does not curse or ridicule her, but utters instead the words 'Gelobt sei Jesus Christus!' to which she replies 'Gelobt sei Jesus Christus in Ewigkeit! Amen' (*Der Fürst der Welt*: 623). Taken in isolation, this conclusion could be viewed as somewhat unsatisfactory. In the light of the later poetry, however, it can be interpreted as meaning that both Beatus and Maria Michaela have at last glimpsed the true Gospel – she by acknowledging her failure to love properly and thus bearing some of the guilt and responsibility for her sister's execution, and he by recognizing in the contrite woman a deep spirituality that has laid aside all ambition. When, in the folk-tale, the orphan adopted by Mary opens the door of the forbidden thirteenth chamber, what is revealed is not just the Holy Trinity, but the Holy Trinity as that 'Feuer, welches das Herz der Welt ist' (*Der Fürst der Welt*: 541) that all-embracing self-sacricial love from which most of us shrink in fear and panic, but which is, in Mitterer's view, the creative force behind all forms of being throughout the universe. At the end of the novel Maria Michaela rediscovers this secret – too late to prevent her own tragedy, but an indication to the reader of Mitterer's deep religious insight and profound moral conviction.

Notes

[1] Quotation taken from dust cover of the 1988 Böhlau edition, from which all my quotations from the text are cited. This edition also contains a useful 'Zeittafel' and a complete list of Erika Mitterer's published works. Only those works mentioned in the above essay are therefore included in my bibliography.

Bibliography

Brown, G. B. 1990. 'Der Briefwechsel in Gedichten mit Erika Mitterer – monologue, dialogue, or duet?' In H. Herzmann and H. Ridley (eds), *Rilke und der Wandel in der Sensibilität*, Essen, Die blaue Eule: 107-120
Mason, Eudo C. 1953. 'Rilke's Correspondence in Verse with Benvenuta and Erika Mitterer', *German Life and Letters*, 7: 199-203
Mitterer, Erika. 1930. *Dank des Lebens*, Frankfurt am Main, Rütten and Loening
—. 1935. *Gesang der Wandernden*, Leipzig, Staackmann
—. 1945. *Wir sind allein. Ein Roman zwischen zwei Zeiten*, Vienna, Lückmann
—. 1951. *Die nackte Wahrheit*, Innsbruck, Österreichische Verlagsanstalt
—. 1974. *Entsühnung des Kain. Neue Gedichte*, Einsiedeln, Johannes Verlag
—. 1977. *Alle unsere Spiele*, Frankfurt am Main, Knecht. 1988. English translation *All Our Games*, Camden House
—. 1985. *Das verhüllte Kreuz. Neue Gedichte*, St. Pölten. Niederösterreichisches Pressehaus
—. 1988. *Der Fürst der Welt* (1940), new and revised edn, with introduction by Roman Rocek, Vienna, Böhlau
Rilke, R. M. 1957. *Briefwechsel in Gedichten mit Erika Mitterer* (1950), *Sämtliche Werke*, vol. 2, Wiesbaden, Insel: 279-321
Wigmore, J. 1991. '*Vergangenheitsbewältigung* in Austria: the Personal and Political in Erika Mitterer's *Alle unsere Spiele* and Elisabeth Reichart's *Februarschatten*', *German Life and Letters*, 44: 477-487

'Die Liebe zu den Modellen':[1] Barbara Frischmuth's Myths

Mererid Puw Davies

Medusa

In Barbara Frischmuth's (b. 1941)[2] short story 'Älter geworden...' (1989 [1988]), a male tourist is sightseeing in a Roman museum where he admires a painting of a beautiful woman, only then to experience 'tiefes Erschrecken' when he encounters: '"Medusa" ... ein tatsächlich im Raum als Körper vorhanden seiendes Wesen ... Mit halb geöffneten violetten Lippen und jenem Schlangenhaar ... Und ... sein Blick [fällt] noch einmal auf das "Bild einer Frau", und er hätte fast aufgeschrien, die Ähnlichkeit erkennend zwischen der Schönen und der Häßlichen' ('Älter geworden...': 105-6).

'Medusa' is another visitor to the museum whose appearance – mental disturbance is implied – petrifies the man. First, she is monstrous, challenging the cultural and aesthetic order. Second, and worse, her presence exposes the contingency of this order, as she deconstructs the distinction between her chaotic self and the ordered image of the 'Figura di donna', the portrait of a beautiful woman. Third, 'Medusa' challenges the man's subject position by resisting and returning his gaze. And fourth, the man's terror recalls Sigmund Freud's interpretation of Medusa's head as a displaced and terrifying image of castrating maternal genitalia.[3]

I begin my discussion of Frischmuth's uses of myth by focusing on this epiphanic moment partly because this event is typical of Frischmuth's use of myth when addressing her major themes: gender identity and relations; intertextuality and the question of language. But more importantly, this moment also highlights the dual nature of myth – as a type of textual *content* and as a type of *language* – which marks Frischmuth's writing. Here, I shall briefly explain what I understand by myth as both content and discourse before returning to 'Älter geworden...', and demonstrating the significance of these two types of myth in practice.

In this paper, I shall use the term 'myth' as follows. On the one hand, myth denotes familiar, ritualized narrative material with a variety of explanatory and referential applications. Myth according to this definition could involve brief references to well-known material from the classics or the Bible or extensive re-workings of a theme or figure familiar from such myths. And on the other hand, recent theories suggest an alternative definition of myth as *process* or type of discourse. Following Roland Barthes's theory of 'myth' (1972 [1957]), I shall deploy this term 'myth' in inverted commas to mean a type of language with a particular function and distinctive features rather than to indicate the use of myth as content. Barthes saw 'myth' as a mystifying, totalizing rhetoric, a way of (mis)representing reality which erases difference and history and makes the contingent appear eternal. In Barthes's Marxist analysis, this is a depoliticizing rhetoric which prevents analysis and resists societal and cultural change and it is motivated by the desire of the dominant class to perpetuate existing societal arrangements and prevent any critical analysis of these. Barthes identifies several rhetorical figures characteristic of such 'myth' and I shall refer to these in my analysis of Frischmuth's explorations of 'myth' as linguistic process. And to these rhetorical figures identified by Barthes I shall add a further figure of my own which strikes me as being of the same order. This is the figure of the 'ineffable', since it seems to me that in many literary texts potential disruption is dealt with by claiming explicitly or implicitly that the disruptive event or idea is inexpressible and thus precluding it from representation. This rhetorical move fits well with Barthes's description of 'myth' as a stabilizing, conservative mode of representation.

As I suggested above, 'Älter geworden...' highlights not only the use of myth as content by referring to the classics in a conventional manner, but also the use of 'myth' as discourse. Thus, firstly, the content of this story uses a familiar image from classical myth to symbolize a moment of horror as economically as possible. In this way, the narrator does not need to go into descriptive and analytic detail to evoke the visage of the other, frightening museum-goer as her terrifying appearance is clearly established by the reference to a monster of classical antiquity. This is a standard, literary use of myth as content.

Secondly however, we can go further and identify the text's use of 'myth' as rhetoric, for the word 'Medusa' is used not as a description of the person who frightens the man, but as a means of avoiding a description or explanation of why she is frightening. It is not a real Medusa who terrifies the man, but something which he calls 'Medusa'; nor is the real monster here the person the man calls 'Medusa', but her challenge to his subjectivity and the threat of castration which she represents. In other words, the text suggests that the disturbing phenomenon experienced by the man is so dreadful that it cannot be expressed in conventional, realistic terms – i.e. that it is ineffable. And in this manner, the disturbance is effectively excluded from the text and replaced by a conventional image which fits more comfortably with cultural order, thus weakening the horrific moment. Or in other words, the naming process by means of myth is a way of re-familiarizing the disturbance, making it safe, analogous to Perseus catching the Gorgon's reflection in his shield; that is, it also becomes 'myth' as discourse. Nonetheless, although this rhetorical twist is an example of the use of myth as content in the service of 'myth' as a conservative, stabilizing mode of representation, in that it weakens and vanquishes disturbance, this creation of a blind spot in the text draws considerable attention to itself and thus hints at the more horrific, underlying meaning. It seems to me therefore that the topos of the ineffable, while being a powerful component of Barthesian 'myth', is also its weak link, since it points so ostentatiously to that which it excludes, and so I shall focus on this topos of the ineffable in my readings of individual texts by Frischmuth.

A survey of secondary literature to date on Frischmuth's work shows that there is ample scope for an analysis of myth based on the theoretical premises I have outlined here. Although critics have pointed out the centrality of linguistic, mythological, literary and societal models to Frischmuth's work, they tend to make the generalizing assumption that her use of such models is gently progressive as part of a project of Frauenliteratur which challenges dated and oppressive cultural norms.[4] Indeed, this assumption is very often made in the context of the common claim that Frischmuth's work itself is 'model' Austrian Frauenliteratur. That is, secondary literature which deals with Frischmuth often appears in publications of an anthological type which aim to give an overview of recent Austrian literature or recent (Austrian) 'women's writing' with reference to exemplary figures such as Frischmuth.[5] Or similarly, individual essays may begin by assuming Frischmuth's exemplary status, as their titles suggest.[6]

Consequently, my analysis of three of Frischmuth's prose texts, *Die Klosterschule* (1979 [1968]), *Das Verschwinden des Schattens in der Sonne* (1980 [1973]) and *Herrin der Tiere* (1986a) is motivated by three questions. First, can we be more rigorous about the way Frischmuth uses such models as myth in her writing? Second, what can Frischmuth's writing teach us in more general terms about contemporary myth as both content and discourse? Given the assumption made by most critics that Frischmuth's use of models is in some way progressive or that it at least marks a move away from the more oppressive uses of tradition, I shall consider the political implications of her uses of such old cultural models as myth. And third, what makes this very varied body of work seem exemplary to many critics?

Die Klosterschule
Frischmuth's first published book, *Die Klosterschule*, bears witness to the Austrian avant-garde tradition of *Sprachskepsis* and reveals the workings of the closed linguistic system of Catholic education, consisting as it does of a montage of the various types of language which make up the world of the convent school: readings from Catholic journals, rules and regulations, lessons, reprimands and so forth. The montage technique demonstrates how this system works – and also, by means of parodic juxtapositions, how it may be used to deconstruct itself.

As far as myth – i.e. easily identifiable reference to well-known bodies of material – is concerned, there is surprisingly little use of the Christian myth, if this is defined as Biblical material, in *Die Klosterschule*. However, *Die Klosterschule* explicitly exposes 'myth' as an oppressive and dehistoricizing rhetoric, since the 'myths' of Catholic education, in line with Barthes's 'myth', rely on notions of the universal and the eternal: '[Gott] hat in Seiner Weisheit und Allmacht die Welt nicht nur erschaffen, sondern Er erhält sie auch im Dasein. In der stofflichen Welt wirken Naturgesetze, die Gott gegeben hat (Siehe Bohrsches Atommodell!)' (*Die Klosterschule*: 67). And just as for Barthes, 'myth' tends to proverbs and tautological, lapidary statements, so this kind of discourse abounds in *Die Klosterschule*: 'Das Herz Jesu in sich und sich im Herzen Jesu sein lassen. Zu vielen Zeiten eine Andacht zum Herzen Jesu verrichten. Glauben, daß das Herz Jesu das Herz Jesu ist' (63).

Another rhetorical figure identified by Barthes as part of 'myth' as discourse which is used frequently in *Die Klosterschule* is 'identification', and the schoolgirls are the objects of just such a process. The novel opens with a performative 'wir': 'Wir, Angehörige der katholischen Jungschar, Zöglinge des Klosters, Schülerinnen der Ober- und Unterstufe …' (7), and this identification is maintained throughout in order to demonstrate how such a rhetorical process works normatively to erase cultural difference: 'Hättet ihr nicht Lust [euren schwarzen Brüdern und Schwestern … euren braunen Brüdern und Schwestern … euren gelben Brüdern und Schwestern], diesen armen Wesen, die wie ihr Kinder Gottes sind, beizustehen?' (31) However, the schoolgirls do not take over this normative familial discourse, but use another rhetorical figure of 'myth', exoticism, which Barthes calls 'une figure de secours' when 'identification' fails: 'Es ist auch noch die Rede von Kümmeltürken, Hottentotten … von der Faulheit der Neger … Ansonsten interessieren uns noch die Tiere des Urwalds' (18-19). That is to say, the schoolgirls' rejection of 'identification' in favour of 'exoticism' suggests that the official rhetoric based on 'identification' has failed. Indeed, official Catholic 'myth' is constantly subverted when the children use it in such performative contradictions as this and spawn parodic versions and eccentric associative chains. Thus, during the daily walk, the girls have to practise their English: 'wir formen mit dem Munde Wörter, die wie englische ausgesprochen werden könnten' (15).

The major taboos of the official Catholic 'myth' focus on the body and sexuality, and many passages of *Die Klosterschule* illustrate how taboos surrounding these areas are enforced through the topos of ineffability associated with 'myth' as discourse, such as in the euphemistic 'Anstandsstunde' in which the girls are given instruction on chaste courtship. However, *Die Klosterschule*'s eccentric juxtapositions ensure that precisely these taboo topics of the body and sexuality constantly re-emerge. Even the Bible is read only for 'die bestimmten Stellen, die interessanten Stellen' which involve sexuality and precipitate extravagant fantasies. Indeed, at one point, the narrator is punished for such

'Geschichtenerzählen' and gets detention in compensation for which she gorges herself on jam sandwiches. Each pupil's food supplies are numbered: 'Jede Schachtel, jede Dose, jedes Glas ist mit einer Nummer versehen. Ich habe 122. Unter dieser Nummer kann man bei Brandgefahr die Feuerwehr rufen' (47). This is a particularly important crux as we are seeing two sets of rules interfering by coincidental association and setting off subversive associations, since fire is a traditional symbol of physical desire and danger that has here been displaced onto the officially sanctioned act of eating, which is carried to anti-social and immodest extremes.

In conclusion therefore, it seems that while the ideological restrictions of language cannot be overcome in any final sense, *Die Klosterschule* renders transparent the rhetorical figures of Catholic 'myth' by means of montage and alienation effects which render its normally invisible internal contradictions evident. This parodic narrative technique also devalues Biblical myth which traditionally legitimized Catholic rules and regulations. By citing Biblical myth incompletely, inaccurately or out of context, and juxtaposing it with less revered types of language, *Die Klosterschule* divests the Christian myth of its traditional aura and thus it ceases to be a sacred and essentially different type of narrative. Because *Die Klosterschule* does not focus on the content or message of Biblical myth but on its rhetorical uses, the text demotes Biblical narrative from transcendent myth to the instrument of a transparently oppressive, discursive 'myth'.

Das Verschwinden des Schattens in der Sonne
Frischmuth's first novel, *Das Verschwinden des Schattens in der Sonne*, written five years after the *Erzählung Die Klosterschule*, demonstrates an increased interest in the content of myth for its own sake, as the novel consists of the first-person narrative of a young woman who travels to Istanbul to conduct research on the myths and literature associated with the religious order of the Bektashi.[7] However, as in *Die Klosterschule,* myth as content is nonetheless shown to be inextricable from 'myth' as discourse, which again is critically exposed. It seems to me that Edward W. Said's concept of 'Orientalism' (1995 [1978]) is particularly useful in illuminating the type of 'myth' as discourse which this novel exposes, as Said characterizes Western discourse about the 'East' – and in particular, the discourse of the Orientalist academic – as a 'myth' in which the 'Orient' is figured as the absolute Other: '... because of Orientalism the Orient was not (and is not) a free subject of thought or action' (1978: 3). Furthermore, as Said describes it, this Western construct is inextricably linked with rejection, antagonism, exploitation and colonialism.

The narrator of *Das Verschwinden des Schattens in der Sonne* lives with Sevim, a young Turkish woman, and Turgut, Sevim's cousin, and is fascinated by the myths and history of the Bektashi which permeate the narrative. The turning-point of the novel comes towards its end and is formed by a conversation between the narrator and Sevim in which Sevim accuses her of failing to engage with the realities of Turkish life. Soon after, Turgut is shot at a political demonstration and the narrator is devastated at her own failure to understand anything at all. I shall begin by considering the significance and function of myth for this novel and subsequently analyse its uses in terms of the 'myth' of Orientalist rhetoric.

Most simply, in this novel, myth is celebrated for its aesthetic appeal since the narrator is far more fascinated by it than she is by contemporary Turkey. However, myth has a more complex function in the narrative, being portrayed both as an ordering factor in the episodic, non-linear main narrative and as potentially subversive and disorderly. The former, ordering function is the one which first meets the eye since the Bektashi myths punctuate the main narrative in a chronological sequence, beginning with the founding myths of the Bektashis and then their history, and the final passage of myth describes the integration and vanishing of the individual into the divine. In contrast to the episodic main narrative, the contrapuntal passages of myth provide an ordered, linear development, progressing from founding myth to divine apotheosis. Thus, myth ensures narrative order as it dictates a secure, patriarchal and religiously-founded world view.

However, this first impression is disrupted by other, more subversive aspects of Bektashi spirituality. The Bektashis were a small sect within Islam, now officially disbanded in Turkey, with unconventional, near-heretical practices, such as the de-segregation of the sexes (Schimmel: 432). Furthermore, the ecstatic practices of trance and dance in Islamic mysticism (the original 'whirling dervishes') which were associated with groups such as the Bektashi, are often considered to represent an anti-rational subversion of dominant discourses. For instance, this imagery is used in some Arab women's writing today in a way which parallels Western feminist searches for alternative cultural economies (see Accad 1993). Therefore, this sub-text also implicitly questions the authority of myth as a secure, patriarchal means of ordering the world and the novel.

The final passage of myth cited, in which the soul is lost in divine experience, represents a fantasy of integration, which is described in terms of ineffability: 'eine Beteuerung des Ungewissen ... weil das Wort nicht imstande war, diesen Vorgang zu beschreiben' (*Das Verschwinden des Schattens in der Sonne*: 114-5). However, the depiction of this fantasy of integration is not motivated by the narrator's successful integration into Turkish life, but follows her realization that her fascination with these myths has prevented such integration and it is here that the 'myth' of Orientalism is exposed in

Frischmuth's novel. It seems to me therefore that Orientalism is in fact the unpleasant truth which this displaced evocation of the 'ineffable' seeks – unsuccessfully – to silence.

Frischmuth's narrator, despite her extreme sympathy for all things Turkish, is unable to grasp the reality of modern Turkish life, due to her Orientalist academic training and misplaced expectations that the modern city of Istanbul will principally teach her about classical Persian poetry. Indeed, the text deliberately makes it clear that it is the very celebration of myth which beguiles the narrator and blinds her to societal reality so that her fascination with myth is actually a symbol of the impossibility of real integration and an indication that she is unconsciously but inevitably mired in the Western Orientalist 'myth'.

Thus, *Das Verschwinden des Schattens in der Sonne* places more emphasis on myth as content than *Die Klosterschule*, endowing it with an important aesthetic, narratological and structural function as well as subversive potential. But like *Die Klosterschule*, *Das Verschwinden des Schattens in der Sonne* also refers critically and conspicuously to 'myth' as discourse and exposes its workings without, however, suggesting that there is any easy escape from it. And as in *Die Klosterschule* it is implied that 'myth' as discourse – here, Orientalism – relies strongly on a fascination with myth as content – here, the Bektashi myths – for its effect. Significantly however, the narrator fails to write her planned dissertation, suggesting that the 'myth' of academic Orientalism falls short of omniscience, just as the Catholic 'mythologies' in *Die Klosterschule* are revealed to be fallible. While the narrator is unable to overcome Orientalist 'myth', she is equally unable to fulfil its expectations.

Demeter

Frischmuth's engagement with myth in the 1980s was influenced by certain feminist theories which sought to reclaim ideas and myths believed to be matriarchal, and in this period Frischmuth abandoned her earlier, critical investigation of de-politicizing and stabilizing discursive 'myths' for a less complex 'Liebe zu den Modellen'.[8] In the wake of the *Neue Frauenbewegung* of the 1970s and 1980s, notions of matriarchal myth and spirituality were theorized by Heide Göttner-Abendroth (1993 [1980]), drawing on Robert Graves's interpretations of classical mythology (1960 [1955]).[9] According to such theories, in matriarchal antiquity, a female deity represented the cyclic nature of time and eternal renewal and was attended yearly by a 'Heros', a young man who guaranteed fertility and was subsequently dispatched into the underworld. These myths were used by Göttner-Abendroth as part of her critique of modern, technological society and proposed as a utopian alternative.

Herrin der Tiere presents what Göttner-Abendroth, following Graves, considers to be an archaic version of the Demeter myth[10] and consists of loosely linked episodes organized around an anonymous woman, this time the object of third-person narrative. The protagonist has rejected the expectations of mainstream society and abandoned a safe office job to work as a trainee trotting racer on a stud farm at the eastern extremity of Austria. Thus, *Herrin der Tiere* aims to explore an alternative way of life and thereby implicitly sets up binary oppositions, for instance between country life and city life and the society of animals and humans. References to the myth of Demeter are central to this representation of a different life and I shall examine references to the goddess here before going on to consider the implications of Frischmuth's shift of emphasis from 'myth' as discourse onto myth as content.

The cult of Demeter was associated with horses and Graves reports that in pre-Hellenic times, a horse-headed Demeter was worshipped (1960: 62). The protagonist of *Herrin der Tiere* also lives among horses and fantasizes about creatures who are half-horse and half-human and about being such a creature herself. The fertility cult associated with Demeter is also alluded to, for instance in the protagonist's pleasure in touching the corn which she feeds to her horses (Lützeler 1992: 80-1). At the end of the narrative, the protagonist has a sexual encounter with the stranger Viktor, a Hungarian refugee who is subsequently picked up by the authorities and never seen again. Viktor (*nomen est omen*) is the modern equivalent of the transient and dispensable 'Heros' of Graves's myth, since Demeter was the goddess of agriculture, a technology which she entrusted to her 'Heros' Triptolemus. Viktor, too, happens to be an agricultural engineer.

It seems to me that the evocation of myth in *Herrin der Tiere* is qualitatively different from that in *Die Klosterschule* and *Das Verschwinden des Schattens in der Sonne* inasmuch as it is presented as something binding, essential and a-historical – indeed, as 'myth' in the Barthesian sense. For instance, the protagonist's encounter with Viktor is described in terms which suggest that the protagonist is possessed by archaic, unconscious powers: 'Sie beginnen sich zu drehen, wie in einem längst vergessenen Tanz, zu dem eine Figur gehört, die sie in die Knie zwingt, dann ganz zu Boden, sich weiterdrehend, bis die Bewegung einen ganz anderen Rhythmus findet, Musik, die sie aus der Zeit hebt' (*Herrin der Tiere*: 128). And afterwards the protagonist is inexplicably haunted by a sentence: '*Das dreimal gepflügte Feld.* Was will dieser Satz von ihr? Nach all der Zeit' (129). According to Graves, during a wedding Demeter and a lover 'slipped out of the house and lay together openly in a thrice-ploughed field' (1960: I, 89). That is, it is implied that the protagonist is not simply *like* Demeter but that she *is* Demeter. Or in other words, the protagonist is taken out of history by such passages and inserted into a different, 'natural', mystic world. Here, then, we have a text which does not so much expose the workings of 'myth' as discourse, as perpetuate them. In terms of the 'myth' of gender identity, the protagonist's identification with Nature inadvertently reinscribes the traditional binary in which man is equated with culture and woman with Nature, and in which the second term is always inferior.[11]

Furthermore, the myth is transformed and rendered utopian. Graves reports Demeter's rape in the form of a mare by the god Poseidon and given that the horse was also sacred to Poseidon, who invented horse-racing, it seems that Poseidon and his threat to the goddess figure is conspicuous by his absence from *Herrin der Tiere*. This striking omission of an important component of the original myth suggests that the utopian vision of woman living in harmony with animals and Nature is fragile and cannot tolerate threat or disruption. It seems that this omission is a similar silencing of disturbing elements to that identified as the topos of ineffability mobilized in 'myth' as discourse which I considered above.

Conclusion

In conclusion, I shall return to my three initial questions. First, what is the function and significance of myth as discourse and as content for Frischmuth's *oeuvre*? The works discussed here involve differentiated uses of both types of myth which confound simplistic value judgements and move from a position of *Sprachskepsis* and a concern with the manipulative language systems of 'myth' as discourse to a more celebratory and conventional view of myth as content. That is, I have analysed a move from an ironic and revealing political critique of 'myth' to a mode of narration which, in assigning great prestige to myth as content, effectively becomes 'myth' itself.

Second, what can Frischmuth's writing teach us about contemporary myth as discourse and as content? It seems that these two concepts are inextricably linked, for Frischmuth shows Barthesian 'myth' to be all-pervasive and furthermore, she indicates that such 'myth' tends to rely on myth as content to legitimize itself. Similarly, such texts as *Herrin der Tiere* which focus strongly on the themes of myth become 'myth' themselves. However, although there seems therefore to be no possibility of transcending the discourse of 'myth' – and therefore, of dispensing with myth as content – these textual elements may both be destabilized by the use of ironizing repetitions, recombinations and performative contradictions.

And third, what is it about this very varied body of work that makes it appear exemplary? Doubtless, to some extent, Frischmuth's dynamic response to changing, contemporary ideas about myth. However, to claim that these responses are typical of contemporary Austrian women's writing is misleading. Frischmuth's writing may, however, be more compatible with the cultural mainstream in that, when it challenges normative 'myths', it does so more discreetly than the writing of other authors such as Elfriede Jelinek, for instance, do. Where they exist, Frischmuth's critique or reassessments of myth as both content and discourse are subtle and thus perhaps more easily recovered by the dominant cultural norm. And of course, the very characterization of these texts as 'exemplary' erases their differences and disruptions and attempts to cover over specific, local moments of subversion.

This article was written during time spent as North Senior Scholar at St. John's College, Oxford.

Notes

[1] This quotation is taken from the title of one of Frischmuth's most-reviewed works, *Kai und die Liebe zu den Modellen* (1979).

[2] For biography and bibliography, see Haider 1992 and Renhardt 1992.

[3] In the essay 'Das Medusenhaupt', Freud noted: 'Kopfabschneiden=Kastrieren. Der Schreck der Meduse [sic] ist also Kastrationsschreck, der an einen Anblick geknüpft ist. Aus zahlreichen Analysen kennen wir diesen Anlaß, er ergibt sich, wenn der Knabe, der bisher nicht an die Drohung glauben wollte, ein weibliches Genitale erblickt. Wahrscheinlich ein erwachsenes, von Haaren umsäumtes, im Grunde das der Mutter' (1941: 47).

[4] Many critics note that Frischmuth's prose makes much use of mythology, but this statement is not usually further qualified as much of the secondary writing on Frischmuth consists of general and descriptive overviews rather than close analysis. On the whole, Frischmuth's use of models has been pigeonholed as moderately progressive, for instance by Cella 1982; Daviau 1980; Gürtler 1983; and Stangel 1988. A notable exception to this trend is provided by Eifler (1989). The only study to date devoted to Frischmuth and myth is Lützeler (1992).

[5] For instance, Blum 1986; Blumer 1983; Cella 1982; Daviau 1987; Gürtler 1983; Györi 1988; Kindl 1980; and Stangel 1988.

[6] For instance, Daviau 1980.

[7] Frischmuth provides a list of sources on the Bektashi and Islamic mysticism at the end of her novel, but apart from one reference to Hellmut Ritter, *Das Meer der Seele: Gott, Welt und Mensch in den Geschichten Fariddudin Attars* (no publication details provided), this bibliography is inaccessible to readers not fluent in Turkish. For further information on Islamic mysticism see Schimmel 1975. Schimmel informs us that Ritter's book appeared in Leiden in 1955.

Notes continued

[8] The thesis of a prehistoric matriarchy which preceded later classical civilization remains controversial. See Pomeroy 1973 and Nixon 1994: 9-10.

[9] Frischmuth refers to Göttner-Abendroth 1993 and especially to Graves in her Munich lectures on poetics (Frischmuth 1991).

[10] Göttner-Abendroth 1993: 48-51 and Frischmuth 1991: 64-71. Other 'models' for this text include Hermann Broch's Demeter project, the unfinished novel *Die Verzauberung* ([1935] 1976). See Frischmuth 1986b.

[11] For a more general analysis of the difficulties involved in feminist attempts to appropriate this binary division, see Butler 1990: 36-7.

Bibliography

Accad, Evelyne. 1993. *Blessures des Mots: Journal de Tunisie*, Paris, Indigo and Côté femme

Barthes, Roland. 1972. *Mythologies*, tr. Annette Lavers, London, Jonathan Cape

Bartsch, Kurt (ed.). 1992. *Barbara Frischmuth*, Graz, Droschl

Blum, Marie-Odile. 1986. 'Barbara Frischmuth oder die Weite der Möglichkeiten, die uns offenstehen', in Carine Kleiber and Erika Tunner (eds), *Frauenliteratur in Österreich von 1945 bis heute*, Berne, Peter Lang: 15-26

Blumer, Arnold. 1983. 'Kulturelle Fremde in der Frauenliteratur am Beispiel von Barbara Frischmuths *Die Klosterschule*', in Manfred Jürgensen (ed.), *Frauenliteratur: Autorinnen – Perspektiven – Konzepte*, Berne, Peter Lang: 181-95

Broch, Hermann. 1976. *Die Verzauberung*, in Paul Michael Lützeler (ed.), *Kommentierte Werkausgabe*, 13 vols, Frankfurt am Main, Suhrkamp, vol. 3

Butler, Judith. 1990. *Gender Trouble*, New York, Routledge

Cella, Ingrid. 1982. '"Das Rätsel Weib" und die Literatur: Feminismus, feministische Ästhetik und die Neue Frauenliteratur in Österreich', *Amsterdamer Beiträge*, 14: 189-228

Daviau, Donald G. 1980. 'Neuere Entwicklungen in der modernen österreichischen Prosa: Die Werke von Barbara Frischmuth', *Modern Austrian Literature*, 13: 177-216

—. 1987. 'Barbara Frischmuth', in Donald G. Daviau (ed.), *Major Figures of Contemporary Austrian Literature*, Berne, Peter Lang: 185-206

Eifler, Margaret. 1989. 'Postmoderne Feminisierung', in Mona Knapp and Gerd Labroisse (eds), *Frauen-Fragen in der deutschsprachigen Literatur seit 1945*, Amsterdam, Rodopi: 1-35

Freud, Sigmund. 1941. 'Das Medusenhaupt' in Anna Freud, E. Bibring, W. Hoffer and E. Kris (eds), *Gesammelte Werke*, 18 vols, London, Imago, vol. 17: 45-8

Frischmuth, Barbara. 1968. *Die Klosterschule*, Reinbek, Rowohlt

—. 1979. *Kai und die Liebe zu den Modellen*, Salzburg, Residenz

—. 1980. *Das Verschwinden des Schattens in der Sonne* (1973), Munich, dtv

—. 1986a. *Herrin der Tiere*, Salzburg, Residenz

—. 1986b. 'Leseerinnerungen an Hermann Broch', in Paul Michael Lützeler (ed.), *Hermann Broch*, Frankfurt am Main, Suhrkamp: 25-32

—. 1989. 'Älter geworden...', in *Mörderische Märchen*, Salzburg, Residenz: 101-16

—. 1991. *Traum der Literatur: Literatur des Traums*, Salzburg, Residenz

Göttner-Abendroth, Heide. 1993. *Die Göttin und ihr Heros: Die matriarchalen Religionen in Mythos, Märchen und Dichtung*, Munich, Frauenoffensive

Graves, Robert. 1960. *The Greek Myths*, 2 vols, Harmondsworth, Penguin

Gürtler, Christa. 1983. *Schreiben Frauen anders? Untersuchungen zu Ingeborg Bachmann und Barbara Frischmuth*, Stuttgart, Heinz

Györi, Judit. 1988. 'Barbara Frischmuth', in Horst Haase and Antal Mádl (eds), *Österreichische Literatur des 20. Jahrhunderts: Einzeldarstellungen*, Berlin (GDR), Volk und Wissen: 694-715

Haider, Hans. 1992. 'Vita', in Bartsch 1992: 151-62

Kindl, Ulrike. 1980. 'Barbara Frischmuth', in Heinz Puknus (ed.), *Neue Literatur der Frauen: deutschsprachige Autorinnen der Gegenwart*, Munich, Beck: 144-8

Lützeler, Paul Michael. 1992. 'Barbara Frischmuths Demeter-Trilogie: Mythologische Finde-Spiele in der postmodernen Literatur', in Bartsch 1992: 73-98

Nixon, Lucia. 1994. 'Gender Bias in Archaeology', in Léonie J. Archer, Susan Fischler, and Maria Wyke (eds), *Women in Ancient Societies: An Illusion of the Night*, London, Macmillan: 1-23

Pomeroy, Sarah B. 1973. 'Selected Bibliography on Women in Antiquity', *Arethusa*, 6: 127-57

Renhardt, Maria. 1992. 'Bibliographie', in Bartsch 1992: 163-222

Said, Edward. 1995. *Orientalism: Western Conceptions of the Orient*, Harmondsworth, Penguin

Schimmel, Annemarie. 1975. *Mystical Dimensions of Islam*, Chapel Hill, University of North Carolina Press

Stangel, Johann. 1988. *Das annulierte Individuum: Sozialisationskritik als Gesellschafts-analyse in der aktuellen Frauenliteratur*, Berne, Peter Lang

The Sounds of Silence: Ilse Aichinger's *Die größere Hoffnung, Der Gefesselte*, and *Kleist, Moos, Fasane*

Brigid Haines

Zudringlich werden durch Abwesenheit. (*Kleist, Moos, Fasane,* Aichinger 1991c: 43)

Versuchen, in diesen tödlichen Augenblicken zu Hause zu sein. (*Kleist, Moos, Fasane*: 81)

Like many readers before and since, Ilse Aichinger is both irritated and fascinated by the works of Adalbert Stifter, outraged by the seeming security of his fictional world, but also impressed by the powerful sense of 'Angst' which provides the motor to his writing and gives the lie to that sense of security:

> Ich begegnete Stifter noch einmal an einem nebligen Spätherbstnachmittag in einem englischen Antiquariat. Unter einem Stapel französisch-hebräischer Wörterbücher zog ich einen kleinen Band der Erzählungen Stifters in deutscher Sprache hervor. An eine Papprolle gelehnt, begann ich zu lesen, ich las langsam und gespannt, ich nahm den Band mit und las ihn auf den schaukelnden Omnibussen, angesichts der Baumkronen von Hydepark und Kensington, die sich aus dem Dunst hoben, und der aufblitzenden Kinoreklamen. Noch einmal war ich geneigt, angesichts der ungeheuerlichen Sanftmut des Autors und seiner selbst im Zorn ergebenen Gestalten den Band wegzuschleudern oder liegen zu lassen, aber noch einmal, vielleicht angesichts der Gegensätzlichkeit der Umgebung oder weil ich an einer Wendung meines Sprachverständnisses angekommen war, entdeckte ich die Sätze Stifters. Mit diesen Sätzen hat zu kämpfen, wer sich mit ihnen einläßt, mit ihrer Geduld, ihrer unnachgiebigen Freundlichkeit, bis er die Spannung des 'So und nicht anders', die Linie des Blitzes in ihnen begreift.

Her sense of anger left her; she read on,

> und entdeckte in der Schilderung die Definition der Räume und Landschaften, in der Gelassenheit und Ergebenheit den reißenden, fast verzweifelten Strom der Sprache, ihre Hochkarätigkeit, den Tod zu ihren Seiten. Ich begegnete ihm, nicht dem behäbigen Schulinspektor, dem Schreiber fast devoter Briefe an seine Ehefrau oder seinen Verleger, dem Beipflichter des Wohlverhaltens, sondern einem, der unter das Gesetz geraten ist, der seine Wörter aus dem Schweigen holt, dem einzigen Ort, aus dem sie zu holen sind, ob von Joyce, Conrad oder dem Hofrat Stifter. (*Kleist, Moos, Fasane*: 96-7)

Ilse Aichinger is a writer also much preoccupied with 'Angst', which she sees as productive (she describes Stifter approvingly as 'einer, der Angst genug

hatte', *Kleist, Moos, Fasane*: 96), and with 'Schweigen'. But while Stifter's works seek to engender comfort and a sense of order in author and reader alike (though they are arguably rendered interesting by their failure to do so), Aichinger's texts, particularly the late ones, seek first and foremost to unsettle. Rather than striving for closure, they deliberately work towards openness, and are defiantly oppositional to all structures of dominance, whether institutional, linguistic, or hermeneutic. Their structural openness makes categorization difficult. Attempts to see her works as early examples of *écriture féminine*, for example, which have been slow in coming due to Aichinger's lack of an obvious feminist agenda and her anti-mimeticism, are only valuable if taken also in the context of the postmodernism debate (Schmid-Bortenschlager 1991). For as well as being linked to the Austrian tradition of 'Sprachzweifel' so eloquently represented by Hofmannsthal's Chandos letter, Aichinger, as the following paper will show, exploits the fact that poetic language highlights the free play of the signifier which the language of power, with its insistence on structures and meaning, tries to cover up. Thus it can be argued that her texts do indeed do what Cixous, following Derrida, requires of écriture féminine, in that they 'work on the difference' (Cixous, quoted in Moi 1985: 108): they do not rely on the author as guarantor of meaning or on an illusory transparency of language, but instead suggest multiple, shifting meanings produced within and by language.

The postmodern resistance to interpretation for which Aichinger's works are famous, or infamous, does not, however, mean that they lack focus. In the same article she quotes Grillparzer, who writes in a letter to Stifter that only a fool can be so sure of himself, 'daß ihn der gemeinsame Lärm seiner Zeit nicht ins innere Wanken brächte' (*Kleist, Moos, Fasane*: 93). Stifter's texts, claims Aichinger, are redeemed by a pregnant silence inspired by his fear of the turbulence of his times. Aichinger's texts, which seek both to articulate what has been left silent by others, and to contain silences, are correspondingly rooted in peculiarly twentieth-century concerns, namely the real fear of Nazism and its legacy, and the more generalized fear of totalizing discourses.

Aichinger's early and only novel, *Die größere Hoffnung* ([1948] 1991b), for example, counteracts the silence surrounding the taboo subject of the Holocaust, dealing as it does with the experiences of a group of Jewish and part-Jewish children living in Vienna towards the end of the Second World War. Their hopes and fears and the stark realities of their conditions of existence, for example the degradations of daily life under the anti-Jewish laws, the constant fear of deportation and death, the awful prospect of suicide as a way of avoiding the concentration camps, are vividly presented. Like writers such as Celan and Bachmann, Aichinger finds ways of articulating what George Steiner calls 'the world of the unspeakable' (1985: 15), and she does it by telling her story from (to borrow the title of our conference) the perspective of an Other Austrian – a female Jewish child, this perspective being underscored by the biographical knowledge that Aichinger herself is also that other of the other: a Jewish *survivor* of the Holocaust (as well, of course, as being other in de Beauvoir's sense by virtue of being female). As Sigrid Weigel argues, Aichinger's achievement in the novel is to have found a language with which the persecuted may speak rather than writing about them as victims (1987: 12). The narrative technique can be usefully contrasted with that employed by Jurek Becker in his story 'Die Mauer', about a child's experience in the Lodz ghetto. Becker keeps a tighter control of meaning by using a dual narrative structure: the narrator writes of his own experiences as a five-year-old with the hindsight of an adult who has survived the terrible experiences of the Holocaust; according to David Rock, 'the adult perspective establishes distance, so avoiding sentimentality, and reminds the reader of the historical dimensions of the story' (Becker 1993: 26). Aichinger, by contrast, uses an anonymous and ageless third person narrator who sees things with the eyes of a child. The effect is far from being sentimental, however: the child's view liberates the reader from the known narratives of the Nazi period, with their moral certainties and unexplored blind spots, into the realms of naked experience, fantasy and dream, and exposes the so-called realities of the adults as learned ideology (for example the tragic suicide of the grandmother turns out to have been avoidable when the soldiers she was convinced were coming to get her do not turn up, Lorenz 1981: 65). The child's view allows the Holocaust to be fictionalized while avoiding the twin dangers of sensationalism and despair: the central character Ellen, who is tragically blown up by a bomb at the end of the story, reflects the horrific events going on around her in dreams and play, but never stops searching for 'die größere Hoffnung', some kind of spiritual or poetic transcendence.

Aichinger's next works are also resolutely opposed to the prevailing values of the post-war restoration period, with its fictions of the 'Stunde Null' and the 'Kahlschlag'. In 'Aufruf zum Mißtrauen' (1946) she exhorts her readers to guard against the reemergence of totalitarianism not in institutions or international relations but in the self and in interpersonal relations: 'Kaum haben wir stammelnd versucht, wieder "ich" zu sagen, haben wir auch schon wieder versucht, es zu betonen. Kaum haben wir gewagt, wieder 'du' zu sagen, haben wir es schon mißbraucht! Und wir beruhigen uns wieder. Aber wir sollen uns nicht beruhigen!' (1990a: 17).

Several stories in *Der Gefesselte* (1953) continue the theme of the space of the personal in the face of social pressure in a way that is very reminiscent of Kafka (though Aichinger claimed in 1983 never to have read much Kafka, *Kleist, Moos, Fasane*: 102). For example the eponymous hero of 'Der Gefesselte', finds that over the course of time the rope bonds, which he wakes up one morning to find have been used to restrain him, give him, paradoxically, strength and courage; it is when they are removed that he can no longer fulfil his public role. The woman in 'Seegeister' is faced with the alarming prospect that whenever she removes her sunglasses, she literally starts to fade away; this is tolerable so long as the summer lasts, but what will happen in the winter? And the man in 'Wo ich wohne', who finds that the physical location of his flat keeps going down a floor but refuses to tell anyone about it, realizes too late (when he reaches the cellar) that his conformism has left him no room to complain.

Nevertheless, while her work remains oppositional and engaged, prepared to question the new self-assurance of post-war German and Austrian society, it is for the most part[1] not didactic, for that would mean to impose closure. 'Schweigen' is not merely something to be overcome, it is also valued positively. Her advocacy of 'Schweigen' arises partly out of a suspicion of the German language which had, to use Rüdiger Görner's phrases, 'sich versprochen, leergesprochen' (Görner 1986: 12), and partly because, despite writing against the grain of history, she does not wish to install new narratives in place of old ones. The 1987 volume *Kleist, Moos, Fasane* demonstrates the full spectrum of her attitudes to 'Schweigen'. Part I, which is composed of autobiographical sketches, shows that children, as in *Die größere Hoffnung*, can articulate taboos and retain a sense of wholeness ('Die Kräfte der Kindheit hielten die Welt zusammen', *Kleist, Moos, Fasane*: 13). Part II, entitled simply 'Aufzeichnungen 1950-85', works to undermine adult narratives: it consists of powerful aphorisms which thematize dream, play, searching, and in particular the positive possibilities of openness, rupture, and difference, for example 'Nur wenn wir wissen, daß alles offenbleibt, kann ein Dialog zustandekommen' (*Kleist, Moos, Fasane*: 59); 'Nichts erscheint so sehr Heimat als das, wovon man Abschied nimmt. Es scheint, daß der Abschied zuerst war. Auch Mütter werden zu Müttern im Augenblick der Trennung' (47); and 'Ich kann das eine Wort nur verstehen, indem ich ein anderes dafür suche' (69). Part III contains essays on the works of other writers and contains many direct references to 'Schweigen'. In the essay on Conrad, Aichinger writes disparagingly about the modern age, 'in dem alles erzählt und nichts angehört wird' (91). The close relationship of language and silence is stressed, true language being that which contains silence (112), though what can be said must always be viewed with suspicion (114). In her poetological essay 'Das Erzählen in dieser Zeit' she stresses the ethical imperative not to be silent: 'So liegt auch heute für den Erzählenden die Gefahr nicht mehr darin, weitschweifig zu werden, sie liegt eher darin, daß er angesichts der Bedrohung und unter dem Eindruck des Endes den Mund nicht mehr aufbringt' (*Der Gefesselte*: 9), the task of writing being, however, not to create meanings, but 'Die Stummheit immer wieder in das Schweigen zu übersetzen' (Stettler 1984: 36). Just as Aichinger cultivates 'Schweigen' in her own work ('Ich schreibe, weil ich keine bessere Form zu schweigen finde', Aichinger, quoted in Weigel 1987: 11), so it is also what she admires in others, for example Georg Trakl (*Kleist, Moos, Fasane*: 98-101), and other recent unnamed writers who incorporate 'Stille' into their works' ('Stille ... ist für mich eine Form von Engagement', Aichinger, quoted in Moser 1990: 27). And in the Conrad essay she writes that, 'Um wieder notwendig zu werden, müssen [die Wörter] die Lautlosigkeit zurückgewinnen, aus der sie notwendig entstanden' (*Kleist, Moos, Fasane*: 91).

Aichinger's own texts, particularly the late ones, incorporate 'Schweigen', 'Stille' and 'Lautlosigkeit' through the many devices they employ to 'work on the difference': parables, surreal and playful effects, fantasy, dream form, myth, linguistic experimentation, the anthropomorphising of abstract nouns and the taking literally of figures of speech, as well as a blurring of boundaries, a modernist lack of a sovereign perspective and an increasing refusal to narrate. The rest of this paper comments briefly on how Aichinger works towards openness with reference to four of the most significant of these stylistic devices, namely the use of paradox and metonymy, and the treatment of time and perspective, though the historical focus mentioned above should always be born in mind. Aichinger prefers to see herself as a 'Vermittlerin' rather than an 'Erfinderin' (Lorenz 1981: 48), though, as Andrea Reiter argues in the case of *Die größere Hoffnung*, what she is conveying is often not meanings but the states of mind engendered in the victims of history through their ordeals (Reiter 1996: 241).

Die größere Hoffnung abounds in the use of paradox, for example '"Warum spielt ihr im Dunkeln?" "Wir sehen besser so!"' (152), and 'Man behält nur das, was man hergibt' (139). These paradoxes and Ellen's constant questioning raise universal questions regarding life, suffering, death and hope. But no answers are provided. Neva Šlibar, writing about Aichinger's poetry, quotes Paul Geyer, who writes that the paradox can be seen as a weapon against system building. Paradoxes are 'Figuren des Widerstandes gegen die Machtergreifung der Logik des Entweder-Oder. Die Geschichte dieses Widerstandkampfes ist *auch* eine Geschichte des abendländischen Denkens. Eine Geschichte von unten, sozusagen' (Geyer's emphasis). Šlibar comments, 'Genau dies entspricht Aichingers Poetik unaufhörlicher Verunsicherung und Verweigerung' (1993: 58).

Sigrid Schmid-Bortenschlager, taking as her starting point the title of the volume *Kleist, Moos, Fasane* (which are street names remembered from Aichinger's Vienna childhood), has described Aichinger's use of metonymy rather than metaphor as a general principle, 'nicht mehr die Ähnlichkeit verbindet die Ausdrücke, sondern die Kontiguität im Raum, in der Zeit, im Text'; 'Aichinger ersetzt die klassische Struktur der Ähnlichkeit durch eine Struktur der zufälligen Nachbarschaft, sie hebt damit einen Grundsatz der klassischen Logik auf und ersetzt die Vergleichbarkeit durch eine – von außen gegebene oder aber auch individuell bedingte – Beliebigkeit' (Schmid-Bortenschlager 1991: 88, 90). For example, chapter three of *Die größere Hoffnung* ends with a song by three characters who join the children in their attempt to leave the country, the 'Pestverkünder' Augustin who claims that 'Die Pest ist ausgebrochen, aber niemand bemerkt es' – an obvious reference to Nazism (73); 'der Mann mit der Weltkugel', Kolumbus, a dreamer; and König David, a boy who preaches and breaks windows with his sling, 'eine alttestamentarische Figur, die die Leute mit dem Zeichen der Kristallnacht, den zerbrochenen Fensterscheiben, konfrontiert und sie zwingt, sich damit auseinanderzusetzen' (Weigel 1987: 18-19). The metonymic dissonance created by bringing together these completely unrelated figures confounds the reader's expectations of authorial intent and leaves him or her searching for connections.[2] But connections are what Aichinger is at pains to avoid; as she famously wrote, 'Niemand kann von mir verlangen, daß ich Zusammenhänge herstelle, solange sie vermeidbar sind.' (1991d: 12).

The element of arbitrariness is also introduced by Aichinger in her treatment of time, where she tends to eschew chronology in favour of 'eine schwebende Gegenwart' (Werner Weber, quoted in Moser 1990: 86). Apart from the progression from 'Die große Hoffnung' (the desire to escape) in Chapter 1 to 'Die größere Hoffnung' of the final chapter, the novel does not stress the forward movement of time but focuses on episodes; it has rightly been called a 'Stationendrama'. The stories in the volume *Der Gefesselte* employ a different technique: they 'spielen alle deutlich vom Ende her und auf das Ende zu' (*Der Gefesselte*: 10). The most striking example of this is 'Spiegelgeschichte', the story of a woman's life told backwards from the moment of her funeral (she died from the effects of a backstreet abortion) to her birth. Released from the constraints of narrative chronology, new meanings can emerge, new connections can be made. For example the central character's request to the abortionist is 'Mach mir mein Kind wieder lebendig!' The narrator comments, 'Das hat noch keine von der Alten verlangt. Aber du verlangst es. Der Spiegel gibt dir Kraft. Der blinde Spiegel mit den Fliegenflecken läßt dich verlangen, was noch keine verlangt hat' (68). While, however, the feminist critic Regula Venske goes so far as to say that the story achieves a more far-reaching '"Entmannung" im Sinne einer Absage an männliche Ordnungsprinzipien' than any explicitly feminist text could (1991: 119), I would argue that this approach still ties down the story too much. For though it could be argued, using Irigaray's philosophy for example, that the principle of chronology that is being challenged in the text is masculine,[3] this is not a point made by the text itself, which instead suggests multiple interpretations but commits itself to none of them.

After *Der Gefesselte* Aichinger became increasingly suspicious not just of narration as an organizing principle, but also of perspective; in a recent interview she wrote:[4] 'Jemand hat mich einmal gefragt, wie ist ein Baum eigentlich wirklich und ich dachte: von links, von rechts, von oben, von unten, oder wenn man drinnen steckt oder wenn man oben – ja, wie ist ein Baum wirklich? Das interessiert mich immer noch. Und nicht nur ein Baum' (Steinwendtner 1993: 13). To put this in terms of silence, all descriptions are partial and have their blind spots, which causes them to leave something unsaid. This even applies to descriptions of the self, of which Aichinger is very wary. Trying to describe the self is, she writes, like looking in the mirror but not managing to capture the right facial expression (1990b: 23); she is not a psychological writer, since to probe the psychology of fictional characters means tying them down in language. This is why, Aichinger claims in one of her most enigmatic formulations, she prefers definitions, which paradoxically do not impose limits, to descriptions: 'Definieren grenzt an Unterhöhlen und setzt dem Zugriff der Träume aus' (1991d: 12).

I have employed the word 'Schweigen' to enable me to bring together two different but related aspects of Aichinger's work. Firstly she articulates what others are afraid to, and urges her readers to resist 'natural', i.e. dominant discourses, for example in the following uncharacteristically unambiguous rallying cry: 'Wenn immer von "Gott" die Rede ist oder von "Geist": dem muß gekontert werden' (Aichinger, quoted in Bartsch and Melzer 1993: 8). Such statements make her of enormous interest to feminism, particularly of a postmodern kind, but this is only one context within which her work can be discussed. For I have also tried to show some of the ways in which she refrains from articulation, and sows the seed of doubt in her readers about whether language or the languages that we have at our disposal, are adequate to articulate reality at all. Unlike some feminist writers and critics, she does not propose a feminine counter-language which might subvert the symbolic order, but turns instead increasingly to a private linguistic world, which explains why her work has never been given the attention it warrants. In her later works, with which I have not engaged here, she pushes the possibilities for open-endedness to the extent, some say, of incomprehensibility, which is perhaps unfortunate: 'So bewirkt paradoxerweise gerade Aichingers Offenheit für die Vielfalt der möglichen Blickpunkte und Aussageweisen, daß ihre Schriften dem Leser hermetisch verschlossen erscheinen' (Ratych 1979: 435), though Andrea Reiter has recently argued that just because these works cannot be tied down to one meaning it does not follow that they are not meaningful (1996: 220). Aichinger remains an enigmatic and provocative writer, but an extremely important one nonetheless. Though often almost wilfully obscure, at its best her use of language is, because of its openness, extraordinarily suggestive; as the writer Elisabeth Reichart expressed it: 'Ilse Aichinger bleibt der Sprache gegenüber wachsam, mißtrauisch. Sie entläßt sich nicht in die Bequemlichkeit, sondern setzt von Werk zu Werk erneut ein Maß an Unbedingtheit, vor dem mir schwindelt und das mich reicher macht' (1991: 40).

Notes

[1] The stories in *Der Gefesselte* are an exception: they have justifiably been called 'lehrhaft', Weigel 1987: 30.

[2] It is interesting to note that Aichinger did not bother to correct printers' errors to the typescript of *Schlechte Wörter* because she found them creative. This demonstrates 'wie distanziert Aichinger selbste der Form ihrer Texte gegenüber steht - als seien sie nicht einmal endgültig abgeschlossen', (Lorenz 1981: 42).

[3] For example: 'in sexual difference, ... femininity is experienced as a space that often carries connotations of the depths of night (God being space and light), while masculinity is conceived of in terms of time'. See Whitford 1991: 167.

[4] On Aichinger's request this interview was conducted in writing. See Steinwendtner 1993: 13.

Bibliography

Aichinger, Ilse. 1990a. 'Aufruf zum Mißtrauen' (1946), in Moser 1990: 16-17
—. 1990b. 'Die Vögel beginnen zu singen, wenn es noch finster ist' (1952), in Moser 1990: 23-4
—. 1991a. *Der Gefesselte* (1953), Frankfurt am Main, Fischer
—. 1991b. *Die größere Hoffnung* (1948), Frankfurt am Main, Fischer
—. 1991c. *Kleist, Moos, Fasane* (1987), Frankfurt am Main, Fischer
—. 1991d. *Schlechte Wörter* (1976), Frankfurt am Main, Fischer
Bartsch, Kurt and Gerhard Melzer (eds). 1993. *Ilse Aichinger*, Graz, Droschl
Becker, Jurek. 1993. *Five Stories* (1980), ed. David Rock, Manchester, Manchester University Press
Görner, Rüdiger. 1986. 'Die versprochene Sprache: Über Ilse Aichinger', *Neue Rundschau*, 1997, 4: 8-21
Lorenz, Dagmar C. G. 1981. *Ilse Aichinger*, Königstein (Ts.), Athenäum
Moi, Toril. 1985. *Sexual/Textual Politics*, London, Methuen
Moser, Samuel (ed.). 1990. *Ilse Aichinger: Materialien zu Leben und Werk*, Frankfurt am Main, Fischer
Ratych, Joanna M. 1979. 'Zeitenthobenheit und Welterfahrung: Gedanken zum Hermetikbegriff in Ilse Aichingers Dialogen', *Modern Austrian Literature*, 12, 1979: 423-36
Reichart, Elisabeth. 1991. 'Die innere Landkarte: An Ilse Aichinger', *Literatur und Kritik*, 259/260: 35-40
Reiter, Andrea. 1996. 'Die Erfahrung des Holocausts und ihre sprachliche Bewältigung: Zu Ilse Aichingers *Die größere Hoffnung*', *German Life and Letters*, 49: 236-42
—. 1996. 'Ilse Aichinger: The Poetics of Silence', in Arthur Williams, Stuart Parkes, Julian Preece (eds), *Contemporary German Writers, Their Aesthetics and Their Language*, Berne, Lang
Schmid-Bortenschlager, Sigrid. 1991. 'Der Ort der Sprache: Zu Ilse Aichinger', in Walter-Buchebner-Gesellschaft (ed.), *Das Schreiben der Frauen in Österreich seit 1950*, Vienna, Böhlau: 86-94
Šlibar, Neva. 1993. '"Definieren grenzt an Unterhöhlen": Ambiguisierte Paradoxie in Ilse Aichingers Gedichten', in Bartsch and Melzer 1993: 55-87
Steiner, George. 1985. *Language and Silence*, London, Faber
Steinwendtner, Brita. 1993. 'Ein Paar Fragen in Briefen: Gespräch mit Ilse Aichinger', in Bartsch and Melzer 1993: 7-13
Stettler, Luzia. 1984. 'Stummheit immer wieder in Schweigen zu übersetzen, das ist die Aufgabe des Schreibens', in Moser 1990: 36-40

Venske, Regula. 1991. *Das Verschwinden des Mannes in der weiblichen Schreibmaschine: Männerbilder in der Literatur von Frauen*, Hamburg, Luchterhand

Weigel, Sigrid. 1987. 'Schreibarbeit und Phantasie: Ilse Aichinger', in Inge Stephan, Regula Venske and Sigrid Weigel (eds), *Frauenliteratur ohne Tradition? Neun Autorinnenporträts*, Frankfurt am Main, Fischer: 11-37

Whitford, Margaret (ed.). 1991. *The Irigaray Reader*, Oxford, Blackwell

Inszenierungen des unendlichen Gesprächs:
Zu Friederike Mayröckers langer Prosa

Andreas Kramer

Die österreichische Schriftstellerin Friederike Mayröcker (geb. 1924) hat gegenwärtig in der literarischen Öffentlichkeit, in Kritik und Forschung einen Status, der von Gegensätzen und Widersprüchen gekennzeichnet ist. Einerseits ist ihr literarischer Rang im großen und ganzen unbestritten, was sich u.a. in zahlreichen Auszeichnungen niederschlägt und zur Quasi-Kanonisierung in neueren literaturgeschichtlichen Darstellungen geführt hat (Venske 1991: 273; Clausen und Singelmann 1992: 472-3). Gelegentlich begegnet man sogar Apostrophierungen wie der, daß Mayröcker eine der 'bedeutendsten deutschsprachigen Schriftstellerinnen der Gegenwart' (Luserke 1995: 438) sei oder daß ihr Werk 'zu den größten Herausforderungen' an Kritik und Germanistik gehöre (Kastberger und Schmidt-Dengler 1996a: 9); solche Aussagen deuten vielleicht durch die superlativische Form darauf hin, daß es sich hier eher um Kompensationsleistungen als um sachlich-nüchterne Feststellungen handelt. Auf der anderen Seite ist Mayröcker, wiewohl in einem großen Verlag und einigen kleinen Verlagen veröffentlichend und auf dem literarischen Markt vielfältig präsent, selbst bei den an moderner Literatur Interessierten immer noch eher eine Angelegenheit von Insidern, also doch relativ unbekannt und ungelesen.

Die Gründe hierfür scheinen mir zunächst in der öffentlichen Wahrnehmung von Mayröckers Literatur zu liegen. Ein Rezensent des Bandes *Stilleben* (1991) beschreibt Mayröckers Arbeiten als 'Expeditionen in nichterkundete Territorien der Sprache', deren Charakteristika das 'erfinderische Spiel mit Wortkonstellationen' und die 'kombinatorische Sprachphantasie' seien (Hinck 1991). Mit 'Konstellation' und 'Kombination' werden in dieser Rezension, die für viele andere stehen mag, Schlüsselworte der Avantgardeprogrammatik in der deutschen Nachkriegsliteratur abgerufen und bestimmte Leseerwartungen geweckt, nämlich daß Mayröcker eine Tradition der Arbeit an der Sprache fortsetzt, die Wirklichkeit als Sprachwirklichkeit wahrnimmt und die (man denke an die Konkrete Poesie) im Grunde einfach entschlüsselt werden kann. Gleichzeitig aber erwähnen nahezu alle Kommentatoren die untergründig dunkle, schwierige, unverständliche Sprache in Mayröckers Arbeiten, die sogenannten halluzinatorischen oder Traum-Passagen in der Prosa, in denen inhaltliche und thematische Logik außer Kraft gesetzt werden, und legen damit nahe, daß Mayröcker eine schwer lesbare, unzugängliche, hermetische Autorin sei (Luserke 1995: 452).[1] Der Stellenwert der hermetischen Literatur aber ist im

deutschen Sprachraum immer noch von Hugo Friedrichs einflußreicher Studie über *Die Struktur der modernen Lyrik* (1956) bestimmt: als prototypisch modern gilt immer noch das dunkle unverständliche poetische Sprechen.
   Mayröcker wäre also einerseits avantgardistisch-experimentell, andererseits typisch modern, also dunkel. Diese beiden Schablonen der literaturkritischen Wahrnehmung heben unterschiedliche Aspekte der Mayröckerschen Texte hervor, während sie andere vernachlässigen. Gemeinsam ist beiden eine exklusive Auffassung von literarischer Moderne. Sicher steht Mayröcker in der Tradition der sprachexperimentellen Avantgarde dieses Jahrhunderts, doch es gibt ebenso starke Bezüge zur emphatischen Moderne von Hölderlin und Kleist über die Romantik hin zum Surrealismus und zu Samuel Beckett. Aus der grundlegenden Schwierigkeit für die Kritiker, Mayröckers Werk einem Modernebegriff zuzuordnen, resultiert auch die Unmöglichkeit, ihm eine unmittelbare politische oder weltanschauliche Haltung abzuziehen. Und aufgrund derselben Schwierigkeit kommt es wohl auch zu der Verlegenheitsbehauptung, ihr Werk stehe in der deutschsprachigen Gegenwartsliteratur ohne Vergleich da (Luserke 1995: 442), obwohl sich Verbindungen zu anderen Autoren herstellen lassen und es doch schon Wirkungen auf das Werk anderer, meist jüngerer Autoren gibt, wie etwa Marcel Beyer, Ulrike Draesner, Thomas Kling.
   Aus dieser komplizierten Situation heraus läßt sich wohl das Bedürfnis nach Auslegung und Kontextualisierung von Mayröckers Werk erklären, das sich in dem starken Anwachsen der Sekundärliteratur in den letzten Jahren niederschlägt. Doch auch hier ist die Situation nicht eindeutig. Die sich mit Gegenwartsliteratur befassende Literaturwissenschaft beruft sich oft auf die Autorenpoetik, was im Falle Mayröckers zu Komplikationen führt, da bei ihr Prosa und Poetik schwer zu trennen sind. Die Autorin bewegt sich zwischen den zwei schon angesprochenen poetologischen Polen, dem sprachkonstruktiven und dem romantisch-surrealistischen: 'Fundstücke, Tätowierungen, Entschlüsselungen von Welt : simultane Netzwerke : betörend das Wissen, daß Innovation vollkommen uneingeschränkt bleiben müsse, daß das Spontane nie dem Prinzip des Maßvollen untergeordnet werden dürfe, daß andererseits die Kontrolle über das Schweifende (also die eigentliche poetische Substanz) nie erlahmen dürfe' (1983: 29). Zwar mag der Oberflächeninhalt dieser Passage eindeutig bestimmbar sein, doch ist nicht zu verkennen, daß diese Passage überwiegend literarisch ist, nicht begrifflich; daß die Autorin Bilder aus heterogenen Bildfeldern sowie semantisch unvereinbare Wortkombinationen benutzt; daß der Inhalt dieser Passage also durch ein literarisches Verfahren generiert wird und somit nicht uneingeschränkt als poetologisches Statement genommen werden darf (was in der Praxis aber doch zumeist geschieht und sodann zu den angesprochenen Komplikationen führt); und daß schließlich das, wovon und worüber diese Prosa spricht, nicht zu trennen ist von der spezifischen Art und

Weise, wie diese Prosa spricht. Dieses gilt für alle Texte aus den inzwischen auf vier Bände angewachsenen *Magischen Blättern* (1983-1995); und da einige dieser Gelegenheits- oder Auftragsarbeiten in literarische Veröffentlichungen wie *mein Herz mein Zimmer mein Name* (1988), *Stilleben* (1991) und *Lection* (1994) inkorporiert wurden, fallen im Prinzip auch diese unter diese Klausel.

Im Diskurs der Germanistik selber setzt sich diese Polarität fort. Mayröckers Werk, wo es denn als solches betrachtet wird, oder Teile davon (meist die Arbeiten der letzten anderthalb Jahrzehnte) werden meist zu stark auf die avantgardistische (und das heißt im oben angesprochenen Sinne: sprachexperimentell verengte) Tradition zurückgeführt. Dem stehen Mayröckers durchaus historisierende Selbstaussagen entgegen, die ihren Schreibimpuls u.a. damit erklärte, sie wolle die historischen Voraussetzungen überwinden, indem sie 'post-dadaistisch' und 'postsurrealistisch' schreibe; genau dies implizieren auch Mayröckers zahlreiche positive Verweise auf männliche Kollegen wie Samuel Beckett oder Arno Schmidt (Mayröcker 1991: 51; 1995: 90), aber auch verborgenere Einflüsse wie etwa der Gertrude Steins sind auszumachen (Kramer 1993: 230-49; Riess-Beger 1995: 94-101). Entweder wird Mayröckers Werk also mit den Traditionen der Avantgarde vernetzt und erklärt, was die Eigenart ihrer Arbeiten gewiß nur zum Teil zu beschreiben vermag; oder aber es wird in einen ganz anderen, in einen wissenschaftlichen Diskurs eingetragen, und zwar den des Radikalen Konstruktivismus (Schmidt 1989) oder aber den der Dekonstruktion (Riess-Beger 1995). Beide Ansätze berühren sich in ihrer Auffassung von Sprache als unabgeschlossenem Sprachspiel, aber während Siegfried J. Schmidt in seiner konstruktivistischen Lektüre Mayröckers diese Offenheit zur Voraussetzung von Sinn erhebt (im Sinne von 'Erfahrungen machen im Text und außerhalb'), schließt eine dekonstruktivistische Lektüre die Möglichkeit einer eindeutigen Sinnfixierung in Sprache, ja, eines eindeutigen Sinns schlechthin, aus. In beiden Fällen wird vorausgesetzt (und befolgt) eine postmoderne Textpraxis, in der genuin literarische 'Aussagen' außerliterarischen 'Aussagen' untergeordnet oder an die Seite gestellt werden; Ziel ist dabei einmal die durchgehende Ästhetisierung heterogener, d.h. poetischer und szientifischer Sprachformen, und sodann die wechselseitige Erhellung dieser 'Aussagen', während ihre Form weitgehend außer Acht bleibt (hierzu grundlegend Habermas 1985: 219-47).

Der Befund wäre also, daß sich Mayröckers dunkle, schwierige Literatur einem genuin hermeneutischen Zugriff widersetzt. Daraus kann man zunächst noch keine Option zugunsten einer antihermeneutischen Methode (Konstruktivismus oder Dekonstruktion) ableiten; im Gegenteil, Mayröckers Literatur scheint etwas anderes nahezulegen, nämlich die Notwendigkeit einer Ergänzung der traditionellen Hermeneutik, die ja auf dem einheitlichen Sinn insistierte (Petersen 1991: 63).[2] Im Folgenden möchte ich einige solche materialspezifischen

Überlegungen zu Mayröckers langer Prosa anbieten. Ich möchte zunächst zeigen, wie diese Literatur überhaupt verfährt; sodann prüfen, ob sich der Begriff der 'Textur' zur Beschreibung dieses neuen Typus von literarischem Text eignet; und schließlich, über die Verfahrensanalyse hinaus, überlegen, was diese neue Schreibweise unter literarhistorischen und texttheoretischen Gesichtspunkten bedeuten kann.

'Wortknüpfkunst'
Unter Berufung auf erzählerische Aussagen wie 'auf keinen Fall eine Story zulassen!, das Äußerste ein *Erzählverlauf, wie Lebenslauf*, also keine Geschichte, keine Lebensgeschichte' (1985: 121; Hervorh. der Autorin) hat man versucht, Mayröcker als dezidierte Nicht-Erzählerin zu beschreiben (Schmidt 1984a). Erzählen im strukturierten Sinne setzt immer schon eine Wirklichkeit voraus, von der sich erzählen läßt. Diese Voraussetzung ist in der modernen Literatur systematisch untergraben worden, und auch Mayröcker gehört dieser Tradition an. Was allerdings übersehen wird, ist die Tatsache, daß prononcierte Erzählverweigerung noch nicht die Abwesenheit des Erzählens überhaupt bedeutet. Das Erzählen mag noch so sehr reduziert sein, ein 'Erzählverlauf', den das Zitat ja immerhin konzediert, eine 'Erzählhaltung' und ein 'Erzählverhalten', die Mayröcker in einem Interview anführt, wären durchaus beschreibbar (Schmidt 1984b: 267-8). (Dem würde auch nicht entgegenstehen, daß sich in den letzten Büchern zunehmend Erinnerungspassagen und Ansätze zu narrativen Sequenzen finden.) Die in der Forschung gelegentlich formulierte Alternative 'Erzählerin oder Nichterzählerin?' ist also eine Scheinalternative.

Anders sieht es aus bei der Frage, worum es sich bei Mayröckers Arbeiten denn eigentlich handle. Kaum fügen sie sich dem herkömmlichen Gattungsschema ein, Autorin und Verlag verzichten in der Regel auf einen Untertitel. Die Bezeichnung 'Texte' scheint zu kurz zu greifen und läßt darüber hinaus an den avantgardistischen Purismus der 60er Jahre denken, von dem sich die Autorin explizit losgesagt hat. 'Roman' oder 'Erzählung' implizieren erkennbare narrative Strukturen und sicher ein Minimum an Nacherzählbarkeit, also eine wie auch immer mimetische Grundhaltung. Gegen ein solches 'Nachzeichnen' spricht sich die Autorin ausdrücklich aus (Schmidt 1984b: 273). Und ihre Bücher, was immer in ihnen gesagt wird, lassen sich nicht paraphrasieren. Stoff, Material, Thema werden dem poetischen Verfahren unterworfen, welches integraler Bestandteil von Bedeutung wird und mitunter derart dominiert, daß es zur eigentlichen Bedeutung wird. Von der Vorrangigkeit des 'Verfahrens' haben in der Literaturtheorie zum ersten Mal die russischen Formalisten gesprochen, deren Einsichten parallel zu den Arbeiten des Futurismus entstanden, und in der Geschichte der Literaturtheorie (über die diversen nationalen Strukturalismen bis zum Poststrukturalismus) hat der Verfahrensbegriff immer ein Korrektiv zu weltanschaulichen, geistesgeschichtlichen oder essentialistischen Interpretationen gebildet.

Die Bezeichnung 'Prosa' dürfte für Mayröckers Arbeiten noch am angemessensten sein, wobei meine Bezeichnung 'lange Prosa' deskriptiver und neutraler zu sein scheint als der wertende Ausdruck 'große Prosa' oder gar 'Großepik' (Schmidt-Dengler 1996: 164). Gleichwohl stellt sich das Problem, daß Teile aus der langen Prosa vorab in anderer Form, als Auftrags- oder Gelegenheitssarbeit, veröffentlicht wurden, was bedeutet, daß bei Mayröcker die Grenze zwischen 'literarischer' und 'expositorischer' Prosa fließend ist und daß dadurch das literarische Verfahren um so zentraler wird.

Es handelt sich in der Regel um eine außerordentlich stark modulierte Prosa. Die Sprechhaltung überformt die Erzählhaltung. Dementsprechend finden sich zahlreiche, in normaler Prosa ansonsten eher unübliche typographische Hervorhebungen, etwa der Gedankenstrich, Kapitälchen, Kursivierungen, Doppelpunkte (stets exakt in der Mitte zwischen zwei Wörtern) und Schrägstriche. Auf der textuellen Ebene gibt es die Leitmotive, Wiederholungen, Zitate und Neologismen, die auf den Sprechcharakter dieser Prosa verweisen, aber gleichzeitig auch den konstruktiven, den Verfahrensaspekt, also den Kunstcharakter mitvergegenwärtigen.

Dieser Kunstcharakter von Mayröckers 'Wortknüpfkunst' (Mayröcker 1983: 57) ist wieder in den Blick geraten (Beyer 1996). Hinzuzufügen wäre, daß die metaphorische Gleichsetzung von Text und Textilie nicht erst in *Lection* beginnt, sondern im Werk der Autorin schon länger ein Motiv ist (z.B. Mayröcker 1988: 203). Mayröcker spricht in der Prosa 'mütterlicherseits' davon, daß ihr die Handarbeiten ihrer Mutter wichtige Arbeitsanstöße waren und poetologische Prinzipien einschlossen wie 'das Mustern, das Probieren, das Arrangieren, das Kombinieren, das Kopieren, das Experimentieren, das Collagieren' (1987: 152).

Beyer hat im Zusammenhang seiner Untersuchung zum Metaphorisierungsprozeß den Begriff 'Textur' vorgeschlagen, den übrigens auch die Autorin benutzt hat. 1980 sprach sie, wenn auch eher en passant, von der Rolle der Erinnerung beim Schreiben und beschrieb die Verwandlung 'vom erinnerten Urbild zur poetischen Textur' (1983: 11). M.E. ist der Begriff 'Textur' auch über seine metaphorische Bedeutung hinaus zur Charakterisierung der Machart von Mayröckers Literatur brauchbar. In der neueren Literaturwissenschaft beschreibt der Begriff solche 'unverständlichen' Texte der Moderne, die folgende Merkmale aufweisen: sie haben keine konsistenten (z.B. narrative oder thematische) Strukturen; sie brechen mit dem realistisch-mimetischen Prinzip und stellen demnach keine 'Aussagen' dar und keine 'Identifikationsmuster' bereit; sie sind selbstreflexiv und autothematisch, genauer: sie verweisen den Interpreten auf das Verfahren, nach dem sie hergestellt sind; und sie machen eine hermeneutisch eindeutige Interpretation unmöglich (Baßler 1994: 17). Das läßt sich an einem längeren Beispiel aus *Lection* zeigen:

> ich bin außerstande zu reagieren, ein Entsagen alles in allem so mag es sein, ein ENTSÄBELN ENTSACHEN, ein Absagen Aufsagen Überantworten Verzerren womöglich, ein sich von etwas Loslösen Lossagen eine Verweigerung ein Abgesang, ein sich *Entschuhen*, wie damals, er hatte sich *entschuht*, B. hatte sich *entschuht*, damals, in diesen landläufigen Gewölben, sepiafarbenen Wiesenpanoramen, was immer das heißen mag, er zog sich um, das Gebüsch war seine Umkleidekabine, und wie auf ein Signal sahen die Umstehenden weg, erinnerst du dich, sage ich zu Helene, er stand im Schatten dieses Gebüsches, entledigte sich der Wanderhose und zog die feierlich wirkende schwarze Hose über, im Morgenlicht, also der Text als vernetztes Fuchsienrot, der Text als funkenschlagende Rosenwolke, als milchiger Schatten abwärtsrieselnd den Baum, den knorrigen Stamm des Baumes im Garten unter dem Fenster, der Text als tränengesprenkeltes Hegelpärchen, -bärtchen, wohin?, oder ist es eine ZITTERWUT eine ZITIERWUT also daß man sich nur noch zeigen kann in der WORTVERKLEIDUNG : in der Sprache anderer, weil man sich zurückgenommen hat in eine äußerste Lautlosigkeit Sprachlosigkeit Schweigsamkeit weil man sich zurückgezogen hat in diesen äußersten Winkel aus welchem man nur noch hervorzulugen vermag, schon beinahe teilnahmslos das Geschehen ringsum betrachtend, die Vielzahl der Standpunkte einer vibrierenden Welt, usw. (1994: 110-11)

Der Eindruck des parataktisch Ruhelosen, des Insistierenden dieser Darstellung entsteht durch die genau gesetzten, zuweilen verblosen Sprechperioden, die durch Kommata abgetrennt rhythmische Wirkung erzielen. Gleiches tun die phonetischen Assoziationen zu Beginn und der rhetorische Katalog gegen Ende der Passage. Der Gestus des Fragens und der Gebrauch von Phrasen wie 'nicht wahr' oder 'usw.' erhöhen die Unsicherheit und Instabilität des Dargestellten. (Andere von Mayröcker häufig gebrauchte Mitel sind der Konjunktiv, als-ob-Sätze; Fragesätze wie 'oder wie soll ich sagen?'; Selbstkorrekturen und Neuansätze in der Form von 'ich meine'.) Die typographisch hervorgehobenen Signalwörter und der phonetische Wechsel zu Nachbarwörtern ('ZITTERWUT' und 'ZITIERWUT') heben das Bedeutete gleich wieder auf. Auch einzelne Wörter haben eine präzise Funktion, die über ihre lexikalische Bedeutung hinausgeht: das mehrfach benutzte 'wie' stellt Ähnlichkeiten her; das 'also' suggeriert einen kausalen Zusammenhang, der semantisch so nicht nachvollziehbar ist, der aber Sinn macht (als Verweigerung von Sinn) im Licht der dunklen Metaphern, mit denen der 'Text' charakterisiert wird. Dieser semantischen Verflüssigung entspricht die thematische: der sanfte Wechsel von der beschriebenen, besprochenen Erinnerung an das Umkleiden zur zentralen Metapher der Passage, 'WORTVERKLEIDUNG', die die beiden wichtigsten Bild- und Gegenstandsebenen von *Lection* noch einmal metaphorisch vereinigt: die Textilien mit der Reflexion auf den Text selber. In dieser Passage (und das ist qualitativ neu in *Lection*) sind (relativ unmetaphorische, relativ 'narative') Erinnerung und (relativ metaphorische) Spracharbeit so stark verschränkt, daß die eine nicht ohne die andere gelesen werden kann. Dieser Prozeß wird in *Lection* derart zugespitzt, daß es sich sogar verbietet, hier poetologische Statements von 'realistischen' Sequenzen zu trennen (Beyer 1996: 148). Das führt auch der Text weiter vor, indem er anschließend die Ungewißheit anspricht, ob das sprechende Ich über eine, seine Sprache verfügt. Erzählsubjekt und erzähltes Objekt lösen sich, der Tendenz nach, in gleicher Weise und gleichzeitig auf. Die Leitmotive in dieser Passage sind selbstverständlich mit dem Gesamttext verbunden und garantieren ästhetische Kohärenz dort, wo der Text 'inhaltlich' auseinanderzufallen droht.

Verfahrensanalytisch gesprochen: das von Mayröcker verwendete lexikalische Material und der Thesaurus, dem sie entstammen (das 'Paradigma'), lassen sich durchaus beschreiben, ebenso wie die syntagmatischen Verknüpfungsregeln, denen sie unterworfen sind. Eine genetische Analyse dieser texturierten Prosa hätte zudem noch die Tatsache zu berücksichtigen, daß Teile der zitierten Passage in anderer Abfolge und mit leichten Variationen unter dem Titel 'ENTFACHUNG' 1992 separat publiziert worden sind (jetzt Mayröcker 1995: 38-44).

Wofür ich mit dem Begriff der Textur plädiere, ist im Grunde ein neuer Typ von moderner Prosa, der sich eben von tradierten Strukturen lossagt. Baßler hat eine signifikante Zunahme von texturierten Texten in der Moderne festgestellt und verschiedene Typen von expressionistischen Prosatexturen inventarisiert; eine ähnliche Arbeit steht für die Nachkriegsprosa noch bevor. Deutlich geworden sollte sein, daß Texturen weniger zur dekonstruktiven Lektüre einladen (wie soll man weiter verflüssigen, was ohnehin schon flüssig ist?) als vielmehr zur Überlegung auf die Prozeduren der Herstellung von Sinn. Texturen sind nicht unverständlich und hermetisch; sie sind auch nicht einfach dekodierbar; sondern sie machen Sinn, indem sie konventionelle Sinnerwartungen unterlaufen.

'denn es geht ja kreuz und quer beim Lesen'
Texturierte Prosa läßt sich als Verfahren und Verknüpfung beschreiben. Texturen sind keine einfachen 'Aussagen' oder literarische 'Identifikationsangebote', gleichwohl entfällt die Bedeutungsfrage nicht, sondern stellt sich in verschärfter Form. Texturierte Prosa läßt sich u.a. auch dadurch verstehen, daß man ihre Referentialisierungen untersucht, also fragt: 'Wie und in welchem Modus wird gesprochen?' und 'Was wird gesprochen?' Bei Mayröckers Prosa kämen etwa Traum, Halluzination, Zitat (Eigen- oder Fremdzitat), autobiographische Erinnerung in Betracht. Die am häufigsten gebrauchte Referentialisierung ist jedoch das Gespräch, als Monolog, Dialog oder Polylog. Alle diese Formen werden, wie nicht anders zu erwarten, unterlaufen und verflüssigt. Gleiches gilt

für die Frage nach dem, was gesprochen wird. Selbst die höchst texturierte, unverständlichste Prosa ist Teil historischer Diskurse und damit selbst diskursiv besetzt, und sei es nur im Diskurs 'Unverständlichkeit'. Selbstverständlich sind in der modernen Literatur Verbindungen und Übergänge zwischen diesen beiden Typen von Referentialisierung möglich.

Diese Referentialisierungen erlauben, mehr als die strukturale Verfahrensanalyse, Vermutungen über die Bedeutung dessen anzustellen, was die Texturen tun, und das heißt Vermutungen über die hermeneutischen Prozeduren, die sie inszenieren.[3] Ich möchte hier nur einige Beispiele geben. Unter den zahlreichen Stimmen in Mayröckers Prosa haben die Briefe eine besondere Funktion. Vor allem in *mein Herz mein Zimmer mein Name* können sie, wie Juliane Vogel gezeigt hat, als Kontrafaktur zur romantischen Briefliteratur gelesen werden, wie sie vor allem von Frauen gepflegt wurde. Zwei Dinge sind m.E. jedoch wichtig: erstens sind diese Briefstimmen, wie dekonstruiert sie bei Mayröcker auch sind, Teil des Leitmotivs 'Gespräch', was männliche ebenso wie weibliche Stimmen umfaßt. Und zweitens ist die Brieflichkeit mehr als der Ausdruck 'hermeneutischer Verständigungsspiele' (Vogel 1996: 82), sie ist Teil einer umfassenderen Diskurses über das 'Gespräch' seit Ende des 18. Jahrhunderts und als solcher nicht ohne weiteres zu reduzieren auf die Geschlechtszugehörigkeit der Diskursteilnehmer. Das 'Gespräch' steht symptomatisch für den Niedergang des alten Repräsentationsmodells von Sprache, wonach sprachliche Zeichen Ausdruck von Gedanken sind, die die Welt logisch und vernünftig darstellen, sie wiedervergegenwärtigen können sollen und uns sagen, wie wir sie verstehen sollen. Mit Herder und schärfer noch in der Romantik, bei Schleiermacher und den Schlegels, gilt Sprache nur im Gespräch als wirklich, gilt das 'Gespräch' als Garant einer neuartigen Hermeneutik des mehrstimmigen und potentiell unendlichen Dialogs (siehe Frank 1990: 40-6).[4]

Als Sonderfall des Gesprächs steht bei Mayröcker die fiktionale Anrede an den Leser, der ihren Text rezipiert, wie etwa in der folgenden Passage aus *Lection*:

> Denn das Schreiben, geliebter Leser müssen Sie wissen, setzt das Gemüt mit seinen gemachten Revolutionen, freien Vorstellungen, feurigen Ausdrücken und anderen bunten Verästelungen in Sehen / Unruh / Glut und Lüsternheit, es nimmt den Kopf ganz *als in Arrest*, setzt den Menschen in ein Schwitzbad der Passion ... Das zu Sagende zu Schreibende : eigentlich etwas in Übereinstimmung mit dem Leser – daß sich nämlich die meisten Dinge von selbst verstehen, daß darüber zu sprechen zu schreiben sich erübrige, daß man gemeinsam auf solche Weise eine Art Plateau gewinnen könne, von wo aus sich die Gedanken in größerer Wucht und Freiheit der Sicht bewegen, sage ich, *eine Art Jagdplateau*, sage ich ... (1994: 41-2; Hervorh. der Autorin)

Die Anrede an Leser gibt sich (außerhalb der zitierten Passage) als Kolportage zu erkennen, die Autorin zitiert aus der *Mythoscopia Romantica* (1698) des Zürcher Pastors Gotthard Heidegger. Dessen wortreiche Warnungen vor dem Schreiben (die ja Mayröckers Schreiben recht akkurat beschreiben) münden in eine lehrhafte Reflexion auf Sagen und Schreiben; ein Wechselspiel der Redeweisen wird hier dargestellt ebenso wie eines der Leseweisen.

Gleichzeitig wird der Diskurs über 'Schreiben' fortgesetzt, und wie nebenher auch Derridas Unterscheidung zwischen Rede und Schrift aufgehoben. Für Derrida ist das schriftliche Zeichen nur das Supplement des Supplements, der gesprochenen Sprache: es 'erübrigt' sich, wörtlich genommen, in jedem Falle, ist aber dennoch alles andere als überflüssig, denn nur 'gemeinsam' können schreibender Autor und lesender Leser das Plateau eines wilden, dezentrierten Denkens erreichen (oder ihm jedenfalls Nach-'Jagen', wie der erste Satz von *Lection* behauptet).

Ein weiteres Beispiel. In nahezu allen Texten Mayröckers finden sich Bilder des Plötzlichen, mit denen die Autorin Momente der Eingebung zu evozieren scheint und Augenblicke der Verwandlung von gelebter Erfahrung in Geschriebenes festhält (z.B. 1995: 67). Auf den ersten Blick mag man hier an eine moderne Anknüpfung an einen romantischen Topos denken, etwa bei Eichendorff, in dessen Prosa das Plötzliche ebenfalls als Sprechereignis (Stille, Schrei) oder aber als Wetterphänomen (Sturm, Wetterleuchten, Blitz, was den Topos von der poetischen Inspiration hervorruft) dargestellt ist. Doch gibt es eine entscheidende Neuerung: diese Momente bei Mayröcker sind nicht nur als Sprech- und Wetterereignisse referentialisiert, sondern auch als Körperereignisse. Oft beschreiben sie einen berauschenden, zuckenden, konvulsivischen Körperzustand, fast durchweg unter Bezug auf den Augenblick der poetischen Inspiration. Am prominentesten sind hier die offenen und kryptischen Erwähnungen von Mayröckers Pfingsterlebnis 1939, welches der Autorin zu ihrem ersten Gedicht verhalf; es wird mehrfach emphatisch, ja enthusiastisch gefeiert (1983: 87; 1987: 140 und 188).

Wie überlegt und sorgfältig Mayröcker hier vorgeht, kann ich hier in zwei Schritten nur andeuten. Der moderne ästhetische Diskurs über das Schöne ist hier in vermittelter Form aufgenommen. Erst nach dem Verschwinden des klassisch Schönen kommen, von den Romantikern bis zur surrealistischen Generation, körperliche Grenzzustände zur ästhetischen Geltung und bringen im literarischen wie theoretischen Diskurs Neues hervor. Walter Benjamin sprach anläßlich von Goethes *Wahlverwandtschaften* von 'Erschütterung' und 'Unruhe des Herzens', und für Breton war das Konvulsivische Hauptmerkmal des Schönen (Bohrer 1981: 83-4). Die Plötzlichkeits-Emphase in der modernen Literatur führt zu spezifischen Texten. Im 18. Jahrhundert, mit Rousseau beginnend, wird die reine freie Subjektivität entdeckt und gefeiert, in der Romantik bildlich und symbolisch überhöht, gleichzeitig ins logische Extrem getrieben. Darauf antwortet das 20. Jahrhundert mit einem Rekurs auf mythologische Denkfiguren (Bohrer 1983: 215). In der Nachmoderne ist dieser Augenblick nun reine Sprache geworden. Der Diskurs 'Plötzlichkeit' formuliert nun, wie bei Mayröcker, die Widersprüche, die der Sprache inhärent sind. Damit hat der Augenblick fiktionalen Charakter gewonnen, und genau diese Fiktionalität leitet die utopische Phase der ästhetischen Rezeption ein (Bohrer 1983: 217), für Autor und Leser (in der Phantasiearbeit). Je mehr der Text auf die Spannung zwischen utopischem Augenblick und textuellem 'Momentum' reflektiert, desto intensiver (laut Bohrer) diese Glücksgefühle; als Beispiel führt er Proust an, bei dem 'die "Augenblicke" des Lesens mit den "Augenblicken" der Erinnerung im utopischen Glück identisch' geworden seien (217). Etwas Analoges sehe ich bei Mayröcker am Werk, in der radikalen, aufs Schreiben und Lesen bezogenen Binnenperspektive, die Wirklichkeit nur als subjektive Sprachwirklichkeit anerkennt. Fast müßig zu erwähnen, daß somit die Utopie inhaltsleer, geschichtslos, fiktiv geworden ist, anders ausgedrückt: Fiktion und Geschichte decken sich nicht. Damit ist auch der Status von Utopie anders geworden: sie wird reduziert, gleichzeitig radikalisiert, da vormals teleologisches oder gar eschatologisches Denken durch Sprache ersetzt wird. Ein 'ästhetisches Mythologem' tritt somit an die Stelle der geschichtlichen Utopie. In dieser Linie der emphatischen, ästhetischen Moderne steht Friederike Mayröcker.

Wie bereits oben bei der Reflexion auf den Texturbegriff, den Gesprächsdiskurs und die Plötzlichkeits-Metaphern erwähnt, gebraucht und verknüpft Mayröcker bestimmtes Sprachmaterial in ihrer bildlichen *und* begrifflichen Bedeutung und kompliziert damit eindeutige Bedeutungszuschreibungen. Durch Referentialisieren lassen sich diese Materialien mit vorgängigen und parallelen Diskursen vernetzen, ohne daß sie jedoch auf diese reduzierbar wären, eben weil sie in den texturierten Text eingewoben worden und mit ihm verknüpft sind. Die Metapher vom Text als Gewebe, welche die Autorin erwähnt, ist zentraler Bestandteil der poststrukturalistischen Texttheorie, seit Roland Barthes sie in seinem Essay 'Der Tod des Autors' (1968) benutzt hat. Das hat in der Folge zwei Ausfaltungen erfahren, die Intertextualitätstheorie Julia Kristevas (unter deutlich feministischem und psychoanalytischem Vorzeichen) und Derridas Begriff des 'texte général', den dann auch Foucault verwendet hat. Gemeinsam ist diesen Ansätzen, bei aller Divergenz im einzelnen, eine Abwertung des intendierten *einen, einheitlichen* Textsinnes und ein Plädoyer für semantische Entgrenzung. Dies läßt sich durchaus, wie Manfred Frank gezeigt hat, mit der romantischen Hermeneutik des unendlichen Gesprächs verbinden (1990: 38-105). Dies soll nicht heißen, daß Mayröcker irgendwie vom Diskurs des Poststrukturalismus oder der romantischen Hermeneutik beeinflußt wäre (obwohl es hier wichtige Verbindungen zu zeigen gäbe), sondern lediglich, daß ihre texturierte Prosa im Horizont dieser Diskurse verstanden werden kann. Dementsprechend würde ich, von dem Verzicht auf traditionelles Erzählen und der starken Autothematisierung des Schreibens bei Mayröcker ausgehend, nicht von einer 'verweigerten Kommunikativität' (Luserke 1995: 445) in ihren Arbeiten sprechen,[5] von einem neuen Typ von Kommunikativität, einer Inszenierung des potentiell unendlichen Gesprächs im Text mit dem Leser. Die Gesprächssituation ist derart texturiert, daß der Leser sich aller 'Dunkelheit', d.h. allen Anforderungen an traditionelle hermeneutische Erwartungen zum Trotz, zur Antwort verpflichtet fühlt. Schleiermacher drückt diesen Sachverhalt auf eine stellenweise mayröckerisch anmutende Art aus:

> Denn die unmittelbare Gegenwart des Redenden, der lebendige Ausdruck, welche die Teilnahme seines ganzen geistigen Wesens verkündigt, die Art, wie sich hier die Gedanken aus dem gemeinsamen Leben entwickeln, dies alles reizt weit mehr als die einsame Betrachtung einer ganz isolierten Schrift dazu, eine Reihe von Gedanken zugleich als einen hervorbrechenden Lebensmoment, als eine mit vielen anderen auch anderer Art zusammenhängende Tat zu verstehen, und eben diese Seite ist es, welche bei der Erklärung der Schriftsteller am meisten hintangestellt, ja großenteils ganz vernachlässigt wird. (Schleiermacher 1977: 316)

Wie dieser Typ von Gesprächsinszenierung, der die Hermeneutik ebenso wie die Dekonstruktion auf die Probe stellt, im einzelnen texturiert ist und welche literarhistorischen Folgen daraus zu ziehen sein werden, muß noch offen bleiben. Das Gespräch über Mayröckers Literatur aber dauert an.

Notes

[1] Luserke beschreibt die Machart der Mayröckerschen Prosa und ihre Polyvalenz. Herkömmliche Analyseverfahren, wie etwa die Parallelstellenmethode, schieden deshalb aus. Das ist m.E. so nicht richtig. – Im übrigen widerspricht schon der Gebrauch der Licht- und Helligkeitsbilder in Mayröckers Prosa dem Eindruck des Dunklen; 'einige sehr dunkle Stellen mischen sich mit einigen sehr hellen Stellen' (Mayröcker 1988: 337)

[2] In den weiteren Erwähnungen Mayröckers im Kapitel 'Weltverlust und Subjektivismus' verfährt Petersen reduktiv und ordnet Mayröckers Prosa kurzerhand dem surrealistischen Roman zu (211; 288)

[3] Möglicherweise ließe sich auch von der literarischen 'Simulation' des Gesprächs reden, doch müßte dazu der von Baudrillard u.a. gebrauchte allgemeine Begriff der Simulation für die Literaturwissenschaft präzisiert werden.

Notes continued

[4] Auf die Parallele zwischen romantischer Briefliteratur und neueren Dialogizitätsmodellen weist Riess-Beger hin (1995: 144)

[5] Gegen Ende seines Aufsatzes konzediert Luserke allerdings, daß Kommunikation in Mayröckers Texten teilweise durch typographische, stilistische und syntaktische Signale wiederhergestellt wird (1995: 454)

Bibliography

Baßler, Moritz. 1994. *Die Entdeckung der Textur: Unverständlichkeit in der Kurzprosa der emphatischen Moderne, 1910-1916*, Tübingen, Niemeyer

Beyer, Marcel. 1996. 'Textur: Metpahorisierung und Ent-Metaphorisierung in Friederike Mayröckers Lection', in Kastberger und Schmidt-Dengler 1996b: 140-50

Bohrer, Karl Heinz. 1981. *Plötzlichkeit: Zum Augenblick des ästhetischen Scheins*, Frankfurt am Main, Suhrkamp

Clausen, Bettina und Karsten Singelmann. 1992. 'Avantgarde heute?', in Klaus Briegleb und Sigrid Weigel (Hrsg.), *Gegenwartsliteratur seit 1968*, München, Hanser: 455-87

Frank, Manfred. 1990. *Das Sagbare und das Unsagbare: Studien zur deutsch-französischen Hermeneutik und neueren Texttheorie*, Frankfurt, Suhrkamp

Friedrich, Hugo. 1956. *Die Struktur der modernen Lyrik: von Baudelaire bis zur Gegenwart*, Hamburg, Rowohlt

Habermas, Jürgen. 1985. *Der philosophische Diskurs der Moderne: Zwölf Vorlesungen*, Frankfurt am Main, Suhrkamp

Hinck, Walter. 1991. 'Komödienhafter Sternhaufen: Friederike Mayröcker hat aus Gesprächen ein "Stilleben" gewonnen', *FAZ*, 31. Mai: 34

Kastberger, Klaus und Wendelin Schmidt-Dengler. 1996a. 'Vorwort', in Kastberger und Schmidt-Dengler 1996b: 9-10

— (Hrsg.). 1996b. *In Böen wechselt mein Sinn: Zu Friederike Mayröcker*, Wien, Sonderzahl

Kramer, Andreas. 1993. *Gertrude Stein und die deutsche Avantgarde*, Eggingen, Edition Isele

Luserke, Matthias. 1995. 'Ein unsteter Zyklus Schreibkunst: Betrachtungen zum Werk von Friederike Mayröcker', *Euphorion*, 89: 438-54

Mayröcker, Friederike. 1983. *Magische Blätter*, Frankfurt am Main, Suhrkamp

—. 1985. *Das Herzzerreißende der Dinge*, Frankfurt am Main, Suhrkamp

—. 1987. *Magische Blätter II*, Frankfurt am Main, Suhrkamp
—. 1988. *mein Herz mein Zimmer mein Name*, Frankfurt am Main, Suhrkamp
—. 1991. *Magische Blätter III*, Frankfurt am Main, Suhrkamp
—. 1994. *Lection*, Frankfurt am Main, Suhrkamp
—. 1995. *Magische Blätter IV*, Frankfurt am Main, Suhrkamp
Petersen, Jürgen H. 1991. *Der deutsche Roman der Moderne: Grundlegung – Typologie – Entwicklung*, Stuttgart, Metzler
Riess-Beger, Daniela. 1995. *Lebensstudien: Poetische Verfahrensweisen in Friederike Mayröckers Prosa*, Würzburg, Königshausen und Neumann
Schleiermacher, Friedrich. 1977. *Hermeneutik und Kritik mit einem Anhang sprachphilosophischer Texte*, hrsg. Manfred Frank, Frankfurt, Suhrkamp
Schmidt, Siegfried J. 1984a. '"Der Fall ins Ungewisse": Anmerkungen zu einer Nicht-Erzählerin', in S. J. Schmidt (Hrsg.), *Friederike Mayröcker*, Frankfurt am Main, Suhrkamp: 13-23
—. 1984b. '"Es schießt zusammen": Gespräch mit Friederike Mayröcker', in S. J. Schmidt (Hrsg.), *Friederike Mayröcker*, Frankfurt am Main, Suhrkamp: 260-83
—. 1989. *Fuszstapfen des Kopfes: Friederike Mayröckers Prosa aus konstruktivistischer Sicht*, Münster, Kleinheinrich
Schmidt-Dengler, Wendelin. 1996. 'Lektionen: Zur großen Prosa der Friederike Mayröcker', in Kastberger und Schmidt-Dengler 1996b: 151-66
Venske, Regula. 1992. 'Kritik der Männlichkeit', in Klaus Briegleb und Sigrid Weigel (Hrsg.), *Gegenwartsliteratur seit 1968*, München, Hanser: 267-76
Vogel, Juliane. 1996. 'Nachtpost: Das Flüstern der Briefstimmen in der Prosa Friederike Mayröckers', in Kastberger und Schmidt-Dengler 1996b: 69-82

Hilde Spiel and the Possibility of a Multicultural Society:
Die Früchte des Wohlstands and *Mirko und Franca*

Andrea Hammel

Hilde Spiel is one of the best known female Austrian writers who was exiled by the Nazis and lived in Great Britain. She was born in Vienna in 1911 and died there in 1990. Both her parents came from Jewish families but had converted to Catholicism. Her family background, her identification with Austria as well as her later exile initiated her extensive interest in multiculturalism which is reflected in her literary and journalistic work.

Her first novel, *Kati auf der Brücke*, was published in 1934, but by then Spiel already knew that she would not be able to stay in Austria for very much longer. Spiel's journey into exile was very different from the horrific escapes of many other refugees. For her the civil war in 1934 was more of a shock than the Anschluß itself. She knew that she wanted to leave the country but was very pragmatic about it and decided that she should finish her studies first. Pursuing these studies did not prevent her from engaging in a lively social life – falling in and out of love frequently – and even frequenting the bars of Vienna with fashionable young men irrespective of their political conviction. She knew, however, about her own ability to compromise her ideals and later called this time before her exile a murky time; this fear of slow corruption was one reason for her emigration.

After the completion of her doctoral thesis she came to England and there she married the journalist and writer Peter de Mendelsohn. It was her husband who encouraged her to change her language for writing (Spiel 1991a: 155). Spiel started working for the *New Statesman* and continued to pursue her literary career. In 1939 *Flute and Drums* was published in English by Hutchinson but the novel was still written in German first and then translated by Spiel with the help of her husband and a friend, Eric Dancy. This was Spiel's first fictional treatment of the theme of fascism, in this case dealing with the Italian variety. After this a complete language switch occurred and she started to work on a historical novel about Vienna in English which was called 'The Fruits of Prosperity'. This project remained unfinished during the war and only extracts which were translated into German were published in *Die Zeitung*, a London exile journal, between 1941 and 1943, and, in April 1946, in the cultural supplement of *Der Zeitspiegel*, a publication of the Free Austrian Movement in London. It was published for the first time in book form as *Die Früchte des Wohlstands* in 1981, translated by Hilde Spiel herself.

During the war the family's situation remained financially precarious and the couple did not want to move exclusively in exile circles. They tried as much as possible to align themselves with British writers and intellectuals. However, their attempts to be accepted fully by British intellectual and literary figures failed. Spiel describes her utter astonishment when friends suggested at the end of the war that they would now return to Austria: 'Da wußten wir und gestanden's uns doch nicht ein: neun Jahre der Einfügung in die englische Welt waren vergeblich gewesen' (Spiel 1991a: 206).

Spiel continued to live outside Austria for another eighteen years. As early as 1946, however, at the earliest possible opportunity, she asked the *New Statesman* for accreditation to go to Vienna as a correspondent where she kept a diary of her return written in English and from which several newspaper articles originate. A German version was eventually published in 1968 in Munich under the title *Rückkehr nach Wien: Tagebuch 1946*. Until then Spiel's only novel about the exile theme had been *The Darkened Room*, (1961, *Lisas Zimmer* 1965) in which the main characters exemplify in a narrative form Spiel's theoretical views about exile as an illness – a view further elaborated on in her 'Psychologie des Exils' (Spiel 1976: 27-33). In 1963 Spiel returned to Austria to live there permanently.

Hilde Spiel's other fictional involvement with the exile problem appears in her play *Anna & Anna* (Spiel 1989). It features a doppelgänger motif employing Anna 1 who stays in Vienna during the Nazi period and Anna 2 who emigrates to London. The two protagonists can be seen as representing the individual stories of those who stayed behind and became, therefore, inevitably implicated in National Socialism and of those who left Austria with a feeling of alienation and guilt at having abandoned a part of themselves as well as often having left behind friends and relatives.

Edward Timms suggests the two Annas also represent the two Austrias: under Nazi rule and in exile in London (Timms 1995). During the war Spiel seems to have been a staunch supporter of the stance taken by the Free Austrian Movement promoting the distinctiveness of Austria from Germany in a cultural and political sense. Her name appears on a list of delegates representing Austria at the Seventh International PEN Congress in September 1941. Since January 1938 the Austrian PEN in London had been recognized as the official representative of Austria in the international PEN community (Amann 1984: 66). The Moscow Declaration on Austria of the 30 October 1943 was an important document to Hilde Spiel. It begins as follows: 'The Governments of the United Kingdom, the Soviet Union and the United States of America are agreed that Austria, the first free country to fall victim to Hitlerite Aggression, shall be liberated from German domination' (quoted in Berkley 1988: 333). Spiel included the declaration in the original film script of *Anna & Anna* and insisted on having it read out *completely* at the play's performance at the Burgtheater. In her interview for the German TV series 'Zeugen des Jahrhunderts' with Anne Linsel in August 1988, Spiel points out how significant the last paragraph of the declaration was to her (Linsel 1992: 109). 'Austria is reminded, however, that she has a responsibility which she cannot evade for participation in the war on the side of Hitlerite Germany, and that in the final settlement, account will inevitably be taken of her own contribution to her liberation' (Berkley 1988: 333). Spiel is obviously very critical of the Austrians' participation in their own liberation. This is made clear in *Rückkehr nach Wien* where she writes about the insincerity and self-pity of many Austrians who consider themselves only as victims of the National Socialists, never as colluders or perpetrators.

What makes Austrian culture so distinctive? For Spiel, there were probably many different features, but the possibility of a multicultural society does seem to be the most important. In the interview with Anne Linsel she describes why Austria is special: 'Es setzt sich zusammen aus der Vielgestaltigkeit der Einflüsse, die sich in eineinhalb Jahrhunderten – mit Ausnahme der sieben Jahre des Anschlusses – in Österreich manifestierten' (Linsel 1992: 81). Her non-fictional writing includes a book on the Viennese Jew Fanny von Arnstein, often described as Spiel's masterpiece, and a large part of her essays are about issues concerning cultural difference and understanding. Even one of her last works *Vienna's Golden Autumn* (1987) gives a good impression of her vision of a multicultural Austria. She examines the period from 1866 to 1938 in the light of its cultural diversity and especially in view of the Jewish contribution to Austrian life: 'Dieses liberale, stark jüdisch durchsetzte Bürgertum war eben die letzte Selbstverwirklichung universalen Österreichtums, ehe es an Traditionalismus da, nationaler und sozialer Unrast dort scheiterte' (Spiel 1988: 41). The post-war Austria by comparison had lost its 'Urbanität und Weltoffenheit' which had been replaced by 'gleichmacherische Provinzialität' (Spiel 1988: 25).

For Spiel the height of Austria's multicultural society coincided with the reign of Franz Joseph I. One of Spiel's prime concerns is to show that the Austrians of Jewish descent have been an integral part of Austrian society for many centuries. She even argues that at times it was only the assimilated Jews who saw themselves first and foremost as Austrian nationals and who felt a real duty to the Austrian state because most of the other Austrian citizens would claim to have their roots in one of the distinct ethnic parts of the Austrian monarchy. On several occasions she cites a scene from Franz Theodor Csokor's play 'Die 3. November 1918' to support this view: After the Austrian defeat Oberst von Radosin commits suicide. He is buried by his comrades Orvanyi,

Ludoltz, von Kaminski, Zierowitz, Sokal und Vanini. Everybody throws some earth into the grave accompanied with the words 'Earth from Hungary', 'Earth from Poland', Earth from Carinthia', 'Slovenian earth', 'Czech earth', 'Roman earth' while they pay their last respects to von Radosin. Finally, it is the turn of the Jewish army doctor Dr Grün who hesitates a moment but then throws the earth and says simply: 'Earth from Austria' (Spiel: 1988: 223).

For Spiel the ascent of Jewish participation in society is integrally linked with the ascent of liberalism which she sees to have developed in the early part of the nineteenth century and to have been universally accepted from 1848 onwards (Spiel 1988: 41). Spiel realizes that the irrational reverence for German culture above any others created problems for the Jewish intellegentsia and that the *laissez-faire* policy linked to nineteenth-century liberalism led to economic chaos like the stock market crash on 9 May 1873. This interrupted the liberal phase for a decade. After the recovery in 1883 a polarization occurred in Austrian society. On the one hand, there was, according to Spiel, the liberal, anticlerical, rational bourgeoisie and, on the other hand, there were the lower classes who had been turned to racial hatred by the nationalist parties and the clergy.

Die Früchte des Wohlstands (1981) portrays this division as well as the possibility for a multicultural society. In the extracts of her diary which were published in 1988 she writes in her entry for 2 February 1942: 'Arbeit am Roman. Ich mag ihn, aber was wird man dazu sagen? Es ist doch au fond eine Unverschämtheit, das Buch auf Englisch zu schreiben' (Spiel quoted in Strickhausen 1990: 31). Indeed, it seems strange to imagine a young Austrian exile going to the British library in London to research nineteenth-century Austrian history.

The novel has three main strands: firstly, the history of an assimilated Viennese Jewish family, secondly, the crisis of the liberal bourgeoisie, and thirdly, the consequences of Austria's rapid industrialization. The narrative is framed by two historical events, the world exhibition in Vienna in 1873 and the burning of the Ringtheater in 1881. Stephanie and Milan embody the generation in which the fruits of prosperity seem ripe and ready to be picked. Stephanie's family comes from an assimilated Jewish background, her father Carl Benedict had come to Vienna from Moravia in 1843 with high hopes of becoming a teacher or a doctor. As no university would accept him because of his Jewish background, he became a textile merchant. Although his career turned out to be successful and prosperous Carl Benedict always regretted that he was not allowed to enter a profession and that 'Dieser klare Geist, dieser tiefe Ernst, diese Entschlossenheit ... nichts anderem dienen [sollten] als dem Schacher mit Waren' (*Die Früchte des Wohlstands*: 40). As a consequence he has high hopes for his children. His wife Marie comes from an even older assimilated family and despises her husband's trade to a certain extent although she is happy to use the money he earns to pay for her own taste in fine art and music. Milan, on the other hand, comes from a Croatian farming family. His family is not poor, either, but his circumstances and education are necessarily very different to Stephanie's. As a younger son from a rural background he travels to Vienna to seek his fortune. Contrary to the newly arrived Carl Benedict in the 1840s, Milan, in the 1870s, has no feigned or genuine aspirations to look for anything but wealth.

Rapid industrialization has brought wealth to Vienna and the world exhibition is only one outward sign of this development albeit the most obvious one. The negative aspect of increasing industrialization is the rapid, often destructive pace of modern life and the corrupt business men who make their profit from other people's misfortune. Spiel shows how the little investors are ruined and how the profiteers are often to be found in public offices. As an image for growing industrialization Spiel uses the railways which cut through the landscape and interrupt the social order in all provinces of the Habsburg Empire but at the same time bring the different parts of Austria closer together:

> In jenem Jahr rollten viele Züge.
> Sie rollten durch das träge, mährische Flachland, das stille, satte, pflaumenfarbige Slawonien, durch die ungarische Ebene, die blau im Himmel verrann, und durch die grünen und goldenen steirischen Wälder.
> Die Züge bäumten sich auf. Viehherden längs der Schienen, noch ungewohnt des Lärms, der durch ihre Weiden riß, stoben verstört davon. Bauern, die Furchen tretend hinter ihren schweren Gäulen, beschatteten die Augen mit der Hand und starrten. Die Züge, dampfend und zischend von feurigem Rauch, stampften durch den hellen Tag, durch die stille, sternenlichte Nacht, dahin zur Stadt, zur Stadt, zur fernen Stadt des Kaisers. (*Die Früchte des Wohlstands*: 5)

A train carries Milan to his hopeful future in Vienna, but the railway brings about his near downfall as well. He is conned out of all his money by a dubious investment in the Galician railway. Although his loss is due to a criminal profiteer, even respectable investors like Carl Benedict lose money due to the fall in value of railway shares after the stockmarket crash in 1873. Ultimately though, the financial chaos manages to bring people of different ethnic and social backgrounds together such as Milan and Carl Benedict. Milan starts working for Carl and as he is a child of the new era, a natural salesperson with his eyes firmly on success, he rises fast in Benedict's firm and eventually even marries his daughter Stephanie. It is really the boom and bust atmosphere which weakens old, hierarchical structures and works in favour of a certain kind of multiculturalism.

It has been argued that Spiel is advocating a natural homogeneity of the Habsburg monarchy without any conflicts (Fliedl 1995: 125). In my opinion this is not really the case. Spiel rightly points out that the economic success of the Habsburg empire did contribute to keeping it together in the later decades of the nineteenth century. This worked not only in the geographical sense but also to pacify middle-class subjects such as the Benedicts for whom economic success acted as a substitute for liberal freedom and real political participation. Actual conflicts are incorporated in the novel. Milan's brother-in-law has to give up his position in the civil service because of national and ethnic problems and Milan has to lend him money. The most broadly illustrated conflict is the fate of the Orthodox Jew Simon Wolf who was at one point Milan's teacher. It is shown how the less fortunate in the new society are looking more and more for scapegoats. Antisemitic and nationalistic thinking spreads among these groups. Simon Wolf is beaten up by a group of young thugs and the police turn out to be more sympathetic to the perpetrators than to the victim.

Carl Benedict and Milan behave charitably towards Wolf and employ him in their enterprise as an accountant. It is made clear that charity in the end remains useless in view of the increasing differences in wealth and opportunity in society. Ethnic separatist tendencies are suppressed which leads to political radicalism rather than a solution of the conflicts. The political structure is shown to encourage the search for scapegoats rather than reform. In turn, it is first and foremost the Jewish industrialists who are blamed for the social injustices. Hilde Spiel shows the intertwining of social and economic factors well, although she sometimes seems to idealize rural life – the escape to Milan's hometown in Croatia is shown as their only chance to escape the hedonistic ways of city life – or to schematize people from the provinces like Milan. The possibilities of nineteenth-century Austrian multiculturalism such as social and ethnic mobility are exemplified by the main characters in the novel. At the same time she shows its limits: the widening economic division in society ultimately prevents the functioning of a multicultural Austria. Spiel explains the inconsistency of the political system and its ruler which opens up and closes down opportunities at the same time:

> Das österreichische Pendel schwang in diesem Jahr 1876 so munter wie eh und je. Wie immer schlug es ein wenig heftig nach der ungarischen Seite aus... Es war eine konfuse, eine unzulängliche Staatskonzeption. Bald sollte sie ein neues Jahrhundert durch Methoden ersetzen, die dem Staate weit wirksamer dienten als die Politik des Irgendwie. Gemessen an dem Leid, das diese neue Ordnung über die Menschheit bringen sollte, waren die Leiden der alten Schlamperei freilech nur Nadelstiche. (*Die Früchte des Wohlstands*: 164)

In this way Spiel connects nineteenth century Austrian history with the contemporary events in Europe. Other references include singers marching into Vienna singing 'Die Wacht am Rhein' being cheered or booed by the watching crowds. This incident induces the Jewish bourgeoisie to have visions of 'zerbrochene Fensterscheiben, niedergetrampelte Zäune, eingestoßene Türen, in deren Öffnung ein Gewehrknauf erscheint, eine heulende Menge' (278).

But this connection was not obvious enough for the British publishers. While novels directly relating to the rise of National Socialism frequently found publishers – as indeed *Flute and Drums* had – this novel remained unpublished until 1981. It was published one year after *Mirko und Franca* which was written as a filmscript in the 1970s, made into a film in 1979 and was broadcast for the first time on Austrian television on 27 November 1986. The filmscript was turned into the novella by Spiel herself after the film had been made. This might account for the simplicity of the language which indicates more than it describes (Strickhausen 1996: 303).

Mirko und Franca (1980) is set in Trieste which has a very multicultural history. The novel works on three levels: firstly, it shows the history of the city under its various influences and their consequences on the present political situation. Secondly, it features the love story between the young Mirko from Koper in Yugoslavia and the Italian girl Franca. Franca suffers from mental illness which is the connection to the third level of the novel, the investigation into modern psychiatric treatment.

Hilde Spiel wrote *Mirko und Franca* after she had returned to Austria. In both *Anna & Anna* and the second part of her autobiography *Welche Welt ist meine Welt?* (1990) she explains the gap between those who went away and those who stayed behind and the impossibility of bridging it again. The critic Rita Mielke describes the emotional state of the returning exile as feeling very close and very far away at the same time and the sense of resolve to fight against prejudice and fixed hierarchical structures which this experience produces (Mielke 1994: 140). This ambiguous state is embodied by the coastal city of Trieste which after the Second World War belongs to Italy, but the majority of the surrounding countryside is Yugoslavian. Right at the beginning of the book the post-war state is made clear as the Yugoslavs come across the border to Trieste on Saturdays to buy what they cannot purchase at home. The main protagonist Mirko is part of the weekly shopping migration. It is shown how the people of Trieste fear a Balkanization of their city while at the same time needing the trade from the incoming buyers because there is not much other economic activity left. The Yugoslavs and Mirko, as the singled out representative, are shown as a little coarse but active and dynamic whereas the Trieste of the 1970s and its inhabitants are relics from the past. The foster father of Franca, the Commendatore Bauer-Bonfante is – like his name – still inherently linked to the old Austrian monarchy. Franca's past – she has been physically abused by her stepmother and sexually abused by her father – keeps her trapped so that the Commendatore suggests to Mirko: 'Franca hat keine Zukunft. Keine vorhersehbare jedenfalls' (*Mirko und Franca*: 23). In this way Spiel keeps the love story between the two young people interwoven with the history of the city.

After their first brief encounter Mirko wants to meet Franca again and eventually the Commendatore allows him to do so. Spiel uses the Commendatore's description of the way to his villa for an exposé on the eventful history of Trieste: 'Es fahre eine Tram nach Opicina... An der Piazza Oberdan könne er sie erreichen... Oberdan. Ein Name aus der Geschichte dieser Stadt' (*Mirko und Franca*: 26). Trieste still offers the background for such disparate people as the patriarchal monarchist Bauer-Bonfante, the naive genius Mirko, the abused Italian girl Franca, the gallery owner Guiseppina and the chic Graziella to meet. It is of course the sometimes naive Mirko who believes in a positive outcome: 'Was nicht ganz tot ist, kann man doch zum Leben erwecken' (*Mirko und Franca*: 46). Here, the third level of the novel comes in: the Italian psychiatrist Franco Basaglia who reformed psychiatric hospitals from being enclosed mental asylums to places for open, patient- and community-centred care. Franca is one of those patients who would have been locked up before but is now allowed to live under the care of the Commendatore. The problem with this kind of care is the overprotective nature with which the Commendatore bestows it. This is not really what Basaglia's reform movement advocated. According to the psychiatrist the patients should learn to come to terms with his or her traumatic past and this process is vital for their recovery (*Mirko und Franca*: 116f).

Can there be parallels between two novels which are set more than a hundred years apart and were written more than thirty years apart? I would like to argue that they are both part of Hilde Spiel's lifelong project on multiculturalism and that they also indicate her way of dealing with history and narration. Spiel wants to show that European history has always been multicultural while being antisemitic, racist, class bound and misogynist at the same time. Additionally Hilde Spiel's historical narration does not only focus on political developments on a large scale but also on individuals' stories. Although the novels are very different, parallels can be drawn between the way the relationships between the male and the female main characters in both novels are interwoven with the ideal of multiculturalism.

In *Die Früchte des Wohlstands* the Viennese upper-middle-class Jewish woman Stephanie does marry Milan from a Croatian farming background but their relationship is difficult. Stephanie does not love Milan but succumbs to her father's will. He hopes that the marriage will help Stephanie 'den Fluch meiner Rasse abzustreifen' (*Die Früchte des Wohlstands*: 132). In the same way for Milan it is probably not love but obtaining what has seemed unobtainable – to be accepted by the rich urban family to such an extent that he can marry one of its members – that makes him marry Stephanie. For the majority of the plot their relationship is not very successful due to their disparate backgrounds and expectations. Stephanie fantasizes about the young composer with whom she had been romantically involved. Milan finds comfort in the arms of big blonde women. Only when they finally manage to communicate with each other does their relationship start to have a chance to develop.

In *Mirko und Franca* it is also the lack of communication which hinders the two lovers – again from very different backgrounds – to have a successful relationship. Mirko is not told about Franca's traumatic past and therefore makes a series of wrong assumptions which lead to him having a relationship with the flamboyant Graziella. Franca has a relapse and Mirko withdraws from the artistic community in Trieste completely. Only when Franca starts talking about her background do things begin to look better. It can be argued that Spiel sees communication and the ability to face up to personal and historical past as the ultimate prerequisites for a possible multicultural society.

The two novels have very different endings: Stephanie and Milan perish during the burning of the Ringtheater in Vienna while Mirko and Franca end up sitting on the patio of a country house talking with each other about their past lives. The negative ending of *Die Früchte des Wohlstands* is motivated by the incomplete understanding between Milan and Stephanie – Milan never really accepts her as a Jewish woman – but also by the description of political reality: the incomplete understanding of the political structure of the Habsburg Empire as well as the lack of communication between different ethnic and social groups. It is also noteworthy that this novel was written during the Second World War while millions were being murdered by the Nazis. In the end it shows the destruction of a multiculturalism which never managed to understand its own dynamics and therefore had no chance to survive. It is perhaps easier to dissect Austrian nineteenth-century multiculturalism, but Spiel tries to use this knowledge and especially her exile experience to show more contemporary possibilities: with regard to the Second World War she manages to consider the fault of Austria as well as the sins against Austria. In *Mirko und Franca* she portrays the divisions between Eastern and Western Europe, between communism and capitalism while at the same time narrating a very private love story. In this novella there is an open ending with a tentative indication of hope.

Spiel's understanding of the failure of pre-war Austria was that multiculturalism was not the product of bombastic economic expansion but something as fragile and human as the exile experience she was undergoing. Her insistence on fully remembering the Moscow Declaration came with the realization that only by criticizing the barren Austria that had been could the multicultural seeds distilled by the exile process return with the chance of growing.

The real quality of both books lies in the author's demand for communication at both levels – public and private. Hilde Spiel's idea of a multicultural society would have included people from different backgrounds and with different histories actually talking to each other. At the same time she does not neglect the importance of societal structures which must be able to facilitate such communication. In her stories Spiel shows us that multicultural society has to come to terms with the past. If the European people cannot come to terms with the whole of European history, the negative as well as the positive moments, then there is no future. Hilde Spiel considered herself 'eine Europäerin auf der steten Suche nach der verbindenden Erläuterung, dem einenden Wort' (quoted in Mielke 1994: 138); her personal story as well as her fictional stories might just be one of the important parts of European history which have been neglected for too long.

Bibliography

Amann, Klaus. 1984. P.E.N. *Politik Emigration Nationalsozialismus. Ein österreichischer Schriftstellerclub*, Vienna, Hermann Böhlaus Nachfahren
Berkely, George E. 1988. *Vienna and its Jews*, Cambridge (MA), Abt Books
Fliedl, Konstanze. 1995. 'Hilde Spiel's Linguistic Rights of Residence', in Robertson, R. & Timms, E. (eds), *Austrian Exodus*, Edinburgh University Press
Linsel, Anne. 1992. *Hilde Spiel Die Grande Dame: Gespräch mit Anne Linsel*, 'Zeugen des Jahrhunderts', Ingo Hermann (ed.), Göttingen, Lamuv Verlag
Mielke, Rita. 1994. 'Nachwort', in Spiel 1994: 138-48
Spiel, Hilde. 1976. *Kleine Schritte*, Munich, Ellermann Verlag
—. 1987. *Vienna's Golden Autumn*, London, Weidenfeld and Nicolson
—. 1988. *Glanz und Untergang. Wien 1866-1938*, tr. Hanna Neves, Munich, Paul List Verlag
—. 1989. *Anna & Anna*, Vienna, Kreymayr und Scheriau
—. 1991a. *Die hellen und die finsteren Zeiten*, Reinbek, Rowohlt Verlag
—. 1991b. *Die Früchte des Wohlstands*, Frankfurt am Main, Ullstein Verlag
—. 1994. *Mirko und Franca*, Frankfurt am Main, Ullstein Verlag
Strickhausen, Waltraud. 1989. 'Im Zwiespalt zwischen Literatur und Publizistik. Deutungsversuch zum Gattungswechsel im Werk der Exilautorin Hilde Spiel', *Publizistik im Exil und andere Themen: Exilforschung*, 7, Munich, edition text und kritik
—. 1990. 'Hilde Spiels historischer Roman *Die Früchte des Wohlstands*', *Exil*, 10

—. 1996. *Die Erzählerin Hilde Spiel oder 'Der weite Wurf in die Finsternis'*, New York, Peter Lang

Timms, Edward. 1995. (unpublished) 'Austrian Literature in a Schizophrenic Age: Exile and Reintegration', paper presented at a conference on 'Austria 1945-1995: Fifty Years of the Second Republic', European Institute, London School of Economics

Marginalization and Memories:
Ceija Stojka's Autobiographical Writing

Susan Tebbutt

1) The Hybridity of Culture

In *The Location of Culture* (1994) Homi Bhabha argues that culture is located at the periphery, at the intersection of the paths of people of different cultures. Identity is not merely constructed in terms of membership of one nation, but exists at the intersection of many boundaries, in terms of gender, religion or ethnic group. The articulation of cultural differences involves an awareness of these subject positions and the border areas where different cultural groups within a society intersect and interact. Bhabha argues: 'It is only when we understand that all cultural statements and systems are constructed in this contradictory and ambivalent space of enunciation, that we begin to understand why hierarchical claims to the inherent originality or 'purity' of cultures are untenable, even before we resort to empirical historical instances that demonstrate their hybridity' (Bhabha 1994: 37).

Scant attention has been paid by British Germanists to the hybridity of contemporary Austrian writing. Austrian women have been marginalized, and almost no attention at all has been paid to works in the last quarter of the twentieth century by women writers from ethnic minority groups in Austria.[1] Zeyringer (1992), who emphasizes the Herculean task of selecting representative works for his overview of Austrian literature in the 1980s, tries to include a wide range of writers, but does not make any reference to Ceija Stojka (born 1933), who is the first Austrian woman writer of Roma origin.[2] I would like to focus here on Stojka's two autobiographical works, firstly *Wir leben im Verborgenen: Erinnerungen einer Rom-Zigeunerin* (1988), in which she narrates her memories of the Holocaust, and secondly *Reisende auf dieser Welt: Aus dem Leben einer Rom-Zigeunerin* (1992), where the emphasis is on the post-war years. In order to appreciate Stojka's work it is necessary to look first at how the Roma have been marginalized in Austrian society and literature.

2) Roma in Austria: a Socially Marginalized Group

Today there are between 20,000 and 25,000 Roma/Gypsies living in Austria (Liégeois and Gheorghe 1995: 7), with the largest number living in the Burgenland.[3] Persecution of the group dates back many centuries and reached its zenith in the Nazi period, when pressures on the Gypsies (who were seen as 'asocial') mounted. From 1939 onwards Austrian Gypsies were rounded up and sent to concentration camps like Dachau, Buchenwald and Ravensbrück, or to Mauthausen in Austria itself. In December 1942 Himmler decreed that all those remaining in Europe of mixed Gypsy blood should be deported to Auschwitz, and from March 1943 Sinti and Roma were sent to the so-called 'Gypsy camp' in Auschwitz-Birkenau, which was finally dissolved on 2 August 1944, with 3,000 Gypsies murdered on the night of 2/3 August 1944. Of all the concentration camps, Auschwitz had the largest population of Gypsies from all over Nazi-occupied Europe. In total, some half a million European Roma were murdered in the Holocaust, of whom almost 7,000 came from Austria.[4]

In Austria, as in most European countries, the marginalization of Gypsies did not cease at the end of the war. It is only in the 1990s that the Austrian authorities have begun to re-examine the Nazi period of their history and acknowledge their complicity in the genocide of the Roma minority. Although the Austrian government now recognizes the Roma as an ethnic minority group, anti-Gypsyism is still rampant in the country, as manifest in the 1995 bomb attacks in the Burgenland, in which four members of the Roma ethnic group died.[5] It is against this background of persecution, discrimination and misconceptions that I would like to look at the representation of Gypsies/Roma in literature.

3) Images of Gypsies/Roma in Literature

'Gypsies' have traditionally been portrayed in literature by non-Gypsies as demonic or exotic creatures, and are generally seen in stereotypical terms rather than as individual members of an ethnic group with its own history, tradition and culture.[6] Austrian writing by 'Gypsies' cannot be seen as yet another example of *Migrantenliteratur*[7] since the majority of Roma in Austria are not migrants at all, but Austrian citizens whose families have lived in the country for generations, if not centuries.

Only a dozen or so works exist in German by members of the Roma community. This is due in part to the fact that Romani is an oral language without a standardized written form, and there is thus no tradition of writers proficient in writing in their mother tongue who might then choose to write in German. It can also be explained by the fact that until the early twentieth century the majority of Roma led a nomadic life and were unable to read or write. Although the Roma find themselves between two cultures, just like the migrant writers, they themselves actually belong to both cultures. Stojka is breaking new ground in the history of Austrian literature in that she offers insights not only into the Roma culture and perspective but also into the border areas where the experiences of minority and majority community overlap.[8]

4) Ceija Stojka's Memories

Although story-telling and music formed an important part of her childhood, Ceija Stojka did not come from a family with a tradition of writing, and was in fact herself banned by the Nazis from attending school. After 1945 she returned to school voluntarily and learnt the rudiments of reading and writing. Her writing is driven by the strong desire to communicate about her ethnic group and its experiences. In her first work, *Wir leben im Verborgenen*, written over forty years after the end of the war, when she felt she could no longer remain silent about the past, the key theme is the persecution of Roma during the Nazi period. *Reisende auf dieser Welt*, whilst also dealing with specific Roma issues, is more personal in tone, and reflects on problems, such as the drug addiction of her son, which are not peculiar to members of the Roma community. Both works are edited by free-lance writer Karin Berger and include transcripts of Berger's interviews with Stojka. In *Wir leben im Verborgenen* Berger asks Stojka numerous questions, not only about the Holocaust but also about her childhood and upbringing, the nomadic way of life, the Romani language, and attitudes to Roma today, whereas in *Reisende auf dieser Welt* the dialogue revolves almost exclusively round Stojka's growing interest in promoting Roma music. I would like to look at the ways in which the different facets of Stojka's identity as a Roma, a woman and an Austrian are reflected and interwoven in her writing, examining the intersection between the Roma minority and the majority society (it is important to stress that this is not a Roma/Austrian clash, since Stojka is both a Roma and Austrian). I will then look at the feminine perspective in Stojka's writing, and finally at the ways in which she highlights her Austrianness and her sense of *Heimat* and reflects on the act and purpose of writing.

4.1) The Minority Perspective

Stojka begins *Wir leben im Verborgenen* with the words: '1939 fuhren wir Rom noch mit Wagen und Pferden frei in Österreich herum' (15). There is no sense of conflict between the minority and majority community. The contrast between these relatively care-free days and the later years of persecution, fear, and terror is stark. 1939 was the year when the introduction of new laws meant that Gypsies were prevented from moving from town to town. Stojka describes vividly how members of her family were effectively caged in like dangerous animals: 'Die Gestapo legte ein spanisches Gitter um unser kleines Holzhaus und verbot uns, uns außerhalb dieses Gitters aufzuhalten. Ja, wir spürten Auschwitz schon in der Freiheit' (17). Suddenly the family was 'nirgends mehr sicher' (18), the number of police raids increased drastically, and the Gypsies were rounded up and deported to labour and concentration camps.

Given that the Romani language is traditionally treated by its users as a type of 'secret language', and speakers are generally reluctant to reveal it to outsiders, it is striking that on over a dozen occasions Ceija quotes what her mother said in Romani, usually at moments of high tension or despair, when her mother is praying to God for the safety and survival of her children and trying to reassure them. Once in Auschwitz and behind the electrically-charged barbed wire fence, the mother says in Romani: '"*Chutilen dume mindig gaj murie zocha.*" (Haltet euch immer an mir fest.) Die SS-Männer schrien: "Im Laufschritt Marsch", sie schlugen uns auf den Rücken und preßten uns dann in eine Baracke' (*Wir leben im Verborgenen*: 21). The warmth and humanity of the mother is in stark contrast to the brutal behaviour of the SS. When the family arrives at Bergen-Belsen, the first impressions are horrific: 'Gleich hinter dem Tor lagen ein paar Tote, der Brustkorb war ihnen aufgeschlitzt, Herz und Leber fehlten ihnen. Mama sagte; "*Na da ra murie scheej!*" (Keine Angst, mein Kind.) Nur ein paar Schritte vor der Baracke lagen die Toten, daß man sie gar nicht zählen konnte, einer über dem anderen, jung und alt, manche lebten auch noch' (56). After the murder of Ceija's father in Dachau his remains are returned in an urn, and her mother puts the bones in a handkerchief and ties it round her neck, but the cloth and its contents are later confiscated by the Nazis, who show as little sensitivity here as they do when asked to allow a three-day wake. Ignorance of and insensitivity to the culture of the Roma is prevalent.

Ceija Stojka had the number Z6399 (Z standing for *Zigeuner*) tattooed on her arm. Like the Jews, the Gypsies/Roma were persecuted, classified and dehumanized during the Nazi regime, but whereas there are numerous literary representations of the experiences of Jews, the experiences of Gypsies have been so marginalized by historians and authors that it would be easy to forget the genocide of half a million Roma in the Holocaust. The tattoo constitutes an all-too-visible reminder of the persecution of Stojka's ethnic group.

The facts relating to illness, disease, deprivation, hunger, maltreatment, beating and abuse in Auschwitz, Ravensbrück and Bergen-Belsen are in many respects similar to those to be found in other female survivors' testimonials[9], but Stojka's account is remarkable for its explicit and uncompromising descriptions of the suffering. She portrays the way in which the Nazis deprive their victims of all human dignity, even when the victims are dead, recalling the stench of the rotting corpses lying by the massive latrine: 'Dort sind immer die Toten gelegen, oft mit dem Gesicht zur Wand, mit offenem Mund, und die Scheiße ist ihnen hinein. Wenn ein Mensch normal stirbt, sogar unter einem Leid stirbt, dann hat er wenigstens noch eine gewisse Würde in sich' (*Wir leben im Verborgenen*: 99). It is important to note that Stojka does not only portray her minority group as victims. She skilfully deconstructs the stereotypical image of the Roma as thief, showing how concentration camp inmates may be reduced to stealing the blanket covering a dead body, because their need is so great. Roma may thus occasionally resort to thieving, but the criminal act must be understood in its wider socio-historical context.

What images are conveyed of Roma after the war? In the opening pages of *Reisende auf dieser Welt* it appears as if the Roma who survived the Holocaust returned to Austria to lead an idyllic life in harmony with nature, without a care in the world:

> Gemeinsam kamen wir in Wien gut an. An einem schönen Platz, dicht neben dem Prater, machten wir Rast. Dort lagerten schon mehrere Roma, insgesamt drei Familien.... Ohne lange zu fragen, machten die Frauen ein großes Lagerfeuer.... Das Lagerfeuer leuchtete und funkelte, und aus den Töpfen drangen die wunderbarsten Düfte. Später wurde eine große Decke auf das grüne Gras gebreitet, darüber kam ein weißes Tischtuch. Das Essen wurde in die Mitte gestellt, und jeder konnte sich nehmen soviel er wollte. (*Reisende auf dieser Welt*: 19)

Despite these very harmonious, romantic images of the ethnic group (in which it is striking how Stojka never questions the male and female roles), the continuity of anti-Gypsyism in the post-war period is incontrovertible. Prejudice may no longer be officially sanctioned at government level, but is still widespread at a personal level. Stojka often has to put up with insensitive, offensive comments, be they triggered by the tattoo on her arm: 'Na, Sie ham aber a scheene Telefonnummer!' (*Wir leben im Verborgenen*: 104), or simply out of the blue. She recounts an incident in the market when she has just received 150 eggs. A total stranger hurls verbal abuse at her: 'Du dreckige Zigeunerin, du lebst noch? Dich hat der Hitler vergessen!' and then smashes all the eggs to pieces (104).

Stojka is particularly worried about how her children may be subject to discriminatory treatment: 'Solang man nicht weiß, daß sie [the children] Zigeuner sind, ist alles okay. Aber wie es jemand erfährt, ist es vorbei', and also recounts how such prejudices can be held by the very young: 'Wie meine Enkelin in der Schule gesagt hat, sie ist eine Zigeunerin, haben die Kinder geglaubt, sie ist eine Hexe und macht etwas Böses' (*Wir leben im Verborgenen*: 148). This is a telling example of how even in the last quarter of the twentieth century many people are misinformed about the Roma minority, associating 'Gypsies' with the possession of supernatural evil powers.

Discrimination at work is also prevalent. Stojka explains how one of her nieces does not dare to admit in public that she is a Roma: 'Ich schwör dir, sie ist eine gute Sekretärin, alle haben sie gern, aber wenn die wissen würden, sie ist eine Zigeunerin, wäre sie keine drei Wochen mehr dort' (*Wir leben im Verborgenen*: 149). She also recounts how some members of the Roma community may even adopt the tactic of passing themselves off as Persian or

Yugoslavian when looking for a job, hoping to avoid discrimination. In *Wir leben im Verborgenen* Stojka exposes the oppression of the minority by the majority community, whereas in *Reisende auf dieser Welt* she is concerned to establish her ethnic group as an important cultural force, rather than as an oppressed group: 'Man hat uns [the Roma] für Vielerlei gebraucht. Man hat dieses Romantische gebraucht, das Verträumte, Verspielte, man hat unsere Tänze und unsere Musik gebraucht. Und das seit hunderten Jahren, aber kein Mensch kennt und weiß etwas von den Leuten, die diese Musik gemacht haben.... Wer soll unsere Kultur weitertragen? Ich bin bereit, ich mache es' (*Reisende auf dieser Welt*: 172).

Surprisingly, Stojka expresses an understanding of the behaviour of neo-Nazis: 'Sie [the neo-Nazis] müssen "Heil" schreien, um sich zu bestätigen. Nur so hat man Ehrfurcht vor ihnen, denn sonst wären sie ja ganz normale Bürger. Für mich sind sie Wesen ohne Seele, ich bedaure sie' (*Reisende auf dieser Welt*: 173). She feels that it is the Roma who need to change and be more willing to defend themselves:

> Ich sage, die Rom hier in Österreich nehmen sehr wenig Stellung zu ihrer Person, sie verteidigen sich nicht. Wenn sie jetzt hören, daß zum Beispiel ein Gadjo [non-Gypsy] sagt: Der Scheiß-Zigeuner, dann könnte ihm der Zigeuner ja sagen: Du, warum sagst du das? Ich sag zu dir ja auch nicht, du bist ein Zweitbezirkler oder du bist ein Gadjo von Aspang. Ich bin halt ein Zigeuner, na bitte. Aber viele übergehen solche Bemerkungen und tun, als hätten sie nichts gehört. Das finde ich falsch. (*Wir leben im Verborgenen*: 153)

Rather than expending energy on abusing right-wing extremists, she prefers to take a positive course of action and promote the Roma culture through its music. In the interviews with Karin Berger in *Reisende auf dieser Welt* collected under the title 'Solange es Roma gibt, werden sie singen', Stojka talks of the very strong sense of community, and how they spend whole evenings telling stories and singing: 'Unsere alten Lieder kann man nur so beschreiben, daß man sagt, für uns sind sie wie Gedichte. So wie sich ein anderer in Gedichtform ausdrückt, sich etwas Schweres von der Seele schreibt, so drücken wir uns in den Liedern aus. Die Roma konnten ja nicht lesen und schreiben' (*Reisende auf dieser Welt*: 140-1). In the same way that the songs express the culture of the group, so Stojka's own autobiographical writing helps to communicate a more differentiated image of the Roma.

4.2) Feminine Perspectives
Heinemann, in her doctoral dissertation on woman prose writers of the Holocaust (1981), argues that the best-known authors writing about the Holocaust are men,

and that the best known work by a female writer, the Diary of Anne Frank, 'stops short before the fate of the characters assumes the cataclysmic quality of the Holocaust experience' (Heinemann 1981: 290). Heinemann questions whether it is possible to isolate specifically female themes and a female style of writing, pointing out that the use of self-effacement rather than self-dramatization in autobiographical writing (often a feature of female writers' style) may be attributed to a refusal to take responsibility for surviving. When a Holocaust work is self-effacing, however, this may be due either to the female socialization of the author or to the Holocaust experience endured. Stojka is definitely self-effacing in her portrayal of suffering, and although she turns the spotlight on her mother (who assumes a pivotal role in the family after the death of the father), she does not over-dramatize the mother's actions either.

The impact of Hitler's racial policies on women is seen in the account of how sterilization is offered to the Roma women as an alternative to extermination. On the day when the sterilization is to be carried out there is no electricity, which Ceija's mother sees as an act of mercy on the part of God. Stojka makes the reader aware of the way in which the authorities were prepared to infringe the individual rights of women to make decisions about their own bodies.

Her experiences as a *daughter* and woman are represented in *Wir leben im Verborgenen*, but in *Reisende auf dieser Welt* it is primarily as a *mother* that she is writing, finding herself at the age of eighteen with two babies and no husband, reacting in a resilient and positive way, attempting to keep her family intact just as her own mother had. The portrayal of her desperate attempts to help her son Jano kick his addiction to drugs is extremely moving. On the first night of the treatment she sleeps at Jano's feet and sings to him in Romani and German, but on the second day she does not let him sleep, massages his body to get some colour back into him and even chews his food for him: 'Kleine Bissen Butterbrot mit Milch kaute ich und steckte sie ihm in den Mund. Ob er es bemerkte? Ich glaube nicht. Ich nahm einen Schluck Milch und ließ sie in seinen Mund hineinfließen' (*Reisende auf dieser Welt*: 82). Stojka is very open in her portrayal of Jano's addiction, and her account bears witness to the intensity of a mother's love for her son.

4.3) The Austrian Dimension
There is a strong sense of geographical location in both works, with frequent references to specific towns, streets and places, like the *Kongreßbad* in Vienna. Stojka was born in Austria, but like many members of minority groups had to adopt a pragmatic attitude when forced to leave her home country. It is striking that she refers to Auschwitz with bitter irony as the 'neue Heimat' (*Wir leben im Verborgenen*: 21).

Just as the inclusion of Romani makes her writing distinctive, so the Austrianness of her language is significant. The very names of the children, Hansi, Karli and Kurti, Mitzi and Ossi have the diminutive suffix -*i*, which immediately makes them sound Austrian. Stojka uses diminutive forms (or compounds including them) such as 'Strohflankerl' (*Wir leben im Verborgenen*: 57), 'Marterl', 'Schwammerlsuppe', 'Schößel', and 'Eßsackerl' (*Reisende auf dieser Welt*: 28, 47, 62 and 75). Austrian or South German words and expressions to do with food slip in unobtrusively, such as 'eine gute Jause', 'Guglhupf' and 'Kaiserschmarrn' (*Wir leben im Verborgenen*: 16, 49 and 78) or 'Melange' (white coffee) (*Reisende auf dieser Welt*: 70). The choice of words like 'Scheibtruhe' (wheelbarrow) and 'Krampen' (pick-axe) (*Wir leben im Verborgenen*: 32 and 60), 'Fauteuil' (armchair) (*Reisende auf dieser Welt*: 38) or the Austrian variants 'übernachtig', 'manchesmal', 'Zünder' (matches) and 'Tempelhüpfen' (hopscotch) (*Wir leben im Verborgenen*: 51, 63 and 44) all bear witness to Stojka's Austrian background. It is, however, not only in these individual words or phrases that Stojka's Austrian origins are evident. She describes her attempts to extract an identity card from an official in Jois, where her mother had lived, but 'in diesem kleinen Dorf Jois dachte damals niemand an die verschwundenen und nie zurückgekehrten Menschen' (*Reisende auf dieser Welt*: 32). In post-war Austria a veil had been drawn over the Roma murdered in the Holocaust, which enabled anti-Gypsyism to thrive. The official is quoted as saying: 'Mia san ka Bett'lamt und scho gor net für eich' (34-5).[10] The conversation is significant, because the dialect is not a barrier to Stojka's understanding, but the official does not identify with Stojka and considers her to be 'other', alien, different, inferior, whereas she perceives herself as both Roma and Austrian, and reminds the official that her mother had owned a house in the village.

4.4) Reflecting on Reflections

Like many other members of persecuted groups writing about the Holocaust, Stojka had not previously even discussed her experiences with close members of the family, and the act of narrating, although in many ways therapeutic, is also painful: 'Ich könnte dies nicht ein zweites Mal erzählen, denn in meinen Gedanken erlebe ich jetzt alles, als wäre es gestern passiert. Wenn ich alle meine Gedanken niederschreiben könnte, wäre dies sicher ein endloses Buch der Leiden. Doch meine Gedanken laufen schneller als meine Hände alles zu Papier bringen können' (*Wir leben im Verborgenen*: 20). In conversation with Karin Berger she reflects on the initial difficulties of narrating her memories: 'Papier ist geduldig.[11] Es hat mit dem Schreiben halt recht gehapert, aber wie ich einmal begonnen hab, sind die Erinnerungen nur so herausgeschossen' (*Wir leben im Verborgenen*: 97).

The immediacy of Stojka's account is evident in her description of how the writing affects her emotionally: 'Aber Auschwitz habe ich ein zweites Mal erlebt. Manchesmal hab ich sogar aufgeschaut und mir gedacht, Hilfe, der kommt jetzt auf mich zu mit seinen Stiefeln. Hoffentlich sieht er mich nicht' (*Wir leben im Verborgenen*: 98). Stojka is motivated to write about the Roma perspective on Auschwitz, because although she feels she has 'alles auf meinem Film im Kopf. Und der täuscht mich nicht' (102), it is important that the 'film' is processed into literary form, so non-Gypsies can appreciate just how an Austrian Roma woman experienced the Holocaust.

5) Conclusion

Given the alarming rise in the incidence of racist attacks on Roma in Austria in the 1990s, I feel it is important in any consideration of contemporary Austrian women's writing to recognize the contribution of Stojka's autobiographical writing, in order to highlight new images of a marginalized group whose members' identity and experiences are far from being homogeneous.

Stojka herself argues that: 'wir müssen hinausgehen, wir müssen uns öffnen, sonst kommt es noch so weit, daß irgendwann alle Romani in ein Loch hineinkippen' (*Wir leben im Verborgenen*: 154). Although many of her experiences are specific to members of the Roma community, Stojka is also writing from the point of view of an Austrian woman. Non-Roma readers may thus see her both as a Roma, as different, but also as a fellow woman or as a fellow Austrian. *Wir leben im Verborgenen* and *Reisende auf dieser Welt* reflect Ceija Stojka's position at the intersection of a number of identities and add to the richness of both Roma and Austrian culture.

Notes

[1] The two most scrutinized post-war Austrian writers are male, Thomas Bernhard and Peter Handke.

[2] Roma is the collective term for all members of the Romani community, but is also used specifically to refer to Roma of Eastern European origin. In the German-speaking countries the 'Gypsies' are referred to as 'Sinti' (Western European Roma, mainly living in Germany) and 'Roma'. The term 'Zigeuner' is rejected by most German-speaking Roma, since it became degraded during the Nazi period and associated with Hitler's racist policies.

[3] The statistics are for 1994 and are taken from Liégeois and Gheorghe (1995: 7). Figures include both Austrian Roma who have lived in the country for generations, and more recent arrivals from Eastern Europe.

Notes continued

[4] Some 90,000 Sinti and Roma from Yugoslavia, 35,000 from the USSR, 15,150 from France and 15,000 from Germany were among those murdered in concentration camps. The information is taken from Köpf (1994: 65). The actual number of fatalities is generally considered to be much higher than the official figures.

[5] Media interest soon subsided after the initial outrage.

[6] One of the very few exceptions is Erich Hackl's *Erzählung* entitled *Abschied von Sidonie* (1989), which is based on extensive research into the case of an Austrian Roma girl who was deported to and died in Auschwitz.

[7] *Migrantenliteratur*, originally referred to in Germany as *Gastarbeiterliteratur*, has become an important strand in contemporary German literature since the 1960s.

[8] There are few contemporary German-language works by Sinti or Roma, and only one by a German woman writer, *Zwischen Liebe und Haß: Ein Zigeunerleben* (1985) by Philomena Franz. Other works by Sinti in Germany are *Da wollten wir frei sein: Eine Sinti-Familie erzählt* (1983), recorded and edited by Michail Krausnick, and Alfred Lessing's picaresque autobiographical account of surviving the Holocaust, *Mein Leben im Versteck* (1993). Apart from Ceija Stojka, the only other Austrian Roma writer is her brother Karl, whose account *Auf der ganzen Welt zu Hause:* (1994) records key events over sixty years of his life.

[9] See for example the accounts of surviving Auschwitz by Kitty Hart (who was born in Poland) *Return to Auschwitz* (1981), by Helen Lewis (born in Czechoslovakia) *A Time to Speak* (1992) and Italian Giuliana Tedeschi, *There is a Place on Earth* (1992).

[10] The High German version of this utterance would be "Wir sind kein Bettelamt und schon gar nicht für euch".

[11] Anne Frank expressed the same sentiment in her diary.

Bibliography

Bhabha, Homi K. 1994. *The Location of Culture*, London, Routledge
Franz, Philomena. 1985. *Zwischen Liebe und Haß: Ein Zigeunerleben*, Freiburg, Herder
Fraser, Angus. 1995. *The Gypsies*, 2nd edn., Oxford, Blackwell
Hackl, Erich. 1989. *Abschied von Sidonie*, Zurich, Diogenes
Hart, Kitty. 1981. *Return to Auschwitz*, London, Sidgwick and Jackson

Heinemann, Marlene E. 1981. 'Women Prose Writers of the Nazi Holocaust', Ph. D. dissertation, Indiana University, Ann Arbor

Köpf, Peter. 1994. *Stichwort: Sinti und Roma*, Munich, Heyne

Krausnick, Michail (ed.). 1983. *'Da wollten wir frei sein!': Eine Sinti-Familie erzählt*, Weinheim, Beltz

Lessing, Alfred. 1993. *Mein Leben im Versteck: Wie ein deutscher Sinti den Holocaust überlebte*, Düsseldorf, Zebulon Verlag

Lewis, Helen. 1992. *A Time to Speak*, Belfast, Blackstaff

Liégeois, Jean-Pierre and Nicolae Gheorghe. 1995. *Roma/Gypsies: A European Minority*, London, Minority Rights Group

Stojka, Ceija. 1988. *Wir leben im Verborgenen: Erinnerungen einer Rom-Zigeunerin*, ed. Karin Berger, Vienna, Picus

—. 1992. *Reisende auf dieser Welt: Aus dem Leben einer Rom-Zigeunerin*, ed. Karin Berger, Vienna, Picus

Stojka, Karl and Reinhard Pohanka. 1994. *Auf der ganzen Welt zu Hause: Das Leben und Wandern des Zigeuners Karl Stojka*, Vienna, Picus

Tedeschi, Giuliana. 1992. *There is a Place on Earth* (orig. Italian 1988), tr. Tim Parks, London, Random House

Zeyringer, Klaus. 1992. *Innerlichkeit und Öffentlichkeit: Österreichische Literatur der achtziger Jahre*, Tübingen, Francke

Ruth Beckermann und die jüdische Nachkriegsgeneration in Österreich

Andrea Reiter

In einer Rezension von Ruth Beckermanns *Unzugehörig* heißt es abschließend: 'Erst nachdem diese jüdische Nachkriegsgeneration durch die typischen Stadien von Zionismus-Begeisterung und antifaschistischem Engagement gegangen war, konnte sie sich mit dem beschäftigen, worum es wirklich ging: Mit den Erfahrungen der Eltern und der Bedeutung der Judenverfolgung und -vernichtung für die Gesellschaft heute' (Heenen-Wolff 1990). Dieses Urteil, wiewohl auf den Essayband von 1989 gemünzt (*Unzugehörig. Österreicher und Juden nach 1945*: 119ff), trifft auf Beckermanns Biographie generell zu. Wie zu zeigen sein wird, ist sie geradezu ein Modellbeispiel für diese Entwicklung.

1952 als Kind jüdischer Überlebender des Holocausts in Wien geboren, spürte sie schon früh den Konflikt zwischen jüdischer Privatsphäre in der Familie und der nicht-jüdischen Öffentlichkeit. Einem Abenteuer gleich versuchte sie, in ihre Umgebung, die sie als spannend empfand, einzutauchen: 'Man wollte unbedingt dazugehören und gab die Schuld an den Schwierigkeiten, die man damit hatte, den Eltern. Die Rebellion gegen das Ghetto-Dasein der Eltern, wie wir ihre Zurückgezogenheit damals nannten, begann. Ihre Lebensweise war uns peinlich' (*Unzugehörig*: 119).[1]

Später, als Teen, schärfte die Lektüre Sartres den Blick für das eigene Anderssein. Die 'Réflexions sur la question Juive' gaben der Jugendlichen die Argumente zur Bestimmung des eigenen Standortes. Ferienaufenthalte in Israel begünstigten die Ausprägung romantisch-zionistischer Ideen und einer jüdischen Identität. Die Jahre 1968ff brachten eine erste Politisierung für die damals gerade 17jährige. Wie Beckermann in einem Interview bestätigt, wurde die Affiliation mit der Linken noch verstärkt durch ein späteres Ereignis, nämlich die 1976 mitgemachte Besetzung der Arena, des ehemaligen Schlachthofgeländes von St. Marx in Wien, und ihre Umwandlung in ein alternatives Kulturzentrum: Es gab 'eine Phase nach '68, in der Zeit der "Neuen Linken" wo ich meinte, inzwischen so angepaßt zu sein, daß alles Jüdische kein Problem mehr für mich wäre' (Bretschneider 1988: 34). Während Intellektuelle wie Jean Améry den in der Linken aufkeimenden Antizionismus schon früh als verkappten Antisemitismus durchschauten, dauerte das Rendezvouz der jüngeren Generation mit der Linken auch in Deutschland länger. In Österreich änderte 1986 der kontroversielle Präsidentschaftswahlkampf Kurt Waldheims schlagartig die Situation. Während 'alles, was mit der Zeit der Verfolgung zu tun hatte' für das Kind noch 'mit großer Angst und Scham verbunden' war, und aus diesem Grund auch die Eltern nicht darauf angesprochen wurden, brachten die Ereignisse der achtziger Jahre ein Umdenken. Erst dann, schreibt Beckermann, 'begannen wir, über solche Gefühle nachzudenken' (*Unzugehörig*: 120, 121). Die Zugehörigkeit war nicht mehr selbstverständlich politisch-ideologisch determiniert, sondern mußte neu erkämpft werden.

Der bis dahin in Österreich nur unterschwellige Antisemitismus manifestierte sich nun offen, nicht zuletzt auf höchster Politikerebene: Der damalige ÖVP-Minister Michael Graff ließ sich dazu hinreißen, den Präsidentschaftskandidaten seiner Partei zu exkulpieren, solange man ihm nicht nachweisen könne, daß er sechs Juden eigenhändig umgebracht habe. Die Führung das Wahlkampfes gegen die Einmischung des Jewish World Congress, der Waldheim der Kriegsverbrechen beschuldigte, galt der Mobilisierung des Volkszornes, wie auch Beckermann ihn in ihrem Film *Die papierene Brücke* festgehalten hat. Den Eindruck der Ereignisse auf die jüdische Minderheit in Österreich beschreibt die Autorin so: 'Die 1986 einsetzende antisemitische Welle rief ebenso die Erinnerung an die vielen nazistischen und antisemitischen Skandale der vergangenen vierzig Jahre hervor wie an persönliche Kränkungen, zu denen die meisten Juden geschwiegen hatten. Die Frage nach jüdischer Existenz in Österreich stellt(e) sich neu.' (*Unzugehörig*: 110) Auch das zwei Jahre später aus Anlaß der 50. Wiederkehr des November-Pogroms, der Kristallnacht, und des Anschlusses Österreichs an das Dritte Reich begangene sogenannte Bedenkjahr bewirkte eher die Verfestigung antisemitischer Ressentiments. Wie im Fall von Alfred Hrdlickas Holocaust-Denkmal auf dem Albertina-Platz, das einen knienden, straßenwaschenden Juden zeigt, geriet das öffentliche Gedenken leicht zur Demütigung derjenigen, derer gedacht werden sollte. Am Rande sei hier vermerkt, daß Ruth Beckermann ihre Kritik an diesem Denkmal bereits zu einem Zeitpunkt äußerte, als bei Politik und Kunstkritik noch eitel Freude darüber herrschte. Das Verhalten des Künstlers in der sogenannten 'Hrdlicka-Affäre' im vergangenen Jahr, ausgelöst durch Hrdlickas offenen Brief an Wolf Biermann, in dem er diesem als Reaktion auf die Kritik des Liedermachers an der aus der SED hervorgegangenen PDS und ihrem Vorsitzenden Gregor Gysi die 'Nürnberger Rassengesetze an den Hals' wünschte, hat zwar mit Beckermanns Kritik am Kunstwerk unmittelbar nichts zu tun, zeugt aber von demselben Mangel an Sensibilität des Künstlers, der sich auch in der Ästhetik seiner Skulptur niederschlug.[2] Nicht nur die historische Situation der Juden in Österreich (Spiel 1994) war bekanntlich anders als in Deutschland. Während die nationalsozialistische Vergangenheit die Verfassung und Politik der jungen Bundesrepublik Deutschland weitgehend prägten, die Schuld am Massenmord an den Juden einbekannt wurde und die Regierung eine bewußte Abgrenzung zur Vergangenheit vorgab, geschah in Österreich nichts dergleichen. Die Zweite Republik präsentierte sich überzeugend als erstes Opfer Hitlers, das als solches weder seine demokratische Glaubwürdigkeit unter Beweis zu stellen hatte, noch die Wiedergutmachung der Verbrechen an den Juden betreiben zu müssen glaubte. Dazu paßt, daß die Rückkehr der Emigranten (Matejka 1984) bzw. die Rückerstattung 'arisierten' Vermögens (Knight 1988) verzögert wurden.

Das offizielle Judentum in Österreich reagierte auf diese Situation damit, daß es sich ein *low profile* verordnete. Stillhalten statt Einmischen war bis in die jüngste Vergangenheit weitgehend die Parole (Embacher 1995), für die nicht zuletzt die Person Hans Weigels steht. Vor allem aber verhinderte die Zersplitterung innerhalb der Jüdischen Gemeinde aufgrund gegensätzlicher (auch politischer) Interessen eine wirksame Vertretung jüdischer Anliegen im Nachkriegsösterreich. Schon bevor der Waldheim-Wahlkampf den Antisemitismus in Österreich wieder an die Oberfläche spülte, entwickelten Ruth Beckermann und ihre Generation unter dem Eindruck des zunehmenden Antizionismus in der Linken eine Identität, die sich von der vorangehenden absetzt: Selbstbewußt nahmen sie ihr Anderssein nicht nur an, sondern faßten es nunmehr positiv, produktiv: 'Der Zerfall der Linken und unser spezielles Zerwürfnis mit ihr brachte uns endlich in die Nähe von uns selbst' (*Unzugehörig*: 126).

Ruth Beckermanns Weg von der Identifikation mit den 'Anderen' über den Zionismus, vom Aufgehen in der linken Ideologie zur (Neu-)Entdeckung des Judentums läßt sich auch als Phasen unterschiedlich empfundener Zugehörigkeit interpretieren. Als bewußte Jüdin und Frau führt sie heute ein Leben als Intellektuelle, die zwar, was das Geistige anbelangt, Österreich als ihre Heimat anerkennt, Zugehörigkeit aber nicht geographisch auffaßt. Geprägt von der österreichischen Kultur, insbesondere der Literatur der Jahrhundertwende, verbringt sie einen Teil des Jahres in Paris und macht nach wie vor viele Reisen. Daß diese allerdings auch mit ihrem Verhältnis zu Österreich, d.h. zu Wien, zu tun haben, verrät die Bemerkung, daß sie sich im Ausland nicht 'mit den Nuancen der Gemeinheit hier d.i. in Wien, die man genau spürt, weil man sie ja genau kennt, auseinandersetzen' müsse. 'In Frankreich gibt es genug Antisemitismus, aber der fällt mir nicht so auf. Ich verbinde damit nichts. Während natürlich hier jede Kleinigkeit ein ganzes Assoziationsfeld eröffnet' (Reiter 1996). Ralph Giordanos Zugehörigkeitsgefühl, das er durch die positive Resonanz auf seine Bücher, insbesondere *Die Bertinis*, in Deutschland bestätigt glaubt (Giordano 1992: 108ff; 119ff), empfindet Beckermann jedenfalls nicht. Aber auch Lea Fleischmanns kategorisches *Dies ist nicht mein Land* scheint sie nicht unterschreiben zu wollen. Es verwundert zwar nicht, daß sie nicht mehr an den Schutz als öffentliche Person glaubt, wie dies etwa Stefan Zweig noch tat. Dennoch hängt sie an dem Land ihrer Kindheit in ähnlicher Weise wie dieser. Ihr Zugehörigkeitsgefühl scheint, zumindest ursprünglich, eher dem Wolfgang

Hildesheimers vergleichbar zu sein, der sich an seine Verbundenheit mit dem Volk der Juden immer dann erinnert fühlte, wenn er einen traf (Schultz 1986: 225). Dies wurde ihr anläßlich ihrer Filmreise nach Osteuropa bewußt: Als 'Heimatsuche auf jüdisch' kommentiert sie in *Die papierene Brücke* ironisch ihre Emotionen anläßlich des koscheren Schächtens der Hühner durch den Rabbiner, dessen Zeugin sie wurde. Die Nähe zur Natur und die Selbstverständlichkeit der täglichen Verrichtungen erinnerten sie an Erfahrungen, die sie als Kind während der Ferien auf dem Land machte. Was das Heimatgefühl betrifft, so scheint sie es unter dem Einfluß ihres Vaters, der nach dem Krieg nach Wien kam, entwickelt zu haben. Ihre Mutter, die aus der Emigration in Israel ins Nachkriegsösterreich zurückkehrte, habe diesen Aufenthalt dagegen als lediglich provisorisch und temporär aufgefaßt. Auf sie trifft auch zu, was die Tochter in *Unzugehörig* generell für die Juden im Österreich nach 1945 feststellt: 'Eine innere Entscheidung dafür, ein klares Ja zum Hierbleiben gab es nicht' (*Unzugehörig*: 102f; 1987).

Die Identität des Kindes prägte dieser Umstand dahingehend, daß es zunehmend 'das Leben im Land der Mörder und in der Nähe der Toten ... [als] einen paradoxen psychischen Vorteil' aufzufassen begann. Es wirkte 'wie eine Garantie des Nicht-Vergessens' (*Unzugehörig*: 126). Und da war noch ein Grund: 'In gewisser Weise', glaubt Beckermann, schütze der Antisemitismus 'vor der Konfrontation mit der Überlebensschuld und vor der unerträglichen Frage nach dem Sinn des Lebens nach dem Überleben' (127).

Ruth Beckermann, Jüdin und Frau, verbindet wie Anna Mitgutsch (1995: 17f)[3] mit der Besinnung auf das Judentum keine feministische Position. Nur im Negativen gebe es 'eine Verbindung zwischen Feminismus und Antisemitismus, bei Weininger und auch bei anderen. Es gibt aber auch den Antisemitismus in der Frauenbewegung und den Antifeminismus bei den Juden' (Beckermann in Reiter 1996). In ihrer Rezension von *Unzugehörig* kritisierte Erica Fischer, daß die Autorin nur von 'Juden', nicht aber von 'Jüdinnen' spreche (Fischer 1989: 9). Dem ist entgegenzuhalten, daß die Isolierung der Minderheit der Frauen innerhalb der jüdischen Minderheit diese zusätzlich schwächen würde. Instinktiv scheint Beckermann sich diesem Problem zu verweigern, das freilich die Stellung der jüdischen Frauen in der Diaspora generell betrifft.

Welche literarischen Formen entsprechen nun der kritischen Auseinandersetzung mit der eigenen Identität und mit Österreich? Für Beckermann begann sie mit einem historischen Essay, der das Buch *Die Mazzesinsel* einleitet und der der untergegangenen Welt der Juden in der Wiener Leopoldstadt nachspürt. Bis in die Entwicklung des Filmessays sollte dieses Genre in den nächsten Jahren zu Beckermanns bevorzugtem werden, einen Umstand, den sie auch im Gespräch reflektiert:

> Ich glaube, daß ich einen persönlichen Bezug brauche, wenn ich etwas schreibe. Mein Zugang ist kein wissenschaftlich-objektiver, sondern ein sehr subjektiver. Das kann man entweder unterdrücken oder man kann es für sich fruchtbar machen.... Mich interessiert, was so etwas in mir auslöst. Einerseits gibt man etwas von sich anderseits lernt man bei der Beschäftigung mit einem bestimmten Thema wieder einen Teil von sich kennen. Es ist ein Dialogisieren mit dem Material oder mit der Welt. (Reiter 1996)

Beckermann faßt dementsprechend den Essay als Genre, das ihr erlaubt, von eigener Erfahrung ausgehend, zu versuchen, den Holocaust und das Überleben ihrer Eltern für die eigene Identität zu verarbeiten. Einen Einfluß des Poststrukturalismus oder der französischen Philosophie, wie sie die Beziehung Beckermanns zu Frankreich, insbesondere zum französischen Film nahelegten, verneint sie. Dagegen bekennt sie sich zum Vorbild Jean Amérys, der bis heute 'ein geheimes Losungswort' darstelle. Schon die 16jährige bewunderte ihn als 'Teil einer Gegenwelt, die sich nicht allein gegen die Dumpfheit der anderen richtete, sondern gegen die Anpassungsversuche der Eltern an diese Scheinwelt.' (Beckermann 1993: 191) Später bezeichnet sie Améry als Schriftsteller, der 'zur Familie gehört':

> Ich habe das nie genau analysiert, aber bei Améry ist es klar, daß es die Erfahrung, die Thematik ist, die mich anzieht, auch die Radikalität und der Schmerz, den ich empfinde, daß er in Brüssel gesessen ist und daß er auch in Frankreich nicht diesen Zugang sich verschafft hat, obwohl es möglich gewesen wäre. (Reiter 1996)

Für Beckermann ist Essayismus Experiment, von dessen Ergebnis sich überraschen zu lassen sie durchaus bereit ist, wie in ihrer Stellungnahme zu *Nach Jerusalem*, dem Film über die Fahrt von Tel Aviv in die israelische Hauptstadt, deutlich wird: 'Ich habe eben das Konzept dieser Straße gewählt, um auch mich selber einzuschränken und das zu sehen, was wirklich auf diesem Weg passiert; und nicht den Weg zu wählen von einer Person zur anderen, von der Stelle zu der Stelle.' (Reiter 1996) In diesem Film Beckermanns werden die vermittelten visuellen Eindrücke kaum kommentiert. Die Reise von Tel Aviv in Richtung Jerusalem, in deren Verlauf sich ein Panorama der kulturellen Vielfalt im modernen Israel, der Konflikte aber auch der positiven Interaktion zwischen Israeli und Palästinenser, zwischen Judentum und Islam entfaltet, wird nicht so sehr verbal als visuell erzählt. Im Sinne des Genres des Filmessays verlagert sich die Narration also in die Bilder. Wie Beckermann unter dem erklärten Einfluß Chris Markers *Sans Soleils* eine sehr persönliche Form des Dokumentarfilms entwickelt, läßt sich anhand von drei ihrer jüngsten Filme erkennen.

Die Filmtrilogie, deren Abschluß *Nach Jerusalem* darstellt, wird zusammengehalten durch das Forschungsinteresse der Regisseurin. Der erste Teil *Wien retour* folgt noch dem traditionellen dokumentarischen Muster. Der Film zeigt eine Montage des erzählenden Leopoldstädter Kommunisten, Franz Weintraub, und historischen Bild- und Filmmaterials. Die Tonspur wird dominiert von der Narration Weintraubs, der dem Zuseher seine Geschichte von der Ankunft in Wien 1924 bis zu seinem erzwungenen Exil erzählt und sozusagen als Nachsatz noch über den Verbleib seiner Familie berichtet.

Beim mittleren Teil der Trilogie, *Die papierene Brücke*, handelt es sich um den autobiographischsten von Beckermanns Filmen. Auf den Spuren der Erzählungen ihres Vaters reist sie nach Osteuropa, also gewissermaßen in die eigene Erinnerung. Sie erklärt nicht nur zu Beginn ihr persönliches Interesse an der Reise, sondern ist auch im Laufe des Films als Interviewerin präsent. Mit dem Film erzählt sie zwei unterschiedliche Geschichten, diejenige ihres Vaters in Osteuropa und diejenige, die ihrer Großmutter bestimmt gewesen wäre, hätte sie sich ihr nicht entzogen. Oma Rosa stellte sich stumm und überlebte in Wien. Der zweite Teil von *Die papierene Brücke* dokumentiert die Pausengespräche der jüdischen Komparsen in einer Hollywood Rekonstruktion des Lagers Theresienstadt für die ABC-Fernsehserie 'Krieg und Erinnerung'. Beckermann, Kind und Enkel der einst Verfolgten und Davongekommenen, steht nicht nur im Zentrum dieses Films, sondern sie bildet mit ihrer Person auch die Klammer, die seine beiden doch recht unterschiedlichen Teile zusammenhält.

Den genannten Filmen gemeinsam ist der Umstand, daß sie nicht nur die Bilder des Verlorenen heraufbeschwören, sondern daß sie das Verlorene zum Anlaß eines eigenständigen Kunstwerkes machen (Muschg 1981: 51). Dies gilt ebenfalls, wenn auch auf eine andere Weise, für den abschließenden Teil der Trilogie. Beschwörung sei die eigentliche Absicht des Essays, kritisierte einst Reinhard Baumgart (1957: 604). Eine Beschwörung in Bildern im positiven Sinne ist Beckermanns Filmessay *Nach Jerusalem*:

> Ich hatte mit Israel viel zu tun, da meine Mutter dort in der Emigration war und ich als Kind die Sommer dort verbrachte. Zuerst hatte ich eine sehr emotional geprägte Beziehung zu diesem Land, die als Kind natürlich eine sehr schöne war und dann später – in den 70er und 80er Jahren –, eine sehr kritische. Dann wollte ich mir dieses Land anschauen, wollte sehen, wie es wirklich ist. Was ist aus den Träumen geworden? (Reiter 1996)

In diesem Film zieht sich die Regisseurin gänzlich zurück in die Auswahl und Organisation der Eindrücke. Waren in *Wien retour* die Bilder noch weitgehend Illustrationsmaterial des Textes und ergänzten sie diesen in *Die papierene Brücke*, indem sie die unausgesprochenen Sehnsüchte der Autorin ausdrückten ('die Landschaft zog mich in sich hinein' lautet ein charakteristischer Bildkommentar), so stehen sie in *Nach Jerusalem* für sich, fungieren also nicht mehr als Metaphern wie in den vorangegangenen Filmen, sondern 'bilden eine eigene kontrapunktische Ebene'[4] Bildschnitt und Musik gewinnen nunmehr den Rang von *Erzähl*techniken. Tschaikowskis *Symphonie melancholique*, von der zwischen Lokalgeräuschen, Interviews oder Radio-Meldungen immer nur ein bis zwei Takte des Themas zu hören sind, bildet das einigende Element für die unterschiedlichen Szenen und Bilder. Indem sie eine gewisse Stetl-Atmosphäre evoziert, verbindet diese Musik darüber hinaus auch das 'neue', reale Israel der Intifada, der Multinationalität mit den Träumen der europäischen Juden. Der Titel ist dabei durchaus programmatisch gemeint: 'Das Nicht-Ankommen in Jerusalem', schrieb mir die Autorin:

> war von Anfang an Konzept. Damit wollte ich zeigen – wie auch in der Doppelbedeutung des Wortes *nach* im Titel angedeutet –, daß es ein Jerusalem gibt, das Sehnsucht bleiben sollte. Versucht man dort anzukommen wie die religiösen Fanatiker, für die die Bibel ein Grundbuch zu sein scheint, wird ein Kreuzzug daraus. Außerdem soll der Film auch den Schwerpunkt der Argumentation von Jerusalem weg verlagern. Auch ohne ein geeintes Jerusalem gibt es ein Israel.[5]

Wen will die Regisseurin mit ihren Filmen ansprechen? Alle und niemanden, meint sie im Gespräch. Und auf Nachfrage erklärt sie, daß sie mit *Nach Jerusalem* ein alternatives Bild des Landes liefern wollte, das das aus den Massenmedien bekannte, wenn nicht korrigiert, so doch ergänzt. Beckermanns bisherige Filme waren alle essentiell Reiseberichte: In *Wien retour* geht es um die Reise aus dem Stetl nach Wien, in *Die papierene Brücke* um eine in die Gegenrichtung, und *Nach Jerusalem* stellt die Reise nach Israel dar. Die Vorliebe für den Reisebericht ist kein Zufall; auch der Essay stellt als Form gewissermaßen eine Reise in unbekannte Sphären des Wissens und des Bewußtseins dar.

Warum schreibt Beckermann also Essays und nicht nur sie? Auch mehrere ihrer österreichischen und deutschen jüdischen KollegInnen halten sich an das Genre.[6] Warum schreibt sie keine Romane beispielsweise? Warum fühlt sie sich durch das relativ ungeläufige Genre des Filmessays angesprochen?[7] Nicht zufällig wird Jean Améry mit seinen autobiographischen Essays bekannt. Mit seinem ersten, 'An den Grenzen des Geiste' (1964), machte er sich diese Form zur Lebensform, die der zunehmenden Vorläufigkeit seiner Existenz entsprach.[8] Könnte man also die These wagen, daß der Essay ein dem durch den Holocaust geprägten jüdischen Schicksal angemessenes Genre ist, angemessener jedenfalls als die mit Adornos bekanntem Verdikt belegten Gedichte? Es scheint einiges dafür zu sprechen, insbesondere was die zweite Generation betrifft. Während Reinhard Baumgart das 'Stilgesetz des Interessanten' (1957: 599) für die Popularität des Essays nach 1945 verantwortlich macht, liegt die Aktualität dieser Form für die Generation nach Améry in seiner Verquickung des

Persönlich-Erlebnishaften mit dem allgemein Gültigen, des Ephemeren mit dem Bleibenden. Es ist die 'Struktur der Erinnerung', die sich im 'methodisch unmethodischen' Verfahren niederschlägt, wie Adorno das treffend bezeichnete (1981: 21), die dem Anliegen dieser Autoren entgegenkommt. Der Essay könnte damit als Prototyp des sogenannten 'konzentrischen Schreibens' angesehen werden, das der amerikanische Germanist Thomas Nolden jüngst in seinem gleichnamigen Buch als Charakteristikum der 'Jungen jüdischen Literatur' bezeichnete. Wie im Essay ist der Ansatzpunkt des konzentrischen Schreibens die Gegenwart, 'die ohne Bezug auf die Shoah freilich nicht zu denken ist und auf die das Schreiben deshalb unwillkürlich bezogen ist' (1995: 63f). Den Kindern der Holocaust-Überlebenden erlaubte die abwägend-offene Form des Essays, Positionen im Schreiben zu klären. Diese die Kritikfähigkeit fördernde Skepsis ist jedoch nicht die 'Standortlosigkeit', die Baumgart dem Essay in den fünfziger Jahren fälschlich attestierte (1957: 599). Die Freiheit vom System, die sich in der assoziativen Denkbewegung der Essays genauso spiegelt, wie im Perspektivenwechsel und in der subjektiven Argumentation, eignet sich zur Identitätssuche von Beckermanns Generation. In gewissem Sinne könnte man bei dieser Literatur auch von Therapie sprechen (Muschg 1981): Die Kinder der Überlebenden bedienen sich des Essays als literarischer Form, um mit dem fertig zu werden, was ihre Eltern erlebten, ohne daß sie sich, wie etwa im Erlebnisbericht gänzlich entblößten. Stellvertretend für viele meint Beckermann daher: 'ich habe in acht Jahren drei Filme gemacht und zwei Bücher und habe mich darin mit diesem Thema beschäftigt und bin durch sämtliche Depressionen gegangen, die dazugehören. Jetzt ist es für mich anders. Irgendwann hat man etwas für sich verarbeitet, und es kann mich jetzt nicht mehr so leicht erschüttern, was damit zu tun hat' (Reiter 1996).

Symptomatisch ist in dieser Hinsicht die Reihenfolge von Beckermanns Werken, die das graduelle Anwachsen ihres jüdischen Selbstbewußtseins spiegelt. Ursprünglich ging es ihr darum, sich ihrer Wurzeln zu vergewissern. Die zumindest in Film und Erzählung wieder erstandene Leopoldstadt in *Wien retour* (1983) lieferte das Bildmaterial für *Die Mazzesinsel* (1984). *Die papierene Brücke* (1987) stellte den Übergang von der Sichtung des Verlorenen zur Auflehnung gegen das Bestehende dar. Der Film zeigt den Vater Beckermanns, wie er bei der Anti-Waldheim-Demonstration in Wien angepöbelt wird. Mikrophon und Kamera helfen der Regisseurin, ihre Sprachlosigkeit zu kompensieren: 'Die Videokamera war dort für mich wie eine Waffe, die einzige Möglichkeit, mich zu wehren' (Bretschneider 1988: 37). *Unzugehörig* (1989) bringt schließlich die Standortbestimmung der im Nachkriegsösterreich geborenen Jüdin. *Unzugehörig* ist nicht nur, aber auch eine Abrechnung: Die Sprache ist nunmehr selbst zur Waffe geworden, die im Film noch weitgehend fehlte; die Anklage z.B. gegen Alfred Hrdlickas Skulptur ersetzt die Bilder der

Sprachlosigkeit derjenigen, die alles verloren hat (z.B. *Die Mazzesinsel*). Die Auseinandersetzung mit dem Land, aus dem die Eltern und Großeltern vertrieben worden waren und das dennoch für die jungen Juden zu einer Art Heimat geworden war, erfolgt nicht von ungefähr Ende der achtziger Jahre: Die Ereignisse in den vorhergehenden Jahren (Waldheim-Wahlkampf 1986 und Bedenkjahr 1988) haben nicht nur die jüdische Bevölkerung in einen 'kollektiven Schock' versetzt (*Unzugehörig*: 106), sondern haben auch die aufgeklärte nichtjüdische junge Generation zur Auseinandersetzung mit der nationalsozialistischen Vergangenheit Österreichs veranlaßt (z.B. Haslinger 1987).

Nach Jerusalem (1991) schließlich arbeitet Material auf, das in *Die papierene Brücke* anklingt. Beckermanns jüdisches Selbstbewußtsein ist nun so weit gefestigt, daß sie sich Kritik auch an ihrer zweiten Heimat leisten kann. Das ungetrübte Bild der Kindheit wird hinterfragt. Die Solidarität, namentlich die mit dem Staat Israel, die Jean Améry noch jede Kritik aus Pietät gegenüber den ermordeten Kameraden verbat (Schultz 1986: 75), läßt sich im Zeitalter der Intifada nicht mehr kommentarlos aufrechterhalten. Das heißt nicht, daß Beckermann in das Horn der Antizionisten bliese, die in den Palästinensern die Juden der Juden zu erkennen glauben. Sie führt vielmehr vor, daß ein *modus vivendi* besteht zwischen den Juden als Besatzungsmacht und der moslemischen Minderheit, der nicht nur Konfrontation heißt. Im Gegensatz zu den herkömmlichen Berichten zeigt Beckermanns Film gerade diese Seite der Beziehung.

Exemplarisch und mitunter explizit führen Beckermanns bisherige Arbeiten das Problem der Identität der zweiten Generation vor. Als eine der ersten warf Helen Epstein in ihrem Buch *Children of the Holocaust* (1979) anhand von Interviews mit Kindern von Überlebenden die Frage nach der sekundären Traumatisierung auf. Peter Sichrowsky tat Ähnliches mit österreichischen und deutschen Jugendlichen (1985). Beckermann selbst beweist, daß es nicht nur die unmittelbaren Erfahrungen der Eltern sein müssen, die die Reaktionsmuster der Kinder prägen. Als sie in Czernowitz von der Miliz inhaftiert und, anscheinend weil sie fotographiert hatte, verhört wurde, fühlte sie sich zwanghaft an die 'Erlebnisse der Elterngeneration' erinnert (1985: 85). Die Traumatisierung betrifft also die jüdische Nachkriegsgeneration generell, auch wenn die Eltern, wie Beckermanns eigene, nicht im Lager waren. Allein der Umstand, Jude oder Jüdin zu sein, machte bereits die Kriegsgeneration zu einem Teil der durch den Holocaust geprägten Schicksalsgemeinschaft, die nun in ihre Kinder als Kompensation für das Verlorene nicht nur hohe Erwartungen setzten (*Unzugehörig*: 10), sondern die ihnen auch durch die Erziehung ihre Einstellung zur jüngsten jüdischen Vergangenheit mitgaben. Ob die Kinder sich diese aneignen oder dagegen revoltieren, um eine Auseinandersetzung mit ihr kommen sie nicht herum. Ob man allerdings dabei in Anlehnung an viele Überlebende der Lager von einem Verhaltens-'Syndrom' der zweiten Generation sprechen kann, das sei dahingestellt (Niederland 1989). Jüngste Beiträge der Psychotherapie zum Thema scheinen dies aufgrund von Fallstudien eher zu verneinen. Viele Faktoren bestimmen die Psyche des Individuums, obwohl nicht geleugnet wird, daß die Holocaust-Erfahrung eine der prägendsten ist (Cooper 1995). Auch Beckermann sieht das so: 'Das ist wirklich sehr individuell. Es kommt immer auf die Konstellation an, wo die Eltern waren, ob sie beide die gleichen Erfahrungen machten, wie sie zueinander stehen, wann sie sich kennengelernt haben' (Reiter 1996).

In jedem Fall hat Beckermann als Intellektuelle den Vorteil, daß sie ihre Gefühle artikulieren kann, zuerst mit Hilfe von Photographien vom ausgelöschten jüdischen Wien (Die Mazzesinsel) und später schriftlich und im Film. Im Unterschied zur Meinung, die in der Rezension von Unzugehörig im *profil* (Anon. 1989) vertreten wird, ist deshalb auch das Autobiographische an diesem Essay gerade das Wesentliche. Er gehört damit in eine Gruppe ähnlicher Werke, wie *Dies ist nicht mein Land* von Lea Fleischmann, oder die Essay-Bände Chaim Nolls *Nachtgedanken über Deutschland*, und *Leben ohne Deutschland*. Sowohl Fleischmann als auch Noll äußern Gedanken wie Beckermann in bezug auf Deutschland, die letztendlich doch immer wieder zum Holocaust zurückführen. Beide ziehen sie allerdings, im Gegensatz zu Beckermann, die Konsequenz aus ihrer Kritik und verlassen das Land; Fleischmann übersiedelt direkt und Noll über Italien nach Israel. Dennoch kommt Noll, so weit er auch flüchtet, aus seinem Deutsch-Sein nicht heraus. Aber 'man muß ja nicht heraus', stellt Beckermann für sich fest: 'Das Angenehme, wenn man nicht hier lebt, ist, daß man sich das mitnehmen kann, was einem gefällt, seine Literatur, seine Musik ... Ich liebe Wien, und ich werde nie im Leben eine andere Literatur so verstehen, wie ich einen Schnitzler verstehe. Das ist ganz klar' (Reiter 1996).

Ruth Beckermann will nicht flüchten. Nachdem sie sich literarisch und filmisch zu einem jüdisch-österreichischen Selbstbewußtsein durchgerungen hat, scheint sie die Auseinandersetzung sogar zu genießen.

Notes

[1] Lea Fleischmann, deren Buch *Dies ist nicht mein Land* beinahe zehn Jahre vor *Unzugehörig* erschien, behielt Ähnliches in Erinnerung (Fleischmann 1980).

[2] Das Gutachten von Karl Müller für die Disziplinarkommission im Bundesministerium ergab allerdings, daß Hrdlicka disziplinarrechtlich nicht zu belangen war.

Notes continued

[3] Anna Mitgutsch hat erst vor kurzem ihre jüdische Identität (wieder)entdeckt.

[4] Persönliche Mitteilung Beckermanns vom 9. August 1996.

[5] Persönliche Mitteilung Beckermanns vom 25. März 1996.

[6] Das gilt für die bereits genannte Lea Fleischmann (1980) und den Journalisten Henryk M. Broder (1986) genauso wie in jüngster Vergangenheit für den in der DDR aufgewachsenen Chaim Noll (1992 und 1995); zur Situation in Österreich siehe auch 'Die jüdischen Literaten' *Illustrierte Neue Welt*, Jänner 1996: 15.

[7] Während es unter der Kriegs- und Vorkriegsgeneration unter den österreichischen Juden durchaus Theaterschriftsteller (George Tabori, Hilde Spiel) und Romanciers (Fred Wander, Ilse Aichinger) gab und gibt, fällt auf, daß Robert Schindel einer der wenigen österreichischen jüdischen Romanschriftsteller unter der Nachkriegsgeneration ist, der, nachdem er als Lyriker begonnen hatte, 1992 seinen vielbeachteten Roman *Gebürtig* publizierte. Bezeichnend für die enge Verbindung unter den jungen Wiener jüdischen Schriftstellern ist übrigens, daß beispielsweise Beckermann und Schindel sich gegenseitig in ihren Werken nennen. Die Filmemacherin verewigt den Schriftsteller als Komparsen bei der Theresienstadt-Nachstellung in *Die papierene Brücke*. In *Gebürtig* spielt Schindel ebenfalls auf dieses Ereignis an, das Esther Lichtblau, eine 'Wiener und Czernowitzer Filmemacherin' im Film festgehalten habe.

[8] Robert Musil läßt Ulrich im 62. Kapitel des *Mann ohne Eigenschaften*, in dem es um die 'Utopie des Essayismus' geht, ähnlichen Gedanken nachhängen.

Bibliographie

Adorno, Theodor W. 1981. 'Der Essay als Form', *Noten zur Literatur*, Frankfurt am Main, Suhrkamp
Anon. 1989. Rezension von Ruth Beckermanns *Ungehörig*, 26, 26. Juni
Baumgart, Reinhard. 1957. 'Die Jünger des Interessanten', *Merkur*, 11: 599-604
Beckermann, Ruth. 1984. *Die Mazzesinsel. Juden in der Wiener Leopoldstadt 1918-38*, Wien, Löcker
—. 1985. 'Erdbeeren in Czernowitz', in Christoph Ransmayr (Hrsg.), *Im blinden Winkel. Nachrichten aus Mitteleuropa*, Wien, Brandstätter
—. 1987 *Die papierene Brücke. Filmessay*
—. 1989. *Unzugehörig. Österreicher und Juden nach 1945*, Wien, Löcker
—. 1991. *Nach Jerusalem. Filmessay*
—. 1983. *Wien retour. Dokumentarfilm*

—. 1993. 'Unter der Bank gelesen. Jean Améry und Österreich', *Das jüdische Echo*, 42: 190-99
Bretschneider, Jürgen. 1988. 'Heimatsuche auf jüdisch. Die österreichische Regisseurin Ruth Beckermann', *Film und Fernsehen*, Mai: 34-7
Broder, Henryk M. 1986. *Der ewige Antisemit. Über Sinn und Funktion eines beständigen Gefühls*, Frankfurt am Main, Fischer
Cooper, Howard. 1995. 'The Second Generation "Syndrome"', *Journal of Holocaust Education*, 4, 2: 131-46
Embacher, Helga. 1995. *Neubeginn ohne Illusionen. Juden in Österreich nach 1945*, Wien, Picus
Fischer, Erica. 1989. 'Ein Dialog fand nie statt. *Unzugehörig* – Ruth Beckermann über das Verhältnis von Juden und Österreichern nach 1945', *Deutsche Volkszeitung/die tat*, 24. November: 48
Fleischmann, Lea. 1980. *Dies ist nicht mein Land. Eine Jüdin verläßt die Bundesrepublik*, München, Heyne
Giordano, Ralph. 1992. *'Ich bin angenagelt an dieses Land'. Reden und Aufsätze über die deutsche Vergangenheit und Gegenwart*, Hamburg, Rasch und Röhring
Haslinger, Josef. 1987. *Politik der Gefühle. Ein Essay über Österreich*, Darmstadt, Luchterhand
Heenen-Wolff, Susann. 1990. 'Ruth Beckermann, *Ungehörig*', Norddeutscher Rundfunk, 28. Juli
Knight, Robert. 1988. *'Ich bin dafür, die Sache in die Länge zu ziehen'. Die Wortprotokolle der österreichischen Bundesregierung von 1945-1952 über die Entschädigung der Juden*, Frankfurt am Main, Athenäum
Matejka, Viktor. 1984. *Widerstand ist alles. Notizen eines Unorthodoxen*, Wien, Löcker
Mitgutsch, Anna. 1995. 'Frauenfeindlichkeit und Antisemitismus. Statement zur Podiumsdiskussion bei der Eröffnungsveranstaltung des Symposiums *Frauen im Exil*', *Mit der Ziehharmonika. Literatur, Widerstand, Exil*, 4: 17f.
Muschg, Adolf. 1981. *Literatur als Therapie? Ein Exkurs über das Heilsame und das Unheilbare. Frankfurter Vorlesungen*, Frankfurt am Main, Suhrkamp
Niederland, William G. 1989. *Folgen der Verfolgung. Das Überlebenden-Syndrom Seelenmord*, Frankfurt am Main, Suhrkamp
Nolden, Thomas. 1995. *Junge jüdische Literatur. Konzentrisches Schreiben in der Gegenwart*, Würzburg, Königshausen und Neumann
Noll, Chaim. 1992. *Nachtgedanken über Deutschland. Essay*, Reinbeck, Rowohlt
—. 1995. *Leben ohne Deutschland. Essay*, Reinbek, Rowohlt
Reiter, Andrea. 1996. Unveröffentlichtes Interview mit Ruth Beckermann in Wien, 21. Februar

Schultz, Hans Jürgen (Hrsg.). 1986. *Mein Judentum*, München, dtv
Sichrowsky, Peter. 1985. *'Wir wissen nicht, was morgen wird, wir wissen wohl, was gestern war'*, Köln, Kiepenheuer und Witsch
Spiel, Hilde. 1994. *Glanz und Untergang. Wien 1866 bis 1938*, München, dtv

Anna Mitgutsch's *Abschied von Jerusalem*:
An Austrian Writer's Presentation of a Divided City

Margaret Stone

Ever since the publication of her first novel *Die Züchtigung* (1985) which was widely acclaimed as a key work of post-1945 Austrian literature, Anna Mitgutsch has been recognized as one of the significant Austrian writers of the post-war period. She has received several important literary prizes[1] and has, to date, published five novels of which *Abschied von Jerusalem* is her most recent work. It appeared in spring 1995, ten years after *Die Züchtigung*, which had turned the hitherto unknown author into a celebrity.

Her latest book is also extremely topical: a novel about the tensions, suspicions, hostilities, violence, aggression and terrorism in present-day Israel, and especially in Jerusalem, one of the world's trouble spots of which we are once again reminded on an almost daily basis in our news bulletins and newspapers. The novel does, however, deal with a good deal more than the present political situation in Israel. In all five novels by Anna Mitgutsch we find as one of her major themes the difficulty, if not impossibility, of forming close and lasting human relationships, of understanding, in the fullest sense of the word, one's fellow human beings, and especially those closest to us. Many of her characters live in disharmony, they are unable to feel at home and secure in the country, culture, society and family they find themselves in and they search in vain for a *Heimat*. Mother and daughter illustrate this theme in *Die Züchtigung*, so do Janna and Sonja in *Das andere Gesicht* (1986). In *Ausgrenzung* (1989) a young mother is fighting for a place in society for herself and above all her handicapped child, only to find that Austrian society rejects them both. The main character in her next novel *In fremden Städten* (1992) is again a woman, this time an American, who has remained a stranger in Austria, her husband's country. She has lost her roots, her *Heimat*, and worst of all, as a writer in a foreign land, her own language, her mother tongue. She perishes in the desparate attempt to regain them both.

For her latest book Mitgutsch chose Jerusalem both as the setting and as one of the major themes, a city which has for many centuries been a melting-pot of different peoples and cultures, a city where different races and traditions have uneasily lived side by side or clashed in open hostility, where to this day unresolved conflicts continue to flare up. Jerusalem is more than an interesting setting for the action and for the characters to take the reader on a guided tour. As the dust cover suggests, the city seems to be 'nicht nur Schauplatz, sondern heimliche Protagonistin'. Mitgutsch, who like Dvorah, the main character of this novel, has returned to her Jewish roots, knows Israel, and especially the city of Jerusalem, extremely well. Dvorah may well speak on behalf of the author when she expresses her feelings about Jerusalem: 'Die Stadt war meine größte Sehnsucht, die sich nie erfüllte, weil ich nie wußte, was ich eigentlich von ihr wollte. Jedesmal, wenn ich hier bin, schleiche ich um sie herum wie eine hungrige Katze, zwänge mich zwischen ihre Mauern, dränge mich auf, nicht unwillkommen, aber doch nur geduldet' (*Abschied von Jerusalem*: 109).

Mitgutsch provides the reader with a very detailed, vivid and colourful picture of present-day Jerusalem. Her descriptions are informative and accurate like those in an intelligent guide book, but her atmospheric and often highly poetic images and metaphors also create another dimension which transcends the level of tourist sights and the city's multi-national crowds of sightseers and pilgrims as well as the everyday lives of its wary and suspicious inhabitants. And yet, although divided in so many ways, Mitgutsch also presents Jerusalem as one of the greatest achievements of mankind, a city where a divine spirit has manifested itself most clearly. By following Dvorah on her wanderings and experiencing the city through her eyes and her reactions, we as readers also become enthralled, we too may have our spirit lifted, catch a glimpse of perfect beauty and gain a deeper insight into the puzzling contradictions and mysteries of Jerusalem and its inhabitants.

It is one of the great merits of this novel that it has succeeded in creating this other dimension which is, after all, what distinguishes serious literary works with a foreign setting from travel books written first and foremost for information and entertainment. It would, nevertheless, help the reader who has never been to Jerusalem and who knows little about it, if the publishers had printed a map of the city on the inside covers of the book and perhaps even included a glossary of the many historic places mentioned and of the Hebrew and Arabic words used.[2] Mitgutsch did, however, explain in the discussion session after the reading from the novel at this conference, that it had not occurred to her to include a map of Jerusalem, because she did not want even parts of her novel to be read at the level of a guide book. It is interesting, in this context, that the dust cover does not show a picture of Jerusalem but rather the rolling sand dunes of the desert.[3]

This many-faceted picture of Jerusalem is the setting for a love story between Dvorah, an (almost) middle-aged Austrian academic, living and working in New York, but who is a frequent visitor to the city, and the much younger Sivan, who claims to be Armenian and to work as an interpreter for a U.N. film team. However much Dvorah wants to believe in this identity, she has to face the fact that in all probability he is a Palestinian terrorist. The reader arrives at this conclusion sooner than the narrator who desparately tries to find plausible explanations for Sivan's actions and eventual disappearance.[4]

The love story between those two unequal partners is by no means just a pretext to provide a plot with tension, suspense and romantic interest, it is embedded in the geographic, historic and cultural settings of Jerusalem. Their relationship, the love of two human beings whose age, education, background and committment to their own community are so vastly different, reflects and is symbolic of life, of love and hatred, of trust and betrayal in the divided city of Jerusalem itself. For brief moments Dvorah's and Sivan's love for each other transcends these problelms, but the author seems to suggest that no human love could be strong enough to overcome personal, cultural and political differences of such magnitude and achieve a 'happy end'. She seems to be equally realistic and pessimistic about the chances of the inhabitants of Jerusalem living together in peace and harmony, as demonstrated by the still ongoing *Intifada*. At a deeper level the warring factions may have more in common than they are ever prepared to admit. As one of the Arab traders in the Suk puts it to Dvorah, very likely expressing Mitgutsch's own point of view: 'Wir sind einander ähnlich, die Juden und wir, ... nur will es keiner sehen' (*Abschied von Jerusalem*: 110).

The novel succeeds in fusing the two levels: the personal, the love story of Dvorah and Sivan, and the general, the much wider picture of Jerusalem, divided in so many political, social, religious, economic and cultural ways. Even the uninitiated reader who has never visited Jerusalem or Israel, will be captivated and fascinated and take away the impression that s/he has been given a genuine insight into this complex city.

The book does, however, require careful reading, because the story line does not unfold in a linear fashion. Indeed, as one reviewer remarked, 'es ist nicht leicht, sich im Labyrinth dieses Romans zurechtzufinden' (Anon. 1995). The author creates a kaleidoscope of fragments from the different strands of the novel, a colourful mosaic of life in Jerusalem as well as of Dvorah's and Sivan's relationship, interspersed with frequent flashbacks to the past lives of some of the characters, especially of the female protagonist, i.e. memories of her childhood and youth, her relatives, especially her Jewish grandmother, her life with her French-Jewish lover in a kibbutz, and with her Austrian husband and their visit to Israel and especially Jerusalem. All these memories are closely linked to Dvorah's encounters with typical representatives of the different ethnic groups in the city and with her attempts to come to terms with what has happened to her. The narrative device used by the author is quite an ingenious one. When Dvorah tries to leave the country, the airport police take away her passport and keep her waiting. She recalls her experiences and is wondering how much they might already know about her and what to tell them about herself and her background and how much to admit about her contacts and what has happened to her in Jerusalem, especially about her relationship with Sivan.

Dvorah was baptized Hildegard (*Abschied von Jerusalem*: 75) by her Catholic family, after her paternal grandmother. Even as a child, already vaguely aware of her other roots, she felt uncomfortable with it (115). Nowhere in the novel does Mitgutsch indicate that Hildegard means 'battle maid', and she may well have chosen it because of its traditional connotations. It does, however, stress an important aspect of Dvorah's character, her determination in the past to fight for her Jewish heritage, and now in Jerusalem her fight with her own conscience and her feelings of guilt, shame and fear which are mirrored by the divided city. When opting for her Jewish heritage, transmitted to her by her maternal grandmother who used to call her 'Bienchen', she chose Dvorah as her new name, the Hebrew form of Deborah ('honey bee'): 'Dvorah heißt Biene, ich habe mir meinen Kindernamen zurückgeholt, und sie ist auch Deborah, die Richterin und Prophetin' (81). It also means eloquence, 'honeyed words' in Hebrew, and Dvorah, telling her own story while she is waiting to be interviewed by the Israeli secret police, does indeed show great narrative skills in telling it. Her friend Channa agrees that this name suits her (76). Officially, however, she ist still Hildegard, as stated in her passport. Her surname is never mentioned. Her two names underline the struggle with her two identities and reflect the many conflicting identities of the inhabitants of Jerusalem. She attempts a critical analysis of her divided background and life and tries to discover the truth and to arrive at a 'judgment' about herself and her lover, as well as about the divided city of Jerusalem and its inhabitants. In the end she fails, but this failure is presented as inevitable. Mitgutsch seems to have come to the conclusion that ultimate insight and truth are beyond our reach, especially in an infinitely complex place like Jerusalem. At the beginning of the novel Dvorah says about this city: 'und immer gab es mehr als eine Wahrheit, die für die Fremden und die, nach der man lebte' (17).

Like all other Mitgutsch heroines, Dvorah, too, remains the outsider she has been all her life, in her native country of Austria and with her family there, in Israel on previous occasions, and in America, where she now lives and works. Her attempts at becoming more than a tourist in the Holy City, at establishing close relationships with her Jewish friends there, for whom Jerusalem is home, also fail. To them, however, only West Jerusalem is familiar territory, East Jerusalem means danger and is to be avoided, as they frequently point out to Dvorah, admonishing her again and again to be 'vorsichtig'. They all distrust the Arabs, but have adjusted to the climate of fear and unease created by the frequent terrorist attacks and the arrests or shootings of Arab suspects.

The story is set in contemporary Israel. East and West Jerusalem are united again after the Six-Day War in 1967. Until then the only crossing point between East and West Jerusalem was the 'The Mandelbaum Gate', hence the title of Muriel Spark's novel of 1965.[5] Mitgutsch has set her novel in contemporary Jerusalem troubled on an almost daily basis by the Intifada. As the author is very ready to admit, the descriptions of Jerusalem and surrounding areas are based on her own intimate knowledge which she has acquired on frequent visits over many years. The novel reveals her deep and very personal commitment to and fascination with the city, and this transmits itself to the receptive reader.

We follow Dvorah's wanderings through both West and East Jerusalem. At the beginning of her account she admits: 'Ob ich noch einige Tage hierbleibe oder nicht, ändert nichts an der Tatsache, daß ich auf der Flucht bin. Oder auf der Suche, das ist die andere Seite derselben Bewegung' (*Abschied von Jerusalem*: 8-9). She tries to trace Martha, a distant Jewish relative who disappeared during the Nazi period, she is in search of her own origins and her personal and cultural identity, in search of the history of her people and the religious and cultural monuments they created, and later on in search of her lover who has disappeared and whom, she fears, the Israeli police has shot dead during a terrorist attack. At the same time she is fleeing from the Israeli secret police, as well as from her own feelings of shame and guilt. Yet she knows this will be in vain: 'ich will ja gefunden werden, warum ginge ich sonst fast täglich am Polizeigebäude vorbei, wenn ich mir nicht sehnlich wünschte, diesem Zustand ein Ende zu setzen?' (9).

Dvorah's observations and contacts introduce the reader to the explosive political and cultural situation in this city which is home to Jews, Arabs, Armenians and other Christian communities, who all live behind invisible dividing lines beyond which there is 'enemy territory'. At first Dvorah tries to ignore this reality, despite the repeated warnings of her friends. She ignores it, because she does not belong anywhere. In their eyes she behaves like an inquisitive, rather naive and ignorant tourist, who is therefore taking great risks. She does, however, soon realize that people's attitudes and especially their political views depend, above all, on their ethnic origin. Everybody living in Jerusalem automatically sizes up anyone they meet according to these divisions: 'Erst sag mir, bist du Moslem, Jude oder Christ, dann können wir weiterreden.' The local inhabitants don't even have to ask: 'sie erkennen sich auf den ersten Blick' (*Abschied von Jerusalem*: 25). Tourists are also scrutinized in this way. The answers to very simple questions soon reveal the information necessary for their categorization: 'Woher kommst du, wo lebst du, besuchst du Verwandte in Israel?' (25). Even just asking the way may reveal a person's identity: 'Jedes Wort hat hier Bedeutung, kein Straßenname, kein Torbogen ist neutral, für manche gibt es drei Bezeichnungen, Codewörter verschiedener Völker und Glaubensrichtungen' (280).

Mitgutsch is clearly very knowledgeable about the current political situation in Israel, but political comment and analysis are, of course, not her main concern in this novel. She assumes that her readers are reasonably well informed about Israel and does not try to give a remedial lesson in middle eastern politics. As a creative piece of writing the novel gives the reader, on almost every page, an insight into the way the divisions in Jerusalem constantly affect its inhabitants' whole way of life, how they interact with other people, how they think and feel. This is a more effective way of conveying a sense of history, of introducing the reader to the complex realities of modern Jerusalem than straightforward political explanations and comments.

The novel opens with the narrator's summary of the tense atmosphere of the Old City of Jerusalem, the Eastern Arab quarter, and this is mirrored by Dvorah's own feelings of unease and suspicion. By contrast West Jerusalem, the more modern, Europeanized Israeli part, is less threatening. Here she is just one of thousands of anonymous tourists no one is particularly interested in. The two halves of the city, co-existing uneasily side by side, are mirrored by the two sides of Dvorah's character and background, by her Jewish roots and her western upbringing and outlook. Sivan, too, is a divided character, who tries to give himself a false identity. He is Dvorah's lover, but almost certainly also a Palestinian terrorist who deceived, used and betrayed her, yet he also treated her in a very tender and sensitive way and showed himself as a very likeable young man genuinely in love with an older woman. After Dvorah recalls their declaration of love for each other, she adds: 'Aber wer immer er in Wirklichkeit war, ein Lügner, ein skrupelloser Verführer, ein Terrorist, dieser Augenblick war die reine Wahrheit, so verstellt sich keiner, er sprach die Wahrheit ... Inzwischen hat sich alles verzerrt, wie eine Landschaft unter Wasser' (44). The reader, therefore, cannot but share Dvorah's ambiguous feelings about her lover, as about Jerusalem itself.

During the discussion after her reading from this novel, Mitgutsch confirmed that her characters were meant to be complex, and she added: 'Meine Sympathien sind gleichmäßig verteilt. Ich mag alle meine Charaktere.' She did, however, admit that the initial motivation for writing this novel was 'die tendenziöse Berichterstattung im Westen' about events in Israel. One review pointed out an interesting fact in this context: 'Ohne Frage steht die Autorin auf der israelisch-jüdischen Seite, bringt aber in den Dialogen mehr, ja fast ausschließlich, die arabische Argumentation einer revoltierenden Minderheit, die sich gegen die "jüdischen Besatzer" auflehnt' (Anon. 1995).

For centuries Jerusalem has attracted people in search of something, from power and riches to more spiritual treasures. In this novel Mitgutsch takes a very pessimistic view of any personal claims of having found religious and spiritual enlightenment and fulfilment in this divided city.

> Hier in Jerusalem werden die Suchenden aus allen Himmelsrichtungen zusammengeworfen, und manche gehen weg in dem Glauben, beinahe etwas gefunden zu haben, halten es fest in den Händen wie falsches Gold, das leuchtet, solange es Tag ist, aber dann ist es doch bloß eine Fata Morgana aus einem arabischen Märchen, und sie gehen mit leeren Händen und verklärten Gesichtern davon. (*Abschied von Jerusalem*: 114)

The experience of Jerusalem wears off and people's lives and attitudes are not fundamentally changed.

What about Dvorah? By the end of the novel she has certainly undergone a 'learning process' about herself as much as about other people and about the city itself and what divides it, but she too has not found 'salvation', and her future in the hands of the Israeli police is a rather uncertain one. Mitgutsch leaves the reader's natural curiosity about Dvorah's fate unsatisfied, but admitted in reply to a question from the audience after her reading: 'Es ist fast unvermeidlich, daß sie bei der Paßkontrolle aufgehalten wird.'

The novel contains many descriptive and very evocative passages which captivate Jerusalem's beauty, mystery and enchantment. Mitgutsch is, above all, fascinated by the effects the changing light has on the colours of the city:

> Im Licht der niedrig stehenden Sonne brach aus den Steinen der Mauer ein Leuchten hervor, als wäre ihre Haut durchscheinend geworden und legte die feinen rötlichen Adern frei. Sie liefen auseinander in einer heftigen goldgelben Flamme, ein kurzer Brand, der zu einem bräunlichen Rot verglühte, während sich bereits schwarze Schatten zwischen die Ritzen schoben. Die Zinnen waren so hoch über uns, daß sie uns den Himmel verdeckten, sie staken verkehrt in seinem kühlen Türkis wie in klarem Wasser. (*Abschied von Jerusalem*: 86)

After her reading Mitgutsch talked about 'Das Erschreiben einer Stadt'. Channa, one of Dvorah's Jewish friends, tells her about the many layers of the city: 'du kennst diese Stadt ja noch gar nicht, man muß sie vorsichtig öffnen, Schale um Schale, dahinter ist immer noch etwas, man wird nie fertig mit dieser Stadt' (*Abschied von Jerusalem*: 24). Mitgutsch also admitted that she lived with a constant longing to revisit Jerusalem, even to settle there, but that she was afraid she might be disappointed if she moved to Israel on a permanent basis. Dvorah seems to reflect the author's own feelings when she admits: 'Die Stadt war meine größte Sehnsucht, die sich nie erfüllte, weil ich nie wußte, was ich eigentlich von ihr wollte' (109).

The novel is also characterized by an artistic device which Anna Mitgutsch uses with great skill and to considerable effect. From page one she introduces a whole series of keywords which spread like an intricate pattern throughout the novel. They link the main character Dvorah with many others and with the city of

Jerusalem, and they also, often in a contrapuntal way, reinforce the main themes of the novel, especially that of the 'divided city' and its 'divided' population.

Throughout her stay Dvorah is haunted by anxiety and fear. She experiences the whole gamut of emotions, from mild anxiousness to mind-numbing terror, about herself and her future, her lover Sivan, the mysterious threats posed by East Jerusalem and by the inhabitants in the Arab territories, by Sivan's friends during her 'abduction' to Ramallah, and finally by the Israeli secret police. Fear is presented as an essential part of the atmosphere of Jerusalem which affects not just Dvorah, but all its inhabitants and all visitors who venture beyond the tourist areas and outgrow tourist attitudes and expectations. Khaled, the red-haired Arab shopkeeper who makes a pass at Dvorah tells her: 'du hast dich zu tief in etwas hineingewagt, das du nicht kennst, aber du weißt nicht, was du fragen mußt, und mit der Antwort kannst du nichts anfangen' (32). Dvorah flees from his shop 'um mich mit meiner Angst und Verwirrung unter die schiefgewachsenen Pinien unterhalb der Stadtmauer am Zionsberg zu verkriechen' (33). She also realizes 'daß die Gewalttätigkeit, die ich fühle, als wären sie gegen mich gerichtet, allgegenwärtig ist in dieser Stadt und nicht zu trennen von ihrer Verführung' (34).

Another key emotion is a feeling of shame, which is experienced by the narrator and the divided city and its inhabitants. Dvorah feels a deep sense of shame because of having been deceived, betrayed and despised by Sivan, his friends and other Arabs. She feels ashamed of her love affair which violates traditonal and cultural expectations and moral codes, a love affair between a middle-aged European woman of Jewish descent and an Arab in his early twenties. As a Jew she is also constantly reminded by the city of the shame of being in the wrong camp, of being just a tourist, a stranger and a woman who fraternized with 'the enemy'.

Jerusalem's shame is its inability to solve its problems, the unwillingness on all sides to compromise, with the inevitable result of bloodshed, suffering, the constant fear of terrorist attacks, and all the other evils that result from the divisions within the city. Dvorah even likens Jerusalem to a treacherous swamp: 'der mich nichts angeht und den ich niemals verstehen werde' (*Abschied von Jerusalem*: 29). Sivan's suggestion of putting Jerusalem under a UN mandate and thus imposing an impartial higher authority, is strongly opposed by Dvorah who is expressing the majority view of the Jews in Jerusalem and in Israel as a whole then and now: 'Niemals, wehrte ich ab, Jerusalem bleibt jüdisch' (28).

Linked with the feeling of shame is the motif of longing. The vast majority of Jerusalem's inhabitants long to live in peace and security, as does Dvorah. But she also yearns for her lover and for love in general, for a *Heimat*, for peace of mind and a sense of purpose in life. She is filled with longing for Jerusalem whenever she is away from it, and she feels its magnetic pull which draws her back as soon as she has returned to her place of work at an American unversity:

> wenn es mir doch gelingt abzureisen, sehne ich mich nach dieser Stadt. Aber wenn ich dort bin, sehne ich mich genauso wie eine unglücklich Verliebte, die demütig darauf wartet, aufgenommen zu werden, nicht mit den Trampelpfaden der Touristen abgespeist, sondern hinter die Steinmauern und Zypressen gelassen zu werden, wo sich das verborgene Leben vollzieht. Wie eine Kaktusfrucht ist diese Stadt, sagt Channa zärtlich. (*Abschied von Jerusalem*: 36)

Among the most interesting themes in the novel are truth and deception. They, too, are intricably linked with each other. When did Sivan tell Dvorah the truth, when was he lying? Will her account of their love affair to the secret police be the truth and nothing but the truth, or inevitably an edited, manipulated version of it? Does she know the truth about Sivan? Has she arrived at the truth about herself, about Jerusalem? These are vital questions in the context of the novel, but the author has no easy, straightforward answers, in fact she seems to suggest that there are none. Very near the end of her story Dvorah sums up her experiences in Jerusalem:

> Die Spannung, in der ich in den letzten Wochen lebte, hat sich aufgelöst. Etwas ist endgültig. Es ist sinnlos geworden, weiterhin auf den Fragen, die offengeblieben sind, zu beharren. Es gibt auch niemanden mehr, der zweifelsfrei die Wahrheit kennt. Sogar die Angst ist weg. Grundlos, das weiß ich. Jetzt kann ich bleiben oder gehen. Ich bin nicht klüger geworden, nur ein bißchen ärmer und nüchterner. (*Abschied von Jerusalem*: 277)

The city itself remains, ultimately, inscrutable. There are many 'truths' depending on which group one belongs to, whether one is a resident Jew, Arab, Armenian or member of another Christian community or just a tourist on a short visit. According to the author, the latter is the least likely to discover the truth about the city or about herself or himself. Dvorah's Jewish friend Nurit, a non-conformist and rebel by nature, tries to tell her that it is a western misconception to believe that there is only one truth which excludes all others: 'Es gibt nicht bloß eine Wahrheit, behauptet sie, es gibt viele und alle zugleich. Unsere Mentalität ist orientalisch, wir handeln nicht mit Ideen, sondern in Geschichten und Gleichnissen, wir reden Poesie und halten eine Balance zwischen den Gegensätzen' (50-1). Throughout the novel there seems to be an echo of Pontius Pilate's famous sceptical question: 'What is truth?'

Closely linked to the themes of truth and deception is the related pair of 'Sein und Schein', perhaps a somewhat overused concept in German literature and thought, but it permeates the whole novel and applies to its characters as well as its setting. The narrator summarizes this important aspect of the novel, when she refers to her wanderings through the 'Altstadt': 'Die Oberfläche der Dinge verdunkelte sich unter dem Gewicht ihrer verborgenen Bedeutung, sie wurden von ihr schier absorbiert. Alles erinnerte an etwas anderes, und nichts war, was es schien' (37). This is a deeply disturbing experience for Dvorah, but possibly also for the reader who follows through this train of thought. This is a key passage, and all major aspects of this novel might be discussed under the heading of 'Sein und Schein'.

Just as the appearance of the city of Jerusalem is deceptive, so is that of its inhabitants, at least for an outsider like Dvorah: 'Aber vielleicht sind sie alle Agenten und Terroristen, Kollaborateure und Spione, von der einen oder anderen Seite bezahlt, von beiden zugleich, oder sie machen es aus reinem Vergnügen an der Verwirrung. Es gibt die unwahrscheinlichsten Kombinationen, und jeder weiß mehr als ich' (29). Even the lovers at first misinterpret each other's outer appearance. Dvorah mistook Sivan for a Jew: 'ein junger eifriger Jude, der auf sein Stadtviertel stolz ist' (25). Sivan who claimed to be Armenian, thought Dvorah was an Arab: 'du warst so schön' (26). Throughout their relationship they hide their true selves, their true identities from each other. They feel the need to protect themselves by clinging to *Schein*, and this contributes to the tragic end of their love. Dvorah herself acknowledges this: 'Ich habe es lieber incognito zu leben und nie ganz das zu sein, was ich scheine' (138).

The problem of appearance and reality is also applied to Dvorah's family and their attempts to hide and forget their association with the Nazi regime and the fact that Dvorah's grandmother was Jewish. This theme is taken up in Dvorah's flashbacks to her childhood and youth, triggered off by her experiences in Jerusalem and her search for Martha and her own identity. Mitgutsch's presentation of Austria through Dvorah's memories also clearly shows this conflict between *Sein* and *Schein*. After 1945 the majority of Austrians tried to forget their involvement with the Nazi regime and presented themselves as *Opfer* rather than *Täter*. This interpretation of Austria's recent history was assisted by becoming enshrined in the State Treaty of 1955.

It is another interesting aspect of the novel that victims and perpetrators are very often two sides of the same coin, as is illustrated by different members of Dvorah's family and, above all, by Sivan. It is also true of many other events in this divided city which bring grief and suffering, but at the same time instil feelings of hatred and revenge and thus fuel the cycle of terrorist hostilities. Heinz Hartwig highlights this aspect of the novel in his review: 'Anna Mitgutsch gelingt es ... die private Liebesgeschichte geschickt und mühelos in die politische Ebene zu heben und an Hand ihrer Heldin Dvorah ein Stück österreichischer Verdrängungsgeschichte zu zeigen.... Diese Mischung zwischen Täter und Opfer innerhalb einer Familie darf man, symbolisch überhöht, durchaus auf die "Familie Österreich" bezogen verstehen' (Hartwig 1995).

With *Abschied von Jerusalem* Mitgutsch has moved forward into new territory with a new setting and a new subject matter. This novel is the work of a mature Austrian writer at the height of her artistic power who is also deeply committed to her Jewish origins and culture. It is, to my mind, her best book to date and deserves much greater public recognition than it has so far received.[6]

Notes

[1] *Landeskulturpreis Oberösterreichs* (1985), *Brüder Grimm Preis der Stadt Hanau* (1985), *Claassen-Rose* (1986), *Südtiroler Lesepreis der Stadt Bozen* (1990), *Anton Wildgans Preis* (1992), *Förderpreis für Literatur* (1996).

[2] As the reviewer in *Die Welt* put it: 'Die reiche Ortskenntnis der Autorin spiegelt sich im Vokabular wider, aber hier fehlt ein Glossar, denn was dem Israeli und dem Jerusalemer selbstverständlich ist, bleibt einem deutschen Leser oft unbekannt und unverständlich' (Anon. 1995).

[3] The subtitle of Michael Wildt's review (Wildt 1995) would, therefore, not be taken as a compliment by the author: 'Anna Mitgutsch ist als Reiseleiterin keineswegs unbegabt.' In the same discussion session Mitgutsch also admitted that her original title for this novel was *Kains Träume*, but the publishers persuaded her to change it to *Abschied von Jerusalem*.

[4] Wildt (1995) does not do the novel justice when he suggests: 'Vielleicht sollte man Anna Mitgutschs Erzählung als gelungene Stadtbeschreibung lesen, denn als Liebesgeschichte scheitert sie daran, daß sie eine Spannung aufrechtzuerhalten versucht, die längst keine mehr ist.' Even if the reader guesses the truth about Sivan quite early on, this does not necessarily mean that the story becomes boring!

[5] Mitgutsch claims not to have read *The Mandelbaum Gate* before writing *Abschied von Jerusalem*. Muriel Sparks's novel is set in the early 60s, and like Mitgutsch she explores the different ethnic and cultural groups in the city, then strictly divided into East and West Jerusalem with very few people crossing from one side to the other. One of the few who does so regularly is Freddy, a British Consulate official who tries very hard to understand this complex city and the conflict between the Jews, Arabs, Armenians and other Christian communities. Muriel Spark, too, creates a vivid and most evocative picture of Jerusalelm, its beauty, its roots in ancient history, its spiritual dimension, and its present-day divisions. As in *Abschied von Jerusalem* a trip through the desert to Ramallah provides a crucial turning point in the action. At the end Freddy leaves Jerusalem, his stay there has changed his life, he has learnt much about the city and its inhabitants, but like Dvorah, he has remained an outsider and he never quite understood the complexities and age-old mysteries of this city.

Notes continued

[6] Although the novel achieved only modest sales figures when it first appeared in 1995, the paperback edition (rororo), published in November 1996, was an instant success, with 12,000 copies sold in three months. An English translation of the novel will appear in New York in the autumn of 1997

Bibliography

Anon. 1995. 'Suche nach dem Ich. Schwaches Licht in friedloser Nacht? Anna Mitgutsch schrieb einen Jerusalem-Roman', *Die Welt*, 6 April
Hartwig, Heinz. 1995. 'Lebenslüge, Spurensuche, Verleugnung.' *Kleine Zeitung*, Klagenfurt, 6 May
Mitgutsch, Anna. 1995. *Abschied von Jerusalem*, Berlin, Rowohlt-Berlin
Spark, Muriel. 1967. *The Mandelbaum Gate*, London, Penguin
Wildt, Michael. 1995. 'Der Trost von Fremden', *Frankfurter Allgemeine Zeitung*, 27 April

Der unbewohnbarste Ort: Über den Begriff der Grenze bei Anna Mitgutsch

Petra Günther

Der folgende Beitrag will der Frage nachgehen, welche Rolle die Grenze bzw. das Bild von der Grenze im Werk Anna Mitgutschs spielt. Berücksichtigung finden ihre bislang fünf Romane, von der *Züchtigung* (1985) über *Das andere Gesicht* (1986) und *Ausgrenzung* (1989) bis zu *In fremden Städten* (1992) und *Abschied von Jerusalem* (1995). Wenn hier die Topographie der Grenze in den Blick genommen wird, soll allerdings keine positivistische Milieuschilderung stattfinden, vielmehr soll untersucht werden, wie der soziale, historisch konkrete Raum der Grenze sich in den Texten als Zeichenraum manifestiert. Ein besonderes Augenmerk wird dabei auf den Zusammenhang gerichtet, der zwischen der literarischen Raumdarstellung und der Verortung des Weiblichen besteht.

Im folgenden Zitat aus der *Züchtigung* ist von der Grenze (noch) nicht die Rede:

> und aus den Spiegeln sah sie mich an mit ihrem irren Blick und vom Weinen verwaschenen Zügen. Da blieb mir das Triumphgeschrei im Hals stecken, ich stürzte zur Tür, aber die Tür hatte keine Klinke, ich hätte es wissen können, nicht einmal ein Schlüsselloch zum Hineinspähen, und ich schlug meinen schlaflosen Kopf auf die schimmernden Fliesen. Auch die Tapetentüren zu den inneren Räumen fand ich nicht mehr. Warum hatte mir keiner gesagt, daß die Häuser der käuflichen Liebe keine Tapetentüren haben, keine Träume, von deren Ufern man ins mondverzauberte Meer hinausrudern konnte zu neuen Inseln und fernen reineren Gipfeln? (*Die Züchtigung*: 198-9)

In der angeführten Passage steht das Raum-Erlebnis im Mittelpunkt: die klaustrophobische Anmutung im Innern eines Spiegelkabinetts. Der Ort der Erzählerin wird markiert durch spiegelnde Wände und Türen ohne Schloß und Klinke, ein Entrinnen ist weder als Ausbruch nach außen noch als Rückzug nach innen möglich, Fluchtversuche enden an der Wand. Die räumliche Konstellation von Spiegel, Wand und Tür dient als eine Beschreibung für den Ort der Frau und entwirft ein Verhältnis von innen und außen, dem sich die Frau ausgesetzt sieht. In topographisch ähnlicher Funktion erscheint das Bild der Grenze.

'Grenze' in der *Züchtigung* meint zunächst die geographisch konkrete Staatengrenze: 'Zu Mittag war sie an der Grenze. Wohin, fragte der Zöllner. Pässe waren damals nicht nötig, um über die Grenze zu kommen. Nach Altötting, sagte sie und ging um den Schlagbaum herum' (*Die Züchtigung*: 15). Öfter jedoch als die deutsch-österreichische Grenze, die als erste im Roman erwähnt wird, gerät die tschechische Grenze in den Blickpunkt: 'Der Krieg brach aus. In dem kleinen Dorf an der tschechischen Grenze änderte sich nichts, als daß jetzt Feldpostkarten kamen, aus Polen, aus Frankreich, aus Griechenland' (*Die Züchtigung*: 41). Sie, nämlich die tschechische Grenze, gilt als Gebiet größter Abgelegenheit, hierher stammen die Eltern der Erzählerin (36), später verbringt Vera als Kind dort Ferien (195, 209), in einer 'gottverlassene[n]' Gegend (189), 'wo [einem] nur Hasen und Rehe in den Weg liefen' (194). Historisch-politische Bedeutung besitzt die 'Grenze' auch in einer Szene aus der unmittelbaren Nachkriegszeit:

> Wenn wir über die Donau mußten, begann ich schon bei der Haltestelle auf dem Brückenkopf zu zittern, denn mitten auf der Brücke war ein Holzverschlag, die Zonengrenze, an der fremde Soldaten 'Idis' kontrollierten ... [Ich] mußte zuschauen, wie meine Mutter hinter der Wand des Holzverschlags verschwand und vielleicht nie wieder herauskam, während ich in der Straßenbahn wartete. Das Heruntergekommenste, eine Frau, die sich mit fremden Soldaten einließ. (99-100)

'Grenze' wie 'Wand' sind hier gleichermaßen mit Abtrennung, Bedrohung und Fremdheit konnotiert. Neben die historisch-politische Bedeutungsfunktion tritt 'Grenze' als Begriff zur Kennzeichnung psychischer Befindlichkeiten:

> Und die mörderische Wut, die Versuchung, der eigenen lauernden Verzweiflung nachzugeben, wo die Grenzen zu einem anderen Ich schwach sind und leicht zu zertrampeln, wo der Selbsthaß unvermutet in die Zerstörung umschlagen kann, ich habe sie erlebt und auch die tiefe Scham danach. (*Die Züchtigung*: 156)

> Selbstzerstörung hieß mein Forschungsprojekt, Selbstmord in der Literatur, Regression, Ich-Verlust, Über- und Unterschreitungen der Ich-Grenzen. (178)

In *Das andere Gesicht* findet sich die Topographie von 'Grenze' weiter ausgebaut. 'Grenze' erscheint zunächst noch einmal als konkret geographisch-politischer Begriff, als die Rede auf die Flucht von Janas Familie (nach dem Zweiten Weltkrieg?) kommt (*Das andere Gesicht*: 67), wobei die exakte zeitliche und räumliche Verortung im unklaren belassen wird; klar wird nur, daß die Grenzüberschreitung den Eintritt in eine neue Sprachgemeinschaft nach sich zieht. Häufiger wird das Wort 'Grenze' zur Bezeichnung psychischer Dispositionen benutzt, ist die Grenze zwischen Wirklichkeit und Wahnsinn gemeint – oder vorsichtiger ausgedrückt: die mögliche und dann wieder unmögliche Passage zwischen verschiedenen Bewußtseinszuständen (*Das andere Gesicht*: 61, 73, 81-2, 297). Genauere Informationen über diesen diffusen

Schwellenbereich sind spärlich: 'Jenseits der Grenze, in meinem Reich, sprach man eine andere Sprache, nichts galt, was den andern unumstößliche Wahrheit war, und niemand durchschaute meine Gesetze' (73).

Jana erzählt hier von sich selbst, später sieht auch Sonja sie als Grenzbewohnerin: 'Da begriff ich, daß sie an der Grenze lebte, in einem Bereich, der ihr nicht mehr den Schutz vor den ständigen Reizen der Wirklichkeit bot, der mich vielem gegenüber, das ihr schon unerträglich schien, immun machte' (*Das andere Gesicht*: 145). Widersprüchlich bleibt, ob sich jenseits der Grenze der Bereich des Eigenen oder des Anderen erstreckt. Während sie weiter oben diesbezüglich von 'meinem Reich' spricht, bemerkt Jana an späterer Stelle: 'Unzählige Male bin ich an diese Grenze des anderen herangegangen, ich habe Bruchstücke davon in mir selbst wiedererkannt, die Angst, den Verlust jeden Sinns und jeder Bedeutung, aber den Zutritt hat es mir nie gewährt' (*Das andere Gesicht*: 179).

Zum einen treten hier das Eigene und das Andere nicht mehr vollkommen trennscharf auf, zum zweiten scheint im jenseitigen Gebiet Anarchie ('Verlust jeden Sinns und jeder Bedeutung') zu herrschen, während vorher noch von 'meinen Gesetzen' die Rede war. Und vollends fragwürdig ist, welche Sprache, wenn überhaupt, dort Geltung besitzt. Behauptet Jana erst: 'Jenseits der Grenze, in meinem Reich, sprach man eine andere Sprache' (*Das andere Gesicht*: 73), so bedeutet hier die 'andere Sprache' gerade Janas eigene Sprache, die eben anders ist als die Sprache der Anderen. Die Bemerkung vom 'Verlust jeden Sinns und jeder Bedeutung' (179) jedoch impliziert den Zusammenbruch jeglichen sprachlichen Systems. In beiden Fällen wird 'Grenze' im Zusammenhang mit (dem Vorhandensein bzw. dem Fehlen von) 'Gesetz' (und Sprache) gedacht, so wie es später im Roman noch einmal heißt: 'Lange Zeit warst du berauscht von diesem Wort, du hättest nicht gezögert, jedes Gesetz, jede Grenze in seinem Namen zu überschreiten' (206).

'Grenze' wird als Synonym für den topographisch ebenfalls bedeutsamen Begriff der 'Schwelle' benutzt: 'Ihr Haus war kein Tempel [...] es [war] ein Haus wie alle andern in jenem Land, mit hoher Schwelle, als überschritte man eine Grenze' (*Das andere Gesicht*: 225). Die Grenze kann aber nicht nur, wie bei diesem Haus einer Priesterin, am Eingang des Hauses verlaufen, sondern auch mitten hindurch: 'Als wollten wir unsere Unterwürfigkeit beweisen, nahmen wir nur drei Räume in Besitz, zogen eine Grenze zwischen uns und der Dunkelheit der hinteren Räume, überließen sie den Geistern der Toten' (281). Im 'Geisterhaus', das Jana und ihr Sohn Daniel bewohnen, trennt die Grenze Lebende und Tote. Die Grenze kann die Nähe des Todes signalisieren:

> Vom Ende her betrachte ich mein Leben als eine schrittweise Einübung in den Tod. In meiner Kindheit war mir der Tod als Nebelmann erschienen, der Gesichtslose, der sich

nie überlisten ließ, sich mir zu zeigen. Fasziniert und wohl auch voll Sehnsucht nach den verlorenen Menschen und Dingen übte ich mich als Grenzgängerin. (*Das andere Gesicht*: 304-5)

Für Mitgutschs dritten Roman ist das Motiv der Grenze sogar titelgebend, und in der eindringlichen Schlußpassage des Buches finden sich auf nur zweieinhalb Seiten fünfzehnmal das Wort 'Grenze' oder verwandte Bildungen wie 'Ausgrenzung', 'Grenzfall', 'Schmerzgrenze' und 'Grenzgänger' (*Ausgrenzung*: 263-5). In der '*Ausgrenzung*', in deren Mittelpunkt eine Mutter, Marta, und ihr behindertes Kind Jakob stehen, bedient sich Mitgutsch also bewußt und prononciert des räumlichen Begriffs der Grenze, um die gesellschaftliche Diskriminierung, die Mutter und Kind erfahren, zu bezeichnen. Zunächst taucht auch in diesem Roman die 'Grenze' noch einmal als geographisch-politische Staatengrenze auf, als von einem Ausflug 'über die Grenze in den Süden' (*Ausgrenzung*: 55) die Rede ist. Später dient sie an einer Stelle zur Veranschaulichung eines sozial-ökonomischen Sachverhalts: Im Rahmen der Scheidungsauseinandersetzungen zwischen Marta und ihrem Mann Felix droht dieser mit der Heimeinweisung des gemeinsamen Sohnes, 'wenn ihr [Martas] Einkommen unter eine bestimmte Grenze fiele' (170).

Als 'Grenzgänger' erscheint zunächst Jakob, dessen Behinderung Ärzte und andere Fachleute als Autismus diagnostizieren: 'Kein Wunder, daß diese Grenzgänge zwischen zwei Wirklichkeiten anstrengend für ihn waren' (*Ausgrenzung*: 161), dessen weitere Entwicklung jedoch die Eindeutigkeit dieser Diagnose erschüttert: 'Das Kind ist ein Grenzfall, deshalb ist es so schwer, ihn einzuordnen, hatte sie Lehrern und Pädagogen gegenüber oft erklärt' (263). 'Die Ausgrenzung, in der sie sich seit langem befanden' (263), betrifft nicht nur das Kind, sondern erstreckt sich auch auf Marta, beide sind konfrontiert mit der 'Grenze, die sie [Marta] und Jakob von den anderen trennte' (263).

Diese Situationsbeschreibung ruft zumindest drei Fragen hervor. Erstens: Wer sind die anderen? Zweitens: Befinden sich Marta und Jakob allein auf der gegenüberliegenden Seite der Grenze? Und drittens: '[...] wer hatte die Grenze gezogen?' (*Ausgrenzung*: 263). Damit ist die Machtfrage gestellt. Ex negativo läßt sich antworten: Die Macht liegt nicht in Martas Händen. 'Die Grenze war ihnen auf den Fersen, und Marta wußte, es würde ihr nie mehr gelingen, sie abzuschütteln, oder sie zu verlassen; und sie abzuschaffen, lag nicht in ihrer Macht' (263).

An dieser Textstelle erscheint die Grenze personifiziert und beweglich, beinahe autonom, doch schon eine Seite später wird klar, daß die Grenze nicht aus sich heraus existiert und wer die Macht in Händen hält: 'Die unentwegte Gefahr im Ungeschützten, die Abgründe, die bei jedem Schritt aufklaffen konnten, die Grenze, die immer die anderen zogen, nie jene, die über ihr zu Fall kamen' (*Ausgrenzung*: 264). Darüber, wer die anderen sind, erfährt man nicht mehr, als daß sie diejenigen sind, die die Grenze ziehen, die Herrschaft innehaben. Es gibt kein Leben ohne die Grenze, höchstens für Momente die Illusion eines herrschaftsfreien Raumes: 'An solchen Tagen war die Zukunft weit weg und belanglos, an solchen Tagen gab es die Grenze nicht' (263).

Marta und Jakob befinden sich auf seiten 'jene[r], die über ihr zu Fall kamen', sind also nicht alleine: 'Die Grenze, an der Marta sich so lange alleine mit Jakob gewähnt hatte, war dicht bevölkert' (*Ausgrenzung*: 264), aber eine Solidarisierung dieser Gruppe der Grenzgänger kommt nicht zustande: 'die Grenzgänger erkannten einander nicht, aus Mißtrauen, aus Angst, und weil sie der Versuch so zu sein wie die andern ganz in Anspruch nahm [...] Wenn wir, die wir an der Grenze leben, einander erkennen könnten, dachte sie, wären wir nicht so einsam und verwundbar' (264-5). 'Das Leben an der Grenze' gestaltet sich jedoch noch diffiziler als bisher schon dargestellt: 'die Grenze war heimtückisch, oft ging sie mitten durch einen hindurch, der glaubte, ihr entronnen zu sein, und machte ihn sich selber zum Fremden' (264). Die Grenze verläuft nicht allein außen an den Menschen entlang, sondern kann zum inneren Bestand der Persönlichkeitsstruktur werden, erscheint als Bild für den psychischen Zustand der Schizophrenie. Das Bild von der Grenze soll durch den Vergleich mit einer anderen räumlichen Bildvorstellung verdeutlicht werden, 'die Grenze [wuchs] wie eine Mauer wieder rund um sie auf' (263), und wird schließlich hinsichtlich seiner Schlüssigkeit und seines Aussagewertes problematisiert: 'Aber Marta wußte auch, daß das Bild von der Grenze nicht stimmte, diese Illusion einer Demarkationslinie, an der es sich recht und schlecht leben ließ; sie war der unbewohnbarste Ort, der Pranger, an dem man immer allein stand, ausgesetzt, von den anderen verworfen' (265). In *Ausgrenzung* wird das Bild von der Grenze also nicht nur bewußt und extensiv benutzt, sondern auch auf die Grenzen seiner Aussagekraft, auf die ihm inhärente Aporie befragt.

Mitgutschs vierter Roman, *In fremden Städten*, arbeitet zwar auch schon im Titel mit einer räumlichen Vorstellung, doch das Motiv der Grenze findet sich nur noch vereinzelt. Wie in den vorhergehenden Romanen steht eine Frau im Mittelpunkt des Geschehens. Wie Vera in der *Züchtigung*, Sonja und Jana in *Das andere Gesicht* und Marta in der *Ausgrenzung* macht Lillian in diesem Roman auch Grenzerfahrungen, zunächst als Amerikanerin in Österreich, dann, zurückgekehrt, als Amerikanerin in den Vereinigten Staaten. Explizit und in der Wiederholung des Ausdrucks fast aufdringlich wird Lillian als 'die archetypische Fremde' (*In fremden Städten*: 33, 215) bezeichnet. Ihr verwischen sich die 'klaren Grenzen zwischen Wirklichkeit und Träumen' (42), die 'Grenze' markiert zunächst vor allem die Sprachgrenze zwischen Österreichisch/Deutsch und Amerikanisch/Englisch: 'Man ist in Sicherheit, man spricht die eigene

Sprache, und sie trägt, die Grenze ist passiert, schwebend noch in einem Vakuum wartet man auf die Ankunft' (54).

Lillian – und das hebt sie in markanter Weise von den bisherigen Protagonistinnen ab – will Schriftstellerin werden, und ihre Reflexionen über die Möglichkeit und Unmöglichkeit dieses Vorhabens, ihren Ort als schreibende Frau zu finden, nehmen in dem Roman breiten Raum ein. Gegen Ende des Romangeschehens versucht sie sich im Ferienhaus ihrer Schwester, das auch von ihrem Vater bewohnt wird, einzurichten, und zwar in der Mansarde: 'Von jetzt an würden alle Gehäuse gleich aussehen, kleine Zimmer mit einem Bett und unterschiedlichem Komfort, Tisch, Sessel, Kleiderschrank, die Zimmertür die Grenze ihres Reiches' (*In fremden Städten*: 230-1).

In *Abschied von Jerusalem* (1995), Mitgutschs bislang letztem Roman, wimmelt es geradezu von Grenzen. In der Topographie Jerusalems als geteilter Stadt spiegelt sich die Zerrissenheit der Hauptfigur Dvorah. Die zahllosen Grenzen verlaufen – wo nicht sichtbar – darum nicht weniger wirksam (*Abschied von Jerusalem*: 17, 61, 86, 97, 156, 188, 218, 249, 271). Jeder in Jerusalem, jeder in Israel geht und fährt 'mit seiner Landkarte im Kopf' (250) – jeder, der dazugehört. Die Aufhebung der Grenzen ist eine Illusion für Touristen, ein Moment in der Dämmerung: 'Ich beobachte, wie die Grenzen verfließen, besonders am Abend, wenn sich die Straßen mit Flaneuren füllen, und wie untertags jeder wieder seiner eigenen Wege geht und die Grenzen respektiert', (101). Die Liebe scheint für einen Augenblick einen Ort 'jenseits der Sprachen' (221), jenseits aller politischen und persönlichen Grenzen zu ermöglichen, doch 'das Unheil war schon zu nah' (165). 'Grenzenlos' erscheinen allenfalls, wie hier, der Himmel über der Wüste oder die Wüste selbst: 'Am Nachmittag lag die Wüste ausgebleicht und grenzenlos unter dem zitronenfarbenen Himmel' (142), aber sie bieten kaum einen bewohnbaren Ort.

An der Grenze entlang läßt sich Mitgutschs Werk erkunden. Die Grenze erscheint als Grenze zwischen Ländern, zwischen Sprachen, zwischen Träumen und Wirklichkeit, Wahnsinn und Wirklichkeit, zwischen dem noch Sagbaren und dem schon Unsagbaren, zwischen Eigenem und Fremdem, zwischen dem Eigenen und dem Anderen. Eine ausführlichere Analyse würde den signifikanten Zusammenhang des Grenzbildes mit anderen bei Mitgutsch sich wiederholt findenden topographischen Begriffen wie dem der (Spiegel-)Wand hervortreten lassen. Welchen Sinn macht es nun, die topographische Untersuchungsperspektive der Grenze zu verfolgen? Daß sich anhand der Topographie von Texten die 'unterschiedlichen *Orte* der Geschlechter in der abendländischen Kulturgeschichte' ablesen lassen, hat Sigrid Weigel in ihren *Topographien der Geschlechter* eindrucksvoll dargelegt (1990: 11). Die Opposition 'männlich/ weiblich' wird räumlich häufig auf das Gegensatzpaar 'innen/außen' gespiegelt, der Begriff des Männlichen gleichgesetzt mit dem bekannten, heimatlichen

Gebiet, der des weiblichen mit dem unbekannten, fremden (vgl. Kane 1995: 528). Angesichts der vorzufindenden Annahme einer bipolaren (Raum-)Struktur gewinnt der Topos der Grenze besondere Relevanz, in ihm manifestiert sich in räumlicher Anschauung die Trennung zweier Bereiche. Wenn die Grenze also einerseits das Augenmerk auf die Differenz richtet, markiert sie doch andererseits die gemeinsame Schnittstelle einer Opposition und wirft die Frage nach Übergangsmöglichkeiten auf. Zudem muß der Begriff der 'Grenze' nicht zwangsläufig allein als eine (mehr oder minder durchlässige) Linie gedacht werden, mit ihm verbindet sich häufig auch die Vorstellung eines ungenau umrissenen Grenzgebietes, Niemandsland genannt. Sind die Übergänge als grenzüberschreitende Schwellenbereiche per se von besonderem heuristischen Interesse (vgl. Weigel 1990: 23, 33, 214, 217), so kommt ihnen abermals gesteigerte Bedeutung zu, wenn man nach dem Ort des weiblichen Subjekts fragt. Indem die Aufklärung die Konstitution des vernünftigen Subjekts als die des männlichen Subjekts vornimmt, gerät 'die Weiblichkeit – bzw. die Frau als Verkörperung von Weiblichkeit – häufig zur Vorstellung des Anderen schlechthin' (Weigel 1990: 119). Lokalisiert wird Weiblichkeit dann entweder '*außerhalb* der Grenzen', oder Frauen erscheinen als Verkörperung von Grenze und Grenzüberschreitung (vgl. Weigel 1990: 119-120). Während also die Bildvorstellungen von Weiblichkeit frei flottieren, ist der historisch-reale Platz von Frauen gerade durch Begrenzungen gekennzeichnet (vgl. Bovenschen 1992: 24, 38). Verschärft stellt sich die Situation schreibender Frauen dar:

> der Ort, von dem aus Frauen schreiben und sprechen, [läßt sich] so kennzeichnen: Indem Frauen teilhaben, teilnehmen an der herrschenden Sprache, ... sind sie an der bestehenden Ordnung beteiligt; sie benutzen dann eine Sprache, Normen und Werte, von denen sie zugleich als 'das andere Geschlecht' ausgeschlossen sind. Als Teilhaberin dieser Kultur dennoch ausgegrenzt und abwesend zu sein, das macht den spezifischen Ort von Frauen in unserer Kultur aus. (Weigel 1989: 8-9)

Läßt man die Protagonistinnen in Mitgutschs Romanen Revue passieren, so haben sie zumindest einen Teil ihres erwachsenen Lebens im intellektuellen Milieu zugebracht oder ringen um künstlerischen Ausdruck. Dabei wird die Suche nach einer stabilen eigenen Position als Krise erfahren: Vera leidet in der *Züchtigung* während ihres Literaturstudiums an Magersucht, Marta (in *Ausgrenzung*) wird als Intellektuelle von der Familie ihres Mannes abgelehnt, Lillian (*In fremden Städten*) scheitert in ihren Bemühungen, eine Existenz als Schriftstellerin aufzunehmen, Jana in *Das andere Gesicht* kann eine eigene Sprache nicht artikulieren und findet deshalb als Frau, als Künstlerin keinen eigenen Ort: 'Aber sie war keine Fremde wie zum Beispiel ihre Mutter ... Sie sprach keine andere Sprache als die unsere ... Wie hätte sie unser Leben, unsere ganze Kultur mit den Augen einer Fremden sehen können, wenn sie nichts besaß, das anders genug war, um uns von außen zu betrachten' (*Das andere Gesicht*: 312). Hier ist das Dilemma noch einmal auf den Punkt gebracht: Es gibt kein Draußen, kein 'jenseits der Grenze', das sich als Beobachtungsposition, als Ausgangspunkt beziehen ließe. Was das prekäre Verhältnis zur Sprache betrifft, ähnelt Jana in auffälliger Weise Martas Sohn Jakob.

Das Krankheitsbild des Autismus klingt bereits bei der Darstellung Janas in *Das andere Gesicht* an – 'Schon als Kind weigerte sie sich, ich zu sagen' (209). Wie zwischen Marta und Jakob gibt es auch zwischen Jana und ihrem Sohn Daniel eine 'Geheimsprache' (252), die den Vater des Kindes – hier Achim, dort Felix – ausschließt. Sowohl Jana als auch Jakob geraten in die Mühlen des psychiatrisch-professionellen Therapiebetriebes, ihre jeweilige Besonderheit wird als auffällige Abweichung diskriminiert und pathologisiert, die therapeutischen Eingriffe werden als auf Beherrschung und Domestizierung gerichtet geschildert. Jana wie Jakob kennen eine eigene 'Welt ohne Deutung und Sinn' (*Ausgrenzung*: 91), den 'Verlust jeden Sinns und jeder Bedeutung' (*Das andere Gesicht*: 179), beide leben in der Wirklichkeit der anderen 'wie in einem fremden Land mit einer schwer erlernbaren Sprache' (*Ausgrenzung*: 161-2). Der (mißglückende) Spracherwerb (des Kindes) wird als (verweigerter) Eintritt in die symbolische Ordnung dargestellt, Jakobs Ausdrucksweise als semiotisch charakterisiert: 'Alle anderen [Wörter] kamen und gingen, sie formten sich nicht zu Sätzen, sie wurden nicht Sprache, sondern erschienen wie Zeichen für etwas Unbekanntes aus einem geheimnisvollen Land' (*Ausgrenzung*: 44). Der abstrakte Verweischarakter von Sprache bleibt Jakob weitgehend fremd: 'Da fiel es ihr wieder auf, daß Jakobs Sprache anders war. Er verstand keine Abweichungen, keine Variationen, er konnte noch immer nicht abstrahieren und liebte doch zugleich alles Abstrakte, Linien, Zahlen, Farben und Töne' (158).

Jakob findet sich im syntaktischen System nicht zurecht: 'Er setzte die einzelnen Zeichen zu Wörtern zusammen und vergaß dabei den Sinn des gewonnenen Satzes. Als wäre jedes Wort eine Hülle, ein Säckchen, aus dem man die kleinen und großen Symbole herausschütteln konnte, eins wie das andere, Zeichen und Sinn' (*Ausgrenzung*: 185). In der Welt, die durch symbolische Zeichen konstituiert wird, bleibt er am Rande: 'Daß diese Linien für etwas anderes standen, daß Zahlen und Buchstaben Symbole waren, erfüllte ihn mit Unbehagen, er nahm es nur widerwillig hin' (230). Noch präziser formuliert ist im Roman von 'Jakobs Sprachverständnis ..., das keine Metaphern kannte' (244), die Rede. Jakob wird, in einer weiteren Parallele zu Jana, von Marta als Künstler gesehen (104, 231, 242).

Auch Lillian erweist sich als Verwandte Janas und Jakobs, auch sie hat Schwierigkeiten, ich zu sagen: 'Einen einfachen Satz, dachte sie, der mit Ich beginnt, das müßte dir doch gelingen' (*In fremden Städten*: 34). Identität und Sprache erscheinen in mehrfacher Hinsicht gekoppelt. Identitäts- und Schreibkrise fallen zusammen, doch beginnen Lillians Schwierigkeiten, in der Sprache zu sich, zu ihrem Ich zu finden, nicht erst mit ihrem letztlichen schriftstellerischen Versagen. An der Barriere zwischen Mutter- und Fremdsprache erlebt sie Probleme, die Jana in *Das andere Gesicht* und Jakob in *Ausgrenzung* schon vor ihr hatten, sie ist sprachlos (*In fremden Städten*: 16, 35), die – sprachlich – Unterlegene: 'Den Kampf um Worte verlor sie immer, und ihr Verstummen glich einer Kapitulation' (28). Sie findet sich in der Sprache nicht wieder: 'Sie fehlte in jedem Satz' (35). Oder noch einmal topographisch ausgedrückt: 'Kein Ort gehörte ihr' (73), sie ist eine 'Leerstelle' (124), ein 'weißer Fleck' (149, 207). Und nicht erst das Leben im Ausland, die Ehe mit Josef ('seiner Ordnung einverleibt', 16), die Konfrontation mit der Fremd- als Alltagssprache scheinen der Ursprung ihrer sprachlichen und existentiellen Krisenerfahrung zu sein: 'Sie konnte sich nie genau entsinnen, wann die Ohnmacht, sich der Dinge durch Sprache zu bemächtigen, begonnen hatte. Beim Umgang mit dem Manuskript ihres Vaters oder später, als die fremde Sprache im Alltag die eigene verdrängte?' (103). Die Geschichte des Sprachverlusts, die den Fallbeispielen Jana, Jakob und Lillian eingeschrieben ist, reicht tiefer, berührt ein kategorielles, nicht hintergehbares Erlebnis von Ausgeschlossensein. Ist (diesen) Personen in solchen 'Fällen' die Rede vom Ich in der Welt unmöglich, gerät auch das Streben nach Identität zum schier aussichtslosen Unterfangen.

Die Verortung der schreibenden Frau scheint einer Aporie gleichzukommen. Einmal, 'weil die Frau nicht aufgeht in dem ihr zugewiesenen Ort im Symbolischen' (Weigel 1989: 210), zum anderen, weil sprachliche Äußerungen doch nur im Rahmen der symbolischen Ordnung möglich sind. So ist die schreibende Frau weder innerhalb noch außerhalb der symbolischen Ordnung zu Hause und auch an keinem dritten Ort, der die Dichotomie von Innen und Außen außer Kraft setzte, sondern stets dem Verstummen nah. Mit der Sprache auf die symbolische Ordnung zurückgeworfen, positioniert sich die Frau als Autorin an den Übergängen zwischen dem Schweigen und dem Schreiben bzw. Reden. Diesen Transitbereich gilt es zu durchstreifen. Die Grenze mag der 'unbewohnbarste Ort' (*Ausgrenzung*: 265) sein, sie ist zugleich der mögliche Ort der Frau in der Kunstproduktion.

Bibliographie

Bovenschen, Silvia. 1992. *Die imaginierte Weiblichkeit. Exemplarische Untersuchungen zu kulturgeschichtlichen und literarischen Präsentationsformen*, Frankfurt am Main, Suhrkamp

Kane, Michael. 1995. 'Entgrenzung, Grenzüberschreitung und Ausgrenzung um 1900 oder "Gender, Geography and Orientation"', in Anne Fuchs und Theo Harden (Hrsg.), *Reisen im Diskurs. Modelle der literarischen Fremderfahrung von den Pilgerberichten bis zur Postmoderne*, Tagungsakten des internationalen Symposions zur Reiseliteratur. University College Dublin vom 10.-12. März 1994, unter Mitarbeit von Eva Juhl, Heidelberg, Universitätsverlag C. Winter: 521-41

Mitgutsch, Anna. 1987. *Die Züchtigung* (1985), München, dtv

—. 1991. *Das andere Gesicht* (1986), München, dtv

—. 1992. *Ausgrenzung* (1989), München, dtv

—. 1992. *In fremden Städten*, Hamburg, Luchterhand Literaturverlag.

—. 1995. *Abschied von Jerusalem*, Berlin, Rowohlt

Weigel, Sigrid. 1989. *Die Stimme der Medusa. Schreibweisen in der Gegenwartsliteratur von Frauen*, Reinbek, Rowohlt

—. 1990. *Topographien der Geschlechter. Kulturgeschichtliche Studien zur Literatur*, Reinbek, Rowohlt

Offene, utopische Stadt: Zur Darstellung Roms in Ingeborg Bachmanns Kurzprosa

Christina Ujma

> Die Faszination: Rom als offene Stadt, keine ihrer Schichten kann als abgeschlossen betrachtet werden, sie spielt alle Zeiten aus, gegeneinander, miteinander, das Alte kann morgen neu sein und Neueste morgen schon alt.[1]

So schrieb Ingeborg Bachmann in dem Fragment 'Ferragosto', entstanden vermutlich in den fünfziger Jahren. Die Verwobenheit der Vergangenheit mit der Gegenwart, die Tatsache, daß in Rom die Geschichte sehr lebendig ist, wurde aber nicht immer so positiv beurteilt: 'Die Preise sind hoch und die Spuren der Barbarei überall. Auf den Terrassen morschen die Oleanderkübel zugunsten der weißen und roten Blüten; die möchten fortfliegen, denn sie kommen gegen den Geruch von Unrat und Verwesung nicht auf, der die Vergangenheit lebendiger macht als Denkmäler' (IV: 30). Das sagte Ingeborg Bachmann in ihrem 1955 erstmals veröffentlichten Essay 'Was ich in Rom sah und hörte'. Eine seltsame Beschreibung von Rom, Sehnsuchtsziel von Generationen deutscher Dichter und Denker, sowie Wahlheimat von Ingeborg Bachmann. Rom hat in diesem Essay nicht den Charakter, den es in der literarischen Tradition hat – Ort stolzer, antiker Vergangenheit und wenig bemerkenswerter Gegenwart. Es ist diese Überlieferung, mit der sich Ingeborg Bachmann im Essay auseinandersetzt und die sie, um es mit Walter Benjamins *Geschichtsphilosphischen Thesen* zu sagen, gegen den Strich der Überlieferung bürstet, die ja auch immer die Überlieferung der Sieger ist.

'In Rom sah ich, daß der Tiber nicht schön ist', so lauten die ersten Worte des Essays 'Was ich in Rom sah und hörte', in dem Bachmann einleitend die Insel Tiberina evoziert, die Tiberinsel, die, geformt wie ein Schiff, seit der Antike der Ort der Kranken und der Beladenen ist. Weiter geht es mit einigen unfreundlichen Bemerkungen über das wichtigste Symbol der Stadt, den Petersdom, dessen protzige Monumentalität auf Italienisch kommentiert wird: 'Chiesa granne, divozzione poca' – große Kirche, wenig Andacht.

Lakonisch werden auch die monumentalen Ruinen der Antike kommentiert, die die Romreisenden der Vergangenheit, nicht zuletzt Goethe, so sehr in Begeisterung versetzten. Positiv wird lediglich das 'verräterische wilde Gras' auf dem Forum vermerkt. Die Tempel und Paläste sind zerfallen, sind Vergangenheit, konnten sich nicht behaupten. Eine Ausnahme gibt es allerdings: 'Säulen sind vom Tempel der Venus stehen geblieben – von diesem Tempel und keinem anderen'(IV: 32). Ironisch verweist Ingeborg Bachmann darauf, daß die Buchstaben S.P.Q.R., Senatus Populusque Romanus, die einst von der Macht des antiken Rom kündeten, sich in der Gegenwart 'von dem Wappenschild der vorüberfahrenden Autobusse, von der Platte eines Kanaleinstiegs' ablesen lassen.

Mit einem Gang durch die Viertel am Tiber setzt Ingeborg Bachmann die Demontage des klassischen Rombildes fort. Es sind drei Orte, an denen sie die Geschichte Roms in beklemmenden Bildern lebendig werden läßt. Der erste ist der Palazzo der Beatrice Cenci, jenes berühmten Inzestopfers, das zusammen mit Mutter und Brüdern den schändenden Vater umbrachte und dafür hingerichtet wurde. Am zweiten Ort, im jüdischen Ghetto, findet sie die Spuren der jüngsten Barbarei – der deutschen Okkupation Italiens in den letzten Jahren des Faschismus – lebendig; 'Die Alten erinnern sich ihrer Freunde, die mit Geld aufgewogen wurden; als sie losgekauft waren, fuhren trotzdem die Lastwagen vor, und sie kamen nicht wieder' (IV: 30).

1955, als das Essay erstmals erschien, war es kaum mehr als zehn Jahre her, daß die deutschen Lastwagen vorfuhren und viele der jüdischen Bewohner des Ghettos in die Lager gebracht wurden, trotz massiver Geldzahlungen, die dies eigentlich verhindern hätten sollen. Die präzise Benennung dieser perfiden Greueltat ist eine Herausforderung für ihre deutschen und österreichischen Leser, die sich in den fünfziger Jahren mehrheitlich Mühe gaben, die jüngste Vergangenheit zu verdrängen und von den Verbrechen, die in deutschem Namen in Italien oder anderswo begangen wurden, in der Tat nichts hören und sehen wollten.

Auf dem Campo de' Fiori, dem farbenprächtigen Blumen- und Gemüsemarkt Roms, findet sie keine Romantik, sondern läßt erneut die Vergangenheit lebendig werden, denn auf dieser ehemaligen Hinrichtungsstätte wurde nach der Einigung Italiens, sehr zur Empörung der Kirche, eine Statue zum Gedenken an den häretischen Mönch Giordano Bruno errichtet, der hier im Jahre 1600 verbrannt wurde, weil er es gewagt hatte, den Allwissenheitsanspruch der Kirche im Namen der Philosophie in Frage zu stellen;

> Ich sah auf dem Campo de Fiori, daß Giordano Bruno noch immer verbrannt wird. Jeden Sonnabend, wenn um ihn herum die Buden abgerissen werden, ... wenn der Gestank von Fisch, Chlor und verfaultem Obst auf dem Platz verebbt, tragen die Männer den Abfall, der geblieben ist, nachdem alles verfeilscht wurde, vor seinen Augen zusammen und zünden den Haufen an. Wieder steigt Rauch auf, und die Flammen drehen sich in der Luft. Eine Frau schreit, und die anderen schreien mit. Weil die Flammen farblos sind in dem starken Licht, sieht man nicht, wie weit sie reichen und wonach sie schlagen. Aber der Mann auf dem Sockel weiß es und widerruft dennoch nicht. (IV: 30-1)

Ob der Müll damals wirklich noch unter dem Standbild des ketzerischen Denkers verbrannt wurde, oder ob dieses Bild der dichterischen Freiheit entspringt, wissen wir nicht. Auf alle Fälle aber entsteht so ein beklemmendes Bild, eines, das die Unterdrückung und das Grauen in der Vergangenheit aufsucht und es in die Gegenwart herübertransportiert, ihm damit Aktualität verleiht.

Die Geschichte Roms ist eine Geschichte der Barbarei, dies macht Ingeborg Bachmann in 'Was ich in Rom sah und hörte' an Beatrice Cenci, stellvertretend für die Unterdrückung der Frauen, am Ghetto, für die massenhafte Ermordung der Juden während des Faschismus und an Giordano Bruno, stellvertretend für den kritischen Geist deutlich. Stärker als alle Autorinnen und Autoren zuvor konfrontiert Bachmann die LeserInnen mit der Negation des traditionellen Goethe-Winckelmannschen Italienbildes, mit dem Schrecken, den die Geschichte und vielleicht auch die Gegenwart der Ewigen Stadt birgt.

Bachmann setzt ihr Essay nach der Zurückweisung der Vergangenheit in einem sanfteren Ton fort, denn Rom, die Stadt der Gegenwart, ist auch ihr Thema. Es ist ihre Erzählstrategie, die durch die Italienromantik geprägten Orte in einem ganz anderen Licht erscheinen zu lassen, wie z.B. den berühmten Trevi-Brunnen:

> Wer ein Geldstück in die Fontana di Trevi wirft, um wiederzukommen, fürchtet, es könnte nicht angenommen werden. Aber er kann getrost sein. Nachts setzt sich ein Junge auf den Brunnenrand und pfeift, lockt die andern hervor. Wenn alle sich versammelt haben, legt der Junge die Kleider ab und steigt lässig ins Wasser. Mond belichtet die Szene, während er sich fröstelnd bückt und die Münzen einsammelt. Am Ende pfeift er wieder, und in seinen Händen verschmelzen alle Währungen zu Silber. Die Beute ist unteilbar unter dem Mond, denn der Junge hat das Aussehen eines Gottes gegenüber den andern, die ihre Gestalten billigen Anzügen verdanken. (IV: 33)

Die Poesie und die Göttlichkeit Roms liegt hier also an ganz ungewöhnlichem Orte, in der unbekleideten Gestalt eines italienischen Straßenjungen, dessen Handeln den Vulgärmythen der Italienreisenden, wie dem Werfen der Münzen in den Trevibrunnen, Hohn spricht.

Die Schönheit und der Charme des Alltagslebens ist ein wichtiger Aspekt des Essays, sogar an dem monumental häßlichen römischen Bahnhof Stazione Termini entdeckt Ingeborg Bachmann Faszinierendes:

> Auf dem Bahnhof Termini sah ich, daß in Rom die Abschiede leichter genommen werden als anderswo. Denn die fortfahren, lassen denen, die bleiben, einen Gepäckschein auf Sehnsucht zurück. An den Bahnhof grenzt ja ein Rest der Diokletiansmauer, und gegen die neue schwebende Glaswand gestochen erscheinen drei Zypressen in einer unmißverständlichen Schrift. Das Klassische ist das Einfachste, und alte und neue Texte vertreten es gleich gut. (IV: 32-3)

Ein weiterer Hieb auf die Tradition – Goethes Verdikt 'das Klassische ist das Einfachste', angesichts dieser Bahnhofshalle im scheußlichsten Funktionalstil der fünfziger Jahre erbaut, kann man nur sagen 'armer Goethe', dessen Vision von edler klassizistischer Einfalt und stiller Größe hier zur Groteske verkommt. Seit Mussolinis Rückgriff auf die Antike zur Rechtfertigung seiner Herrschaft und seit seinem Brutaloklassizismus war es für junge Autorinnen und Autoren kaum mehr möglich, sich positiv auf die antike Vergangenheit Italiens zu beziehen. Die faschistischen Säulenalleen und Triumphadler erscheinen nun häufig als ein gigantischer Widerruf des humanistischen Pathos früherer Klassizismusentwürfe.

Über Italien, besonders über Rom schreiben, heißt immer auch, sich in eine Tradition zu begeben, zu der man schon Stellung nehmen muß. Dabei war der entmystifizierende Blick auf Italien, besonders auf Rom, die scharfe Abgrenzung vom Goetheschen Italienerlebnis in den fünfziger Jahren nicht außergewöhnlich. Sie findet sich in Marie Luise Kaschnitz' *Engelsbrücke* (1955) genau wie in Wolfgang Koeppens *Tod in Rom* (1954) und in seinem *Neuen römischen Cicerone* (1958). Der geht allerdings ganz Ciceronemäßig geschwätzig vor, er betont zwar, daß die Geschichte Roms eine von Mord und Totschlag ist, er erwähnt auch Beactrice Cenci, aber ist diesen Ereignissen gegenüber nicht sonderlich kritisch eingestellt, sondern vermischt die Schönheit und die Greuel zu einem bunten, facettenreichen Eintopf. Bachmanns Aufsatz ist auch ein Cicerone, allerdings einer durch die Schattenwelt der Geschichte Roms, die dunklen, verborgenen Schichten der ewigen Stadt, durchaus die Schauplätze eines klassischen Reiseberichts aufnehmend, zeigt er deren verdrängte und vergessene Aspekte auf, konzentriert sich auf das, 'was unter der Erde liegt' und 'nur schwer zu sehen ist'.

Am Ende des Aufsatzes 'Was ich in Rom sah und hörte' sucht Bachmann den protestantischen Friedhof auf, – noch ein Ort der Ketzer, jedenfalls für die römischen Katholiken, der Ort, an dem auch einige Repräsentanten des alten Italienmythos begraben liegen.

> In Rom habe ich in der Früh vom Protestantischen Friedhof zum Testaccio hinübergesehen und meinen Kummer dazugeworfen.... Für den Friedhof, der an der Aurelianischen Mauer Schatten sucht, sind die Scherben auf dem Testaccio nicht gezählt, aber gering. Er hält sich eine große Wolke wie eine Muschel ans Ohr und hört nur mehr einen Ton. In den sind eingegangen ... neben Keats Versen eine Handvoll Verse von Shelley. Von Humboldts kleinem Sohn, der an Sumpffieber starb, kein Wort. Und von August von Goethe auch kein Wort. Von den stummen Malern Karstens und Mareés sind einige Linien geblieben, ein Farbfleck, ein wissendes Blau. Von anderen Stummen wußte man nie etwas. (IV: 34)

Hier wird der hermetische Charakter von Bachmanns Aufsatz deutlich – sie erklärt nichts, beschreibt nichts, sondern evoziert nur Bilder, die der Leser oder die Leserin durch Vorwissen und Kenntnis der Schauplätze entschlüsseln kann oder auch nicht. Wer nicht weiß, was der Testaccio ist, nie auf dem protestantischen Friedhof in Rom war, der hat Schwierigkeiten zu verstehen, auch wenn die Scherben und das Bild vom Friedhof, der dem lebendigen Ton lauscht, den seine toten Bewohner hinterlassen haben, zur Not auch ohne eigene Anschauung als Toterklärung der Tradition zu verstehen ist.

Dabei geht es Ingeborg Bachmann in 'Was ich in Rom sah und hörte' weniger um Sinneseindrücke, um das Sehen und Hören der Stadt der Gegenwart, als um die Stadt als steinerne Metapher, Sinnbild der Geschichte. 'Was ich in Rom sah und hörte' ist denn auch weniger Reiseessay als eine Folge von hoch verdichteten Bildern, eher ein langes Gedicht in freiem Vers. Bachmann selbst beschreibt dies folgendermaßen:

> Den Beitrag für Akzente habe ich schon beendet. Er erscheint dieser Tage, ist aber keine Erzählung, sondern ein formal etwas seltsames Gebilde, für das ich keinen Namen weiß. Es ... handelt sich nicht um eine Rom Impression oder die berüchtigte Wiedergabe der Rom-Eindrücke. Ich habe nur versucht, die 'Formeln' für die Stadt aufzusuchen, ihre Essenz, wie sie sich in bestimmten Momenten ganz konkret zeigt. (Bachmann 1983: 13)

In der Eleganz von Sprache und Stil wird Bachmann der Tradition, die sie attackiert, gerecht, ohne daß dies die Radikalität ihrer Aussagen beeinträchtigen würde. Weit entfernt ist Bachmanns Essay von der wohl berühmtesten Abrechnung mit der Stadt Rom und ihrem Mythos *Rom, Blicke*, die Rolf Dieter Brinkmann in den Jahren 1972-73 schrieb, in der er seinen Haß und seine Abgrenzung in spätpubertären Tiraden herausschrie und damit wohl durchaus den Geist der Zeit traf.

Die Nachbarschaft, in die die Literaturwissenschaftlerin Sigrid Weigel Bachmanns Essay rückt, ist immer wieder die von Benjamins Städtebildern (Vgl. Weigel 1993). In der Tat ist Ingeborg Bachmanns Essay 'Was ich in Rom sah und hörte' durch die Kombination von sprachlicher Eleganz, verdichteter Bildersprache und radikaler geschichtsphilosophischer Aussage in der Nachkriegsliteratur einzigartig. Bachmann knüpft bewußt an die Traditionen der Weimarer Republik an.

Der ungewöhnliche Charakter dieses Essays ist auch Gershom Scholem nicht verborgen geblieben. Der Essayist, Religionsphilosoph und Freund Walter Benjamins widmete Ingeborg Bachmanns Essay 1967 ein Gedicht, in dem er einen poetischen Dialog über den jüdischen Messianismus versucht:

> Im Ghetto sahst Du was nicht jeder sieht
> und was sich draussen allzu leicht vergisst:
> Dass nichts ganz voll erfüllt, was geschieht,
> dass noch nicht aller Tage Abend ist (Zitiert nach Weigel 1996)

Dieses Gedicht wurde erst im Nachlaß des jüdischen Denkers gefunden, zu seinen Lebzeiten wurde es nie veröffentlicht. Neben Reflektionen über die jüdische Tradition und das Ghetto enthält es vor allem die Erkenntnis, daß Bachmanns Sicht auf Rom, das Ghetto und seine Geschichte viel enthält, was nicht jeder sieht.

Für Bachmann hat die scharfe Abgrenzung von der traditionellen Italienrezeption noch eine andere Ursache, sie lehnt damit ein Erbe ab, das ihr nicht nur angetragen, sondern fast aufgezwungen wurde – die Fortsetzung der deutschen Tradition der Italiendichtung. Ehrwürdig ist sie schon, diese Tradition, verbunden mit Namen wie Winckelmann, Goethe und Burckhardt, aber auch belastet mit dem Nichtsehen und Nichthören der Barbarei, mit der Idealisierung von Architektur und Geschichte. Die Gegenwart, die so gar keine Ähnlichkeit mit den Zeiten Goethes hat, in seiner Sprache und seinen Bildern zu behandeln, wäre nicht nur unoriginell, sondern unwahr, wie sie in einem Interview der fünfziger Jahre sagte (Vgl. Bachmann 1983: 15-19).

Sie als Fortsetzerin gerade dieser Tradition zu betrachten, dies stand am Anfang der breiten Rezeption der Dichterin. Ausgerechnet *Der Spiegel* vom 18. August 1954 stellte in einer Titelgeschichte Ingeborg Bachmann vor, auf dem Titel ihr Gesicht, darunter die Schlagzeilen: 'Gedichte aus dem deutschen Ghetto (sic!), Neue Römische Elegien: Ingeborg Bachmann' (Vgl. dazu Hotz 1990: 43-69). In dem dazu gehörenden Artikel wird Bachmann nicht nur als Repräsentantin der deutschen Italientradition gewürdigt, in deren Werk getreu der Tradition durch das Italienerlebnis entscheidende Reifung eintrat, sondern auch als Wiedergewinnung des Anschlusses an internationale Entwicklung, als Herausbildung einer eigenständigen modernistischen Literatur. Constance Hotz faßt dies folgendermaßen: 'Die Aufstiegs- und Angekommenseins-Metaphorik ... stimmt mit dem dominanten bundesdeutschen Zeitgefühl um die Mitte der 50er Jahre überein – hier liefert die Literatur einen willkommenen Beitrag zur Wiederherstellung unterbrochener Zusammenhänge und zur Anschließung an internationale Standards. Die Bachmann-Gedichte sind auch ein Wir-sind-wieder-wer-Ereignis' (Hotz 1990: 95-6).

Ein anderer interessanter Aspekt ist die Unbefangenheit, mit der 1954 *Der Spiegel*, aber auch 1990 Constance Hotz, die Österreicherin Ingeborg Bachmann der bundesdeutschen Literatur zuschlägt. Angesichts der Zuschreibungen, ja Vereinnahmungen Ingeborg Bachmanns, ist es nicht verwunderlich, daß sie in den nächsten 15 Jahren gegenüber jedem Reporter, der sie fragte, beteuerte, kein

Italienerlebnis gehabt zu haben. Die Schroffheit, mit der die deutsche Italien-Tradition oder deren Fortführung abgelehnt wird, hat aber noch einen anderen Grund, es liegt an der veränderten Funktion, die gerade in den fünfziger Jahren Rom für deutsche SchriftstellerInnen und Intellektuelle hatte. Rom bot damals eine andere Lebensweise, Auswege aus dem provinziellen Mief, der im restaurativen Österreich genau wie in der restaurativen Bundesrepublik die geistige Atmosphäre charakterisierte. So war es das intellektuelle Klima Italiens, das internationales Flair hatte und auch diverse Zirkel bot, in denen italienische Künstler und Intellektuelle untereinander oder mit Kollegen und Kolleginnen aus anderen europäischen Ländern diskutierten. Italien faszinierte damals nicht nur Ingeborg Bachmann, sondern übte – nicht nur wegen des Wetters und der Kunstgeschichte wegen – eine starke Anziehungskraft auf viele Schriftsteller aus, zum Beispiel auf Uwe Johnson, Koeppen und Alfred Andersch, um nur die bekanntesten zu nennen. Auch Andersch fand die intellektuelle Atmosphäre der Stadt Rom außergewöhnlich – in einem Essay von 1962 huldigte er ihr 'als einem der letzten literarischen Paradiese dieser Erde' (Andersch 1979: 209).

Römische Künstler-Treffpunkte waren mondäne Cafes, wie das 'Doney' oder das 'Greco', wo Ingeborg Bachmann regelmäßig verkehrte und wichtige Kontakte knüpfte. In der internationalen Kulturzeitschrift *Botteghe Oscure* der Marguerita Caetani veröffentlichte Bachmann bereits 1954 einige Gedichte; Übersetzungen ihrer Lyrik erschienen seit Ende der fünfziger Jahre in verschiedenen italienischen Publikationen. Auch die deutsche Schriftstellergemeinde in Rom traf sich regelmäßig, in Marie Luise Kaschnitz fand Ingeborg Bachmann hier eine ältere Freundin und Kollegin; für eine junge Frau in einem Männerberuf – und das war die Schriftstellerei in den fünfziger Jahren unverändert – ein wichtiger Rückhalt.

Ingeborg Bachmanns Interesse an Italien blieb nicht auf Literarisches beschränkt, Sprache, Kultur und Politik wurden ihr bald vertraut, sie wurde auch zur Vermittlerin zwischen der deutschsprachigen und der italienischen Kultur. So schrieb sie 1954 unter Pseudonym mehrere Artikel über die politische Situation in Italien für die Westdeutsche Allgemeine Zeitung (Vgl. Hapkemeyer 1990: 77). 1961 erschienen ihre meisterhaften Übersetzungen bzw. Nachdichtungen der Gedichte Giuseppe Ungarettis. Durch ihre Kontakte mit Schriftstellern und Verlegern förderte sie die Rezeption der jungen deutschen Literatur in Italien. Die Liste ihrer italienischen Freundschaften und Kontakte enthält fast alle wichtigen Persönlichkeiten der jungen italienischen Nachkriegskultur, am bekanntesten dürften Morante, Pasolini und Feltrinelli sein (Vgl. Mocali 1993).

In Interviews erwähnt Bachmann oft genug ihre Faszination durch italienische Kultur und Politik, im Unterschied zur deutschen Tradition wird ihre Italienbegeisterung nicht so sehr durch sinnliche, als durch geistige Anziehung bestimmt:

> Zur Faszination Roms gehört, für mich jedenfalls, die Tatsache, daß es mir als letzte Großstadt unter den mir bekannten erscheint, wo man ein geistiges Heimatgefühl haben kann. Vielleicht als einer der letzten Orte, wo man ... aufgefangen wird. Rom ist wie die Kolonnaden, eine offene Stadt, und sie übt wohl doch eine besondere Kraft aus, mit diesen ineinander verschlungenen Bildern vergangener Zeiten. Darin liegt vielleicht eine Botschaft, die Botschaft einer auch utopischen Stadt. Rom wirkt nicht nur durch das Bestehende; es wirkt auch durch die in seinem vielschichtigen Dasein bestehenden Möglichkeiten. (Bachmann 1983: 23)

In Rom, so fährt Ingeborg Bachmann fort, kann man allein sein, ohne sich einsam zu fühlen, andererseits vereinnahmt die Stadt das Individuum nicht, sondern läßt ihm seine Individualität.

Obwohl Bachmann seit Mitte der Fünfziger vorwiegend in Italien, meist in Rom lebte, bleiben Wien und Österreich die Schauplätze ihrer Romane und Kurzgeschichten, einzig in 'Das dreißigste Jahr' stellt sie die beiden Städte einander gegenüber. Dem anonymen Helden dieser Kurzgeschichte gelingt es nicht, die utopischen und offenen Züge der Stadt Rom zu genießen. Mit dem Herannahen seines dreißigsten Geburtstages stürzt er in eine tiefe Identitätskrise und flieht von Wien nach Rom, wo er früher glücklich gewesen ist. Die Lösung der Krise durch den Italienaufenthalt gelingt nicht. Kaum zufällig, daß Bachmann auf diesem Punkt beharrt, noch ein Hinweis darauf, daß die alte Italienerfahrung der Deutschen und Österreicher nicht mehr möglich ist. Eine andere Identität findet der Held nicht, im Gegenteil, sein altes, sein jüngeres Ich wird ihm 'aufgezwungen wie eine Zwangsjacke'. Das Treffen mit alten Bekannten, mit alten Liebschaften, wird zum Debakel, mündet in den Aufschrei: 'Haltet Abstand von mir, oder ich sterbe, oder ich morde, oder ich morde mich selber. Abstand, um Gottes willen!' (II: 104).

Der Protagonist des 'Dreißigsten Jahrs' macht in Rom eine traumatische Erfahrung, seine Stadt, die Stadt, in der er glücklich gewesen ist, er hat sie verloren. Aller Anstrengungen zum Trotz, eine Fortsetzung jenes ersten Rom-Erlebnisses will sich nicht einstellen, ebensowenig wie er einen neuen, einen anderen Zugang findet. So beschäftigt sich der namenlose Held in diesem römischen August mit dem Nichtstun, dem dolce far niente, mit Cafeaufenthalten, dem Herumliegen am Strand, zahlreichen Liebschaften und planlosem Müßiggang. Eine Karikatur des damals durch Fellini berühmt gewordenen römischen Dolce Vita, das in seinem Fall gar nicht süß ist, sondern nur dazu dient, die Zeit totzuschlagen. Um im Spätherbst nach Wien zurückkehren zu können, muß er sich Geld von den Eltern kommen lassen. Die Rückkehr ist allerdings genau so fruchtlos wie die Reise nach Rom. War Rom, trotz seiner Schönheit, nicht für eine Erlösung gut, so wird Wien in dieser Geschichte zum Ort, den man fliehen muß. So kehrt der Protagonist bald wieder nach Italien zurück, wo er ziellos herumreist und von der Lösung der Krise weiter entfernt denn je ist. Die

Handlung läßt Bachmann damit enden, daß ihre Hauptperson auf dem Weg nach Mailand schwer verunglückt und sich nach der Genesung vornimmt, ein neues Leben anzufangen. Bachmann thematisiert im Romerlebnis des Protagonisten des 'dreißigsten Jahrs' eine grundlegende Erfahrung aller Reisenden: Augenblicke sind nicht wiederholbar, die Beziehungen mit fremden Städten sind so kompliziert wie die mit Menschen; Vertrautheit und Verstehen sind prekär und nicht von Dauer, mit dem Wandel der Persönlichkeit wandelt sich auch die Stadterfahrung. Auch im Fragment 'Ferragosto' erwähnt sie, daß sich die Stadt Rom manchem Fremden 'in der ersten Begeisterung und Enttäuschung öffnet und wieder verschloß'. Der Fremde, der längere Zeit bleibt, so heißt es im selben Text, kann diese Verschlossenheit überwinden, kann in Rom hören und sehen lernen. Die Erkenntnisse, die die ewige Stadt vermittelt, sind allerdings von besonderer Art: 'Die Unbedeutendheit des einzelnen, der ambienti, diese Stadt kommt so gut ohne irgend jemand Bestimmten aus und gibt grade darum, weil sie die eigene Unwichtigkeit dauernd beweist, weil sie immer mit Maßstäben zur Hand ist, vielleicht noch eine Arbeit [auf, macht] eine Lehre möglich, wie man sie nirgends sonst bekommen kann' (IV: 337). In 'Ferragosto' thematisiert Bachmann die ambivalente Situation derer, die sich dadurch auszeichnen, daß sie beiden Menschengruppen, die die Stadt bevölkern, fremd sind, weder Besuche noch Einheimische sind, aber da sie, wie Ingeborg Bachmann in Rom leben, sich eher letzteren zugehörig fühlen. Sinnbild dafür ist der Ferragosto, der profanste und unbekannteste aller italienischen Feiertage, von dem die Touristen keine Kenntnis haben: 'Ferragosto, die Augustfeiertage, den Römern fast ebenso wichtig wie Weihnachten und Ostern' (IV: 336). Gemeint sind jene Augusttage, an denen der Sommer in italienischen Städten kaum noch auszuhalten ist und die Einheimischen, wenn es ihnen irgend möglich ist, ans Meer fliehen, während die Touristen die leere Stadt erobern. Die 'Andenkenkäufer', die 'Museen- und Kirchenbezwinger in Rekordzeiten' und die 'Chiantihelden', sie werden zum Beispiel dafür, wie man es vermeidet in Rom hören und sehen zu lernen. Dabei ist Rom durchaus eine zugängliche Stadt, in Interviews der Bachmann wird immer wieder die Offenheit Roms herausgestellt, die das Individuum nicht auf eine Identität festlegt, aber trotzdem annimmt. In Italien, in Rom, so sagt Ingeborg Bachmann, habe sie leben und zu ihrem eigenen Lebensentwurf stehen gelernt.

Rom hat ähnlich wie Wien eine Geschichte reich an Kunst wie an Barbarei, aber in den Arbeiten und Interviews ist es immer wieder die Gegenwart Roms, die hervorgehoben wird, das alltägliche Leben, das von ungeheurer Vitalität, aber auch von Freundlichkeit bestimmt ist und damit die Anziehung der Stadt ausmacht, genau wie der ästhetische Reiz, der dem Alltagsleben eigen ist. Schreiben über Italien aus einer anderen Perspektive, als der der Fremden, könne sie allerdings nicht, dafür seien italienische Verhältnisse zu komplex. Dabei ist es nicht so, als hätte Bachmann nicht versucht, Italien zum Thema zu machen, aber die Versuche sind fast alle Fragment geblieben, wie 'Ferragosto'. Aber dann gibt es unter den unvollendeten, mehr oder weniger ausgearbeiteten Stücken des Nachlaßes einige, die Italien thematisieren, nicht nur Ferragosto, sondern auch die Kurzgeschichte 'Portrait von Anna Maria' und die Hommage an Maria Callas. Hier wird die Sängerin zum italienischen Genius hochstilisiert, zur idealen Verkörperung italienischer Kultur und Musik:

> sie war, was ... an die Duse denken läßt: ecco un artista. Sie hat nicht Rollen gesungen, niemals, sondern auf der Rasierklinge gelebt, sie hat ein Rezitativ, das altbacken schien, neu gemacht, ach nicht neu, sie war so gegenwärtig, daß alle ihr die Rollen geschrieben haben, von Verdi bis Bellini, von Rossini bis Cherubini, in ihr nicht nur die Erfüllung gesehen hätten, sondern weitaus mehr. (IV: 342-3)

In dem Stück *Zugegeben* aus dem Jahr 1969, das sie für eine Anthologie über das literarische Profil Roms schrieb und ursprünglich mit einer italienischen Widmung für Marie Luise Kaschnitz versah, thematisiert Ingeborg Bachmann das eigene Leben zwischen Wien und Rom. Es ist dadurch gekennzeichnet, daß sie zwar in Rom lebt, aber immer nur über Wien bzw. Österreich schreibt, und sich im Moment des Schreibens, trotz der römischen Wohnung, in Wien befindet. Was Rom jedoch ihrem Leben zu bieten hat, zählt viel, und mit der Feier dessen beendet sie das kleine Prosastück:

> Zugegeben, daß die Leute hier auch nicht besser sind als anderswo, aber fünf Minuten auf der Straße und ein kleiner Anflug von Wahnsinn, eine Versuchung, das alles ganz aufzugeben, sind dann doch plötzlich abgewendet. Zugegeben, die Leute sind etwas schöner und sehr freundlich ... Zugegeben, daß man hier aufhört, die Dinge allzu ernst zu nehmen; denn in 2500 Jahren ist viel Wasser den Tiber hinuntergelaufen ... Die Leute wissen schon, daß man einfach miteinander auskommen muß. Zugegeben, ich habe hier erlernt, mit den anderen auszukommen. Ich habe es wieder erlernt, aber ich gebe auch zu, wenn die Tür zufällt zu dem Zimmer in dem ich arbeite, dann gibt es keinen Zweifel: Denken ist solitär, Alleinsein ist eine gute Sache. (IV: 340-1)

Nach langer Flucht vor dem Thema hat Bachmann schließlich ihr Romerlebnis in diesem Prosastück thematisiert und publiziert. Sie entwirft eine ironisch distanzierte Vision, aber auch eine, die sich zur gespaltenen Existenz bekennt und das Leben zwischen den Kulturen, zwischen Rom und Wien, als Freiraum und positiven Entwurf charakterisiert.

Notes

[1] Ingeborg Bachmann, 'Ferragosto', in: *Werke*, hrsg. Christine Koschel et al., Bd. IV, München 1978: 337. Die Bachmann-Nachweise erfolgen im folgenden nach der Gesamtausgabe in 4 Bänden im Text, die römische Ziffer bezieht sich auf den Band der Gesamtausgabe, die arabische Zahl bezeichnet die jeweilige Seite.

Bibliographie

Andersch, Alfred. 1979. *Aus einem römischen Winter und andere Reisebilder*, Berlin, Akademie: 209
Bachmann, Ingeborg. 1978. *Werke* I-IV, hrsg. Christine Koschel et al., München, Piper
—. 1983. *Wir müssen wahre Sätze finden: Gespräche und Interviews*, hrsg. Christine Koschel, Inge von Weidenbaum, München, Piper
Hapkemeyer, Andreas. 1990. *Ingeborg Bachmann, Entwicklungslinie in Werk und Leben*, Wien, Österreichische Akademie der Wissenschaften
Hotz, Constance. 1990. *'Die Bachmann', Das Image der Dichterin: Ingeborg Bachmann im journalistischen Diskurs*, Konstanz, FAUDE
Mocali, Maria Chiara. 1993. 'Die Bachmann-Rezeption in der italienischen Literaturwissenschaft und Literatur', in D. Göttsche, H. Ohl (Hrsg.), *Ingeborg Bachmann, Neue Beiträge zu ihrem Werk*, Internationales Symposion Münster 1991, Würzburg, Königshausen und Neumann
Weigel, Sigrid. 1993. '"Stadt ohne Gewähr" – Topographien der Erinnerung in der Intertextualität von Bachmann und Benjamin', in D. Göttsche, H. Ohl (Hrsg.), *Ingeborg Bachmann, Neue Beiträge zu ihrem Werk*, Internationales Symposion Münster 1991, Würzburg, Königshausen und Neumann
—. 1996. 'Der Abend aller Tage', *Die Zeit*, 1. Juni: 26

The Question of Subjectivity in Bachmann's *Frankfurter Vorlesungen* and *Das Dreißigste Jahr*

Ingrid Stipa

What are the psychological, social and political implications of a perception of subjectivity in which the traditional autonomous subject proves to be an illusory substance, ('eine geträumte Substanz') masking an illusory identity (*Frankfurter Vorlesungen*: 42)? In *the Frankfurter Vorlesungen* Bachmann conducts an analytic reading of significant twentieth-century literary texts, from which emerges her own position of the question of subjectivity, a question that will also become the central concern of most of the narratives of her first prose collection, *Das dreißigste Jahr*.

According to this reading of the twentieth-century literary scene, the epistemic shift which dislodges the subject from its central position coincides with turn-of-the century language scepticism exemplified by Hofmannsthal's *Chandos Brief* (1902). In this well known literary document, Hofmannsthal reports that he suddenly finds it difficult to think and speak coherently, even about the most trivial everyday events. Like more complex issues, these too demand judgements based on such binaries as good and evil, or pity and envy. Each attempt to reduce these to a single denominator results in disintegration rather than the desired coherence: 'Es zerfiel mir alles in Teile, die Teile wieder in Teile, und nichts mehr ließ sich mit einem Begriff umspannen' (quoted in Bachmann, *Frankfurter Vorlesungen*: 14).

In addition to Hofmannsthal, Bachmann refers to some novellas by Musil, Proust's *A la recherche du temps perdu*, (1919), Benn's *Rönne, Aufzeichnungen eines Arztes* (1920), Beckett's *L'innomnable* (1953) and Rilke's *Die Aufzeichnungen des Malte Laurids Brigge* (1910). In calling attention to the problematic relationship between the speaking/writing subject and its discourse, all of these works contribute to the construction of the modern conception of subjectivity as it distinguishes itself from that indebted to more conventional systems of thought.

The conventional text generally features an autonomous, omniscient narrator who recounts the events of his or her well-ordered world without indicating any awareness of the constitutive function of language. For this narrator language seems to be nothing more than a transparent medium which simply designates or signifies the objects and events of the world. In the modern text, on the other hand, the narrator or speaking subject recognizes the constructive function of language and with that begins to question his/her autonomy and centrality in the signifying process. Thus, for example, Proust's narrator, Bachmann points out, disappears from the text over extended periods of time, and the chameleon narrators of Hans Henny Jahnn's *Fluß ohne Ufer* (1929) and Beckett's *L'innomnable* defy final identification.

Rilke's *Malte Laurids Brigge*, which Bachmann mentions only in passing, clearly registers the moment of transition from one theoretical position to another. Nostalgia for the 'authentic', the 'real', the 'coherent' subject pervades this text even as Malte's new sense of sight leads him to discover the interdependence of subject, object, and language. He learns that writing is a mutually constitutive process which constructs the object of observation (*das Ding*) while changing the content of consciousness of the writing subject itself: 'Aber diesmal werde ich geschrieben werden', Malte observes, 'Ich bin der Eindruck, der sich verwandeln wird' (Rilke, *Die Aufzeichnungen des Malte Laurids Brigge*: 756). In other words, the modern subject loses the anchor of its fixed identity and is set adrift in a sea of endless possibilities. The subject 'ist abgeschnitten von jeder Bindung, jeder Beziehung in dem es als solches bestimmt sein könnte' Bachmann argues (*Frankfurter Vorlesungen*: 58); formerly posing as the exclusive manipulator of language and meaning, the subject of the modern text appears as the 'Instrument eines blinden Geschehens' (58).

Bachmann begins her own analysis of the subject with the pronoun 'I', the 'I' that stands for Ingeborg Bachmann speaking to an audience of students and scholars. Even in such simple declarative statements as 'Ich sage Ihnen', Bachmann reasons, the pronoun 'I' becomes uncertain the moment it is spoken. 'Der es ausspricht, ist gar nicht mehr so sicher, ob er für dieses in den Mund genommene "Ich" Verbindlichkeiten beanspruchen kann, ob er es decken kann' (*Frankfurter Vorlesungen*: 41). Within the conceptual framework of these speculations, the speaking subject can no longer be reduced to a fixed content of consciousness. The very act of enunciation introduces a breach between speaker and pronoun, so that the listener receives only a rhetorical 'I', the subject of a sentence cut off from the speaker. 'Ein Ich ohne Gewähr', Bachmann puns (*Frankfurter Vorlesungen*: 42); however, it is a pun we are meant to take seriously. The acoustically ambiguous 'Gewähr' redefines the traditional subject within the space of a single term:[1] it tells us that the subject carries no guarantee, that it does not endure beyond the moment of enunciation, and that it cannot presume the phallic authority it had formerly taken for granted. While in this model of subjectivity, the subject's traditional role is greatly diminished it does not, however, disappear altogether from the literary text. The unified, autonomous subject in charge of the production of meaning is displaced by the subject as the 'site of the human voice' ('der Platzhalter der menschlichen Stimme', *Frankfurter Vorlesungen*: 61).

In the lecture entitled 'Über Gedichte', Bachmann discusses Günter Eich's poem, 'Betrachtet die Fingerspitzen' (*Frankfurter Vorlesung*). She finds it to be representative of the shift from the masterful, authoritarian subject of the conventional text to its diffident, modern counterpart. The manner in which the poet has conceived his plan, Bachmann speculates, differs substantially from that of his predecessors of one or two generations before. For example, it is difficult to imagine him (the poet) as a prophet, 'es ist nichts Selbstherrliches, Anmaßendes in der Konzeption seiner selbst'. The place ('der Ort') from which he speaks is not autonomously chosen but assigned to him by the society to which he belongs (*Frankfurter Vorlesungen*: 27).[2] 'Der Ort' is Bachmann's designation for the Lacanian Symbolic, that register of articulation associated with structure, order, analysis and reason, in short, the site where subjects are constructed. It will become the explicit focus of the title story of *Das dreißigste Jahr* (Bachmann 1989a [1966]) of the narrative 'Alles', and of 'Ein Schritt nach Gomorrha'.

In 'Das dreißigste Jahr' the protagonist yearns to erase the cultural blueprint which until this time had determined the pattern of his thoughts. He thinks he can do so by escaping to a different society, to Rome. There, however, he meets up with old friends who force on him 'wie eine Zwangsjacke' their conception of his former self ('seine Gestalt' [18]). Later his attention is drawn to language. In response to the media-generated, clipped, self-assured phrases that characterize the speech of the various Molls the protagonist encounters in Rome and Vienna, he disdainfully jeers 'Eure Gedanken sind gepachtete Bilder eurer Welt'. In the meantime his nostalgic search for his 'authentic' being ('seine wirkliche Gestalt' [20])) repeatedly leads to a dead end: 'Immer denke ich in einem Spiel mit vorgefundenen Spielregeln und einmal vielleicht auch daran, die Regeln zu ändern, das Spiel nicht. Niemals' (25). With this insightful reflection the protagonist admits that perhaps his harsh criticism of Moll had been premature, for, like Moll, his own thoughts cannot be considered entirely original, at least not when one considers the epistemological constraints, of 'the game' into which he, like everyone else, has been born. This discovery leads to ideological speculations that posit the desired escape from the Symbolic prisonhouse as a wish. 'Er hätte sich gern außerhalb aufgestellt, über die Grenze hinübergesehen und von dorther auf sich und die Welt und die Sprache und jede Bedingung. Er wäre gerne mit einer neuen Sprache wiedergekehrt' (31). The subjunctives, *hätte*, and *wäre* simultaneously signify the protagonist's desire for transgressing the established boundaries while clearly signalling the impossibility of so doing.

While 'Das dreißigste Jahr' attempts to demonstrate the impossibility of abandoning individual identity and subjectivity, 'Alles' shifts the focus to society at large. It plays with the possibility of social change by displacing conventional language with a system of communication that has presumably evolved outside the boundaries of the Symbolic. In this story the narrator decides that his newborn son, Fipps, will be the first member of an enlightened human race, that he will, in fact, become the redeemer of present, corrupt society. In the course of his philosophical ruminations, he concludes that all social ills are somehow linked to language: 'alles ist eine Frage der Sprache und nicht nur dieser einen deutschen Sprache, die mit anderen geschaffen wurde in Babel, um die Welt zu verwirren. Denn darunter schwellt noch eine Sprache, die reicht bis in die Gesten und Blicke, das Abwickeln der Gedanken und den Gang der Gefühle, und in ihr ist schon all unser Unglück' (66). If normative modes of expression are at fault, the narrator speculates, then it seems to be simply a question of teaching Fipps a new language, for example the language of the shadows, stones and water. The language of nature, so the reasoning goes, will displace conventional communication along with its traditional mental constructs and perceptual modes implicated in cultural production, social organization as well as in the corruption of society.

In contrast to 'Das dreißigste Jahr' where the lucidity of the protagonist is indicated by the profusion of subjunctives such as, 'Wenn du den Menschen aufgäbest, den alten, und einen neuen annähmest' (35), the narrator of 'Alles', at least in the beginning, clearly believes that it must be possible to escape from the given socio-symbolic order and found a new, enlightened society. His ideology derives from the school of thought which seeks to renew the human race by returning to a presumably more 'natural', more 'authentic' state of being. His thinking recalls the Romantic nostalgia for origins (played out in the obsessive fascination with ruins and ancient languages) and, more recently, at least some aspects of ecological consciousness.

While the narrator's vision may be clouded by Romantic notions of 'origin' and 'authenticity', Bachmann's is not. In the essay 'Dem Menschen ist die Wahrheit zumutbar', she argues that our perception is renewed by the interplay of the possible with the impossible, but at the same time acknowledges that we are confined by the linguistic and cultural constraints which have formed us. Quite predictably then, the narrator of 'Alles' will run up against the linguistic/cultural barrier, and will ultimately become aware of the foolishness of his enterprise.[3] As he tries to educate his son, he soon realizes that he cannot speak the language of nature and that his attempts to invent pure games and fairy tales other than the familiar ones result in nothing but imitations. To the narrator's great disappointment, Fipps grows up to be just another enterprising, rowdy little boy who is capable of anything, 'nur nicht den Teufelskreis zu durchbrechen' (71). And how could it be otherwise? The subject as the site of the human voice ('der Platzhalter der menschlichen Stimme') necessarily speaks and reproduces the culture and society in which it is embedded. This being the case, what is our hope of changing perceptions, cognition, society?

Bachmann writes against the utopian vision of changing society from without, but she by no means rejects the possibility of social change. 'Es gilt weiterzuschreiben', she insists in the *Frankfurter Vorlesungen* (95) precisely because she believes in the redemptive power of the literary text, in its capacity to open new avenues of perception and cognition. For instance, she regards the Enzensberger poem 'Verteidigung der Wölfe gegen die Lämmer' to be exemplary in its capacity to educate the reader 'zu neuer Wahrnehmung, neuem Gefühl, neuem Bewußtsein' (*Frankfurter Vorlesungen*: 19). 'Das Gedicht' she says, 'provoziert in uns einen erkennthishaften Ruck' (34). This cognitive jolt can only come from literary texts in that ordinary, everyday speech has a strictly utilitarian function and consists only of 'Phrasen und sprachlose[r] Gewalt' (22).

Although Bachmann believes that the epistemic shift dismantling the sovereign subject constitutes the primary development in the evolution of Western thought by which modern texts are able to move us toward new modes of perception and cognition, she also recognizes that the sovereign, authoritarian subject of discourse has not entirely disappeared. Among others, it appears in the form of historical figures or statesmen, for example 'wenn Churchill oder De Gaul Bericht erstatten' (*Frankfurter Vorlesungen*: 43). Taking this a step further, we might say that the 'sovereign', 'authoritarian' subject is the socially-sanctioned pose of public discourse in patriarchal culture and hence very much a part of our everyday experience. We need only think of politicians, lawyers, evangelists, football coaches, university presidents, or pompous professors, and the list goes on.

In keeping with the social construct of lived experience, the sovereign subject of Bachmann's fiction is generally a masculine figure. With such notable exceptions as Jordan of *Der Fall Franza* and 'Das Gebell', Ivan of *Malina*, the members of the *Herrenrunde* of 'Irrungen und Wirrungen', (whom Bachmann ironically describes as 'Männer ... unterwegs zu sich, wenn sie abends beinander sind, trinken und reden und meinen' [82]), the masculine protagonist gradually discovers that his subjectivity is neither sovereign nor autonomous but rather figures as a part of the pervasive socio-cultural continuum of which he is a part. In 'Ein Schritt nach Gomorrah' Bachmann takes this one step further. She focuses on the relationship between individuals from the perspective of gender and thereby calls attention to how polarized gender norms limit the possibilities of imagining interpersonal relationships outside the divisive male/female designations.

Precisely what is Charlotte risking in her step toward Gomorrah? The reflection from Mara's skirt which temporarily transforms Charlotte's living room into a world of red and the light in the bar which gives Charlotte the feeling 'in einen Höllenraum gelangt zu sein' ('Ein Schritt nach Gomorrah': 113), unequivocally signal that Charlotte is about to enter the danger zone of a forbidden order, the zone of homoerotic desire, a threat to patriarchal society. Up to this point Charlotte had more or less observed the social norms defining masculine and feminine roles. While she had at times been tempted to undermine the structure of the social institution of marriage ('an der Verfassung zu rütteln' [130]), her rebellious thoughts never went far enough to keep her from submitting to its state ('in den Zustand der Ehe einzugehen und sich darin einzurichten' [129]). Throughout the narrative this conventional order, 'Franz' helle Ordnung' ('Ein Schritt nach Gomorrah': 123), keeps in check the threat of the new order, the danger zone coded red. We readily recognize the former whenever Charlotte glances at her watch, when she rehearses her duties for the next day, when she takes stock of the apartment and realizes that she is unable to connect herself with a single object in it, ('Es war gar nicht daran zu denken, daß jemals etwas mit ihr zu tun haben würde, so lange sie mit einem Mann lebte' [123]), and finally, when she sets the alarm just before dawn at the end of the story.

Charlotte's assertion 'Es war Schichtwechsel, und jetzt konnte sie die Welt übernehmen, ihren Gefährten benennen, die Rechte und Pflichten festsetzen, die alten Bilder ungültig machen und das erste neue entwerfen' ('Ein Schritt nach Gomorrah': 134), seems radical indeed. It declares that the old order will vanish and a new one will take its place, even if only in Charlotte's imagination. At the centre of this revolution lies the question of subjectivity, that is, what it takes to assume a subject position in patriarchal culture. Charlotte's rebellion, however, falls short of undermining the actual structure of the order which determines that individuals become either masters or slaves, subjects or objects, males or females. Consequently her wishful thinking remains within the familiar patterns of binary thought. While the narrative features certain explicit homoerotic moments, these are secondary to the greater temptation of assuming a subject position at the expense of Mara: 'Ich will bestimmen, wer ich bin, und ich will mir auch mein Geschöpf machen, meinen duldenden, schuldigen, schattenhaften Teilhaber. Ich will Mara nicht, weil ich ihren Mund, ihr Geschlecht – mein eignes – will. Nichts dergleichen. Ich will mein Geschöpf und ich werde es mir machen' (128).

Charlotte's imagined rebirth as sovereign subject does not, however, come without its attendant dose of misogyny and self-hatred. As she sees her own feminine self reflected by Mara, she disdainfully observes: 'So also waren ihre eigenen Lippen, so ähnlich begegnete sie einem Mann, schmal, fast widerstandslos, fast ohne Muskel – eine kleine Schnauze, nicht ernst zu nehmen' ('Ein Schritt nach Gomorrah': 119). And later, as she witnesses Mara's obsequious behaviour, her begging for love, she thinks 'mir ist dauernd unklar, wovon sie spricht. Die Sprache der Männer war doch so gewesen in solchen

Stunden, daß man sich daran hatte halten können. Ich kann Mara nicht zuhören, ihren Worten ohne Muskel, diesen nichtsnutzigen kleinen Worten' (121).

From Charlotte's present masculine perspective, Mara's pleading words can readily be dismissed as 'nichtsnutzige kleine Worte' for they lack the precision, mastery, assertiveness and control normally associated with the pose of the 'autonomous' subject. However, useless as feminine speech may seem to be, it provides the ground which allows the masculine 'sovereign' subject and its masterful speech to assume its pose and position in society. In other words, the masculine subject requires the complicity of the feminine in order to exist. Charlotte seems to understand this when, in thinking about her relationship with Franz, she admits that she actively participates in her own subordination: 'Sie betrauerte Franz ... er wußte nicht, daß alles umsonst gewesen war, die Unterwerfung, die sie selber, mehr als er betrieben hatte, weil er hätte gar nicht wissen können, was an ihr zu unterwerfen war' ('Ein Schritt nach Gomorrah': 125). Similarly, Mara declares herself ready to submit to Charlotte's will in exchange for affection: 'Ich will ja alles tun, alles glauben, was du willst. Nur lieb mich! Lieb mich' (134)!

With her imaginary 'Schichtwechsel', Charlotte in no way changes the hierarchical paradigm which governs gender relations but simply claims a position of dominance for herself, not unlike the one held by her husband, Franz. The text as a whole, however, suggests that Charlotte is not entirely unaware of the entrapment of her thoughts in the binary system by which individuals are assigned to the position of the oppressor or the oppressed. Interspersed with her imaginary power-play she conjures up a utopian realm in which the terms masculine and feminine have vanished from general language use and collective social consciousness as signifiers designating opposites. 'Komm, Schlaf, kommt, tausend Jahre, damit ich geweckt werde von einer anderen Hand. Komm, daß ich erwache, wenn dies nicht mehr gilt – Mann und Frau. Wenn dies einmal zu Ende ist!' (125).

Not unlike the utopia envisioned in 'Alles', Charlotte's new society would also be governed by a language other than the one that apprehends the world in polarized terms:

> In ihrem Reich galt ein neues Maß. Es konnte dann nicht mehr heißen: sie ist so und so, reizvoll, reizlos, vernünftig, unvernünftig ... Immer hatte sie diese Sprache verabscheut, jeden Stempel, der ihr aufgedrückt wurde und den sie jemand aufdrücken mußte – den Mordversuch an der Wirklichkeit. Aber wenn ihr Reich kam, dann konnte diese Sprache nicht mehr gelten. ('Ein Schritt nach Gomorrah': 151)

Charlotte's utopia conceives social change as a complete restructuring of society in terms of an unidentified structure and language. She can only say what society will *not* be, precisely because, like the narrator of 'Alles', she envisions a new society completely disconnected from the present. 'Das Reich erhoffen. Nicht das Reich der Männer und nicht das Reich der Weiber. Nicht dies, nicht jenes' ('Ein Schritt nach Gomorrah': 185). Her tears as well as her resigned winding up of the alarm clock at the end of the story reflect the ultimate impossibility of either realizing her utopian dream, an undifferentiated harmonious society, or of taking her turn in the power-play of patriarchal culture.

For a more promising ending than this, we have to return to the story of 'Alles'. One of the direct consequences of the narrator's hypothetical attempt to change society is the breakdown of the relationship between him and his wife, Hannah. While he lives in his philosophical ruminations and spends most of his time brooding over his son's inability to save the human race, she provides the love, care and nurture that children require. In the end, not even the shared grief over the loss of the son is able to bridge the gulf of silence that keeps the two apart. There is however a positive note in this seemingly bleak ending. As the narrator begins to understand the impossibility of passing beyond the limits of language and culture, he also realizes that the responsibility for changing society lies within the individual: 'ja, ich war es. Ja, ich war der erste Mensch und habe alles verspielt, hab nichts getan' ('Alles': 72). The final scene features the narrator as an enlightened, mature individual who accepts his share of the responsibility for the failed relationship with Hannah and, in a larger sense, for his part in perpetuating the ideological gulf between a masculine and a feminine perception of the world. 'Diese Entfernung, meßbar mit Schweigen, wie soll sie jeh abnehmen? Denn in alle [sic] Zeit wird, wo für mich ein Minenfeld ist, für Hannah ein Garten sein' (81). Beginning with the divisive, hierarchical designations 'ein Mann/eine Frau' and their social consequences, men and women are driven into contradictory perceptions of the world, here summarized by the juxtaposition of a minefield and a garden. It seems, therefore, that Symbolic language, as it is conventionally practised, becomes useless in any attempt to bridge the gulf of silence separating men and women, the narrator and his wife.

As we have known since Freud, the signifying process is not limited to verbal exchange but involves the entire body: underneath language 'schwellt noch eine Sprache, die reicht bis in die Gesten und Blicke, das Abwickeln der Gedanken und den Gang der Gefühle, und in ihr ist schon all unser Unglück' ('Alles': 66). Although this language of gestures, glances and emotions is in part implicated in the same socio-cultural continuum as the language of verbal exchange, it is also linked to unconscious drives and primary processes, a pre-discursive psychic space which Julia Kristeva designates as the semiotic (1986: 93). This means that it ultimately has the potential of disrupting and possibly altering the symbolic signifying process. While it is the role of the Symbolic to name, articulate and classify, the semiotic perpetually challenges, disrupts and resists the Symbolic signifying process and as such constitutes the only possibility of ultimately changing the manner in which we use the language of verbal exchange to communicate with each other. As the narrator of 'Alles' thinks about crossing the dark hallway that separates his room from Hannah's he tries to banish all thoughts and words from his mind: 'Ich denke nicht mehr, sondern möchte aufstehen, über den dunklen Gang hinübergehen und, ohne ein Wort sagen zu müssen, Hannah erreichen' (81). With this he contemplates the first step in reaching out, in tearing down 'den Trauerbogen ..., der von einem Mann zu einer Frau reicht' (81), hence the first step in allowing alternative forms of communication rise to the surface of consciousness. The narrator's gesture suggests a willingness to redefine his own subjectivity by moving toward the elimination of the masculine/feminine distinction which keeps men and women apart. 'Ich denke nicht mehr. Das Fleisch ist groß und finster, das unter dem großen Nachtgelächter ein wahres Gefühl begräbt' (80). This true feeling, repressed and buried by the paternal law but also expressed by the body if only obliquely, will become the basis for the non-verbal exchange contemplated by the narrator, an exchange not governed by Lacan's Symbolic, but rooted in the maternal bond, in Kristeva's semiotic.

Notes

1 *Gewähr* means guarantee but we also hear *Gewehr* meaning rifle.

2 A shorter version of this reading of the *Frankfurter Vorlesungen* as well as of the narrative 'Alles' will appear in Stipa, forthcoming.

3 Sigrid Weigel (1989) comes to the same conclusion. Furthermore, she points out that critics have repeatedly taken the phrase, 'no new world without a new language' to substantiate the claim that Bachmann argues for a new language (281). In taking this sentence out of context this argument misses the point. The narrative illustrates the impossibility of founding a new language leading to a new society, and *not* the reverse.

Bibliography

Bachmann, Ingeborg. 1989a. *Das Dreißigste Jahr* (1966), 2nd edn, Munich, Piper
—. 1989b. *Frankfurter Vorlesungen*, 11th edn, Munich, Piper
Kristeva, Julia. 1986. 'Revolution in Poetic Language', *The Kristeva Reader*, ed. Toril Moi, Oxford, Blackwell
Rilke, Rainer Maria. 1966. *Werke*, 6 vols, vol. 6, Frankfurt, Insel
Stipa, Ingrid. Forthcoming. 'Female Subjectivity and the Repression of the Feminine', in Gudrun Brokopf (ed.), *Thunder Rumbling at my Heels: Tracing Ingeborg Bachmann*, Riverside, Ariadne
Weigel, Sigrid. 1989. '"Ein Ende mit der Schrift. Ein anderer Anfang." Zur Entwicklung von Ingeborg Bachmann's Schreibweise', in Christine Koschel and Inge von Weidenbaum (eds), *Kein Objektives Urteil — Nur ein Lebendiges*, Munich, Piper: 265-310.

The Cost of Loving: Love, Desire, and Subjectivity in the Work of Marlen Haushofer

Margaret Littler

It is an irony of the critical reception of Marlen Haushofer (1920-1970) that she was long dismissed as a writer of *Eheromane* and children's books, whereas the recent revival of interest in her work is due in part to its treatment of the incompatability of women's creative work and their reproductive work as wives and mothers.[1] Haushofer's novels expose a sexual division of labour in marriage whereby men can be productive in the public sphere only because women bear responsibility for the domestic realm and personal relationships. If she has enjoyed only belated recognition by feminist critics, it is because her novels offer few positive models of emancipation, her female protagonists becoming less, not more autonomous with regard to the structures of family life. While the female protagonist of her first novel, *Eine Handvoll Leben* ([1955] 1991a) actually leaves her unhappy marriage and chooses a life of independence, those of *Die Tapetentür* ([1957] 1991c), 'Wir töten Stella' ([1958] 1990b), and *Die Mansarde* ([1969] 1992) are unable to exercise a similar degree of autonomy. As recently as 1992 Madeleine Marti drew attention to the bold treatment of lesbian desire in *Eine Handvoll Leben*, but she attributes the subsequent abandonment of the theme to biographical factors, as if having to 'excuse' Haushofer for succumbing to the pressures of 'compulsory heterosexuality' in her later work (Marti 1992: 81). Such a restrictive focus, while seeking to highlight Haushofer's radical status, ends up falling into the same trap as early feminist criticism, looking for strong role models of women who successfully defy the status quo, rather than for more subtle analyses of why it is so necessary, but difficult, to do so.

This, however, is the theme of Haushofer's most ambitious work, *Die Wand* ([1963] 1990a), the dystopian novel of a woman's sole survival of the end of civilization. Far from a 'domestic' novel for women, this is a wide-ranging exploration of the elusive boundary between culture and nature. It ranges from a radical critique of gender relations to a probing interrogation of the integrity of the self, in which it anticipates postmodern feminist writing of the 1980s.[2] It is this aspect of Haushofer's work which has fascinated contemporary writers such as Anne Duden, who sees also in Haushofer's last novel, *Die Mansarde* (1969), an indictment of bourgeois marriage as 'eine Mechanik zur gefahrlosen Verarbeitung des umgetriebenen Wissens, des Unausgesprochenen' (Duden 1986: 110) and in the female protagonist's artistic production the articulation of untamed, female sexuality. In addition to the assertion of specifically female eroticism, however, I will argue that Haushofer constructs in her later works a model of ethical subjective existence based on responsibility and love. I will draw on Luce Irigaray's *An Ethics of Sexual Difference* (Fr. 1984; Eng. 1993), in which the ethical subject is seen as the product of its encounter with an autonomous, primary other, as opposed to an other which is the mere reflection of the self. It is an involuntary ethical response, based on mutual respect and irreducible alterity.[3]

This paper will look briefly at evidence of specific forms of female desire, which are inevitably sacrificed to the cultural constraints of female socialization in *Eine Handvoll Leben* (1955) and *Die Tapetentür* (1957). Rather than an unremitting pessimism, however, I hope to show that, if read in conjunction with more recent (inter)texts, Haushofer's female protagonists may be seen as examples of 'radical female subjectivity' (Weigel 1989: 116ff) which is explicitly linked to a critique of Enlightenment rationality (Venske 1987: 99), *and* to the articulation of a positive ethical relationship to the world.

1) Subjectivity and Female Desire

1.1) Eine Handvoll Leben (1955)

In *Eine Handvoll Leben* erotically charged relationships between women are unusually prominent for a novel of the 1950s, albeit defused to an extent by the retrospective setting among adolescent girls at a convent school (Marti 1992: 52-76). Although the protagonist, Elisabeth, is unable to respond sexually to either of her schoolfriends, Käthe and Margot, she is the *only* one of Haushofer's protagonists actually to turn her back on marriage and motherhood, choosing to live in England as 'Betty Russell'.[4] Only on returning to her former home incognito as a prospective buyer of the house after her ex-husband's death, does she reflect on her convent education and stifled adolescent passions.

The brutal discipline imposed by the nuns at school contrasts starkly with the warmth and sensuality of her early childhood in a woman-dominated household (*Eine Handvoll Leben*: 49). The result of the convent's spartan regime was to make the girls despise their own bodies and to alienate them from their pleasure. In terms of Irigaray's thought, this can be seen as preparation for women's role as the object of men's desire. According to Irigaray, patriarchal culture offers women only a relation of substitution and rivalry, never one of mutual love and respect. The absence of a 'female homosexual economy' (Irigaray 1993: 66;105) means also that there is no possibility of the emergence of a female subject, one which would occupy a self-defined place in the symbolic, not merely provide the bedrock of male subjectivity. Haushofer's narrative forges a connection between socially sanctioned female identity and the obliteration of female desire, Elisabeth's engagement to her husband coinciding with her lesbian schoolfriend's suicide (*Eine Handvoll Leben*: 78).

Elisabeth's increasingly uneasy relationship to her self-image accompanies the process of female identity acquisition: 'Je mehr sie selbst an Substanz verlor, desto strahlender, dichter und übermächtiger mußte ihr Bild werden' (*Eine Handvoll Leben*: 90). Only her voracious reading of 'the classics' counteracts this normalizing process. In particular Kleist's *Prinz Friedrich von Homburg, Das Käthchen von Heilbronn* and *Penthesilea* give her a symbolic space in which to live out her ambivalent sexual urges and desires which she had learnt to suppress: 'Sie konnte lieben und hassen wie Käthchen oder Penthesilea, aber nicht mehr wie Elisabeth' (*Eine Handvoll Leben*: 90).[5]

Female desire does find expression in the novel, both in the schloolgirl's illicit love for her teacher Dr. Elvira (*Eine Handvoll Leben*: 87), and in the suspension of individual identity, an overwhelming empathy with the suffering of humanity, which points beyond the question of gendered identity to Haushofer's more universal cultural concerns:

> Es gab kein Innen und kein Außen mehr, keine Grenze, die sie von den Bettlern und schmutzigen Gassenkindern trennte. Elisabeth war durchlässig geworden, und alle Welt durchströmte sie. Es war, als hätten sich ihr Fleisch und ihre Knochen in Flüssigkeit aufgelöst, die, vom leisesten Anhauch berührt, sich kräuselte, kleine Wellen schlug und langsam wieder verebbte. Manchmal, ohne jeden ersichtlichen Anlaß, spürte sie in der Brust ein Brennen und Feuchtigkeit unter den Lidern. Dieser völlig unpersönliche Schmerz war etwas Neues für sie. Eine winzige Spur der großen Menschenqual Millionen Lebender, Toter und noch Ungeborener durchzuckte sie dann und ließ sie vergessen, daß sie Elisabeth war, eine Person, von deren Einmaligkeit sie bis dahin fest überzeugt gewesen war. (*Eine Handvoll Leben*: 131)

While this erotic dissolution of subjective boundaries may be read as masochistic, it is also open to interpretation in terms of Irigaray's account of female desire, as, 'an openness on the infinite in jouissance ... Body-expanse that tries to *give itself exteriority, to give itself to exteriority* ... To give itself in a space-time without end.... She always wants more, encore, we are told by certain psychoanalysts ... who equate this more with pathology. In fact, this *more* is the condition of sexuate female desire' (Irigaray 1993: 64). The association of erotic ecstacy with a compassionate response to the needs of an as yet indeterminate other is already suggested in the 'evanescence of subject and object' (Irigaray 1993: 185) in Haushofer's first novel.

1.2) Die Tapetentür (1957)
The female protagonist of *Die Tapetentür*, Annette, is a young librarian, who falls in love with the executor of her father's will and gives up both career and

independence for a marriage which stifles her most fundamental instincts. The dual narrative voice exposes the strategies of self-deception by which she denies to herself the damage being done to her personality and the subordination of her erotic needs to those of her husband. She seems to come to terms with Gregor's different sexual desires *and* his lack of insight into her own needs: 'Er kann sich einfach nicht vorstellen, daß Frauen anders lieben als Männer ... Ich muß ihn fast bedauern, daß er dieses schwebende und vielfältige Entzücken nicht kennt' (*Die Tapetentür*: 107).

Annette only experiences this in the company of her female friend, Meta, with whom she relaxes completely in the warmth of female intimacy, while dimly aware of the stirrings of dangerous passions:

> Annette schwamm im lauen Meerwasser, unter einem ewig strahlenden Himmel, Salzgeschmack im Mund und kleine weiße Kräuselwellen vor den Augen, und sie wußte, daß das Wasser unter ihr gefährlich war, voll schwarzer Untiefen und einer tödlichen Kälte. Aber die Kälte drang nicht bis zu ihr herauf. Die Sonne war noch nicht untergegangen, und man mußte sich nicht fürchten, solange es Licht und Wärme gab und die sanften Liebkosungen der salzigen Wellen. (*Die Tapetentür*: 90-1)[6]

At the end of the novel, after a miscarriage and separation from her husband, she throws away the diary she had been keeping, the entries of which alternate with third-person narrative, recognizing that this supposedly authentic record of her marriage had been a medium of self-deception, because formulated in rational discourse which fixed her in a subject position inadequate to her experience: 'Es war vielleicht gleich ehrlicher, beim Schreiben den Eindruck von Spontaneität gar nicht erst aufkommen zu lassen, denn es gab kein spontanes Schreiben; schon die Tatsache, daß man einen Gedanken im Kopf erst zu einem Satz ordnen mußte, machte das Schreiben zu einer ganz bewußten Arbeit' (*Die Tapetentür*: 123-4).

2) Love and the Ethical Subject

The incompatability in these novels of the female subject of language and female desire is inextricably connected in the later novels *Die Wand* and *Die Mansarde* with a more wide-ranging critique of Western rationality, based on the triumph of the subject over the other, nature, and the feminine. This is linked to the affirmation of a maternal ethical stance, despite the fact that *actual* motherhood remains problematic, even undesireable, for Haushofer's characters. Parallels drawn with the work of the German writer Anne Duden in this section are intended to demonstrate ways in which Haushofer prefigures arguably some of the most radical trends in contemporary women's writing.

2.1) Die Wand (1963) and 'Das Landhaus' (Duden 1982)

Die Wand is the story of a widow who accepts an invitation to stay with friends in their hunting lodge in the country. When her friends fail to return from an excursion to the nearby village, she finds herself cut off from the rest of the world by an invisible wall, behind which all life has been petrified, presumably as the effect of some nuclear apocalypse, which she alone has miraculously survived. The narrative is her *Bericht*, written at a time of crisis after two years of this isolation, during which she learns painstakingly to adapt to living off the land and caring for the few animals who are her only companions and source of food.

In Anne Duden's much shorter text 'Das Landhaus', published in the volume *Übergang* (1982), the protagonist-narrator is merely 'house-sitting' in the secluded country cottage of an academic couple who are away working for three weeks. At first, she fears intrusion and barricades herself in at night, but then has an almost mystical experience in the garden which liberates her from fear, the constraints of linear time, individual subjectivity, inner and outer reality, and she is found lying on the floor at the end by someone whose response is: 'Das ist ja wahnsinnig. Komm sofort hier raus' (Duden 1982: 43). The effect of isolation in the house is to make the woman feel subtly changed and detached from her previous life. She loses a sense of the necessity for mundane tasks such as mowing the lawn and cooking. She stops wearing make-up, washing her hair, and changing her clothes, rarely bothering to glance in the mirror: 'Nur ganz selten sah ich in den Spiegel, und wenn, dann äußerst uninteressiert, wie beiläufig auf ein vorübergehendes Wesen' (Duden 1982: 35).

Haushofer's protagonist feels a completely different person at the time of writing from the woman she had been two years previously. She reflects ruefully that, as a wife and mother she had always felt like a 'beast of burden', but her body had been poorly adapted to the role (*Die Wand*: 113). In the two years of her isolation, however, her body has adapted more effectively than her mind to the new conditions of her life: she has lost all sense of her 'Fraulichkeit', gone are her curled hair and rounded hips, and she hardly menstruates. In the mirror she sees an androgynous figure, more like an adolescent boy than a woman (82). Sometimes she feels like an old man, sometimes like a child, or like 'ein sehr altes, geschlechtsloses Wesen', more akin to a tree than to a human being (82).

Ageing is no longer a source of anxiety for her, now that no one comments on her appearance (151), clothing is purely functional (257), and her mirror image is forlorn and superfluous: 'Es sah ganz fremd aus, mager, mit leichten Höhlungen in den Wangen. Die Lippen waren schmaler geworden, und ich fand dieses fremde Gesicht von einem heimlichen Mangel gezeichnet. Da kein Mensch mehr lebte, der dieses Gesicht hätte lieben können, schien es mir ganz überflüssig. Es war nackt und armselig, und ich schämte mich seiner und wollte nichts mehr mit ihm zu tun haben' (230-1). Significantly, she longs not just for

the human *gaze*, but for an amorous encounter, which no man would be equipped to provide. When imagining sharing her isolation with a man, she can envisage only a relationship of dominance and dependence. The only company she craves is that of an older woman, 'eine gescheite, witzige, mit der ich manchmal lachen könnte. Denn das Lachen fehlt mir noch immer sehr' (66).

The woman's identity changes with her location: when in the valley where the house is she still has a sense of being a subject distinct from her natural environment. When up on the 'Alm' with the cow in the summer, she feels a part of the totality of nature (185). While she could still perceive clear boundaries between herself and nature, she had been disconcerted by this fragmentation of her self, but after two years the boundaries are fluid and her identity diffuse. Only the process of writing her 'Bericht' confuses her because language imposes a false identification of the new and the old 'ich': 'Es fällt mir schwer, beim Schreiben mein früheres und mein neues Ich auseinanderzuhalten, mein neues Ich, von dem ich nicht sicher bin, daß es nicht langsam von einem großen Wir aufgesogen wird' (185). Her old, human identity is now decentred, and 'other' in the natural world:

> Als ich weitergehen mußte, tat ich es mit tiefem Bedauern, und ganz langsam verwandelte ich mich unterwegs wieder in das einzige Geschöpf, das nicht hierhergehörte, in einen Menschen, der verworrene Gedanken hegte, die Zweige mit seinen plumpen Schuhen knickte und das blutige Geschäft der Jagd betrieb. Später, als ich die obere Jagdhütte erreichte, war ich wieder ganz mein altes Ich, begierig darauf, in der Hütte etwas Brauchbares zu finden. Ein schwaches Bedauern blieb noch stundenlang in mir zurück. (62)

Instrumental rationality regains its supremacy, but an intimation remains of a different way of inhabiting the world.

A clear parallel can be drawn with Duden's 'Das Landhaus', when the woman experiences a suspension of the subject boundary between herself and her surroundings, inner and outer reality become one, and she enters into a new relationship with the house: 'Hinter und vor den Lidern war es ein und dasselbe ... Küche, Toilette, Schlafzimmer – brauchte ich alle nicht mehr für meine Zwecke, für die sie gebaut und eingerichtet waren. Und natürlich war ich zugleich überall anwesend, also auch in ihnen, und sie in mir' (Duden 1982: 41-2). Like Haushofer's protagonist, she experiences a blissful liberation from the means-ends calculation of rational subjectivity.

Haushofer's protagonist retains the suspicion that this signals madness, but at the same time this madness is justified: 'Vielleicht wäre die einzig normale Reaktion auf alles, was geschehen ist, der Wahnsinn' (*Die Wand*: 187). Yet she begins to write her report in an attempt to preserve her reason, to remain a human subject (7). It remains ambiguous whether she is motivated by a feminine urge to nurture (75), or by a residual faith in the power of 'Vernunft' to keep her and the animals alive (65). Indeed, this turns out to be a false dichotomy in the novel, when the protagonist reflects: 'Es gibt keine vernünftigere Regung als Liebe ... Nur, wir hätten rechtzeitig erkennen sollen, daß dies unsere einzige Möglichkeit war, unsere einzige Hoffnung auf ein besseres Leben' (238). The need to love and nurture is not a result of her actual maternal status, but rather the condition of being alive, even if it represents an intolerable burden (71; 200). This accords with Irigaray's account of ethical subjectivity, indebted to Emmanuel Levinas, for whom 'maternal love' is a paradigmatic example. Whereas the phallocentric reduction of women to maternal function normally implies their 'subhuman' or 'pre-ethical' status, Levinas valorizes the mother's unconditional openness to the offspring's needs as the epitome of an ethical response, in which self-interest is subordinated to care of the other (Grosz 1989: 146). As Haushofer's protagonist reflects on her constant fear for the survival of the animals entrusted to her care: 'Es war eben der Preis, den man für die Fähigkeit bezahlte, lieben zu können' (*Die Wand*: 71). She is in no doubt that the 'wall' is the result of an unethical obsession with knowledge and perverted rationality (75), and the overgrown Mercedes in the yard stands as a sad icon of phallocentric culture (222).

The destructive nature of technological progress is also implicit in Duden's text, as the protagonist marvels at the self-confidence and 'echte wissenschaftliche Autonomie' of the lifestyle of the academic couple in whose house she is living (Duden 1982: 29). The results of their single-minded pursuit of knowledge appear in the news items she sees randomly juxtaposed on the television screen: the stationing of American nuclear missiles in West Germany, the launch of a new warship, and another leak in a nuclear reactor (24). Their bookshelves contain a section on 'Militaria', including a volume named *How to Kill*, incongruously purchased from the 'Survival Store, Los Angeles' (40). The survival of human culture depends on man's insensititivity to the insidious links between progress, violence, and death.

When the woman in *Die Wand* reflects on her own situation as an item of 'News', she recalls how untouched most people were by foreign disasters, because of their inability to imagine 'other' lands and respond to foreign suffering: 'Hätte sich die Katastrophe in Belutschistan abgespielt, säßen wir völlig ungerührt in den Kaffeehäusern und läsen darüber in der Zeitung. Heute sind wir [she and her animals] Belutschistan, ein sehr entfremdetes, fremdes Land, von dem man kaum weiß, wo es liegt, ein Land, in dem Menschen wohnen, die vermutlich gar keine richtige Menschen sind, unterentwickelt und unempfindlich gegen Schmerzen; Zahlen und Nummern in fremden Zeitungen. Keine Ursache, sich aus der Ruhe bringen zu lassen' (*Die Wand*: 45). It is a mark of her complete rejection of her own culture that she spontaneously shoots down the man who appears at the end of the novel and kills both her bullock and

217

her dog. She feels no remorse, as 'Der heimliche Wunsch zu morden muß immer in ihm [the man] schon geschlafen haben' (162), but begins to write her report to counteract the shock of this lack of identification with her own kind.

As a survival strategy for the rational subject, forgetting/repression is a crucial faculty, as seen in the central importance for both Duden and Haushofer of time and memory. In both 'Das Landhaus' and *Die Wand* linear time becomes superfluous once the women find themselves outside of human society (Duden 1982: 41; *Die Wand*: 43-4; 64; 237). Gradually Haushofer's protagonist stops crossing off the days on the calendar, and trying to keep the clocks going, because only the cycles of nature now matter in her life. Time becomes a network sustaining all life and death, in which nothing is ever past or forgotten, both a comforting and a terrifying thought (237).

Even at the start of the novel, however, she feels defenceless against the memories from her past life: 'Ich bin schon jetzt nur noch eine dünne Haut über einem Berg von Erinnerungen' (66). This, and the notion of the inescapable presence of death, is a central motif of Duden's work of the 1980s, both *Übergang* (1982) and *Das Judasschaf* (1985): the body is the irreducible site of suffering, and retains the memory of suffering even when the conscious mind has 'processed' and disposed of it (Duden 1982: 88). For Duden this memory is a collective trauma; the knowledge of the holocaust and the war. Forgetting is a survival strategy, occasionally rendered dysfunctional when rational thought is knocked from its position of authority, whether by physical violence ('Übergang') or by anxiety and disorientation ('Das Landhaus'). Then her protagonists confront the reality of human suffering and brutality, and the enormous work of repression constantly required for human civilization to continue.[7] Then the protagonist of 'Das Landhaus' has to force herself to remember the patterns of everyday life, in order to reinstate the power of 'Vernunft' against the 'Denk- und Wahrnehmungsüberschuß' which constantly threatens her subjective integrity (Duden 1982: 39).

In *Die Wand* this process is seen from the other side, the protagonist's recollections of her previous life being largely those of overwhelming 'Langeweile', from which, she speculates, the end of civilization may be seen as a welcome deliverance: 'Vielleicht war die Wand doch nur der letzte verzweifelte Versuch eines gequälten Menschen, der ausbrechen mußte, ausbrechen oder wahnsinnig werden' (*Die Wand*: 85). 'Wahnsinn' is ambiguous here, implicitly both equated with and opposed to 'Vernunft', resulting perhaps from Haushofer's questioning of the value of Enlightenment rationality while remaining within its discourse.

Alternatively, one could say that she again exposes the false dichotomy between madness and reason, some forms of rationality leading directly to the most insane barbarity. This is not the same as dismissing reason out of hand. A similar ambivalence surrounds Haushofer's attitude to the subject and the symbolic order it inhabits. As her protagonist contemplates the snow-covered pine trees in December, she longs to throw off the old meanings, but cannot escape the nostalgia for Christmasses past: 'Etwas ganz Neues wartete hinter allen Dingen, nur konnte ich es nicht sehen, weil mein Hirn mit altem Zeug vollgestopft war und meine Augen nicht mehr umlernen konnten. Ich hatte das Alte verloren und das Neue nicht gewonnen, es verschloß sich vor mir, aber ich wußte, daß es vorhanden war' (134). On the other hand, her intimation of nature's glory once the effects of culture are forgotten (211), implies not the dissolution of the subject, but the emergence of a new subject-object relation. It seems to anticipate the attitude of 'wonder' described by Irigaray, as the ability to 'behold' without 'taking hold' of or objectifying the object of perception (Irigaray 1993: 13).

2.2) Die Mansarde (1969)

It is this utopian vision which Anne Duden sees affirmed in Haushofer's last novel *Die Mansarde* (1969). This novel returns to the domestic context of bourgeois marriage, but is centrally concerned with the themes of repression and the discovery of a symbolic space for that which is excluded from our culture. A wife and mother of two children withdraws to the attic of their house to work on her illustrations for natural history books. Her husband, Hubert, has become little more than a tolerable companion, who spends most of his leisure time reading military history or visiting the 'Arsenal'. The novel is narrated over one week, in which, mysteriously, extracts from a diary which she had kept 20 years previously arrive daily in the post. The diary is from a time early in her marriage when she had been sent to the mountains to recover from an unexplained psychosomatic deafness which lasted for two years. This past episode is never discussed, but returns in the post like repressed memory, making the woman reflect on how much 'Verdrängung' is crucial to the survival of her marriage. She reads the diary in her attic, then burns it ceremoniously in the cellar, because, 'Gewisse Dinge muß man vergessen, wenn man leben will' (*Die Mansarde*: 195).[8]

The disingenuous narrative voice of the present expresses great compassion with the need for survival mechanisms, especially for Austrians of her generation, for whom 'Verrücktheit' would be a perfectly reasonable response to their recent history: 'Deshalb ist es so wichtig, Geduld miteinander zu haben und jedes Wort zu überlegen und so zu leben, als sei gar nichts geschehen' (*Die Mansarde*: 95).[9] The diaries, however, recall that when she had been banished to the mountains as a young wife, she had not been so tolerant of her husband's insensitivity, when he wrote to her about her coming home, 'als wäre nichts geschehen' (*Die Mansarde*: 123).[10] Like Gregor in *Die Tapetentür*,

Hubert is a 'Meister im Vergessen' (*Die Tapetentür*: 99; *Die Mansarde*: 95), whereas she has to engage in a ceaseless round of domestic chores to keep memory at bay, and even then with only limited success.[11] As Anne Duden puts it, even in the 'Friedhofsruhe' of her marriage, there is little respite from the 'Überschuß an Vergangenheit und Gegenwart' which daily assaults her (Duden 1986: 109). In *Die Mansarde* we read: 'Die große Häßlichkeit und der große Schrecken erreichen uns alle eines Tages. Dann kann man nicht länger davonlaufen und wird an die Wand gepreßt. Es wäre gut, dann taub, blind und gefühllos zu sein, aber damit kann man nicht rechnen' (*Die Mansarde*: 137).

The underlying awareness of mankind's destructive lust for knowledge is as central to this novel as to *Die Wand*, as is clear when the protagonist reflects on the violence done to the world by our symbolic system, and on the inadequacy of symbolic identity for either self-knowledge or a relationship to the world (*Die Mansarde*: 177). She finds an alternative to this deadly conspiracy of knowledge and death in her drawings of birds, insects, and reptiles, her representations based on empathy, not objective knowledge (93). Insects are by nature so 'other', she can identify with the aura of 'Fremdheit' which engulfs them, while acknowledging her projection of feelings onto that which is irreducibly different (94).

It has always been her ambition to depict a bird which is an example of a species, but all she ever manages is forlorn specimens which look as if they must be completely alone in the world (20). She seems constrained to represent only that which is unique and has no place in any taxonomic system.[12] At the end of *Die Mansarde* she draws a tiny dragon, an astonished creature for whose existence there is no basis in reason, nor are its perceptions numbed by consciousness: 'Ein Drache ist ein Wesen, das einsam aussehen darf. Ihm steht es zu. Er wird nicht geboren, ist plötzlich da und weiß nicht, warum, das sieht man ihm an. Er schaut aus, as wäre er unheilbar verwundert' (*Die Mansarde*: 197). Duden sees the dragon as pointing beyond the boundaries of cultural and psychic repression, a 'Sinnbild alles Weggesteckten, der Wildheit und ungezähmten Sexualität, dessen also, was es immer neu zu beseitigen gilt in unseren Breitengraden ... Eine winzige Utopie auf Papier und außerhalb der Denkdomäne' (1986: 114). Its attitude of wonder is also reminiscent of Irigaray's ideal of the amorous encounter, as a non self-conscious corporeal intimacy which nourishes the pre-subjective potential of the lovers: 'On the horizon of a story is found what was in the beginning: this naive or native sense of touch, in which the subject does not yet exist. Submerged in *pathos* or *aisthesis*: astonishment, wonder, and sometimes terror before that which surrounds it. *Eros* prior to any *eros* defined or framed as such. The sensual pleasure of birth into a world where the look itself remains tactile – open to the light. Still carnal. Voluptuous without knowing it' (Irigaray 1993: 185). What Duden interprets as a symbol of all that is victimized and repressed by phallocentric culture can also be cast in the more positive light of Irigaray's notion of ethical erotic exchange: 'Like an amorous impregnation that seeks out and affirms otherness while protecting it' (Irigaray 1993: 186).

This dragon image recalls a prose sketch first published by Duden in 1989 entitled 'Der wunde Punkt im Alphabet', inspired by cultural representations of dragon-slaying. Her self-conscious use of 'Opfer-Täter' diction reverses the conventional sympathies of the onlooker, as she describes the inequality of the contest and names the 'guilt' of the victims as their non-human, 'different' status (Duden 1995: 78). Like Haushofer's protagonist's drawings, 'Dieses Wesen war keine Art und hatte keine Art. Es gehörte zu keiner Spezies, hatte keinen Stammbaum, war überall und nirgends zu finden ... Es war stets Einzelgänger, Einsiedler, Außenseiter' (Duden 1995: 79). Its shameless body doesn't restrict itself to a decent selection of physical attributes, profligately laying claim to an impossible array, even refusing to observe the all-important binary sexual divide: 'Ein einziger Skandal, dieser Drache ... So etwas ist der Körper des Vergehens schlechthin, das corpus delicti. Was Wunder, daß man sich seiner entledigen will' (Duden 1995: 80). It is this unruly body which exceeds classification and representation which makes the dragon such a threat to civilization: symbol of the chaos which must be killed and domesticated before the hero can found the city and claim his virginal bride.[13] The one note of defiance in this desperate scene is the unstoppable scream of the victims: 'Mit weit aufgesperrten Mäulern, die von Blut überströmen – roten klaffenden Wunden ähnlich, die nicht mehr heilen, sich nie wieder schließen werden – und schreien, brüllen, röcheln sie die Sprache der Körper und der Herzen in der den Bildern angestammten Stummheit' (Duden 1995: 84). This image lends poignancy to the ending of Haushofer's last novel, the picture of the dragon figuring 'the material resistance of women's bodies to the cultural constructions that have barred women's pleasure' (Stockton 1994: 50).

Like her contemporary Ingeborg Bachmann, Haushofer's despair of the possiblity of a sexual relation is tempered by a utopian hope for the capacity to love (*Die Wand*: 238).[14] Haushofer's protagonists are all concerned, however, with developing survival strategies for coping with the incompatibility between the sexes, and if her later protagonists appear to acquiesce in deeply unsatisfactory marriages, their critique of the existing cultural order becomes increasingly uncompromising. The fact that a plural, fluid, excessive eroticism transgresses the limits imposed on the female subject points to a rejection of existing notions of rational subjectivity, as does the uncomfortable knowledge of the repression on which our culture is based. At the same time there are moments in her work which open up the possibility of new models of ethical subjectivity and interpersonal relationships, based on non-intrusive love, generosity, empathy, and a tolerance of difference.

Notes

[1] For a critical analysis of Haushofer reception see Venske 1986.

[2] The start of the recent revival of interest in Haushofer coincided with the republication by Claassen Verlag of *Die Wand* in 1983, when it was read primarily as an anti-nuclear novel, finding resonances with the contemporary peace movement. Venske sees even this as a reductive view of the novel's *Zivilisationskritik* (Venske 1986: 51).

[3] For a fuller summary see Grosz 1989: 140-83.

[4] The non-identical nature of the self is signalled in the use of three different names for the protagonist at different stages of her life: the pre-school child 'Lieserl', the schoolgirl and young wife 'Elisabeth', and the mature, single woman 'Betty'.

[5] This is clearer still in the later autobiographical novel *Himmel, der nirgendwo endet*, in which Meta identifies with Kleist's male *and* female characters, but especially with Penthesilea's wild, all-consuming passion ([1966] Haushofer 1991b: 95).

[6] Madeleine Marti notes that this novel is the only one in which the absence of political representation of women is explicitly mentioned (*Die Tapetentür*: 65), but points out also that Annette is unable to allow herself to explore her spontaneous erotic responses to women, or to permit the warm empathy of her friendship with Meta to develop into anything more explicitly sexual. Nevertheless I disagree that this is evidence of any decline in Haushofer's radicalism; there is a devastating criticism of masculinity in the depiction of the heterosexual female dilemma: 'Und der Feind steckt in ihnen, die wir lieben müssen. Ich kann nicht leben ohne Liebe, und ich kann das Unmenschliche nicht lieben' (71). The consequences of this are carried to their logical conclusion at the end of the novel *Die Wand*.

[7] This is my interpretation of the 'Maschinenlärm' which signals the protagonist's status as a worker in a factory, constantly charged with producing and disposing of an excess of experience (Duden 1982: 38-39). It is an image of the subject as a 'machine' for processing perception, an 'industrial' metaphor for repression.

[8] The attic is both traditionally the creative space of artists and the domicile of mad women, as in this novel, where it is the site of the return of the repressed (see Roebling 1989).

Notes continued

[9] This is reminiscent of Duden's autobiographical account of her own experience of growing up as a girl through the devastation of post-war Germany: 'Ich wurde erwachsen, als wäre nichts geschehen' (Duden 1982: 77).

[10] As in *Die Tapetentür*, the dual narrative perspective in *Die Mansarde* serves to expose techniques of self-deception, this time the uncompromising authenticity being accorded to the diary entries, while the resigned wife in the present strives only to preserve the peace in her marriage.

[11] Duden also suggests masculinity's greater facility for forgetting; the female protagonist of *Das Judasschaf* is delivered up to unbearable memory: 'Nichts war mehr zu leugnen, kein einziges Versteck war übriggeblieben, kein Umweg, keine Abzweigung ... Männlichere Lebensaussichten konnte sie bei sich nicht anwenden. Denn es fehlte ihnen, was sie erst noch durch Zusammenstoß mit sich selbst und Versteinerung beseitigen mußte: Gedächtnis' (Duden 1985: 40).

[12] The resort to art as a refuge from rational, symbolic meaning is reminiscent of Anne Duden's *Das Judasschaf*, in which the protagonist finds refuge in art galleries, but also in the Natural History Museum in New York, where she is captivated by picture postcards of an Emerald Snake and a Gecko: 'Ich ahnte, was es mit ihnen auf sich hatte und warum sie mir so gefielen, daß ich schon ein paarmal gedacht hatte: Geschöpfe, richtige Geschöpfe. Es hatte damit zu tun, daß sie selbstverständlich und wortlos vorkamen. Ich empfand Erleichterung und Zuneigung' (Duden 1985: 80).

[13] In her essay 'Women on the Market', Irigaray discusses the 'pure exchange value' of the virginal woman in cementing relations between men (Irigaray 1985: 186).

[14] As Bachmann puts it, until a 'new man' exists, it is as well for the sexes to harbour no romantic expectations: 'Es sollten die Frauen und die Männer am besten Abstand halten, nichts zu tun haben miteinander, bis beide herausgefunden hatten aus einer Verwirrung und der Verstörung, der Unstimmigkeit aller Beziehungen' (Bachmann 1991: 175).

Bibliography

Bachmann, Ingeborg. 1991. *Simultan*, Munich, Piper
Duden, Anne. 1982. *Übergang*, Berlin, Rotbuch
—. 1985. *Das Judasschaf*, Berlin, Rotbuch
—. 1986. 'In Ruhe und Ordnung: unheilbar verwundert. Zu Marlen Haushofers Roman *Die Mansarde*', in Duden and Ebner et al. 1986: 108-14
—. 1995. *Der wunde Punkt im Alphabet*, Hamburg, Rotbuch

Duden, Anne and Jeannie Ebner et al. 1986. *'Oder war da manchmal noch etwas anderes?' Texte zu Marlen Haushofer*, Frankfurt am Main, Verlag Neue Kritik

Grosz, Elizabeth. 1989. *Sexual Subversions: Three French Feminists*, St. Leonards, Allen and Unwin

Haushofer, Marlen. 1990a. *Die Wand*, Berlin, Ullstein

—. 1990b. *Wir töten Stella*, Munich, dtv

—. 1991a. *Eine Handvoll Leben*, Munich, dtv

—. 1991b. *Himmel, der nirgendwo endet*, Frankfurt am Main, Fischer

—. 1991c. *Die Tapetentür*, Munich, dtv

—. 1992. *Die Mansarde*, Frankfurt am Main, Fischer

Irigaray, Luce. 1985. *This Sex Which is Not One* (Fr. 1977), Ithaca, NY, Cornell University Press

—. 1993. *An Ethics of Sexual Difference* (Fr. 1984), London, Athlone Press

Knapp, Mona and Gerhard Labroisse. 1989. *Frauen-Fragen in der deutschsprachigen Literatur seit 1945*, Amsterdam, Rodopi

Marti, Madeleine. 1992. *Hinterlegte Botschaften. Die Darstellung lesbischer Frauen in der deutschsprachigen Literatur seit 1945*, Stuttgart, Metzler

Roebling, Irmgard. 1989. 'Drachenkampf aus der Isolation oder Das Fortschreiben geschichtlicher Selbsterfahrung in Marlen Haushofers Romanwerk', in Knapp and Labroisse 1989: 275-321

Stephan, Inge, Regula Venske, Sigrid Weigel. 1987. *Frauenliteratur ohne Tradition? Neun Autorinnenporträts*, Frankfurt am Main, Fischer

Stockton, Kathryn B. 1994. *God Between their Lips. Women in Irigaray, Brontë, and Eliot*, Stanford, Stanford University Press

Venske, Regula. 1986. '"Vielleicht, daß ein sehr entferntes Auge eine geheime Schrift aus diesem Splitterwerk enträtseln könnte...": Zur Kritik der Rezeption Marlen Haushofers', in Duden and Ebner et al. 1986: 43-66

—. 1987. '"...das Alte verloren und das Neue nicht gewonnen ...": Marlen Haushofer', in Stephan, Venske, and Weigel 1987: 99-130

Weigel, Sigrid. 1989. *Die Stimme der Medusa. Schreibweisen in der Gegenwartsliteratur von Frauen*, Reinbek, Rowohlt

Die Klavierspielerin: on Mutilation and Somatophobia

Tobe Levin

A common theme in African fiction, genital mutilation appears but rarely in European narratives.[1] It occurs, however, in Elfriede Jelinek's *Die Klavierspielerin* (1983) within a context of hatred for the female body: 'Im Sparschwein ihres Leibes steckt sie fest, in diesem bläulich angelaufenen Tumor, den sie ständig mit sich herumschleppt, und der bis zum Platzen prall ist' (300), to give one example of disgust. As Sigrid Löffler notes, Jelinek's fifth novel can be read 'as the story of an unsuccessful artist, as the vivisection of the mother-daughter bond in a claustrophobic petit bourgeois milieu, as the etiology of sex-pathological behaviour, or as a feminist treatment of the theme, "destruction of female sexuality"' (Löffler 1983 cited in Levin 1986b: 436). The latter two concern me here, for, as an activist opposed to genital mutilation, I feel that successful global eradication efforts depend on understanding what factors influence similar practices in Europe.

Mutilating cultures have often openly admitted the rite's aim to negate a woman's pleasure,[2] and Jelinek puts incision to similar symbolic use. In fact, although clearly European, *Die Klavierspielerin* replicates several features of cultural anthropological accounts. In the first instance, of course, Erika is a cutter, someone who relieves unbearable tension, anger or anxiety by razoring her skin (Favazza 1996). Drawing blood from her hands (*Die Klavierspielerin*: 57), she fits the clinical description: 'Ihr Hobby ist das Schneiden am eigenen Körper' (110). Erika enters the literature of tribal rites, however, when enlarging her vagina: 'SIE setzt sich mit gespreizten Beinen vor der Vergrößerungsseite des Rasierspiegels und vollzieht einen Schnitt, der die Öffnung vergrößern soll' (110). This sounds not only like episiotomy but also like introcision, a practice among certain Australian clans to section the perineum.

Naturally, an adult's voluntary knifing differs from the forced excision of children. And yet, shared by both individual and group are a number of features: the surgery's compulsive and ritualistic nature; the razor's association with the father; the complicity of the mothers in suppressing their daughters' sexuality, and the daughters' acceptance of their mothers' teaching. Like African girls looking forward to the rite, Erika has tucked her mother inside herself – 'Mutter und Kind haben die Rollen getauscht' (293) – most strikingly dramatized in what Jelinek calls the 'lesbische Vergewaltigungsszene der Mutter' (51). In this 'parasexual', 'cryptosexual' (293) attack 'wie bei einem Liebeskampf, ... nicht

Orgasmus ist das Ziel, sondern die Mutter an sich, die person Mutter' (*Die Klavierspielerin*: 292). Psychoanalytic and Lacanian critics read this as evidence of an incomplete parting of mother and child, a pervasive textual syndrome theorized by 'the psychologist of narcissism and ego-development', Erika's namesake Heinz Kohut, who 'comment[s] on the destructive effects of a symbiotic mother/ daughter relationship, in which the merger with an idealized object prevents successful separation from the primary other, the mother' (Berka 1994: 231). Now, within the phallogocentric order suppressing feminine alterity, such complicity can only prove dysfunctional.

Jelinek, then, unveils the quisling mother, the one who colludes in her daughters' mutilation in millions of literal cases each year. An estimated 100,000,000 females have undergone clitoral ablation, with 20,000 girls at risk in France, and 10,000 in the British Isles. Such figures reveal a political crisis which feminists have thus far failed to deal with. As Fiddler points out, Jelinek herself 'avoids ... any notion of natural solidarity between women. The "wir sind alle Schwestern" attitude is one which she deplores' (1994: 69). And yet, I aim here to address all campaigners, showing mutilation as a shared oppression, for in Jelinek's text a clitoris or a vagina, when literally and metonymically erased, snuffs out, and paradoxically creates, a female caste based on somatophobia and body-hatred. Those identified as women, wherever they inhabit patriarchal space, have been divided even unto our most intimate bonds, mother turned against daughter, daughter against mother, in Europe as in Africa.

Jelinek thus uses the discourse on women to evoke women's absence from discourse showing that, where two sexes may be expected, we have only one, the male (an echo, perhaps, of the Church fathers for whom women were merely defective men). In Katrin Sieg's terms: 'Woman ... an image with no "substance" ... is revealed as a male phantasma. [Jelinek implies] that women ... cannot speak because they are always already spoken for and about. [She refuses] to represent female identity' (Sieg 1994: 151-2; see also Levin 1991a).

If, however, the female cannot be known, the question becomes, what effect does this have on real lives? 'Language [is] the site at which sexual difference is inscribed and performed', (Sieg 1994: 170) Sieg goes on to remind us: idiom moulds bodies. As Judith Butler contends, '"naturalness" [is] constituted through discursively constrained performative acts that produce the body through and with the categories of sex' (1990: x). Jelinek, reliably denaturing Nature, embodies this challenging assertion in her text, in particular in scenarios of mutilation which ironically construct and deconstruct.

These scenes include, firstly, genital mutilation proper; secondly, metaphors and metonymies of mutilation; and thirdly, gynocidal erasures that conflate women with their genitals, negating both. I start with an example of the third, Erika entering the peep show:

> Hier, in dieser Kabine, wird sie zu garnichts. Nichts paßt in Erika hinein, aber sie, sie paßt genau hinein in diese Kartause. Erika ist ein kompaktes Gerät in Menschenform. Die Natur scheint keine Öffnungen in ihr gelassen zu haben. Erika hat ein Gefühl von massivem Holz dort, wo der Zimmerman bei der echten Frau das Loch gelassen hat. (*Die Klavierspielerin*: 67)

The metonymy making intelligible the link between the first sentence (in which Erika is nothing) and the first clause in the second (in which nothing fits into Erika) is the phallocratic reduction of female to vagina, meaning penile sheath. Erika proves dysfunctional as an encasing, but this in turn only suggests her phallic status. And indeed, she becomes the instrument (in a play on Lacanian thought, whereby the man *has*, but the woman *is*, the phallus), insinuating her whole self into the cell. In a subsequent reversion, now resembling a cyborg, she would logically lack the generous accoutrements both God the carpenter and Mother Nature have bestowed on women: openings. We are left with the impression of a neutered creature, neither giving (shelter) nor receiving (through her entrance hall). In this respect, she differs from 'real women'.

But this extended metaphor continues dismantling the category 'woman':

> Es ist schwammiges, morsches, einsames Holz im Hochwald, und die Fäulnis schreitet voran. Dafür stolziert Erika als Herrin herum.... Der Mann am Eingang nennt sie tapfer gnädige Frau. Bitte kommen Sie doch weiter, bittet er sie gleich in seine gute Stube hinein, in der beschaulich die Lämpchen über Brüste und Fotzen hinweg glühen. Haarbuschige Dreiecke erglimmend herausmeißeln, denn das ist das allererste, worauf der Mann schaut, da gibt es ein Gesetz dafür. Der Mann schaut auf das Nichts, er schaut auf den reinen Mangel. Zuerst schaut er auf dieses Nichts, dann kommt die restliche Mutti auch noch dran. (67)

Erika the totem, opening this passage, has been certified in the preceding lines as sealed. But wait! What do we understand as spongy, decaying, spreading rot if not a process creating holes? Even the phallic woman ends up perforated, she courts the privileges of class and race, illusory inviolability and control, the author tells us: as a 'Hoheit', a 'Herrin', a 'gnädige Frau' in the 'gute Stube', she will no longer be a 'Frau', unlike the charwomen who, we rest assured, are women, 'doch sie sehen nicht so aus' (68). The unstable category of woman dissolves: 'Man würde nicht glauben, daß sie [die Kohut] und die Frauen auf den Fotos ein und demselben Geschlecht angehören, nämlich dem schönen' (126). Yet, while the rubric is being collapsed, the Law (Freud via Lacan) recuperates it, for reduced to her vagina, a female continues to be conflated with lack. Thus, the colloquial 'nothing' opening this text – 'hier ... wird sie zu garnichts' (67) – echoes in the Master Narrative 'Nichts' at its close, the Nothing men see as a woman. Nothing, then, – 'not-woman' – is the counterpart to man, with Jelinek's text seeming to support those who argue for one discursive sex. Women play hide and seek: 'sie [die Frau] taucht immer wieder auf, beschäftigt, wie sie ist, mit dem Verschwinden' (Berka 1993: 135).

These themes – women's complicity with their erasure, a result of the horror their genitals inspire – reoccur in a strongly worded passage, offering Erika's thoughts while Walter Klemmer stalks her:

> Im Gehen haßt Erika diese poröse, ranzige Frucht, die das Ende ihres Unterleibs markiert.... Bald wird diese Fäulnis fortschreiten und größere Leibespartien erfassen. Dann stirbt man unter Qualen. Entsetzt malt Erika sich aus, wie sie als ein Meter fünfundsiebzig großes unempfindliches Loch im Sarg liegt und sich in der Erde auflöst; das Loch, das sie verachtete, vernachlässigte, hat nun ganz Besitz von ihr ergriffen. Sie ist Nichts. Und nichts gibt es mehr für sie. (*Die Klavierspielerin*: 237)

The concluding phrases, from 'le néant' of high philosophy to the larmoyance of daytime soaps, temper with the wit of code-switching the gloom of an otherwise suicidal passage playing with the trope of woman as illness. For although the hyperbole can be read as satire, the nothingness to which woman is consigned both reflects and enacts a gynocidal threat that many females internalize. Concerning the origin of this projection, Jelinek tells an illustrative tale: 'Ein kleiner Bub hat mit seiner Mutter gebadet. Nun rinnt das Wasser in den Abfluß, und er fängt irrsinnig zu schreien an, weil er in diesem schwarzen Loch, in dem das Wasser verschwindet, das schwarze Loch der Mutter sieht, in das er wieder hineingesogen wird. Ein sehr starkes Bild, das mir einleuchtet' (Jelinek 1995: 37).

In *Die Klavierspielerin*, because a woman's whole body inevitably falls prey to her predatory cavity – 'das Loch' takes possession (247), the victim finds Christian complicity attractive: 'Erika liebt den jungen Mann und wartet auf Erlösung durch ihn ... Sie will sich von dem Mann förmlich aufsaugen lassen, bis sie nicht mehr vorhanden ist' (257), clearly a reversal of the little boy's drainage *angst*. If then the male can kill – as 'Erika ... wolle unter ihm ganz vergehen und ausgelöscht sein' (270) –, the man has become the mother. For this nihilism echoes in the relationship with the maternal. As noted, we often find the daughter's wish to rehouse herself in the mother's flesh. At one point she is 'dieser Fisch im Fruchtwasser der Mutter' (73), and again, 'Erika will in ihre Mutter am liebsten wieder hineinkriechen' (95). More frequently, however, the matriarch serves as originating instance: 'diese mütterliche Umschlingung wird sie restlos auffressen und verdauen' (147). Her cannibal progenitor, 'ein Blutegel[,] ... saugt ihr das Mark aus den Knochen' (125), an act of infanticide backing up Jelinek's claim that the mother, too, is male: 'Die Mutter war phallisch, war eben Vater und Mutter in einer Person' (Schwarzer 1989: 54; see also Berka 1993: 143). With the daughter phallic, too – 'Sofort gab der Vater den Stab an seine Tochter weiter und trat ab' (7, cited by Jelinek in interviews with Berka 1993, and Meyer in Jelinek 1995) – and the male maternal, then clearly, the female proper has gone. Sabine Wilke (1993) generalizes from this family constellation, claiming that 'die Übernahme der doppelten Identifikation mit dem Täter und dem Opfer führt also in diesem Text zur absoluten Zerstörung der Frau' (135). After all, 'Erika würde die Grenze zu ihrer eigenen Ermordung gern überschreiten' (*Die Klavierspielerin*: 135), we are assured. Like the vampire, violating boundaries of gender and of life, Erika embodies simultaneously man and woman, the quick and the dead, escaping the structures of the real.

Real, however, is feminine erasure. 99% of the female population of Somalia, and 89% of Sudanese are sewn.[3] And though not so extensively, Erika joins the millions scarred:

> Wenn kein Mensch zu Hause ist, schneidet sie sich absichtlich in ihr eigenes Fleisch.... Kaum verhallt die Türklinke, wird schon die väterliche Allzweck-Klinge, ihr kleiner Talisman, hervorgeholt. SIE schält die Klinge aus ihrem Sonntagsmäntelchen von fünf Schichten jungfräulichen Plastiks heraus.... Diese Klinge ist für IHR Fleisch bestimmt.... SIE setzt sich mit gespreizten Beinen vor die Vergrößerungsseite des Rasierspiegels und vollzieht einen Schnitt, der die Öffnung vergrößern soll, die als Tür in ihren Leib hineinführt. (*Die Klavierspielerin*: 110)

'Um die verborgenen Organe der Frau zu sehen', Jelinek told me (Levin 1991b), 'muß man eben aufschneiden.'

Differing of course from African girls' agony but replicating other classic cases of self-carving, the patient claims it doesn't hurt, an insentience building symbolically on the series of wood-cutting images planted throughout. 'Ganz glattgehobelt' (12) by her mother, the male-invested 'ihr übergeordnete Instanz', Erika winds up 'dort ... wo das weibliche Holz still auf die Axt warten muß' (112). A mere shaft of lumber, Erika lacks feeling. Nonetheless, beyond the distinction between auto-aggression and torture, considerable aspects of socialized mutilation carry over. First, the secrecy: in many instances, initiates are isolated, just as Erika waits to be alone: 'Sie wartet immer schon lange auf den Augenblick, da sie sich unbeobachtet zerschneiden kann' (110). Second, Erika peels off the blade's 'Sunday dress', its 'virginal' protective layers, the utensil metamorphosing into a clitoris embedded in flesh while the Christian Sabbath invokes repression, just as ceremony and suppression fashion initiation rites. Third, the motive covers Erika and Africa. 'Sie ist sich selbst ganz ausgesetzt, was immer noch besser ist, als anderen ausgesetzt zu sein' (110).[4] Control, then, is the issue: rather than risk repudiation or worse abuse by men, African mothers arrange to have their daughters done. And fourth, the urge to torso-modelling is not limited to a single culture: 'Als [die Mutter] ... den aus ihrem Leib hervorschießenden Lehmklumpen betrachtete, ging sie sofort daran, ohne Rücksicht ihn zurechtzuhauen, um Reinheit und Feinheit zu erhalten' (32). Infibulations are performed to beautify an unaesthetic organ and to elevate its owner in the social scale; clitoridectomies also rid the female of the phallic, just as Erika whittles on her femininity.

If, however, knives are needed to carve women, what pre-operative status does the sex retain? Opposing the male is not the female but a multitude, for more than two sexes exist: Holly Devor (1989) talks about several, since 'neither sex nor gender follow[s] slavishly from chromosomal instructions'. Take Turner's Syndrome for instance, a configuration referred to as 45XO or simply XO. 'This individual, thought to be female, will lack internal sexual organs'. XYs, however, who normally become men, may suffer Androgen Insensitivity Syndrome (AIS) or Testicular Feminization: 'In such cases, an XY baby is born with normal-looking female external genitalia, male internal reproductive organs, and a short vagina that does not lead to a cervix or uterus'. Then we have Klinefelter's Syndrome, two or more X chromosomes with a single Y: 'The XXY ... might conceivably make [its victims] females with one Y chromosome or males with an extra X', and finally, we have 'mosaics', 'whose sex chromosomes show variety throughout the body', all abnormalities estimated to occur in three out of every 1,000 births, hence twice as often as Down's Syndrome (Devor 1989: 7-10). And Julia Epstein (1995), adding congenital adrenal hyperplasia, 5-alpha reductase deficiency and 21-hydroxylase deficiency to the list, confirms this figure (1995: 79). Add *Zwangsgeschlechtszuweisung*, or clitoridectomy undertaken routinely on children with ambiguous genitalia, and you can see that African women are hardly alone in being subjected to gendering force.

Other critics of *Die Klavierspielerin* have played variations on somatic dissonance. Reading for its Marxist-feminism, Linda C. DeMeritt notes 'the instrumentalization of the female body and human emotion' (1994: 112). Sigrid Berka (1994), influenced by the 'Deleuzian model', posits the father's absence – D(e)addyfication – as pivotal in Erika's masochistic mother-bond, the relation Barbara Kosta (1993) also privileges. Juliet Wigmore (1990) focuses on bondage as well, drawing parallels between repression of the protagonist's sexuality and the constraints of her musical training. Marlies Janz reads Erika's masochism, with Jessica Benjamin, as an 'Abwehrmechanismus des Selbst' (Janz 1995: 74), i.e. as evidence of a failed gender identification and 'inadequate subjectivity'. Her 'symbolische Selbstdefloration' attempts to create a subject position but one which, ironically, can only inscribe 'castration' (Janz: 74 and 76). Janz sees this as problematic: 'Denn was diese Figur letztlich ausmacht, ist ihre vollkommene Unfähigkeit, sich selbst als Frau zu definieren und über die misogyne Männerprojektion, daß die Frau "das Nichts" und "den reinen Mangel" repräsentiere,

hinauszugelangen' (83). In other words, Erika literalizes psychoanalytic metaphor, undermining its authority. 'Wenn Patricia Jüngers Vertonung des Romans den Zwangscharakter, die Wiederholungen, das Zeremonielle der Selbstzerstörungsakte Erika Kohuts betont, so trifft das wohl den verschwiegenen Gehalt eines Textes, der in seiner Schreibweise noch die Psychoanalyse selber zum masochistischen Ritual erstarren läßt' (Janz 1995: 86).

Elizabeth Wright (1993) agrees: 'Auf den ersten Blick bietet sich dieser Text somit für eine psychoanalytische Lektüre geradezu an', she notes, 'doch erweist er sich sodann solcher Lesart gegenüber als eigentümlich widerständig' (51). Attending to authorial interventions and sensing in their satiric import 'einen wütenden Angriff gegen die symbolische Ordnung *an sich*', (57) Wright explains this resistance to psychoanalysis in terms of Jelinek's aim, 'das Reale des Körpers, seine exzessive Gegenwart, zu erklären' (52), reading the numerous ejected fluids as significant because amorphous; spilling from the body, they mark its fluctuating boundary which leads, like the blood that runs and runs and runs and runs, to 'Auflösung und Dis-Figuration' (55), that is, to 'Lust' in loss.

A feminine longing for pain, implicated in this reading, presents its own vexation, as Allyson Fiddler holds: 'it is surely wrong to see *Die Klavierspielerin* [as] literary proof of the existence of female masochism as a universal gender characteristic' (1994: 149). Nonetheless, Jelinek stresses the mutilation scene's autobiographical anchor:

> Müller: Das grausamste Bild, das Sie erfunden haben, um diesen [Selbst]Haß zu beschreiben, ist eine Selbstverletzung.
> Jelinek: Das habe ich nicht erfunden.
> Müller: Die Frau im Buch zerschneidet sich mit einer Rasierklinge die Scheide.
> Jelinek: Das habe ich wirklich getan. (Müller 1990: 55)

One way or the other, we return to the 'real' with psychoanalyst Annegret Mahler-Bungers (1988). For the clinician, *Die Klavierspielerin* is a 'Krankengeschichte', the symptom being the heroine's failure to develop a 'weibliche Identität' (80), and the narrative an account of masochistic personality formation, for 'Erika Kohut ... beläßt ihre Subjektivität in der Illusion der imaginären Einheit mit ihrem Ideal-Ich aus der Zeit des primären Narzissmus' (Mahler-Bungers 1988: 84). The result of this mother-identification, a need for punishment stemming from guilt, leads Mahler-Bungers to a startling insight: 'Ich möchte die These aufstellen, daß das, was [Erika] fehlt, die *Kastration* ist' (85). Absolving the reader 'von der Vorstellung ... die Kastration sei etwas Reales, also das tatsächliche Abtrennen des Gliedes' (85) she sees it symbolizing difference: 'Der Kastrations-Komplex beginnt mit der Wahrnehmung des anderen Geschlechts und endet mit der Anerkennung des Geschlechtsunterschiedes' (85)

on the part of 'both' sexes, bringing with it mourning for loss and the longing to return to the Same. In other words, Mahler-Bungers's diagnosis, that Erika represents the erasure of sexual difference, allows her to read the piano teacher's mutilation as indeed it is intended when practised in real life. Mahler-Bunger admits: 'Die "Kastration" hätte hier den Stellenwert, den Beschneidungsriten als Initiation der Geschlechtsreife bei Naturvölkern innehaben' (87). To apply the term 'Naturvölker' uncritically to Jelinek makes a rather sad impression, not least because these nature-nigh peoples have been living in London's Brent and Paris's 19th for a good many years and were carrying out real castrations by the millions in the mid-eighties when Mahler-Bungers's piece was written. But not to be peevish – the psychoanalyst is right, to a point. Mutilation occurs, but it doesn't make a woman; it unmakes one.

African women, and specifically those from mutilating cultures, have theorized the gynocidal impetus behind the excision of girls. 'Women can be killed!', Efua Dorkenoo insists (Walker and Parmar 1993: 245), as the noose of a challenged patriarchy tightens, calling for a political reponse. Thus, when Jelinek writes about Erika: 'Der Unterleib und die Angst sind ihr zwei befreundete Verbündete, sie treten fast immer gemeinsam auf' (*Die Klavierspielerin*: 11) and Alice Schwarzer (1989) speculates 'Daß den Frauen die Sexualität zerstört wurde, hat sicherlich weitreichendere Folgen, als wir ahnen', (52) both represent a feminism with broad ecumenical appeal. Few theorists deny the assault on female bodies; what these anatomies, once free of threat, can *mean* remains unknown.

Notes

[1] For an introduction to novels on this theme, see Levin 1986a.

[2] For reasons and rationalizations, see Levin 1980.

[3] See Dorkenoo 1994 for an explanation of the practice of female genital mutilation and for further information about the campaign for its prevention.

[4] Favazza (1996) relates the greater incidence of skin cutting among women than men to the 'ambiguity, paradox, and discontinuity in females' experiences of their bodies' (51). Self-slicing may be an attempt 'to own the body, to perceive it as self (not other), known (not uncharted and unpredictable), and impenetrable (not invaded or controlled from outside)' (51). Note Jelinek: 'es war ihr eigener Körper, doch er ist ihr fürchterlich fremd' (*Die Klavierspielerin*: 111). 'Sie ist für sich selbst tabu' (70).

Bibliography

Berka, Sigrid. 1993. 'Ein Gespräch mit Elfriede Jelinek', *Modern Austrian Literature*, 26, 2: 127-155
Berka, Sigrid. 1994. 'D(e)addyfication: Elfriede Jelinek', in Johns and Arens 1994: 229-254
Butler, Judith. 1990. *Gender Trouble. Feminism and the Subversion of Identity*, London, Routledge
DeMeritt, Linda C. 1994. 'A "Healthier Marriage": Elfriede Jelinek's Marxist Feminism in *Die Klavierspielerin* and *Lust*', in Johns and Arens 1994: 107-25
Devor, Holly. 1989. *Gender Blending. Confronting the Limits of Duality*, Bloomington, Indiana University Press
Dorkenoo, Efua. 1994. *Cutting the Rose. Female Genital Mutilation: The Practice and its Prevention*, London, Minority Rights Publications
Epstein, Julia. 1995. *Altered Conditions: Disease, Medicine, and Storytelling*, New York, Routledge
Favazza, Armando R. 1996. *Bodies Under Siege. Self-Mutilation and Body Modification in Culture and Psychiatry*, Baltimore, Johns Hopkins University Press
Fiddler, Allyson. 1994. *Rewriting Reality. An Introduction to Elfriede Jelinek*, Oxford, Berg
Janz, Marlies. 1995. *Elfriede Jelinek*, Stuttgart, Metzler
Jelinek, Elfriede. 1983. *Die Klavierspielerin*, Reinbek, Rowohlt
—. 1995. with Jutta Heinrich and Adolf-Ernst Meyer. *Sturm und Zwang. Schreiben als Geschlechterkampf*, Hamburg, Ingrid Klein
Johns, Jorun B. and Katherine Arens (eds). 1994. *Elfriede Jelinek: Framed by Language*, Riverside, Ariadne
Kosta, Barbara. 1993. 'Muttertrauma: Anerzogener Masochismus - Waltraud Anna Mitgutsch, *Die Zuchtigung* und Elfriede Jelinek, *Die Klavierspielerin*', in Helga Kraft and Elke Liebs (eds), *Mütter – Tochter – Frauen: Weiblichkeitsbilder in der Literatur*, Stuttgart, Metzler: 243-65
Levin, Tobe. 1980. '"Unspeakable Atrocities": The Psycho-Sexual Etiology of Female Genital Mutilation' *The Journal of Mind and Behavior*, 1, 2: 197-210
—. 1986 a. 'Women as Scapegoats of Culture and Cult: An Activist's View of Female Circumcision in Ngugi's *The River Between*', in Carole Boyce Davies and Anne Adams Graves (eds), *Ngambika. Studies of Women in African Literature*, Trenton, Africa World Press: 205-22
—. 1986b. 'Introducing Elfriede Jelinek: Double Agent of Feminist Aesthetics', *Women's Studies International Forum*, 9, 4: 435-42
—. 1991a. '"Jelinek's Radical Radio: Deconstructing the Woman in Context', *Women's Studies International Forum*, 14, 1 and 2: 85-97

—. 19 Nov. 1991b. Interview with Elfriede Jelinek, unpublished
Löffler, Sigrid. '*Die Klavierspielerin*' ORF Ex-Libris, 1-3, Courtesy of Rowohlt Verlag, 26 March and 2 April
Mahler-Bungers, Annegret. 1988. 'Der Trauer auf der Spur. Zu Elfriede Jelineks *Die Klavierspielerin*', in Johannes Cremerius et al. (eds), *Freiburger literaturpsychologische Gespräche*, vol. 7 'Masochismus in der Literatur', Würzburg, Königshausen and Neumann: 80-95
Müller, André. 1990. 'Ich lebe nicht: André Müller spricht mit der Schriftstellerin Elfriede Jelinek', *Die Zeit*, 26, 22 June: 55-6
Schwarzer, Alice. 1989. 'Ich bitte um Gnade: Alice Schwarzer interviewt Elfriede Jelinek', *Emma*, 7: 50-5
Sieg, Katrin. 1994. *Exiles, Eccentrics, Activists: Women in Contemporary German Theater*, Ann Arbor, University of Michigan Press
Walker, Alice and Pratibha Parmar. 1993. *Warrior Marks. Female Genital Mutilation and the Sexual Blinding of Women*, New York, Harcourt Brace
Wigmore, Juliet. 1990. 'Elfriede Jelinek's Satirical Exposés', in Arthur Williams, Stuart Parkes and Roland Smith (eds). *Literature on the Threshold: The German Novel in the 1980s*, Oxford, Berg: 209-19
Wilke, Sabine. 1993. '"Ich bin eine Frau mit einer männlichen Anmaßung": Eine Analyse des "bösen Blicks" in Elfriede Jelineks *Die Klavierspielerin*', *Modern Austrian Literature*, 26, 1: 115-44
Wright, Elizabeth. 1993. 'Eine Ästhetik des Ekels: Elfriede Jelineks Roman *Die Klavierspielerin*', tr. Frauke Meyer-Gosau, *Text und Kritik*, 117: 51-9

Wasser, hinunter, wohin? Elfriede Jelineks *Kinder der Toten* – ein Flüssigtext

Juliane Vogel

1) Sintflut

In manchen Texten regnet es ungewöhnlich viel. Wasser ergießt sich in so bedrohlichen Mengen, daß die meteorologischen Naturgesetze außer Kraft gesetzt und die in trügerischer Trockenheit Dahinlebenden in Existenz und Gestalt bedroht werden. Hans Leberts Roman *Wolfshaut* (1960) zum Beispiel, dessen Beziehungen zu Elfriede Jelineks neuem Text nicht unbemerkt geblieben sind, hüllt sein sinnbildlich benanntes Dorf 'Schweigen' in einen dichten Regenvorhang ein, Wasser verwandelt die Wege in Pfützen, und nichts, was hier passiert, kann mehr ins Trockene gebracht werden. Eine im Zeichen der Feuchtigkeit geschilderte Landschaft, ein von Regen schraffierter Himmel geben den allegorischen Hintergrund einer Geschichte, im Zuge derer die verdrängten Verbrechen der nationalsozialistischen Vergangenheit nach oben geschwemmt werden.

Die gleichen Niederschläge fallen nun auch in Elfriede Jelineks *Die Kinder der Toten*. Wasser ist das beherrschende Agens auch ihres Textgeschehens. Wie zuvor in Leberts *Wolfshaut* wird auch hier die Wiederkehr des Vergangenen – die unabweisbar gewordene Erinnerung an die Opfer und Täter des Nationalsozialismus – an die Metaphern von Regen und Feuchtigkeit gebunden. Der Text kulminiert in einem durch unmäßige Regenfälle verursachten Erdrutsch, der den Protagonisten österreichischer Gegenwart, den Feriengästen im Gasthof 'Alpenrose', einen schmutzigen Tod beschert. Die Gegenwart wird unter dem Schlamm der Vergangenheit begraben.

Kommt aber das Wasser als Vorbote und Vollstrecker des Untergangs, so trägt es zumeist den Namen der Sintflut und schreibt sich aus heiligen oder klassischen Texten her. Die großen Erzählungen aus der Bibel oder auch aus den Ovidschen *Metamorphosen* werden in Erinnerung gerufen, die zuerst von der großen Wasserkatastrophe, von der regnerischen Beseitigung gottloser Ordnungen berichteten. Darin hatten zürnende Götter die Himmel geöffnet und ihre Schöpfung liquidiert, die ihnen den Gehorsam schuldig geblieben war. Während diese jedoch den Regen als eine pädagogische und letztlich auf die Zukunft gerichtete Maßnahme verstanden hatten, als ein monumentales Purgatorium, das nicht nur das Ende brachte, sondern auch den Anfang einer besseren Gesellschaft, verzichten die neuen Dichter der Sintflut auf eine solche rettende Perspektive. Bei ihnen bringt der Regen weder Katharsis noch

Versöhnung, noch Neubeginn. Auf den Aufbau einer Gesellschaft ohne Schuld darf keine Hoffnung mehr gesetzt werden. Zurück bleibt allenfalls der Schlamm, der Schmutz, dem die schuldverhafteten Kollektive auch nach dem Ende der Regenfälle unrettbar verfallen. Leberts Dorf 'Schweigen' versinkt im eigenen, nunmehr materialisierten Dreck. In Jelineks Text geht die Mure nieder, und die Überlebenden graben sich weiter in sie hinein.

Doch so pathetisch das Sujet der *Kinder der Toten* zu sein scheint, so handelt es sich doch um eine Apokalypse eigener Art. Hier nämlich führen die Komik und das Pathos des Untergangs einen von Satz zu Satz ausgetragenen Partisanenkampf. Die Schrecken apokalyptischer Wasserspiele haben sich so sehr ins Gräßliche und ins Groteske gesteigert, die Stimmen, die von ihnen berichten, so sehr vermehrt, daß sie die dem Stoff ansonsten eigene Erhabenheit durch eine ständig aufbegehrende Widerrede bedrohen. Eine vielfache Rede brandet auf, um seine Wahrheit unter Beweis zu stellen: Das hehre Ereignis des steirischen Weltenendes wird durch sinnloses Sprechen, durch eine atemlose und vielfach aufgespaltene Erzählerstimme seiner tabuisierten Würde entkleidet.

2) Apokalyptisches Gezeter

Dementsprechend lassen sich *Die Kinder der Toten:* die in ihren Wortkaskaden auch viele Bruchstücke und Treibgüter aus religiösen Schriften mit sich führen, als Demontage eines heiligen Textes, genauer gesagt, eines Offenbarungstextes lesen. Hier dringt weder die Stimme des alttestamentarischen Gottes, noch die seines literarischen Stellvertreters durch: auch die monolithische Stimme des Autors wird von den Hochfrequenzen greller Stimmspuren überlagert. Jene auktorialen Instanzen, die einst in ihren Texten mit göttlicher Gebärde Weltuntergänge veranstalteten, werden von Satz zu Satz bekämpft, parodiert und gespalten: Anders als in den mythisierenden Erzählungen eines Hans Lebert und auch eines Christoph Ransmayr, der in seinen Ovid-Roman *Die letzte Welt* ebenfalls eine Vision der Sintflut einarbeitete, sorgt bei Jelinek ein großartiges apokalyptisches Geschwätz und Gezeter für die Verbreitung der Schreckensnachrichten. 'Bleiern ist dieser Richtblock aus Wasser in den rissigen Beton eingepaßt, nichts glitzert, nichts glänzt, wo das doch das liebste Hobby des Wassers ist' (85). Ein monumentales Bild aus dem Vorfeld der Sintflut erfährt seine sofortige Banalisierung, auf der halben Strecke des Satzes kollabiert der heilige Text, um in nur allzu weltlichen Tönen zu enden. Das alte Pathos muß stets dem übersteuerten Deutsch der Slogans, der Jargons und der Medien weichen.

> Es fällt das Wasser. Und das Wasser, zu dem der Schnee in Windeseile schmilzt, fällt auch hinunter. Die Schneeschmelze überlagert sich mit den sich mit jeder Minute noch verstärkenden Regenmengen. Es werden in zwei Stunden, die der Regen jetzt noch weiter fallen wird, über 250 mm gemessen werden, über der Mürz fast 298 mm. Das

sind 300 Prozent der örtlichen Normalwerte. Der heimgesuchte Raum ist wesentlich kleiner als zur Zeit der jüngsten Unwetter, gebietsweise ist der Regen aber sogar noch heftiger. An der Mürz werden Werte registriert werden, die zuvor noch nie beobachtet worden sind. (*Die Kinder der Toten*: 617)

So kündigt sich der alte Vernichtungsmythos der Sintflut in einer sendefertigen Wetteransage an. Ein mit eilfertigen und rekordverdächtigen Zahlen versehener meteorologischer Bericht, eine Jelineksche Stimmenimitation par excellence, meldet eine Apocalypse joyeuse im Zeichen des Wassers. Im Vollzug dieses Untergangs öffnen sich in Jelineks Roman in Szene und Sprache Schleusen, die die biblischen oder antiken sowie auch die literarischen Himmelsergüsse in Ausmaß und Wirkung überbieten.

3) Todesarten. Das böse Wasser

Andererseits darf nicht übersehen werden, daß die Fluten nur eine, wenn auch die dominante Todesart in Jelineks Exekutionstheater darstellen. In geradezu enzyklopädischer Vollständigkeit, dazu in jener Simultaneität, die allen systematischen Darstellungen eignet, präsentieren sich die Techniken des Tötens im Text. Ein phantastisches 'Splattering' hebt an, das seine Abkunft aus der Literatur, bzw. aus den schriftlichen Überlieferungen nicht verleugnen will: Werwolfszenen, wie sie u.a. aus Leberts *Wolfshaut* inspiriert sein mögen, Vampirszenen, wie sie bereits durch *Krankheit oder Moderne Frauen* vorbereitet worden sind, biblische Todesarten, wie etwa der Exitus im Feuerofen (auch hier wirkt der Subtext *Wolfhaut* nach), satanistische Tode, wie in Josef Dvoraks Satanismus-Buch geschildert – im Verein dokumentieren sie, daß sich in Jelineks Text die Todesarten multipliziert haben, um in der Enge der steirischen Seclusio, in der Kürze einer beispiellos verdichteten Zeit miteinander zu konkurrieren. Der einzelne Tod ist kein exzeptionelles, kein definitives Ereignis mehr. In seinen vielfältigen Formen bildet das gewaltsame Sterben eine textumgreifende, reversible und letztlich transpersonale Struktur, die das gesamte Personal von Jelineks Text in Mitleidenschaft zieht. Die aufgestellten Figuren sterben zumeist mehrere Tode, sie werden wiederholt in mörderische Sequenzen verwickelt, die entweder im Staccato des Slapstick oder in unendlicher Dehnung den Exitus herbeiführen.

Dennoch aber faßt die Sintflut diese Schlächtereien im Zeichen des Flüssigen zusammen. In ihrer Eigenschaft als summarisches, massenvernichtendes Tötungsmittel kann sie als eine übergeordnete Form des Mordes gelten: Einmal, indem sie mit Mure und Regen das große Finale bringt: DIE MURE. DIE FURIE, dann aber vor allem deswegen, weil das Buch auf allen seinen Ebenen und von Anfang an von der endzeitlichen Freisetzung von Flüssigkeit, von der Sondierung und Öffnung verborgener und verschlossener Reservoire bestimmt ist. Wasser ist sein großes und alle Erzählung umgreifendes

Thema. Als Element der Auflösung bildet es das Gleit- und Bindemittel des ganzen Textes. Unter den vielen Formen seines Auftretens stellen die himmlischen Wasser der Sintflut ein vergleichsweise harmloses und immerhin aus vielen Traditionen vertrautes Vernichtungsmittel dar. Das noch viel 'bösere' Wasser kommt diesmal von unten, aus der Erde, aus großen und vergessenen Gräbern, und Jelinek scheint hier einer Vernichtungstheologie gefolgt zu sein, die berichtet, Gott habe während der Sintflut nicht nur den Himmel geöffnet, um den überirdischen Ozean, er habe überdies die Erde geöffnet, um den subtellurischen Ozean Toham über den Menschen auszugießen (Vgl. Böhme 1988: 17).

Dieses von unten hinauf dringende 'böse Wasser' ist denn auch der eigentliche Modulator des Geschehens. Es bildet die gallertige Quellmasse, den 'Leichensaft' (228), die 'giftige, erstickliche Maische' (273), in dem sich das in großen und verzögerten Progressionen vorgetragene Thema – die Rückkehr der Ermordeten aus der Erde – ankündigt und realisiert. 'Unter dem Wasserklumpen' hört man, 'wie unten, tief drunten, eine Menschenmasse, ein Menschenmassiv ... heraufkommen möchte, eine Masse, die sich gar nicht erfassen läßt' (105). Die vergessenen, in unterirdischen Reservoirs durchmischten und eingelagerten Toten dringen als flüssige 'Ungestalten' (206) durch 'Abflüsse' (636) und Löcher nach oben. Wässrig sind auch sie, doch ist es nicht mehr reines H_2O, aus dem sie bestehen. Auf ihrem Weg nach oben haben sie dem Wasser, dem ortlosen und absorbierenden Element par excellence, ihre nekrotische Konsistenz mitgeteilt. Vor allem das Klebrige und das Schleimige – jene ekelerregenden Verbindungen von Wasser und Schmutz – bilden die Biomasse der ins 'Leben' zurückdrängenden Wiedergänger und bald auch der Lebenden, die von den Toten heimgesucht und in gleichsam rituellen Morden in ihre flüssigen Bestandteile aufgelöst werden (Vgl. 400). Mischungen aus Blut und Wasser, sowie auch Emanationen des Fettigen – das 'Menschenwachs' (103) – gesellen sich den ringsum waltenden Flüssigkeiten hinzu, der Blutschlamm und andere besondere Säfte tragen die Zersetzungsprodukte ermordeten Fleisches wieder ans Tageslicht. Die Prozesse des Quellens und Rinnens, des Suppens und Tropfens, des Aufplatzens und Schäumens stellen die entsprechenden Prädikate bereit, und am Ende liest sich Jelineks Text als ein Lehr- und Musterbuch, eine Elementenlehre grauenhafter Liquide und entstalteter Materien. Wenn Christian Enzensberger einen 'Größeren Versuch über den Schmutz' schrieb, um dort eine Phänomenologie desselben zu präsentieren (Enzensberger 1968), so folgt ihm nun eine erbarmungslose Steigerung. Gleichfalls könnte man darauf hinweisen, daß Jelineks Text systematisch jenen Aspekt des 'Widrigen' entfaltet, den bereits Karl Rosenkranz ([1853] 1989) als die klassische Szene des Ekels beschrieben hatte. Seinen Ausführungen zufolge zeigt sie das 'Ausströmen trüber Effluvien'. Der Ekel steigert sich gerade dadurch aufs höchste, daß die austretende

Flüssigkeit 'analogisch uns an das Wasser erinnert ... und hier statt seiner eine flüssige, undurchsichtige, etwa noch mit todten verendenden Fischen untermischte Erdauflösung, eine gleichsam verwesende Erde sich darbietet' (Rosenkranz 1989: 313).

Damit aber ist das alte kathartische Projekt der Sintflut ein für allemal zunichtegemacht: Das acherontische Wasser, eine durch verwesende Substanzen verlangsamte Flüssigkeit kann kein reinigendes Wasser sein, da es sich mit dem tödlichen Dreck verbunden hat, den die Einwohner Deutschland-Österreichs vergeblich unter der Erde zu halten suchten. Als 'kontaminierte, eiternde, verweste Masse', als Wiederkehr des 'Abjekten', wie man mit einem von Julia Kristeva im Rahmen einer Psychoanalyse des Ekels geprägten Begriff sagen könnte, transportiert es just jene Vergangenheit, deren Makel nicht mehr abzuwaschen ist.

Doch werden auch andere Wassermythen in diesem 'schmutzigen stinkenden Wasser' (303) zu Ende gebracht. Jener z. B., der vom Ursprung allen Lebens aus Wasser und Feuchtigkeit erzählt, jener von der Ursuppe oder vom Fruchtwasser wird in apokalyptischer Weise gewendet. Denn alles Leben, das in Jelineks Text gezeugt und in Fleisch gekleidet wird, lebt nur das gespenstische Scheinleben der Revenants. Aus dem 'bösen Wasser' steigen Gestalten, die sich bei ihrer Wiederverkörperung in die Überreste anderer Leichen kleiden. *Die Kinder der Toten* sind die Sprößlinge eines nekromorphen Zeugungsprinzips und aus den 'tropfenden Körperfragmenten' (*Krankheit oder Moderne Frauen* 1987: 53) der Ermordeten geformt. 'Wie locker die in ihren Karkassen sitzen, wo doch nicht einmal ihre Glieder zueinander passen' (206), heißt es über die Wiedergeborenen. Deren Hosen 'wirken brettsteif, als wären sie mit gestockten Säften verleimt, und doch bewegen [sie sich] anmutig in ihnen, als wären sie in ihren Hosen gefaßt, eine Quelle, die aus dunklem Erdreich hervortaumelt, einer Hand entrinnt, die die Wassertraube zu sammeln, zu pflücken sucht' (322).

4) Metamorphosen

Was hier geboren wird, ist daher von äußerst unbestimmter Gestalt. Wo alles fließt und abfließt, verwäscht, ist nichts mehr deutlich zu erkennen und alles einem andauernden Prozeß der Umformung unterworfen. Die allgegenwärtigen Flüssigkeiten leiten einen Vorgang ein, der in weiten Teilen des Textes an die Stelle der Handlung tritt und für *Die Kinder der Toten* eine zentrale Funktion erfüllt: sie bewirken eine textumgreifende Metamorphose der Wörter und der Körper. 'Ja, jeder kann sich wandeln, es ist nie zu spät' (132).

Allerdings kann es in diesem apokalyptischen Elementartheater aus dem Mürztal nicht mehr darum gehen, den betroffenen Figuren ein ovidsches Schicksal zu bereiten, sie in Vögel oder in Steine zu verwandeln und die verlassene Form durch eine andere, doch nicht minder gewissen zu ersetzen. Jelineks Metamorphosen sind vor allem destruktive Prozesse und deshalb eher als 'Amorphosen', bzw. als 'Defigurationen' (Rosenkranz) zu lesen, da sie ihren Gegenstand weniger verwandeln als zersetzen bzw. liquidieren. 'Mmhm, Menschengesicht, versuch doch zu bleiben! Oh je, es zerrinnt! Manche Züge sind leider schon fort' (646), heißt es beispielhaft über eins der aus der Erde zurückgekehrten 'Flüssiggesichter' (609). Großartige Sätze sind diesem Schmelzen der Züge, dem Vorgang der Entdeutlichung, der Enstaltung gewidmet: 'Doch wie eine stimmlose stumpfe Sonne aufgeht und diese Frauengestalt da einhüllt, während Schnee fällt und fällt und fällt, lächelt dieses nebelverhangene Gesicht den Förster an' (609). Beständige Verwischung der Umrisse, beständige Wanderung herrenloser Körperfragmente von Leib zu Leib, die Osmosen organischer und anorganischer Liquide, die Morphosen des Gefrierens und Schmelzens – bei alledem bewährt sich das Wasser auch hier als das angestammte Element des Gestaltenwandels. Dieser bedient sich andererseits noch anderer Verfahren: Schindungen, Wucherungen, Blutungen, Beschmutzungen, Verletzungen, die die Halterungen menschlicher Formen, die 'steinern aussehende [...] Styroporschale ihres schmatzenden, verdauenden Leibes' (600) zerstören, zeigen das Prinzip Metamorphose als eine ausgearbeitete Foltertechnik. Gilt hier derselbe Satz aus Ovids Verwandlungsepos, der seine Macht schon in Ransmayrs *Letzter Welt* erwiesen hatte, nämlich: Keinem bleibt seine Gestalt, so nun in weit radikalerer Form.

In dieser Metamorphose ist das fragile Subjekt der Nachkriegszivilisation schon immer den verdrängten Mächten und Formen der Verwesung ausgeliefert. Von Anfang an hat Jelineks Text jene Grenzen überschritten, die dieses gegenüber dem Andrang des 'Abjekten' errichtet. Von Anfang an beherrschen die Mächte der Entdifferenzierung das Geschehen, ohne daß dem eine Phase der Differenz vorausgegangen wäre. Unter seinen Figuren finden sich keine durch klare Grenzen konstituierten Subjekte, aber auch keine durch klare Grenzen umrissenen Körper mehr, die dem Einbruch des Unreinen mit Ekel, Schmerz und Angst begegnen und dem Einsickern flüssiger Menschenmasse den Widerstand gesicherter Individualität entgegensetzen würden: Wie auch in anderen Texten lassen Jelineks Figuren die aberwitzigsten Grausamkeiten und Deformationen ohne Protest über sich ergehen. Zu sagen, wie sie leiden, ist ihnen versagt. Sie sprechen nicht, sie werden gesprochen, und letztlich sind sie nichts als figurale Oberflächeneffekte eines aggressiven nekrotischen Prozesses, der angesichts des Völkermords über jedes Einzelschicksal hinweggeht. In ihren Auflösungen und Vermehrungen, ihrer wechselnden Zugehörigkeit zu den widersprüchlichsten Ordnungen, sei es des Toten oder des Lebendigen, des Flüssigen oder des Festen, des Eigenen oder des Anderen, des Organischen oder des Anorganischen, des Einen und des Vielen, bewegen und verwandeln sich Jelineks Figuren abseits des Identischen und seiner Formen. Das einzige, was sich gleichbleibt in diesem Spektakel der Enstaltung noch auf seiner Gestalt besteht, ist der männliche Phallus, 'diese grelle männliche Fleischwerdung' (118), die, auch wenn ihr Eigner längst schon in Fetzen liegt, seinen weniger wollüstigen als zerstörerischen Geschäften nachgeht und auch im Moment gewaltsamer Auflösung seine Funktionstüchtigkeit bewahrt. Auch in den *Kindern der Toten* erweist er sich als der letzte Fluchtpunkt des vom Wasser bedrohten patriarchalischen Prinzips. Noch im Chaos erhält sich das 'Geschlecht, das ein wenig unterhalb der schleimigen Oberfläche des Stroms liegt', und nach dem 'die Menschenherzen mit Tausenden von Tentakeln ... aus dem flüssigen metallischen Brei ... grapschen' (284). In 'ruckenden' Bewegungen leistet es Widerstand gegen die allseitige Auflösung. Ein geläufiges Theorem wird hier in Szene gesetzt, werden doch im Phallus stets die ordnenden, Gesetz und Sprache stiftenden Mächte symbolisiert, jene, die aus dem grenzen- und konturlosen Zustand präödipaler Existenz herausführen und der entdifferenzierenden Macht der Mutter die differenzierende Macht des Vaters entgegenhalten. Doch dieser kulturstiftende Auftrag ist ihm von Jelinek schon immer abgesprochen worden. Auch wenn sich der Phallus nach wie vor seine Herrschaft in vielen Vergewaltigungsszenarios zu behaupten versucht, vermag er sich gegen das Ungestalte nicht mehr durchzusetzen. Seine Auftritte zeigen ihn in der ganzen Vergeblichkeit seiner Anstrengung, als einen gewalttätigen, mitunter komischen, Automaten im Leerlauf, der unablässig die eine stereotype Behauptungsgeste vollführt (vgl. 385).

Ansonsten aber stürzt auch Jelineks Sprache wie eine Mure über die letzten Dinge hin. Auf 666 Seiten mobilisiert sie den ganzen, wie es heißt, 'Dreck der Dichtung' (89), um den großen Dreck der Vergangenheit loszutreten. Nicht nur daß sie dafür in tausenden von Metaphern den verborgenen Flüssigkeitsgehalt der Wörter freisetzt, um die Festkörpergrenzen von Personen und Dingen aufzuweichen. Nicht nur, daß sie aus den unaufhörlich niederfallenden Kaskaden ihrer Sprache keine einzige menschliche Phsyiognomie, kein einziges kenntliches Gesicht herausrettet. Die Worte stellen darüberhinaus das letzte Lösungsmittel der zersetzten Körper dar: 'Worte werden durch Menschen getrieben, als böten diese keinerlei Hindernisse', heißt es, oder, noch deutlicher, ist die Rede vom: 'Wasser, das, in die Wanne geschleudert, sich in Säure verwandelt, in der die Körper noch eine Weile phantasieren und dann in reine Worte aufgelöst sind' (216). Doch auch diese sind irgendwann nicht mehr lesbar. Wieder und wieder wird berichtet, daß die identifizierenden Aufschriften, die Etiketts und die Namen verblassen, daß sie nicht mehr zu entziffern sind, daß die Chroniken, die von Lebenden und Toten, von Übergangenen und von Siegern berichten könnten, von schmutzigen Wassern ausgelöscht werden. Zuletzt bleibt die 'Schrift des Unartikulierten ...: der Ton eines bis heute anhaltenden Schreis' (388).

Bibliography

Böhme, Hartmut. *Kulturgeschichte des Wassers*, Frankfurt am Main, Suhrkamp
Enzensberger, Christian. 1968. *Größerer Versuch über den Schmutz*, München, Hanser
Jelinek, Elfriede. 1995. *Die Kinder der Toten*, Reinbek, Rowohlt
—. 1987. *Krankheit oder Moderne Frauen*, Köln, Prometh Verlag
Lebert, Hans. 1960. *Wolfshaut*, Hamburg, Claassen
Ransmayr, Christoph. 1988. *Die letzte Welt. Mit einem ovidischen Repertoire*. Nördlingen, Greno
Rosenkranz, Karl. 1989. *Ästhetik des Häßlichen*, 2. Auflage, Darmstadt, Wissenschaftliche Buchgesellschaft

Index

—A—

Aichinger, Ilse, 68, 105-114
Andersch, Alfred, 195

—B—

Bachmann, Ingeborg, 106, 189-210, 221
Becker, Jurek, 107
Beckermann, Ruth, 153-164

—D—

Druskowitz, Helene von, 25-33
Duden, Anne, 211, 214-224

—F—

Fleischmann, Lea, 155, 162-163
Frischmuth, Barbara, 71-103

—H—

Haushofer, Marlen, 15-21, 61-66, 211-224
Hofmannsthal, Hugo von, 64, 106, 201

—I—

Innerhofer, Franz, 61

—J—

Jelinek, Elfriede, 83, 99, 225-242

—K—

Keiderling, Christel, 71, 76, 77, 79
Kerschbaumer, Marie-Thérèse, 64, 65, 68
Kofler, Werner, 61

—L—

Lavant, Christine, 61, 65
Lebert, Hans, 235-237

—M—

Mayröcker, Friederike, 115-127
Mitgutsch, Anna, 61, 68, 156, 167-188
Mitterer, Erika, 83-90

—N—

Noll, Chaim, 162
Nöstlinger, Christine, 35-56

—R—

Ransmayr, Christoph, 236, 240
Reichart, Elisabeth, 15-33, 111
Richter, Jutta, 71, 74, 78, 79
Rilke, Rainer Maria, 83, 86, 87, 201, 202

—S—

Schreiner, Margit, 57-70
Schwaiger, Brigitte, 71, 74, 75, 77
Sichrowsky, Peter, 161
Spiel, Hilde, 129-139, 154
Stojka, Ceija, 141-151

—W—

Winkler, Josef, 61
Wolf, Christa, 31
Wolfmayr, Andrea, 71, 76, 78, 79

Notes on Contributors

Petra M. Bagley is a Senior Lecturer in German at the University of Central Lancashire. She is the author of *Somebody's Daughter: The Portrayal of Daughter-Parent Relationships by Contemporary Women Writers from German-speaking Countries* (Akademischer Verlag, 1996). She is currently working on a book project which has as its theme the boarding-school education of contemporary Austrian writers.

Mererid Puw Davies is Fellow by Examination in German Literature at Magdalen College, Oxford, where she is completing her D. Phil. thesis on the *Blaubartmärchen*, memory and history in recent literature in German by women. Her interests include *Märchen* and fantastic literature, twentieth-century women writers, and feminist theory and criticism.

Allyson Fiddler is Lecturer in German Studies at Lancaster University. Her main interests are in contemporary Austrian literature and women's writing. She is the author of *Rewriting Reality: an Introduction to Elfriede Jelinek* (Berg, 1994) and is currently preparing an article on Austrian dramatist Marlene Streeruwitz.

Petra Günther is writing her doctoral thesis on contemporary German prose fiction at the University of Essen. She has published on Peter Bichsel, Herta Müller, and Sten Nadolny.

Brigid Haines is a lecturer in German at the University of Wales Swansea. She is the author of *Dialogue and Narrative Design in the Works of Adalbert Stifter* (MHRA, 1991), and of articles on Lou Andreas-Salomé, Christa Wolf, Helga Königsdorf, Libuše Moníková, and Elfriede Jelinek. She is currently editing a volume of essays on Herta Müller, and working on a book on critical theory and recent German women's writing.

Andrea Hammel is a research assistant at the Centre for German-Jewish Studies, University of Sussex. She is writing her doctoral thesis on women's exile literature, especially Anna Gmeyner, Martina Wied, and Hermynia Zur Mühlen. She has published on Hilde Spiel and is currently co-editing a volume on *The German-Jewish Dilemma: From the Enlightenment to the Shoah*.

Margaret C. Ives is Reader in German Studies at Lancaster University. She is currently working on a volume of essays on Women Writers of the Age of Goethe. She has also published articles on Gertrud von le Fort and on twentieth-century religious poetry.

Andreas Kramer is a lecturer in German Studies at Goldsmiths College, University of London. His publications include books on the expressionist writer Carl Einstein, and on Gertrude Stein, as well as articles on Hugo Ball, Rolf Dieter Brinkmann, Yvan Goll, Raoul Hausmann, and Robert Musil.

Hubert Lengauer lectures in the Institut für Germanistik at the University of Klagenfurt. He has published widely on Austrian literature of the 19th and 20th centuries. Following his book *Ästhetik und liberale Opposition. Zur Rollenproblematik des Schriftstellers in der österreichischen Literatur um 1848* (Böhlau, 1989), he is now working on a literary history of the *Vormärz* period.

Tobe Levin teaches for the University of Maryland (European Division) and the University of Frankfurt, specialising in African-American and Jewish-American women's writing. Her doctoral thesis focused on Elfriede Jelinek. She has co-edited a special issue of *Women's Studies Quarterly* (Dec. 1992), edits *WISE Women's News*, and serves on the editorial board of the *European Journal of Women's Studies*. Since 1977 she has been active in campaigns against female genital mutilation.

Margaret Littler is a lecturer in German at the University of Manchester. She is the author of *Alfred Andersch (1914-1980) and the Reception of French Thought in the Federal Republic of Germany* (Edwin Mellen, 1991). She has also published on the writers Brigitte Kronauer, Herta Müller, Claire Goll and Unica Zürn and is currently working on postmodern feminist theory and contemporary German women's writing.

Laura Ovenden has recently moved from her post of Graduate Teaching Assistant at the University of Nottingham and is currently working as Lektorin in the Institut für Anglistik at the University of Vienna. She is writing her Ph. D. thesis is on the poetics of Elisabeth Reichart.

Andrea Reiter is a Senior Research Fellow in the School of Research and Graduate Studies at Southampton University. She is the author of *'Auf daß sie entsteigen der Dunkelheit': Die literarische Bewältigung von KZ-Erfahrung* (Löcker, 1995). Her most recent publications are on contemporary Austrian literature (Thomas Bernhard, Ilse Aichinger) and Exile Literature (Hans Sahl, Theodor Kramer). She is currently working on a biography of Hans Sahl.

Mike Rogers is a Lecturer in German at the University of Southampton. His research interests are in Austrian, especially Viennese, literature (Nestroy, Karl Kraus), which have developed via Christine Nöstlinger into an involvement with